The Study of Religion in Canada/
Sciences Religieuses au Canada : 3

The Study of Religion in Canada /
Sciences Religieuses au Canada

The Study of Religion in Canada / Sciences Religieuses au Canada is a series of publications planned as "A State-of-the-Art Review" of religious studies in Canada. Each volume in the series covers a particular geographic region. The aim is to present a descriptive and analytical study of courses, programs and research currently being undertaken in the field of religious studies in Canada. The descriptive aspect of the study takes into account the history, nature and rationale of courses and programs, and statistics concerning enrolments and faculty involved. The analytical aspect of the study is concerned with trends and directions of programs, both projected and actual, the relationship of programs and courses to the training and research of faculty, the appeal of courses and programs, and the relevance of such courses and programs to larger issues in society.

To date there has been no thorough study of the state of the art of religious studies in Canada. Information concerning religious studies has been confined basically to university and college catalogues and course information in guidance counselling offices in high schools. The descriptive and analytical aspects of this study serve to provide valuable information generally not contained in lists of courses, and will aid students, counsellors and educators in both public and private institutions.

This study, the research it has involved and the publication of its results, was made possible by a generous grant from the Social Sciences and Humanities Research Council of Canada.

GENERAL EDITOR: *Harold Coward*   University of Calgary

ADVISORY BOARD: *Bruce Alton*   University of Toronto
Charles Anderson   University of British Columbia
Gordon Harland   University of Manitoba
Harold Remus   Wilfrid Laurier University
Louis Rousseau   Université du Québec à Montréal
Martin Rumscheidt   Atlantic School of Theology

THE STUDY OF RELIGION IN CANADA

Volume 3

Religious Studies in Ontario: A State-of-the-Art Review

Harold Remus, William Closson James and Daniel Fraikin

Published for the Canadian Corporation for Studies in Religion/Corporation Canadienne des Sciences Religieuses by Wilfrid Laurier University Press

1992

Canadian Cataloguing in Publication Data

Remus, Harold, 1928-
  Religious studies in Ontario

(The Study of religion in Canada = Sciences
religieuses au Canada ; 3)
Includes bibliographical references and index.
ISBN 0-88920-206-0

1. Religion − Study and teaching (Higher) −
Ontario. 2. Theology − Study and teaching
(Higher) − Ontario. I. James, William Closson,
1943- . II. Fraikin, Daniel, 1933- .
III. Canadian Corporation for Studies in Religion.
IV. Title. V. Series: The Study of religion in Canada ; 3.

BL41.R45 1992   200′.711713   C91-095675-8

76224

© 1992 Canadian Corporation for Studies in Religion/
    Corporation Canadienne des Sciences Religieuses

Cover design by Michael Baldwin, MSIAD

Printed in Canada

Religious Studies in Ontario: A State-of-the-Art Review has been produced
from a manuscript supplied in electronic form by the authors.

Order from:
WILFRID LAURIER UNIVERSITY PRESS
Waterloo, Ontario, Canada N2L 3C5

Table of Contents

List of Tables

Preface

This state-of-the-art review has been a long time in the making, from the moment in 1982 when it was just a gleam in the eye of Dr. Harold Coward, then President of the Canadian Corporation for Studies in Religion/Corporation Canadienne des Sciences Religieuses, to actual publication. In between, an investigator or investigators had to be found who not only had the experience and interest necessary to undertake the assignment and carry it through to completion but would be willing to engage in a multi-year project and be able to find the time to do so. Given the magnitude of the task in Ontario, dividing responsibilities among three investigators, rather than two (as in Quebec) or entrusting them to only one (as in the other provinces and areas), was deemed wise.

Had we had budget enough and time, there is much more we might have done, and should have done — ways and byways we might and should have explored in order to provide a fuller picture of religious studies in Ontario. As long-time labourers in the vineyard we know or can surmise various "reasonable" or "arguable" generalizations or conclusions. But to demonstrate them from data we might have gathered (but didn't) was not given to us, either by our budget or our calendars. That there are things we might have done differently at the start had we had the hindsight that comes at the end of long labours will doubtless be evident to anyone who has worked on a project of this kind and scope. We must leave them for our reviewers to point out and for future investigators to pursue.

For the three of us time has been the biggest problem: it was (as economists say) an "inelastic commodity," and this meant that the project took considerably longer than we (and the Corporation) had expected and hoped. Other commitments supervened: religious studies as an academic field is of obvious interest and concern to us, but our primary expertise and research interests lie elsewhere, and we could not (and would not) simply abandon them and the learned societies and other fora where they are pursued. One of the original members of the team, Dr. John Hoffman of the religious studies department at the University of Windsor, had to bow out when he saw that the project, because of its length, would conflict with a long-planned sabbatical in Argentina. We are grateful to him for his work in the early stages. The other two authors are grateful that Dr. Daniel Fraikin consented to take his place.

The telephone conference calls among all the state-of-the-art investigators nationwide, their progress reports and the comments on them in sessions at the annual meetings of the learned societies in religious studies, the consultations with colleagues at learned societies meetings in Canada and the U.S.A. — all these were helpful, especially in the early stages. Fundamental to our own study were the working sessions by the three of us at Queen's University, where issues and procedures of analysis were discussed, areas of study and chapters were assigned, and schedules established (which were roughly adhered to; see above, s.v. "Time"). The budget permitted only a few such sessions; subsequent conferring was done while conducting interviews together, at learned society meetings, in writing, by phone, and more recently through electronic mail. Because two of the investigators were located at Queen's, the entering and processing of information from faculty members' curricula vitarum and from the teaching and research inventories they submitted were done there. Appendix A gives information on the gathering and processing of these data.

1

A state-of-the-art review should report on the status quo, assess it, draw some conclusions and make some recommendations, and perhaps venture some predictions. Some readers may have wished for more assessments and recommendations. But, unlike the Quebec review (Rousseau and Despland, 1988), which could begin with 1972 since earlier studies covered the time prior to that date, no such previous work existed for Ontario. We were therefore constrained to devote much space to reporting the status quo, and how it came to be. It was also one of the premises of the study, made clear to all from whom we requested data, that any assessments we provided would be of religious studies in Ontario as a whole, not of individual institutions or programmes or of individuals; we were not functioning as an accrediting agency.

Those who seek "bottom lines" may wish to turn to the final chapter first, or may wish to read nothing but that — a procedure we do not advise since not all the conclusions and recommendations are confined to the last chapter and since, in any case, religious studies in Ontario is too complex to compressed into a single chapter or indeed a single book. Perhaps some authors write their concluding chapter first or have it in their head before they put pen to paper or touch a keyboard. (We wish two or three such had stepped forward at the time investigators were being sought to undertake this study.) That was not true of us, and the first eleven chapters represent cogitations that led to chapter twelve. We would invite readers to follow that route with us.

Some within the field—religious studies professors or students—may think we have given too much attention to religious studies in general, its development and present state, or perhaps that our observations verge on the platitudinous in places. But texts have contexts, and religious studies in Ontario is no exception. Moreover, we did not write only for persons in the field. We address also, and especially, prospective students as well as our colleagues in other university departments, many of whom know little, or know wrongly, about what is still a new field, despite its long lineage. We had in mind, too, administrators in universities and in government agencies (readers in this category dispense funds for higher education and grant monies). And we have kept before us the reading public, and why and how our relatively new, and we believe important, form of scholarship and teaching fits into a changing, pluralistic Ontario, Canada, and world. Accordingly, we have tried to use technical language sparingly, or to explain it when we do use it.

We hope that our efforts will help those within religious studies to a better understanding of our field, in Ontario as well as in its wider historical, cultural, and geographical contexts, so that they, and we, might arrive at more shared understandings and common discourse, interpret it better to others, and in general thus shape our field and determine its direction rather than having it done for us. We hope, too, that our colleagues in other departments might be able to glean from our review who we are, whence we came, why we are in the university, and what we do behind those sometimes strange-sounding course titles. We fondly hope that administrators might perceive, or perceive better, the nature of religious studies as an academic field, like and unlike others in the university, distinct (though in a number of places not cut off) from the study of theology, each having its own reasons for being, each its own sphere and its own approaches to its subject matter, each its own kind of students and purposes.

For those few in the general populace who might chance upon and read our volume we express the hope that they might see better how religious studies can assist in understanding the changing nature and role of religion in Ontario and worldwide and toward a greater appreciation of neighbours who stand in cultural and religious traditions other than their own—to the goal of a more humane society.

2

Each investigator wrote and is responsible for the chapters bearing his name. The differences in our temperaments and writing styles will be evident to readers, withstanding even Harold Remus' editing of the entire manuscript. We each owe much to our working sessions as well as to comments offered to one another on successive drafts of the chapters. We also profited from comments made at an international conference on religious studies at the University of Manitoba in September 1989 and at sessions of the Canadian Society for the Study of Religion/Société Canadienne pour l'étude de la Religion devoted to reports on the review at Université Laval in June 1989 and at the University of Victoria in May 1990. We are grateful, too, to a number of persons who read and commented on (or checked for accuracy) chapters or portions of chapters: Charles Adams, Brian Aitken, Bruce Alton, Roy Amore, Robert Bater, Jo Beglo, Darrol Bryant, Mark Burgess, Oscar Cole-Arnal, John Cook, Harold Coward, Michèle Daviau, Lorne Dawson, Peter Erb, John Franklin, Walter Friesen, John Webster Grant, Ronald Grimes, G. Russel Hatton, Clifford Hospital, C. Douglas Jay, Robert Kelly, David Kinsley, William Klassen, Kay Koppedrayer, Judy MacVicar, William Morrow, Willard Oxtoby, Jordan Paper, Diane Peters, Garry Peters, David Reimer, Peter Richardson, Ben Sheehy, Michael Steinhauser, Randi Warne, and Sandra Woolfrey. If we have omitted anyone, it is not by design, and beg their forgiveness. We make the usual disclaimer absolving these readers of our sins of commission and omission.

This study would not have been possible without the cooperation of faculty, graduate officers, department chairs, and librarians who distributed, filled out, and returned questionnaires. We express our gratitude to them once again. We also express our thanks to a number of these persons for taking time for interviews; so, too, to deans, principals, and other administrators and to students, both undergraduate and graduate, who consented to interviews at the institutions we visited. We trust that in what follows these various persons find that we have not abused their trust. (So as to conceal identities by not revealing the gender of individuals we have sometimes used the plural pronoun ''they'' and ''their'' following an antecedent in the singular, a usage perhaps jarring, but common in everyday speech and well documented in noted writers of English [examples in Miller and Swift, 1988, 44-45].) We hope the various persons we interviewed or spoke to or who provided us with written communications will find we have reported accurately what they imparted to us and that we have provided interpretations that are illuminating, not distorting, and not gratuitous.

To our own institutions and to our long-suffering colleagues we express our gratitude for their support of the project in general and of our efforts individually. Wilfrid Laurier University granted Harold Remus remission of two courses in 1986-87 and provided a grant toward the cost of publication. Michael Perry, Anne-Marie Smith, and Walter Friesen, M.A. students and teaching assistants in the Department of Religion and Culture, carried out research, verification, and proofreading assignments. Jo Beglo, then of the University of Waterloo Library, helped with the design of the first library questionnaire (see chap. 10 and App. A below). Diane Peters of the Wilfrid Laurier University Library designed the second library questionnaire (reproduced in App. A below) as well as assisting with wise counsel and help of various kinds both for Chapter 10 and otherwise. Mark Burgess, a religious studies graduate of Wilfrid Laurier who subsequently earned a master's degree in library science, did the initial gleaning, ordering, and synthesis of data from the first set of questionnaires returned to us by librarians. Linda

Glenn and Alice Croft recorded interview data and transformed manuscripts into computer files. Alice Croft also did the data entry and proofreading of the index compiled by Harold Remus. Cathie Huggins, Administrative Assistant in the Department of Religion and Culture, entered some chapters, and revisions of chapters, in computer files and offered guidance on word processing. Peter Erb provided substantial help in shepherding various versions of several chapters through the computer and, drawing on his experience as a librarian (alongside his professorial duties), offered expert advice for the chapter on libraries. In addition to offering freely and cheerfully (and evangelistically?) of his fund of electronic-networking expertise and knowledge of databases, David Reimer prepared the completed typescript files — skilfully and beyond the call of what was not even his duty — for translation into the final, camera-ready form. The Computing Centre at Wilfrid Laurier lived up to its reputation as a friend to users in need.

Queen's Theological College assisted with the payment of stipends for student assistance. Danielle Michel and Carolyn Sparling Woodall completed most of the data entry after James Wilce, combining computer wizardry with many other talents, helped set up the database and entered much of the data while completing his undergraduate degree in religious studies in 1986. In the second year of his graduate programme in the Department of Religious Studies at McMaster Jim Wilce learned he had cancer. Despite surgery and radiation therapy and chemotherapy, he completed his M.A. degree and began Ph.D. studies, but succumbed to the disease on November 3, 1989 at the age of twenty-six. We are saddened to have lost such a promising young colleague and are grateful for his contribution to the study.

We are grateful also to David Clark of D. M. Clark Systems Ltd. for his generous help in transferring the database from the original, "flaky" programme to a second, sound one and to David Holden for advice on setting up various categories for entering data from faculty c.v.s in the database.

We express our appreciation to Sandra Woolfrey, the wise and perceptive Director of Wilfrid Laurier University Press, and to her knowledgeable staff for advice and guidance in the process of publication.

Finally, we tender a unanimous vote of thanks to Harold Coward and award him the title of "Invisible Hand" who, *pace* Adam Smith, applied for the grants from the Social Sciences and Humanities Research Council that made both the research and publication possible, for which we express our gratitude. In our work with that prodigiously efficient scholar-administrator we have learned the wisdom of Satchel Paige's dictum (slightly edited): "Don't look back, Harold may be gaining on you."

May 1991   Harold Remus, Department of Religion and
                                         Culture, Wilfrid Laurier University
                                    William Closson James, Department of
                                         Religious Studies, Queen's University
                                   Daniel Fraikin, Queen's Theological College

1

Introduction: Religious Studies as an Academic Field

Harold Remus

Ecclesiastes' dictum that "there is nothing new under the sun" (Eccl. 1:9) might with some justice be applied to the academic field called "religious studies." Even casual readers of world literature, past or present, are aware that not only religion, but curiosity about religion and reflection on it — sometimes uncritical or apologetic, sometimes critical or polemical — figure prominently in those pages. Insofar as such curiosity and reflection distance one from unexamined practice and belief they foreshadow religious studies in the twentieth century. Several characteristics of religious studies, however, distinguish it from such adumbrations and warrant for religious studies the adjective "new."

Religious studies is a beneficiary of the development in the last two centuries of academic fields such as philology and linguistics, historiography, anthropology, ethnology, archaeology, psychology, and sociology, which not only extended the purview of the study of religion beyond Western religions to Asian religions and the religions of prehistoric and pre- and proto-literate peoples, but also sought to understand religions on their own terms, apart from confessional or apologetic purposes and with whatever tools modern study of languages, folkways, artifacts, and the like could provide. This purview and approach characterize the way religion is studied in departments and programmes of religious studies today (chaps. 2-4 below).

Theology, too, the queen of medieval sciences and the primal mother of religious studies, changed under the impact of the intellectual ferment of the modern period so that, as pursued in European and some North American

---

universities and in many theological schools, it drew on the resources of the new academic fields as it re-examined and reformulated Christian traditions (see, e.g., Welch, 1972a, 1985a; Schoof, 1970; McCool, 1977; and chaps. 2.4.3 and 3.3 below). Nonetheless, the purpose of theology and theological education remained confessional and professional, committed to a particular religious tradition and to preparing persons for service in that tradition. When Dutch and French universities in the late nineteenth century, and the University of Manchester in the early twentieth century, separated the study of religion from confessional and practical theology (see Sharpe, 1975, 119-36), a significant step was taken on the path toward present-day religious studies. Religious studies came to take its place alongside other departments and fields of knowledge in universities, its faculty judged not by confessional standards or commitment to a religious tradition but on their professional competence in their field as demonstrated in teaching, research, and publication of research (chaps. 2 and 3 below).

As in other fields, so also in religious studies such competence was often achieved in the nineteenth century through study in Europe. As Ph.D. programmes were established in North American universities in the second half of the nineteenth century, however, doctoral candidates studying religion sometimes did so in departments such as philology or philosophy (Remus, 1971, 118-19). The first North American doctoral programme in religion is dated to 1869 (Yale), followed by programmes at a number of other private institutions and, eventually, public universities as well, both in the U.S.A. and Canada (see Welch, 1971, 230-31, Table 12-1; chaps. 2.1.3 and 9 below). Religious studies faculty today commonly hold a Ph.D. in religious studies with specialization in one or more of its subfields (chap. 5 below).

The subfields were at one time largely derivatives of the Protestant seminary curriculum. As universities and Western society and culture generally have become more pluralistic, however, so too have departments of religious studies and the subfields in religious studies (chaps. 2, 3, 8 below). In this development learned societies in religious studies have played a significant role (Remus, 1988, 1662-63). The first of these in North America were established in the late nineteenth century (Society of Biblical Literature and Exegesis, 1880; American Society of Church History, 1888). The largest society, the American Academy of Religion (over 5,500 members), includes in its annual sessions not only traditional areas such as ethics, philosophy of religion, and various aspects of Christianity and Judaism, but also Zoroastrianism, Islam, religions of Asia, new religious movements in North America, African-American religious history, Bahai studies, and thematic or correlating approaches such as ritual studies, science and religion, women's studies, and arts, literature, and religion (see the programmes of the joint annual meetings of the American Academy of Religion and the Society of Biblical Literature, published through Scholars Press, Atlanta, Georgia). In Ontario and in Canada generally learned societies play an important role in religious studies (chaps. 2.7, 3.2.5, and 7.7 below).

Communication of research, whether in meetings of learned societies or through publications, is the lifeblood of modern scholarship. So, too, in religious studies. Many of the important journals in religious studies are European and trace their origins to the nineteenth century. However, many of the North American learned societies in the field also publish journals, the oldest of which, the *Journal of Biblical Literature*, originated in the nineteenth century (1882). The larger societies sponsor publishing programmes that include journals, texts, translations, monographs, and dissertations. In Canada a consortium of learned societies in the field of religious studies — the Canadian Corporation for Studies in Religion/Corporation Canadienne des Sciences Religieuses — has an extensive publication programme (chap. 2.7 below). Some idea of the volume of scholarly publication in the field of religious studies can be gained from the fact that *Religious Studies Review*, established in 1975 by the Council on the Study of Religion (now the Council of Societies for the Study of Religion) as a journal devoted solely to reviews of current scholarly literature in the field, annually publishes critical notes on over 1,200 titles plus review essays of around 100 titles. A recent *Scholar's Guide to Academic Journals in Religion* lists 530 such periodicals (Dawsey, 1988).

The primary institutional locus of religious studies in North America is departments and programmes of religious studies in colleges and universities, and these — faculty, students, curricula, pedagogy, libraries, and the path from past to present — will be the focus of this study (chaps 2-10). However, since religion is studied in various ways in other academic fields, these, too, and their relation to the study of religion in religious studies departments and programmes also receive some attention. Moreover, because some departments and programmes retain ties to theological schools, and much important scholarship in religious studies is carried on by faculty in theological schools,[1] some attention will also be devoted to the relation of theological schools to religious studies (chaps. 3.3, 4.3, 5.1.1.3, 5.2.4, 12.5). Since religion is a subject matter in Bible colleges, these, too, will receive some attention in this study (chap. 11). The final chapter reflects on "the state of the art" and offers conclusions and some recommendations for the future.[2]

Notes

1 Some of the most important journals are published by theological schools, e.g., *Harvard Theological Review* (Harvard Divinity School), *Journal of Religion* (University of Chicago Divinity School), *Interpretation* (Union Theological Seminary in Virginia), *Theology Today* (Princeton Theological Seminary). Recently (1985), Toronto School of Theology began publishing *Toronto Journal of Theology*.

2 Various treatments of the history and nature of religious studies are cited in the chapters that follow, especially Chapter 2. *Inter alia,* Waardenburg's two volumes (1973, 1974) provide an encyclopaedic survey, anthology, and bibliography. Cain, 1987 and Benson, 1987 offer brief general overviews. More specific overviews are, for Europe, the contri-

butions to Welch, 1971, chap. 8, by J. G. Heintz (France), Carsten Colpe (Germany), Ninian Smart (Britain), D. J. Hoens (the Netherlands), and Per Erik Persson (Scandinavia); for the U.S.A., Remus, 1988.

2

Religion and Religious Studies in Ontario

Harold Remus

By 1972, when the second edition of Charles Anderson's *Guide to Religious Studies in Canada/Guides Sciences Religieuses au Canada* appeared, religious studies courses, programmes, or departments were to be found in many Canadian universities (Anderson, 1972, 18) as well as in a number of community colleges (Porter, 1972). Some indication of the rate of growth in that period is that in the five years between the first edition (1967) and the second eight more institutions had been added to the list.

On the one hand, this is not surprising. South of the border the 1960s were a time when "the educational escalator still seemed to be running" (Welch, 1971, vii) and religious studies departments were being established apace, especially in public colleges and universities (ibid., 174, Fig. 9-2). In Ontario, similarly, the 1960s were growth years in university education. While the study of religion in universities may have been a beneficiary of this trend, there are also more profound reasons why such study came to occupy a new place there. The importance of religion, especially Christianity, for understanding Canadian history, society, and culture was emphasized by the Symonds report on Canadian Studies (1975, 108-10) and is evident in studies by historians, sociologists, philosophers, and religious studies scholars (e.g., S. D. Clark 1948; 1962, part 2 [cf. Hiller, 1976-77]; J. Porter, 1965; N. K. Clifford, 1969; Walsh, 1966; Moir, 1972; J. W. Grant, 1972/1988; P. Slater, 1977; Handy, 1977, chaps. 4, 8, 11; Armour and Trott, 1981; Westfall et al., 1985). Most Canadian universities were established by Christian denominations (Wevers, 1956, 160-61), a Christian ethos was assumed and pervasive, and it was not so long ago that courses designed to teach "religious knowledge" or inculcate religion were required in many

---

Notes to Chapter 2 can be found on pages 86-92.

universities. In Ontario the fierce battles that raged between Christian denominations in the nineteenth century (with reverberations into the twentieth) over control and funding, not only of universities but of education generally, are an indication of the importance the people of the province attached to the place of religion in public life.

On the other hand, given the changes in Ontario society designated by terms such as secularization or de-Christianization — the secularization and commutation of the Clergy Reserves in 1854 (Moir, 1968, 257-58; 1972, 182-83), the gradual doing away with Sabbath and blue laws, the displacement of churches as centres of community life, the loosing of ties between churches and political parties, the assumption by government of many of the social welfare activities of churches — it is at first glance paradoxical that the study of religion has come to have an established place in Ontario universities.

Even if the study of religion were conceded a place in the university, another question had to be settled: Which religion — or religions — were to be studied, given the plethora of Christian denominations and the steady proliferation of other religions attendant upon the influx of immigrants from non-Western lands?

The various elements indicated in the preceding paragraphs suggest already why there are in fact departments and programmes of religious studies in Ontario universities and why they have the characteristics outlined in the preceding section: only when the perduring importance of religion in human life was recognized (or recognized anew) by university faculty and administrators and only when the study of religion came to be approached pluralistically and using methods generally accepted in the university could it win and hold a place in Ontario's universities. That story is part of the history of Ontario (and Canadian) society and culture generally and of the history of Ontario higher education in particular.

2.1   The Teaching of Religion: From Christian Establishment to Christian Pluralism

It was only in the latter half of the twentieth century that the Province of Ontario began to establish universities *de novo*. Provincialization of institutions of higher learning established by Christian denominations is also relatively recent; Queen's University (founded 1841) came under provincial control in 1912, but Ottawa (founded 1848) became a provincial institution only in 1965, Windsor (founded 1857 as Assumption College) in 1963, McMaster (founded 1887) in 1957, Wilfrid Laurier (founded 1911) not until 1973 (see 2.6 and Table 2-1 below). The overwhelming majority of the provincial universities in Ontario owe their origins to Christian denominations, and various colleges on university campuses are still church-related. Common to all these institutions of Christian origin at one time was the teaching of (not about) religion, specifically Christianity, with the intent of fostering Christian faith and morals in their students.

The rationale, commonly assumed and sometimes expressed, was clear: Canada — Lower and Upper, French and English — was a Christian nation (J. W. Grant, 1977), "His Dominion" (N. K. Clifford, 1973), and was to remain so. That it owed its founding, continued existence, and prosperity to divine providence was a firmly held conviction among nineteenth-century Canadians, cutting across political persuasions and religious professions (Allen, 1985, and the literature cited in 44, n. 1; Despland, 1977, 526). Although the triumphs of science, technology, and commerce in Victorian Canada were accompanied by a shift in rhetoric from "providence" to "progress," it was a progress commonly conceived as infused with deity so that well into the twentieth century "Progress in Canada was Providence updated" (Allen, 1985, 43).

Related to the providentialist view of Canada was "The Presupposition of Christendom" (J. W. Grant, 1972/1988, 213-15), with Canada added to Christendom as a new province but with stress laid, not on the new as in the republic to the south, but on continuity with the Christendom across the waters (ibid., 214; Handy, 1985, 346-50; Despland, 1977, 527). To counter creeping Americanization and emigration to green American pastures, some clerics in late Victorian Canada advanced the view that Canada was to distinguish itself from the United States through its moral superiority (Kiesekamp, 1973), an argument echoed in nationalist sentiments expressed in the 1960s and 1970s (Despland, 1977, 543).

A Christian nation required a Christian populace, if for no other reason than that religion (i.e., Christianity) was seen as "the only secure basis on which civil authority can rest," as John Beverly Robinson, the Chief Justice of Canada and an articulate exponent of the providentialist view stated early in the Victorian era (Robinson, 1840, 44). Christian religion and Christian morality must therefore be taught in those prime agencies of socialization, the schools, at every level. The principles of Christianity, inculcated through religious exercises and instruction, "should be the basis of a Provincial System of Education," stated Egerton Ryerson, the long-time and influential superintendent of education for Canada West (1844-76) and a Methodist minister (*System of Elementary Education*, 1844; cited in Moir, 1972, 170-71; similar examples from Ryerson in French, 1978, 56; Fiorino, 1978, 62-69). As the first Principal of Victoria College, Ryerson argued that, "If one branch of education must be omitted, surely the knowledge of the laws of the universe, and the works of God, is of more practical advantage, socially and morally, than a knowledge of Greek and Latin" (address, Oct. 21, 1841; cited in Burwash, 1927, 502).

When it came to the question of what kind of Christian instruction was to be included in college curricula, however, Upper Canada Christians were sharply divided. Anglicans especially, and to some degree Church of Scotland Presbyterians, took for granted that a British land and British people would have an established church. Since "in Europe there already existed a society in all important respects Christian, a society of which one's own nation was undoubtedly the highest and purest representative," it was "both natural and legitimate, therefore, to introduce Christianity to new colonies in conjunction with a whole social and economic complex and as part of the normal machinery of government" (J. W. Grant, 1977, 10). For John Strachan, Anglican Bishop of Toronto, "a Christian nation without a religious establishment is a contradiction" (sermon on the death of Bishop Jacob Mountain, July 3, 1825; cited in Henderson, 1969, 91). At his urging, King's College was chartered in 1827 as a publicly-funded Anglican institution with an Anglican professor of divinity. King's was to be "a missionary college," wrote Strachan, through which "the greater portion" of the Canadas would, "through the Divine blessing, be brought up in the communion of the Church of England" (*An Appeal to the Friends of Religion and Literature, in Behalf of the University of Upper Canada*, 1827; cited in W. S. Wallace, 1927, 12). A British government smarting from the loss of the thirteen colonies and with the War of 1812-14 still fresh in memory would have found cogent, too, Strachan's argument that "the teachers of the different denominations . . . are for the most part from the United States" and therefore inclined to render "a large part of the population, by their influence and instructions, hostile to our institutions" (ibid., 13).

Those clergy of supposedly doubtful loyalty whom Strachan dismissed as "uneducated itinerant preachers" who had forsaken "their steady employment" to "betake themselves to preaching the Gospel from idleness, or a zeal without knowledge" (sermon, July 3, 1825; cited in Henderson, 1969, 92), championed another, opposing view of Christian instruction in colleges. It was to be offered in colleges established by the various Christian churches of Upper Canada, with no church or college preferred by the government over another. Their stance was a recognition that in Upper Canada "dissenting" Christians were in the majority. Their most articulate spokesman was Egerton Ryerson, whose devastating reply to Strachan's sermons showed that at least one Methodist minister was neither ignorant nor disloyal (see Moir, 1972, 117). John Beverly Robinson, though a staunch defender of the Clergy Reserves and of the view that the Church of England should be established in Canada, nonetheless argued as early as 1842 that in the remote areas of Canada which the Church of England could not reach Methodists should be supported with land grants and money (Cook, 1972, 90-91).[1]

Robinson's mentor, Bishop Strachan, took longer to persuade. Not until the 1850s, when confronted with growing materialism and what he perceived as "open infidelity," did he recognize Upper Canada's Christian pluralism[2] — *de facto* prior to the resolution of the Clergy Reserves question in 1854 and *de jure* after that — by inviting the "dissenting sects" to join him in creating a Protestant Ontario (Westfall, 1976, 59, citing Strachan's *Charge* of 1856 to the clergy of the Toronto diocese).

They needed no urging. Frustrated by the resistance of Strachan and other King's College supporters to religious equality in education, Methodists had already in 1836 established Upper Canada Academy, which in 1841 became Victoria College, while in 1841 Presbyterians had established Queen's College. Similarly, Roman Catholics had founded Regiopolis in Kingston in 1837,[3] followed by St. Michael's (1852) and Assumption College (1857).[4] (See, further, 2.6 and Table 2-1 below.)

What was to become of King's College, however? Was it possible to teach Christian religion and morals in a publicly funded institution of higher learning without favouring the tenets and piety of one denomination over those of another? The same question confronted the British government at about the same time in Montreal. In endowing the university that would bear his name, James McGill, though a professing Anglican, had said nothing about the teaching of religion, and the royal charter, while calling for "the Education of Youth in the principles of true religion," had not specified which religion was the "true" one. In defending the proposed sole right of the Church of England to teach and practice its doctrines in the college, though exempting non-Anglicans from such instruction or worship, the Governors of the university in 1843 reasoned as follows:

> We do not believe there is, rationally speaking, a choice between the two alternatives, of omitting wholly to establish any system of religious instruction and public worship in the college, or of providing for it by placing the Institution in strict and acknowledged connection with some one recognized form of doctrine (MacMillan, 1921, 148).

The British government, however, interpreted the silence of the testator and the charter's failure to specify further the "true religion" to indicate "a design that Christianity should be taught, not in any single or exclusive form, but in any and every form in which its great fundamental truths and precepts could be imparted to the students" (ibid., 199). In recognition of this principle of Christian pluralism four theological colleges of different denominations came in time to be affiliated with the university, resulting eventually in a cooperative Divinity School (1912) and then an ecumenical Faculty of Divinity (1948), which in 1970 became the Faculty of Religious Studies (see MacMillan, 1921; MacLennan, 1960; Howard, 1963, 77-84; *Brief to the Royal Commission*, 1961, 36-38).

In Toronto the steps taken to resolve the question of the status of King's College and the role of religion in it established a similar but yet distinct pattern of Christian pluralism in religious instruction that persisted for another century not only at what came to be the University of Toronto but elsewhere in the province as well.

The Baldwin act of 1849, which came into effect in 1850, disestablished King's College and placed it solely under government control; the Hincks act of 1853 provided that the actual instruction in what was now to be called the University of Toronto should be provided by a new institution, Univer-

sity College, and by any church-related colleges that might affiliate with the
University; and the Federation act of 1887 brought about actual affiliation
for Victoria and St. Michael's Colleges, with Trinity College finally joining
in 1903 (founded by Bishop Strachan to replace King's College shortly after
its disestablishment, Trinity had its first building in 1851 and its formal
opening in 1852) (Alexander, 1906, 137, 139; W. S. Wallace, 1927, 56-57,
62-65, 136-38). The province's commitment to education in a non-confessional framework is indicated by the designation of the University of
Toronto as "the Provincial University" and of University College as "the
Provincial College." That commitment, a legacy of the Baldwin act, was
evident later as well when denominational universities were provincialized
and new provincial universities established *de novo* (see, further, 2.5 and 2.6
and Table 2-1 below).

2.1.1   The Training of Clergy: Theological Colleges

One result of these various acts was that the teaching of theology and the
training of clergy were delegated to theological colleges established for
those purposes or to faculties of divinity within church-related colleges.
This was one way of responding to the report of a commission on education
appointed by the House of Assembly in 1839 "that it would be wholly subversive of the order of an university, to have within it, chairs for the Professors of different Denominations of Religion" (quoted in Sheraton et al.,
1906, 188) and to its recommendation that denominations establish theological schools for the training of their clergy (ibid.). The establishing of separate theological colleges accorded with a similar but earlier trend in the
United States (Remus, 1971, 115-17). Unlike American seminaries, however, most of which have no connection with universities, the great majority
of theological colleges in Ontario are affiliated in some way with universities (see App. B), and for many years undergraduate arts students and theology students sat together in courses. Such an arrangement was often
regarded as mutually beneficial (e.g., Sheraton et al., 1906, 199), but it persists in only a small number of courses now, though a recent decision by the
Association of Theological Schools allowing the practice under certain conditions may change the picture somewhat.[5] At the graduate level theology
students and religious studies students sometimes take courses together
(see, further, chap. 4.3.1 below).

Another result of the nineteenth-century acts was a Christian pluralism —
sometimes rivalry — in the teaching of Christian theology and training of
clergy (see the list of theological colleges in App. B and the various histories by Alexander, 1906; W. S. Wallace, 1927; Burwash, 1927; Sissons,
1952; Reed, 1952; Edinburgh, 1978; Rawlyk and Quinn, 1980; Vaudry,
1987; Arnal, 1988). Offsetting the rivalry was, first, "a tacit understanding
[among Canadian Christians and churches] that some sort of mutual accom-
modation" was necessary and, second, a "sense of complementarity"

among denominations (J. W. Grant, 1972-73, 347). These factors, together with the emergence of the worldwide ecumenical movement, led to the creation of the United Church of Canada (1925) and the uniting of Union College (formed in 1927 by the Knox College faculty who entered the new church) and the Victoria College theological faculty in Emmanuel College (1928) and, later, to the formation of the Toronto Graduate School of Theological Studies (1944) and its successor, the Toronto School of Theology (1969) (see App. B).

2.1.2   The Teaching of the Christian Religion in Church-Related Colleges and Universities

Robert Baldwin intended his act of 1849/1850 disestablishing King's College to result in the secularization of higher education in Upper Canada. He was ahead of his time: most of his constituents disagreed and expressed their disagreement in various ways (W. S. Wallace, 1927, 56-57, 62-65). To be sure, Free Church Presbyterians welcomed the move, and other Presbyterians as well as evangelical Anglicans depended on the disestablished college for pre-theological training. Nonetheless, "godless" was the epithet repeatedly applied to the new University of Toronto and especially to University College. The church-related universities and colleges saw themselves, by contrast, as assuming Christian commitment on the part of their faculty and students, as seeking to foster a Christian ethos within their walls, and to that end offering both required and elective courses in religion. One of the arguments in favour of moving Queen's and Victoria Colleges to the University of Toronto campus was that the two colleges could thus combine the academic benefits of the University with "the social, moral, and religious influences" of a church-related college (Burwash, 1906a, 51). After the move to Toronto the President of Victoria College, Nathaniel Burwash, saw these aims as realized, not only in the church-related colleges (1906b, 66) but in the University as a whole, with "overflowing congregations of students" attending "university sermons of able preachers of all the churches" (ibid., 65). The novels of Charles Gordon ("Ralph Connor"), himself a graduate of the University of Toronto (1883) and Knox College (1887), reflect the kind of emphatic moral and religious instruction one might expect to receive at the " 'varsity." St. Michael's College sought to "impart a thorough Catholic training, moral and intellectual, so as to fit young men for any position in life" (Sheraton et al., 1906, 192). Similar aims informed ethos and curricula in the other church-related colleges and universities in the province well into the present century with compulsory chapel, required courses in religion, and "religious superintendence" of student life (as a Queen's professor of Latin and Greek in the mid-nineteenth century phrased it; cited in Sheraton et al., 1906, 190).

That these courses aimed at inculcation of the Christian religion is clear. The founders of Trinity College were typical in believing that a university

should (in the words of General Simcoe) "impart religious and moral learning" and provide the basis for secular learning, which (in the words of Thomas Arnold of Rugby) was to be "subordinate to a clearly defined Christian
end" (Macklem, 1906, 138-39). Typical courses in the late nineteenth and
early twentieth centuries were biblical history, biblical literature, church history, Christian doctrine, Christian ethics, apologetics or "evidences" (of
"natural and revealed religion"), and biblical Hebrew and Greek. Some of
these courses were required, others could be taken as "options" (electives).
At the University of Toronto many of these courses came to be designated
as "Religious Knowledge" and persisted as required or elective well into
the present century. Both there and in other universities such courses carried
lingering connotations of inculcation of religion (or of the Christian religion) as their aim, and *parti pris* and want of rigour as characterizing their
pedagogy, even when aims and pedagogy had changed (2.4 and 2.5 below).

2.1.3   University College

How godless was "godless" University College? It was, to be sure, not
under denominational control nor was it supported by denominational funding, nor was there a chapel. Nonetheless, chapel attendance was compulsory, on into the twentieth century, and from the beginning there were
courses treating religion in some way. From 1854 to 1877 all undergraduates were required to take courses in the Department of Metaphysics and
Ethics. The curriculum of 1859 substituted "Natural Theology" and "Evidences of Christianity" for certain Metaphysics and Ethics requirements;
while allowing Honours students some leeway in selection of courses, the
flexibility did not extend to omission of these two courses (Wright and
Alexander, 1906, 83). In 1885 "theological options" (electives) were introduced: Biblical Greek, Biblical Literature, Apologetics, and Church History
(ibid., 84).

Students at University College and the church-related colleges were very
conscious of their respective identities and differences, but these concerned
such matters as modes of dress, clubs, sports, and other badges and bonds of
group loyalty rather than religion as such (see, e.g., *Trinity*, 1952, 19, 37-39,
82-92, 142-148, 159-60; Reed, 1952, 238-39). Graduates of University College — "that secular institution of atheism and the black mass," as Trinity
students feigned to view it (*Trinity*, 1952, 19) — somehow managed to find
their way, in significant numbers, into the ranks of the Christian clergy (see
table, Occupations of Arts Graduates [Men], in Wright and Alexander,
1906, 99). Indeed, in 1885 on the appointment of J. F. McCurdy to teach
"Orientals" in University College, the Trinity student magazine recognized
that "this epithet ['godless'] cannot justly be applied to a College, the students of which are largely drawn from four Divinity Halls and support a
Young Men's Christian Association" (*Rouge et Noir* 4/3 [March 1882], 11;
cited in Moir, 1982, 18).[6]

The faculty of Victorian University College were not noted for their atheism (J. King, 1914, 64, 131), and those who taught religion courses saw themselves as within the Christian fold, as did the renowned Professor of Mental and Moral Philosophy (1871-89), George Paxton Young, though on his own terms (Armour and Trott, 1981, 88-90). John S. Moir's *History of Biblical Studies in Canada* demonstrates that University College faculty who taught Bible and the biblical languages were from the start and for many decades thereafter professing Christians, "scholars of proven piety" (Moir, 1982, 7; also, 6, 15, 16, 23-24 *et passim*).

These were professors in the Department of Oriental Languages. It was in this Department that one sees foreshadowed certain patterns that came to characterize religious studies departments in Ontario.

1. There was, first, the movement to academic specialization and commitment to research for which Germany was noted in the nineteenth century and which drew many British, Canadian, and American students to graduate study there; by the 1880s the same trend was evident in the University of Toronto and the federated colleges. One of these students was James F. McCurdy (1847-1935), "the father of biblical studies in Canada" (Moir, 1982, 25) who, after graduating from the University of New Brunswick and Princeton Seminary, studied in Göttingen and Leipzig (Winnett and McCullough, 1977, 7-8). During his long tenure as professor and head of the Department of Oriental Languages in University College not only did he teach and publish in the area of Hebrew Bible, but his teaching was specialized to the point that he instructed not only in Hebrew but in Arabic and Assyrian as well (Moir, 1982, 15-16).

2. Such specialization was possible in part because Oriental Languages was given departmental status in 1886. From this departmental base McCurdy, who had been carrying the very heavy workload of the Department singlehandedly, argued, successfully, for an additional faculty member. His arguments are instructive. The Department has been serving a "large and increasing number of students" preparing for the Christian ministry. But (said McCurdy) in addition to this service function the Department, in view of the indebtedness of Western culture to the ancient Near East, sees "Orientals" as "a branch of general culture" and therefore of interest and importance to other students as well (McCurdy to James Loudon, n.d., but before July 1895; cited in Moir, 1982, 17).

3. David W. McGee, the professor hired to work with McCurdy, received the Ph.D. from the University of Breslau, but his earlier study had been with McCurdy and with McCurdy's predecessor, Jacob M. Hirschfelder. The next step for the Department of Oriental Languages was to institute a graduate programme so that persons like McGee could continue their studies at Toronto itself rather than go abroad or, as was increasingly the case, to the graduate schools established in the United States in the latter half of the nineteenth century. In 1885 Toronto had approved in principle the granting of the Ph.D. and in 1897 specified the requirements (Wright and Alexander,

1906, 92). The first degrees earned in the Department, granted in 1902, were the first that the University awarded in the humanities at the doctoral level (Alexander, 1906, App. D, 256).

4. These developments in the Department would not have been possible without the cooperation and resources of the federated colleges. Victoria had established a Department of Oriental Languages five years prior to McCurdy's. McCurdy had devised his programme at the request of the principals of Wycliffe and Knox Colleges. Students from the latter, especially, were to be found in large numbers in the courses offered by McCurdy and his colleagues. Faculty appointments in Old Testament at Victoria, Trinity, Knox, Wycliffe, and McMaster (then still located in Toronto) contributed to the scholarly expertise at the University, and the library resources of these colleges were accessible to faculty and students in the University's Orientals Department (Moir, 1982, 6, 16-20; Winnett and McCullough, 1977, chaps. 2 [Victoria College] and 3 [Trinity College]).

These various elements — academic specialization, the granting of departmental status, a conception of religion as a significant element of Western culture and of human experience generally and therefore as a fit subject of study in the university, the development of a graduate programme, and cooperation between university and associated theological colleges — characterize many of the religious studies departments and programmes that came into being in the latter half of the twentieth century in Ontario.

5. One further element proved disturbing in the functioning of the Department of Oriental Languages and required reflection, and the passage of time, before religious studies would be accorded academic status in Ontario universities. This was the question of religious commitment and the purpose of courses in the area of religion. McCurdy, like his colleagues in University College, was a Christian who made no secret of his commitment. In the teaching of courses in the Bible he stated that one aim was "to give college young men and women the right direction, and a sense of relative spiritual values in the most valuable single portion of their education" (cited in Moir, 1982, 1). But what was "the right direction"? And which — and whose — "spiritual values" were to be fostered, and which — and whose — interpretation of the Bible was to be followed?

In the nineteenth century, in the struggles over King's College and the relation between the University of Toronto and the church colleges, these questions had been raised along denominational lines. In the early years of the twentieth century, an era of religious controversy over "'isms'" — Darwinism, Modernism, fundamentalism, higher criticism — they were raised within denominations and figured in an attack on McCurdy's department. As summarized by John Moir (1982, 29-33), the attack took its starting point from ambiguous language in the University Act of 1906 but was motivated by the fundamentalism of the attacker, S. H. Blake, prominent in Toronto as a lawyer, governor of the University, and co-founder of Wycliffe, the evangelical Anglican theological college on the Toronto campus. The act stated that University College was to give instruction in "Oriental Languages and Ethics . . . but not in theology" (sec. 127.2). Also,

> The curriculum in Arts of the University shall include the subjects of Biblical Greek, Biblical Literature, Christian Ethics, Apologetics, the Evidences of Natural and Revealed Religion and Church History, but any provision for examination and instruction in the same shall be left to the voluntary action of the federated universities and colleges (ibid.).

Moreover, none of these subjects was to be required for graduation (sec. 129.1; in Alexander, 1906, App. D, 324-25).

The University, argued Blake, was to teach "secular subjects only" and

> in such a way that the very varied religious convictions of its supporters shall suffer no hurt . . . and no professor has a right to teach anything else. He may be an Anglican, or he may be an infidel, a Methodist or a Roman Catholic, but he must keep his convictions to himself (letter to *Mail and Empire*, Dec. 13, 1906; cited in Moir, 1982, 29).

John Hoskin, who chaired the University Board of Governors, replied that the courses in biblical literature offered by the Department of Oriental Languages involved "no dogmatic teaching" and "no work of interpretation [was] being carried on." "It would seem necessary," he concluded, "that a properly equipped University should take some cognizance of literature which is ranked with the most important any nation has given to man [sic]" (in Moir, 1982, 30). A Committee of the Board of Governors likewise stated (1909) that while University College professors "must not trespass upon the field of Theology," the University nonetheless "not only has the right, but the imperative duty to include in the curriculum of Arts the religious and theological subjects mentioned in the Section [i.e., 129.1]" (*Report . . . 1909*, 8, 14; cited in Moir, 1982, 32). As to whether, and how, the Christian Bible could be taught in University College, the Committee contended that,

> in its opinion, the University Act does not exclude all interpretation of the Bible in University College, and that every discussion of any of its books in the College would not be a teaching of Theology contrary to the statute. In the opinion of your Committee many of the subjects assigned to University College could not be fully and properly taught without the use of the Bible—notably, Oriental Languages, Ethics, Ancient History, and Greek require the assistance of the Bible for their full and proper appreciation. To exclude all discussion of the Bible and literary, historical, linguistic, and ethical sides thereof, whether in the Hebrew, Greek, English, or other version, would be to exclude from the Arts Course of the College an important literary work, an important historical work, an important help to the study of languages, and the greatest code of Ethics known to the world. Your Committee begs, further, to report that, in its opinion, discussions of the books and narratives of the Bible in the study of Literature, Ancient History, Oriental Languages, and Greek may take

place without entering upon the domain of Theology contrary to the stat-
ute. (*Report . . . 1909*, para. 13; cited in Winnett and McCullough, 1977,
15).

Thus, while religion had been affirmed as a legitimate subject for study in
the University, questions of values, interpretation, stance of the professor,
and the purpose of courses in religion were glossed over or touched on only
briefly. Changes in the academic world and in the social and cultural climate of Canada would raise them anew.

2.2   Religious Studies: Secularization and Religious Pluralism

When one looks at a religious studies department in Ontario in the early
1990s, the changes from McCurdy's day — in faculty, curriculum, and
ethos — are unmistakable. Today, the eight to twenty faculty members who
typically constitute a department of religious studies in Ontario almost all
hold earned doctorates from recognized, often prestigious universities.
While most have pursued their graduate studies outside Canada, newer faculty increasingly hold degrees from graduate schools in Quebec and
Ontario. In hiring, tenure, and promotion decisions, faculty are subject to
the same criteria and procedures as faculty in other departments of the university. They belong to a variety of professional societies, Canadian and
international; publish books with a variety of publishers and articles in a
wide range of journals; and serve on various university committees and in
various administrative positions. The religious commitments or affiliations
of the faculty are not immediately evident, either to their colleagues in other
departments or to students. Were they known, they would be seen to range
across the Christian spectrum and to include Judaism, Hinduism, Buddhism,
agnosticism, atheism, and "none of the above." The curriculum likewise
covers a broad spectrum of religions and religious issues, depending on the
size and specializations of the faculty. If asked about their aims in the
courses they teach, faculty members would give diverse answers, but inculcation in or proselytizing for the Christian religion — or any other religion —
would not be among them (see, further, chaps. 3-8 below).

These changes are attributable to changes in the conception and study of
religion, in the attitude of the academy to such study, and in the place of
religion — and what is understood by "religion" — in Canadian, including
Ontario, society and culture.

2.3   Changes in the Nature and Role of Religion

To take the last first, in Ontario as in Canada and the Western world generally, the gothic structures erected by Christians to proclaim a Christian
presence in city, town, and countryside (Westfall, 1976) are today over-

shadowed by office towers and high-rises, or have been converted to restaurants, shops, and other uses, or sit derelict. Some Canadians might continue to work and pray for a Canada that would (again) be "His Dominion," or long for "Toronto the Good." Scholars on royal commissions might cast nostalgic glances back to a time when the Christian Bible instructed many in history, rhetoric, and philosophy of life while "formal religion" gave young people a "stable frame of reference" (M. W. Wallace, 1951, 111-12), and when universities founded by Christians served Christian ends (G. P. Grant, 1951, 124-25; cf. also G. P. Grant, 1986). However, it is significant, and probably symptomatic, that debates over Sunday shopping in Ontario in the late twentieth century focus on questions of "market share," competition, and a day of rest rather than on the sanctity of the Lord's Day and that the requiring of religious exercises in public schools has recently gone by the board. A "steady process of secularization," writes John Webster Grant (1977, 18-19),

> has detached from the control of the churches important instruments through which they once exerted their influence. Philanthropy has long gone, taken over by big business and the state. Politics has been almost completely secularized, despite the religious origins of the CCF and Social Credit. Community life, once dominated by religious societies and even church-sponsored athletic clubs, now has its centre elsewhere. Most significantly of all, the transmission of culture through schools and universities no longer rests on even implicitly religious foundations.

It would be shortsighted to conclude, however, that Canada, or Ontario, is now simply secularized, or religionless, or (as was once facilely asserted of University College) "godless." "Religion," however, no longer has a single (however many-hued) referent: "Christianity." Some idea of the change in the religious landscape that has taken place in only 40 or 50 years in Ontario becomes evident in an autobiographical reminiscence by McGill theologian Douglas John Hall in reflecting on the pluralistic nature of North American society and culture:

> As a child growing up during the 1930s and 1940s in a small southwestern Ontario village, I had absolutely no contact with members of other religious traditions. Until a few Eastern European Roman Catholics began to move into the area . . . even Catholics were more theoretical than real for us. Nearly every person of my acquaintance was either Presbyterian or United Church of Canada. There were a few families of Anglican and Baptist persuasion, though they did not have church buildings in the village; but I cannot recall more than a half-dozen homes where agnosticism had a hearing, and my father's particular variety of skepticism was an embarrassment to us as children in this church-centered environment. I knew no Jews. We heard people speak sometimes of Jewish merchants in the nearby county-town, and the all-too-common image of the Jew prevailed (one spoke freely, for instance, of being "jewed"). As for Muslims, Buddhists, Hindus, and members of other

religious traditions they were as remote for us as were the lands in which
(we might have read) they were dominant. Missionaries from [i.e., to]
India or China who appeared among us periodically provided our only
relatively personal entree into such strange places, and their stories — at
least as they were received by us — almost invariably accentuated the
need to rescue souls and bodies from such benighted heathendom (Hall,
1989, 208).

Today some of the gothic churches built by mainline churches of that era
now serve as houses of worship not only for newer, and growing, Christian
denominations but also for non-Christian religious groups from lands with
largely non-Christian populations and venerable non-Christian religious traditions.

Prior to such developments, the Jewish community had long been at
home in Canada (Craig, 1959; on the history and nature of Canadian Judaism and comparisons with Judaism in the U.S.A. see, further, Schoenfeld,
1978). Though relatively small in number, it has constituted a significant
presence. In Toronto, where the first congregation was founded in 1856
(Kayfetz, 1959, 14),[7] Jewish leaders in 1897 successfully protested an
attempt by Anglicans to introduce the teaching of religion in the public
schools (ibid., 20). Recently B'nai B'rith has been active in Court actions
objecting to a regulation of the Ontario Education Act requiring prayer(s)
and the reading of scripture(s) at the beginning or end of each school day
(Ontario Education Act [1987], Regulation 262, secs. 28, 29; for a history
of religious exercises in Ontario public schools see Schweyer, 1973; Stamp,
1986; further, chaps. 9.5 [and n. 9] and 12.10.3 below).

Groups such as these — Jews, Hindus, Sikhs, Buddhists, Muslims — each
constitute at most one per cent of the Canadian population, though in large
urban centres that figure is higher.[8] Given the Canadian commitment to
multiculturalism and the protection of minority rights by the new Charter of
Rights, the importance of these groups and their influence on public policy
and attitudes regarding the role of religion in public life generally, and in
higher education specifically, is apt to be greater than their numbers alone
would suggest.

On the Christian side, membership in Christian churches as a percentage
of the Canadian population has declined significantly in recent decades as
has church attendance (Bibby, 1987, Tables 1.2 and 1.3). Equally significant, however, is that virtually 90% of Canadians still claim Christian ties
(ibid., Table 3.1) and that according to one study of the 7% professing no
affiliation (ibid.) almost half had, within the next ten years, come to (or
returned to) a Christian affiliation (ibid., 44). Three-fourths of the population profess belief of some sort in a Christian proposition as specific as the
divinity of Jesus (ibid., Table 4-9).

These data tend to confirm Thomas Luckmann's observation that statistical indicators of the role and importance of religion in contemporary society
such as church membership, attendance, and financial contributions are mis-

leading since they do not take account of non-church life-styles and (to borrow O'Toole's terminology [1985, 110]) "systems of meaning and ultimate significance" — what Luckmann calls "invisible religion" (1967). A number of studies have concluded that the evidence for such religion is itself invisible (Bibby, 1987, 41-43, and citing earlier work). However, the dilution and transmutation of Christian beliefs, commitments, traditions, and mores that Bibby has delineated (1987, chaps. 4-5) might in fact be viewed as one manifestation of "a new social form of religion" (Luckmann, 1967, 91).

Assertions of widespread secularization in the West presuppose certain definitions of religion and "decline" therefrom (Johnson, 1980). If one allows a definition of religion broad enough to include the various Canadian phenomena outlined in the preceding paragraphs, there is still much truth in John Moir's dictum of two decades ago that Canada exhibits a "legally disestablished religiosity" (Moir, 1968, 247).[9] The Christian pluralism that became evident in Ontario in the nineteenth century still persists, albeit in a more ramified way, but now it must take its place within a much more inclusive and comprehensive religious pluralism. It is that kind of pluralism that has come to constitute a new matrix for the study of religion in Ontario's universities.

2.4   Changes in the Conception and Study of Religion

The impact on the study of religion of new disciplines and new ways of examining religious texts and phenomena has been noted in Chapter 1. The spirit of critical inquiry which inhered in many of these disciplines — and in the wake of the Enlightenment often focused on religion — proved to be a potent force in secularization (Johnson, 1980, 21-22). By the 1920s that spirit had won general acceptance in Canadian universities (McKillop, 1979, 229). Nonetheless, it operated within a context of "cultural moralism" inherited from the nineteenth century (ibid., 230). In this tension between "intellectual inquiry and conventional wisdom" (ibid., 231) Canadian scholars exercised (in the words of Robert Falconer, President of the University of Toronto) "a disciplined intelligence" that focused on "the education of the will rather than the intellect" (cited in ibid., 232). This academic ethos held true also in the various areas of the study and teaching of religion. Some of these are examined in the following pages.

2.4.1   Biblical Studies

In the study of religion the impact of the new academic fields and the various "isms" of the nineteenth century was felt first and foremost in the way one viewed the Bible. Even prior to the questions "Darwinism" raised about the early chapters of the book of Genesis, European (and especially German) scholars had proposed a rewriting of Israelite history (Wellhausen,

1878; Hahn 1956, chap. 1; Kraeling, 1955, chap. 7). The "Higher Criticism" that so changed the face of biblical scholarship began with critical comparison of sources and traditions in the Hebrew Bible, but came to embrace archaeological, anthropological, sociological, and comparative-religion approaches as well (Hahn, 1956, chaps. 2-6; Orlinsky, 1965, 86-95).

In Ontario, Higher Criticism found both advocates and critics. Some of the latter were situated in institutions of higher learning (Hague, n.d. [1909]; Griffith Thomas, n.d.); many, however, were outraged churchmen standing outside who saw Higher Criticism as gnawing at the innards of Christian institutions of higher learning. In a few cases in Ontario and Quebec these attacks resulted in the ouster of proponents of Higher Criticism (Moir, 1982, 9-13, 34-35). More typical was the vindication, by university administrators and committees of inquiry, of professors under attack. One significant case at University College has been noted in section 2.1.3 above. At Victoria College the blunting of attacks on Professor George Jackson meant, in effect, that Higher Criticism could and would be taught in Methodist institutions of higher education (Moir, 1982, 35-36). At McMaster, a similar case resulted in a statement that "McMaster University stands for freedom, for progress, for investigation. . . . Baptists have ever been ready to accord to all students of the Sacred Scriptures the largest possible measure of freedom consistent with loyalty to the fundamentals of the Christian faith" (cited in ibid., 37).

What proved decisive in Canada was not whether scholars espoused Higher Criticism but whether they advocated their views in violation of "cultural moralism" and did so dogmatically rather than as a subject for investigation (Moir, 1982, 12). The charge to John Scrimger on his installation as professor in Presbyterian College in Montreal in 1882 was typical in enjoining him to be open to the Spirit's leading in interpreting the Bible, even if that did not harmonize with the traditional creeds, but yet not to seek "startling novelties in the way of interpretation" (cited in ibid., 21). Those biblical scholars who showed themselves reverent and Christian in their scholarship and teaching as well as in their personal lives, pursuing (as J. F. McCurdy put it) "a sane and tactful course of Bible teaching" (cited in ibid., 1), with a "tender regard for popularly accepted beliefs," were free to incorporate the new theories into the curriculum (ibid., 23; see, further, Sinclair-Faulkner, 1981).

Biblical studies today, generally and in Ontario universities and theological colleges in particular, is a highly diverse and complex field drawing on diverse methodologies and fields, as a glance at the programmes of the annual meetings of the Society of Biblical Literature or a perusal of the *Journal of Biblical Literature, Catholic Biblical Quarterly*, or *New Testament Studies* will show. So also the self-description of the Canadian Society of Biblical Studies:

The main objective of the Society is to provide a forum for the critical study of the Bible and related literatures and cultures. To this end, it encourages scholars with diverse expertise to engage in common scholarly pursuits, using varying methodologies drawn from philology, archaeology, history, literature and sociology, and covering such areas as Ancient Near Eastern, Jewish, biblical, patristic and classical studies (CFH, 1987c, 13).

Ontario biblical scholars have been pioneers and leaders in the field in various ways. Long before it became popular to draw on sociological theory to understand biblical history, Theophile J. Meek of the University of Toronto took account of social factors in delineating Israelite origins (Meek, 1927, 1936). S. A. B. Mercer, Professor of Hebrew and Egyptology (and briefly Dean of Theology) in Trinity College and the only Canadian present when Tutankhamen's tomb was opened, was instrumental in the finding and publishing of important biblical manuscripts (Moir, 1982, 57-58, 75-76). F. V. Winnett and A. D. Tushingham of the University of Toronto were among the scholars who were involved at an early stage in bringing the Dead Sea Scrolls to light (Schuller, 1989), and archaeologists such as Donald B. Redford and John S. Holladay of the University of Toronto (Moir, 1982, 99) and Norman E. Wagner and Lawrence E. Toombs of Wilfrid Laurier University have made important contributions to the field (Wagner, 1972; Wagner, Toombs, Riegert, 1973; Toombs, 1985). Frank W. Beare's *The Earliest Records of Jesus* (1962) has served two generations of students, his own at the University of Toronto and many throughout North America. The studies by Robert Polzin (Religious Studies, Carleton) of the Deuteronomic History (1980, 1989 cover Deuteronomy-1 Samuel) have pioneered in applying to that corpus a "literary approach" with a "theoretical underpinning" that he calls an "effective historical consciousness" (1980, 218, n. 7). The work of Reinhard Pummer (Religious Studies, University of Ottawa) on the Samaritans (e.g., 1987) occupies an important niche in scholarship on that group. John Hurd of Trinity College, University of Toronto was an early exponent of computerized instruction in New Testament Greek (see chap. 10.2 below). The list could easily be extended.

Biblical scholars at the University of Toronto and its affiliated theological colleges were largely responsible for the formation of the Canadian Society of Biblical Studies in 1933, and the first president was Sir Robert Falconer, then recently retired as President of the University of Toronto (see the history of the society up to 1967 by Macpherson, 1967). Four of the charter members were rabbis; most were Protestant clergy employed either as professors or pastors; all but one were male (ibid., 2). Two decades later little had changed: in 1953 all but five of the now 87 members were Protestant clergymen (sic) belonging to the mainstream denominations, with professors outnumbering pastors two to one; of the five exceptions, one was a woman, one a rabbi, and the other three were university teachers (ibid., 10). It was at that time, however, that Roman Catholic scholars began to appear

on the membership rolls and at the annual meetings; also new was the introduction of bilingual announcements of meetings (ibid.). Only fairly recently
have women and Jewish scholars come to be more numerous in the Society,
where they now play significant roles (cf. 2.4.5 below).

Though most of the older charter members of the Society had been
trained outside Canada, several of the younger ones had received their education in Canada (Macpherson, 1967, 2). This was another step along the
road to the indigenization of graduate study discussed elsewhere in this
study (2.1.3 above; chaps. 5.2.3.2 and 12.10.1 below). The Society's *Bulletin*, established in 1935, became a kind of Canadian journal of biblical studies, publishing the annual presidential addresses as well as some of the
papers delivered at the annual meetings (Macpherson, 1967, 3-4). When
new channels of scholarly publication proliferated in the 1950s, the *Bulletin*
ceased publication for five years (ibid., 12-14). In the meantime, the *Canadian Journal of Theology* had been launched (1955). In its modest way, the
Bulletin, appearing at a time when scholarly publications in religion were
few in Canada, may be said to have contributed to a tradition of scholarly
communication in the field of religious studies that is an important facet of
"the state of the art" today (see, further, 2.7 below). In these various developments as well as in international learned societies, Ontario biblical scholars have played important roles, and continue to do so.

Another direction study of the Bible took in the nineteenth and twentieth
centuries is represented in the Bible colleges established amid the controversies over Higher Criticism. These institutions are considered in Chapter
11.

(On the contribution of Ontario biblical scholars to the study of ancient
Judaism, see 2.4.5 below.)

2.4.2   History of Christianity and Religious History

The spirit of critical inquiry also underlay changes in the way the history of
Christianity was viewed.

"Church History" was a standard item in curricula of Ontario universities and theological colleges in the nineteenth century and much of the
twentieth century and remains so in theological colleges. As conceived and
taught in the nineteenth century, church history was in great part apologetic.
At Knox College in the 1840s, Professor Robert Burns was not atypical in
defining church history as "the history of God's arrangements with our
world, for displaying his own glory, and securing the salvation of his
people" (lecture, November 3, 1848; cited in Vaudry, 1987, 438), and students were to see that "God is to be recognized in all, and the ultimate
ascendancy of his cause and people to be anticipated in all" (ibid.; cf.
chaps. 3.2.3 and 11.4 below).

This kind of history was eroded by the critical historiography practised by the classical historians B. G. Niebuhr, N. D. Fustel de Coulanges, and Eduard Meyer and modern historians such as Leopold von Ranke (Highet, 1947, 472-79), and by the rewriting of the history of early Christianity by critical scholars such as F. C. Baur (Morgan, 1977; Massey, 1977). The contrast between Burns's view of church history and the critical objectivity of the three volumes in the series "The Church in the Canadian Era" (Walsh, 1966; Moir, 1972; J. W. Grant, 1972/1988) will be evident to any reader. *Inter alia*, the writers (in the words of the General Editor) pay attention to how "the Canadian environment has affected the churches and in turn been affected by them" and "concern themselves not only with the institutional development and the devotional life of the church, but also with its public witness and especially with its relation to the development of the Canadian character" (Grant's Foreword to each of the three volumes, viii).

Where the subject is taught in religious studies departments or programmes in Ontario universities today, it is apt to be entitled "History of Christianity" or "Christianity and Western Culture" or subdivided into examination of specific figures and movements, relating them to their cultural and social contexts. "Christendom," rather than churches or "Christianity," is apt to be the subject of investigation in such courses, sometimes following the lead of French historians who combed hitherto neglected sources to reconstruct the history of the "little," the "ordinary" people (Despland, 1978b, 323-27).

In Ontario some of this kind of work has been carried on both in religious studies departments and in theological colleges (e.g., Arnal, 1979, 1985, 1986), but much of it has been conducted by sociologists (S. D. Clark, 1948; Hiller, 1976-77) and by scholars in university departments of history (Westfall, 1976; Allen, 1970, 1985; Rawlyk, 1984). Two decades ago John Webster Grant spoke of "the growing interest in church history evident in many university departments of history" (1972, viii). The influence of the kind of sociological-anthropological analyses of Christian figures and movements pioneered by classicist Peter Brown (e.g., 1967, 1971, 1981, 1982) is evident also in work by religious studies scholars in Canada generally (Maier, 1989, 1991; Friesen, 1988) and in Ontario in particular (Vallée, 1980; Remus, 1986, 1987; Gray, 1988). How much historians of Christianity or of Christendom will learn from historians of religion generally (Despland, 1978a) remains to be seen. One Ontario historian of Christianity observed in a written communication that his courses on the history of religion in Canada perforce include native religious traditions as well as New Religions and other recent religious movements outside the Christian tradition: the lines between "history of Christianity" and "history of religions" become blurred, he finds, when one thinks in terms of "religious history."

2.4.3   Theology — and Religious Studies

Another staple of curricula in Ontario universities in the nineteenth century and on into the twentieth was theology, offered under such titles as Christian Doctrine, Apologetics, and Christian Evidences. The first of these would be taught along general Protestant or Roman Catholic lines or sometimes with a specifically denominational flavour, depending on the institution and the instructor. In Roman Catholic educational institutions, Apologetics was in an Ultramontanist mode. Elsewhere, Apologetics and Christian Evidences were a mixture of William Paley's standard works on natural theology and "evidences" — which young Theobald Pontifex found left "no loop-hole for an opponent" (Butler, [1903], 1948, 32) — and the regnant Common Sense philosophy (see McKillop, 1979, passim).

The "cultural moralism" and "natural theology" presupposed and defended in such courses could not withstand the onslaughts of Darwinism and Hegelian idealism.[10] Though Canadian theologians were less affected (some would have said afflicted) by German theology than their American counterparts, the critical reshaping of Christian theology underway in Germany since Friederich Schleiermacher (see Dillenberger and Welch, 1988, chap. 9) ultimately had its effect in Canada as well (J. W. Grant, 1972, 60-65 [1988, 61-63]). The ascendancy of the "Neo-Orthodox" theology associated with the name of Karl Barth in the 1930s to the 1950s (Dillenberger and Welch, 1988, chap. 12) brought "natural theology" into further disrepute (cf. J. W. Grant, 1972/1988, 152-53). Writing in the first issue of the *Canadian Journal of Theology*, Gerald Cragg, a Montreal pastor (and, later, professor), observed "something approaching a theological renaissance," "world-wide in scope," which "had not left us unaffected" in Canada (Cragg, 1955, 7).

The founding of the *Canadian Journal of Theology* in 1955 was part of that renaissance. It was viewed as a successor to the *Canadian Journal of Religious Thought*, which had fallen prey to the Great Depression. The new undertaking would be a specifically "Canadian Journal of theology. We are confident [wrote the first editors] that every patriotic Canadian who has a sense of spiritual values will want to see our venture succeed" (*Canadian Journal of Theology* 1955, 1). Even as "spiritual" meant "Christian," so did "theology": the new journal was to be "in the service of the Church of Christ" (ibid., 2), and the articles would be oriented to the typical staples of Protestant seminary curricula of the time — "theological or theological-philosophical, Biblical ... historical ... political and social, pastoral and psychological" (ibid., 1).

Fifteen years later the *Journal* ceased publication in favour of a journal entitled, significantly, *Studies in Religion/Sciences Religieuses*. The new publication was to take its place in a changed world, especially a changed academic world in which scholarly study of religion was to be religiously pluralistic as well as both francophone and anglophone.

In his programmatic statement of aims, William Nicholls, the Editor-in-Chief of the new journal, echoed the views of his predecessor but added a number of significant details that foreshadow subsequent discussion of the relation between theology and religious studies and the place of theology in departments of religious studies. In continuity with its predecessor, the new journal would include theological articles, presumably of a kind produced "by academic methods no less rigorous than those employed elsewhere" (Nicholls, 1971, 2). A number of differentia would distinguish such theology from religious studies, however. The venue of theology is "faith" communities, Christian and Jewish, and, in the case of the former, "the theological colleges affiliated to Canadian universities" (ibid.). The purpose of theological scholarships is "essentially" to serve those communities (ibid.). Religion scholarship, while shedding "fresh light on the questions of human existence which religion has always tried to confront," is characterized by "rigour and detachment, a disciplinary and scientific basis" (ibid., 3). Moreover, while religious studies departments in universities "also have a commitment to the study of Judaism and Christianity," they examine them "in the context of the study of all the other religions of the world" (ibid., 2). In doing so they employ "a variety of methodologies" (ibid., 1), "perhaps plac[ing] less emphasis on theology and more on the attempt to understand the religious experience it reflects" (ibid., 2). Such scholarship is both international and, in Canada, increasingly conscious of "Canadian identity," and hence franco- and anglophone (ibid., 1).

Underlying these differentia were issues that are more than "provincial" (i.e., Ontarian and Canadian) and have refused to go away, despite persisting attempts to resolve them. Articles published in the United States with titles such as "The Ambiguous Position of Christian Theology" (i.e., in departments of religious studies [McGill, 1970]), "What is Theology?" (Ogden, 1972), and "Why Theology and Religious Studies Need Each Other" (May, 1984) hint at the issues and indicate the continuing concern with them.

Writing in 1970, Arthur McGill, a Princeton (later Harvard) University professor of religious studies, noted that theology had traditionally served ecclesiastical institutions and proceeded from "a posture of belief." But now (he argued), as pursued in university departments of religious studies, it is an academic discipline that, in contrast to earlier species of the genus, is subservient to no external fora (i.e., it practises "*autonomous inquiry*"), provides public evidence for assertions arrived at by methods commonly accepted in academia, and is not "closed or defensive or compulsively doctrinaire" (McGill, 1970, 105, 118, 133, 134). Moreover, in universities, where such pursuit of knowledge should be — and often is — welcome, "the tradition of rational autonomy is being questioned" (ibid., 133). Theology, so conceived, is thus timely in its arrival on North American university campuses.

Along the same lines, Schubert M. Ogden, a professor of Christian theology at Southern Methodist University, argued in 1972 that underlying "typical modern doubts about the very existence of theology" are

> two closely related propositions: (1) that theology by its very nature involves an appeal to special criteria of meaning and truth to establish some or all of its statements; and (2) that the theologian himself must be a believer already committed to the Christian understanding of reality, and thus to the truth of the statements that theological reflection ostensibly seeks to establish (Ogden, 1972, 38).

He rejects both of these suppositions. Statements about Christian theology may be "special" "in that they arise solely from reflection on the specifically Christian witness of faith," but insofar as they are "meaningful and true" it is "only because they meet the requirements of completely general criteria" of knowledge (ibid., 39). What a Christian theologian seeks to understand and explicate, he emphasizes, is "the Christian witness of faith" (ibid.) — that is, he or she is thus once removed from belief statements about the objects or affirmations of such faith (e.g., the Transcendent or that "Jesus is the Christ"). It is not the case that "the personal faith of the theologian" is "a necessary condition" of such understanding and explication (ibid.), for "theology can be nothing more than a form of human understanding" and, as such, falls in the sphere of "works," not "faith" (ibid., 38). Ogden concludes that "the usual doubts about theology's right" to take a place in humanistic study in academia "pertain not to theology itself, but only to a traditional understanding of it, which can and should be overcome" (ibid., 39).

More recently, another American, William F. May, has replied to common objections to the presence of theologians in religious studies departments. At the time a professor in a theology department in a private, denominational university, he had come to that position from a large public university where he had established a programme in religious studies. His experience in these two worlds led him to the conclusion that theology and religious studies need each other. It is not only theologians, such as himself, who have ties to communities and institutions outside the academic world, he points out. So, too, do other academics. Such "ties sometimes pull and strain academic judgment," but "the person without such ties would be a grotesque on the human scene. The university can ask only whether a person with such ties is free to pursue questions of truth in his or her discipline" (May, 1984, 749). Because some religious traditions include theological reflection or religious thought, study of these traditions entails study of such reflection and thought — and, indeed, theologizing itself, even as philosophy departments include faculty members who philosophize, for in that way students are exposed to the "intellectual vitality" of religion and philosophy (ibid., 750). Christian theology, on the other hand, needs religious studies because it derives from and has been influenced by specific religious traditions and belongs to the genus "religion" (ibid., 753). The kind of theology envisaged would thus "probably be less concerned" with systematizing or defending affirmations of Christian faith and would "probably focus" instead on "common human problems — such as birth, death, politics, human creativity, and destiny" — that is, "theological anthropology" or "problematic theology" (ibid., 751) — and it would learn from religious studies.

Hotly disputing May's rationale for the "doing" of theology in a secular university is a 1986 article by Ivan Strenski of the religious studies department at the University of California–Santa Barbara and American editor of the journal *Religion*. One cannot "do' theology in such a setting because "creative theology, if it is anything at all, is *religion* itself, and not the *study* of religion" (1986, 329). Partly what is at issue is one's perception of the nature of religious studies departments as constituted at present (or in 1986): even as "English departments can have creative writers," or a political science department a "creative" politician (i.e., one actually engaged in politics), so, too, a religious studies department could "hire a 'creative' or 'constructive' theologian, or indeed a holyman or guru, as some have" (ibid.). But creative writers and politicians do not constitute the core of an English or a political science department, whereas, because of the way religious studies has developed in relation to theology but not sufficiently away from it, the core of religious studies departments is not solidly religious studies (ibid. 327-29). The proper locus of theologizing is "living religious communities," not religious studies departments serving as "surrogate religious communities" (ibid., 330).

If one were indeed to do theology in a secular university, then it "would have to be free of apologetics, liturgical expression, commitment or anything else likely to compromise its liberal intentions"; moreover, it would necessarily be "a general human enterprise in (1) method and (2) application" (332), drawing on comparative studies (332) and on "the history of religions for [its] primary data" (334). But then it should not be called "theology," a term with "intrinsic theistic reference"; Strenski proposes instead the designation "hermeneutics" (332).

Still another term proposed for the kind of theology that might be done in a university is "meta-theology" (Harvey, 1970, 28, referring to Victor Preller). It would "not at all understand itself as a servant of a church or of a tradition" but, on the other hand, would not necessarily be "an *ersatz*-theology" just "because it does not take place within or rely upon a concrete religious community" (ibid.). It could be "more strictly philosophical" than many theologies are (ibid.) and/or "in touch with psychology, sociology of knowledge, mysticism, and Marxist humanism, and . . . more agnostic than dogmatic theology usually is" — "a genuinely secular theology" (ibid., 29).

Mutatis mutandis, issues similar to those discussed in the preceding paragraphs arise in connection with Jewish or Muslim theology in a university context. In American Judaism, as Jacob Neusner has written recently, the present generation — in contrast to earlier generations — is producing works of Judaic theology. These are, on the one hand, "evidence of the modernity and secularity of the theologians," but, on the other, "of their participation in the traditional sacred values and in the archaic texts" of Judaism (1988, 323). In a university setting, wrote Neusner in an earlier essay, "the study of Jewish theology, *except* when examined from a comparative or morphological perspective by historians of religion, and *not* as a self-validating system, has no place in the university curriculum" (Neusner, 1970, 179). Theological commitments to exegetical traditions and ties to communities can engender conflict (Neusner, 1985).[11] Indeed, debate over such ties and commitments has come to vex university appointments in Islamic Studies (2.4.6 and chap. 5.2.3.1 below).

In Canada the pages of *Studies in Religion/Sciences Religieuses* have, since its inception in 1971, given seismographic readings of an ongoing debate among Canadian religious studies scholars over the relation of theology — that is, Christian theology — and religious studies. Religious studies scholars in Ontario have figured prominently in the debate and some of the issues raised are similar to those outlined above but also recall nineteenth-century disputes over the place of religion in Ontario universities.

In the institutionalization of religious studies in university departments and programmes (2.5 below), an important element was self-definition, and much of that definition was a *via negativa*: religious studies was not this and was not that, but especially it was not theology (see, e.g., Anderson, 1972, 7-9; Davis, 1974-75, 205; Younger, 1974-75, 233; Wiebe, 1978, 9-10; 1984, 401, 405-06; Riley, 1984, 423-24). A journal that defined itself by the title *Studies in Religion/Sciences Religieuses* could receive public financial support whereas a *Canadian Journal of Theology* could not (Moir, 1982, 102). The kind of theology that religious studies was not was (at least) the confessional, ecclesiastically-linked species from which the American scholars cited at the beginning of this section also distanced themselves — what Charles Davis of Concordia University in Montreal, in an article that inaugurated a spirited debate, labeled "higher catechetics" (1974-75, 206). However, argued Davis, that is only one species of a genus that, since the Middle Ages, has developed into a theology that is autonomous, critical, and non-confessional and does not restrict itself to Christian data. This non-confessional kind of theology is reflection on religion, not the practice of religion. Its emergence points to a "reconvergence of theology and religious studies" (ibid., passim).

Responding to Davis, Gregory Baum (then of St. Michael's College, University of Toronto) agreed that there were lines of convergence but insisted that theology was "part of the Christian religion" and "in fact an act of religion" (1974-75, 222-24). The kind of theology envisaged by Davis, said Paul Younger of the Department of Religious Studies at McMaster University, would be "cut off from its roots in the mythology and ritual of living religion" (1974-75, 232) and incapable of fulfilling "its natural role as the clearest expression each group of human beings can make of the meaning of life as they see it'' (ibid., 232-33). Religious studies, on the other hand, needed to cut its filial ties to theology, but, having done so, "We do not any longer need to disparage theology to keep our jobs, so we should try to kick that habit." Nonetheless, theology and religious studies should not try "to occupy the same bed just now" (ibid., 233).

In the protracted debate over this issue, Charles Davis' major *Gesprächspartner* turned out to be Donald Wiebe, who entered the debate while teaching at Brandon University in Manitoba and persevered in it after moving to Trinity College, University of Toronto. Their exchanges in *Studies in Religion/Sciences Religieuses*, and the contributions of others who became involved in the discussion, raised a number of significant issues, bearing not only on the relation between theology and religious studies but also on the nature of each. What is religious studies — a science an art, a discipline, a field? Does it, and does theology, have certain inescapable premises without which students of either will not be "doing theology" or studying "religion"? Does one need to be an "insider" in order to pursue either of these tasks? What is meant by "theology," and what is the ontological status of its referent(s) or of whatever it is that makes a phenomenon "religious"?

In an early, oft-cited study, Clyde Holbrook argues that religious studies is a field rather than a discipline

> because it has no techniques for investigation or evaluation which are peculiar to it, or which set it apart from other humanistic studies. It is an area to be examined by a diversity of methods which are as appropriate to other fields as they are to religion (1963, 37).

Wiebe (1978, 14), in effect, agreed with Holbrook: a discipline, or a "science of religion," was not possible, he argued (*in extenso*, 1978; re-affirmed by him, 1984, 408, n. 39; 1986, 198, n. 7). Religious studies would seem to be "more an 'interpretative art' than a science" (Wiebe, 1978, 15, citing W. L. King, 1965, 7).

Nonetheless, the study of religion can lay some claim to being "scientific" if the student of religion does not cling to unexamined premises. For "the 'outsider social scientist'" (on the one hand) such a premise would be the precluding of "any possibility of the truth of the 'supernatural explanations' of religion (i.e., religion's interpretation of itself by means of reference to transempirical realities)" (Wiebe, 1978, 16). For "the 'uncritical inner participant'" (on the other hand) the counterpart would be the rejecting of "all possibility of the correctness or truth of the 'reductionistic explanations' of the social sciences" (ibid.). For both the "outsider" and the "insider" a critical — especially a self-critical — stance is essential. Both "must proceed without the assumption of the intellectual, or perhaps better, cognitive superiority of the[ir respective] world view[s]" (ibid.).

It is, presumably, "the 'critical inner participant'" who would thus be in a position to do the "non-confessional theology" that Wiebe in a later essay distinguishes from "confessional theology":

> Confessional theologies presume the *existence* of some kind of Ultimate, Transmundane Reality whereas non-confessional theologies recognize the cultural *reality* of "the gods" (i.e., some Transcendent Reality) and attempt rationally to account for it but without presuming that such an account is possible only on the supposition that "the Ultimate" *exists*. Such a "theoretical theology" or theology proper, therefore, in attempting to provide a rational account of the reality of the gods leaves open the possibility for a reductionistic account. As a truly scientific enterprise, theology must hold God (the Ultimate) as problematic (1984, 403).

With this kind of theology, says Wiebe, he has no quarrel. His frustration is with the kind that he believes Davis and others espouse, namely, a "confessional theology" that accepts "without question, as a condition of study, the existence of an Ultimate Reality" and thus "constitutes a form of religious thought that can only 'infect' the academic study of religion and not complement it" (1984, 421).

Wiebe's colleague at the University of Toronto, Bruce Alton, regards Wiebe's stance as an impossible balancing act

> between (on the one hand) a neutralized theology-as-method which proves, ultimately, to be reducible to philosophy of religion or metaphysics (and which, if it is the latter, many philosophers of religion must suspect is grounded in fideism) and (on the other hand) a theology-as-data so devoid of content that no theologians worth their salt would acknowledge it as truly theological (Alton, 1986, 157).

Wiebe sees religious studies in the 1980s as dominated, albeit subliminally, by "a hidden theological agenda," specifically theology of the confessional variety (1984, 422). What is happening at present, he charges — with an eye to Charles Davis especially (Davis, 1974-75, 1984), but also to the field as a whole — is that this "crypto-theological agenda . . . is being brought out of the closet and proclaimed as the only proper method for the study of religion" (1984, 422). This is "a failure of nerve," a retreat from "the explicit agenda adopted by the 'founders' of religious studies," namely, "as an academic (university) concern" committed "to an objective, detached, scientific understanding of religion uninfected by any sentiment of religiosity" (ibid.; similarly, 401-02 *et passim*).[12]

Davis, in replying to Wiebe, sees quite a bit of sentiment in Wiebe's "emotion-laden language" and "the barely controlled intensity with which Wiebe seeks out every symptom of the theological disease" (Davis, 1984, 393). Davis' "chief thesis," however, "is that a neutral standpoint is a false and illusory ideal" (ibid., 399). He does not wish "to refuse the insights into religious texts, beliefs, and practices that accrue to my study of religion from my own religious experiences and convictions" (ibid., 398). He goes on to say "that the higher levels of religious meaning are accessible only after a personal conversion" (ibid., 399); persons "with no taste for the divine are not in a position to analyze the ingredients of religious experience" (ibid., 394).

This, the "insider-outsider" question, and related issues such as the personal commitment of scholars and their personal involvement with what they are studying and teaching — whether texts, rituals, live subjects — and with students, are central to this particular debate but are important also in religious studies generally (see, e.g., 2.4.6, 2.4.7, and chap. 3.2.3 below) as well as in other fields (Myerhoff, 1978 is a striking example from the social sciences).

In his presidential address to the American Academy of Religion in 1972, Robert Michaelsen, drawing on a long career as a religious studies professor at two large state universities, mulled over such problems, under the rubric of "The Engaged Observer." The religious studies professor, "in all likelihood, in some sense a product of an historic religious community," could choose to leave that religious past behind and identify "whole heartedly with the secularized academic world." But the price might be "existential dis-ease," perhaps trying to live schizophrenically, "professionally in the scientific, academic fraternity, and personally in his own religious world" (ibid.). What Michaelsen hoped for was "detachment with involvement, objectivity with participation," "wholeness," and "integrity" (ibid.). Bruce Alton (1986, 156) agrees with Wiebe that this kind of stance — "participant-observer" — has not been maintained by some religious studies professors, but he disagrees that it is a widespread phenomenon.

Not unrelated to these questions of the nature of theology and religious studies and the stance of the religious studies scholar in relation to what he or she studies is the question of what it is that one studies. A common answer has been that, since most religions have to do in some way with the non-empirical, the transcendent, therefore what one studies is what followers of a religion say — "believe" — about that transcendent element; more broadly, "faith" is expressed not only "in words, both prose and poetry," but also "in patterns of deeds, both ritual and morality; in art, in institutions, in law, in community, in character; and in still many other ways" (W. C. Smith, 1978, 171).

What, then, is the ontological status of that in which one believes? To put it another way, is what believers say *true*? A common answer is Ninian Smart's, paraphrased by Davis (1974-75, 217) as the distinction "between the reality and the existence of the objects of religion." In Smart's own words:

> it is wrong to analyze religious objects in terms simply of religious beliefs. A description of a society with its gods will include the gods. But by the principle of the bracket we neither affirm nor deny the existence of the gods. In order to get over the cumbrous inelegancies that we are likely to run into in trying to maintain this methodological posture, I shall distinguish between objects which are *real* and objects which *exist*. In this usage, God is real for Christians whether or not he [sic] exists. . . . the usage being given to the term "real" only partially corresponds to

ordinary usage, and it is to this extent an artificial usage, a term of art (Smart, 1973, 54).

Wiebe (1984, 407) takes a somewhat analagous statement formulated by R. J. Z. Werblowsky for the International Association for the History of Religions in 1960, and signed by many members of the Association, as "a kind of benchmark" against which to delineate what he sees as "the 'retreat to theology'": *Religionswissenschaft*

> is an anthropological discipline, studying the religious phenomenon as a creation, feature and aspect of human culture. The common ground on which students of religion qua students of religion meet is the realization that the awareness of the numinous or the experience of transcendence (where these happen to exist in religions) are—whatever else they may be—undoubtedly empirical facts of human existence and history, to be studied like all human facts, by appropriate method (cited by Wiebe from *Numen* 7 [1960], 3; on the background of this statement, and subsequent developments, see Sharpe, 1975, 273-93).

An attempt to sort out and clarify at least some of the issues in the Davis-Wiebe exchange was offered by Lorne Dawson, at that time a member of the Wilfrid Laurier religious studies faculty. On the one hand, Wiebe has been misunderstood, partly because he has not made himself clear: contrary to Davis' assumption, Wiebe was not looking "to replace non-reductionist accounts of religion with reductionist accounts. Rather he is simply arguing for the importance of keeping the study of religion open to the possibility of either mode of explanation" (Dawson, 1986, 147). Dawson agrees with Wiebe that "it is unacceptably self-validating to simply declare, as the phenomenologists do, that religious phenomena are sui generis and can be interpreted in terms of their own principles of self-understanding" (ibid., 150). On the other hand, religious studies scholars, including both Wiebe and Davis, have not paid enough attention to "philosophically justified" modes of explanation that would make possible "formal [as opposed to explicitly subjective] openness to transcendence" (ibid., 151). Dawson finds the epistemological basis for doing so in recent philosophical interpretations of social-scientific method, such as that of Martin Hollis (1977):

> if the first lesson of post-positivist philosophy of science is that all systems of thought are conceptually self-referential and rely on certain base assumptions that are apparently tautological, then the second derived lesson is that not all tautologies are empty (Dawson, 1986, 150).

Presupposed here is that "references to the transcendent"—that is, references in a formal but not necessarily ontological sense to "a dimension of reality that is beyond and different from that of our ordinary, daily existence" (Dawson, 1987, 228-29)—set apart that which is "religious" from that which is not. To exclude such references would be to transform what is being studied into something other than "religious." And openness to the possibility of a transcendent referent in explaining religious phenomena can be legitimately maintained because the field of religious studies is necessarily conceptualized and demarcated in terms of such a referent. The concept of references to the transcendent in religious studies is on a par with the concept of rational human agency in a field like micro-economics, or even more rudimentarily the principle of lawfulness undergirding science. It is a conceptual primitive, a given, which can be systematically deleted from the analysis of religious phenomena only at the risk of losing the implicit intersubjective (though perhaps only linguistically so) base of ordinary and scholarly discourse. Only when this is appreciated will the academic study of religion be protected from the distorting effects of the covert ontological commitments of the non-reductionists [i.e., in Wiebe's terminology, the "uncritical inner participant"] or the hard reductionists [i.e., the "outsider social scientist"] (ibid., 242).

Dawson argues this approach at length in articles (1985, 1987) and in his book *Reason, Freedom, and Religion: Closing the Gap between the Humanistic and Scientific Study of Religion* (1988).

There is a distinct contrast between the way religion and theology are viewed in these discussions and the way they were viewed and studied in Ontario universities and colleges in the nineteenth century and well on into the twentieth. There is, to be sure, continuity between this tradition (and its roots in the long tradition of theology generally) and present-day religious studies courses treating the history of Christian thought or representative theologians or even "doing theology." But it is the discontinuity — in aims and methods and the definition of "theology" — that has helped make it possible for Ontario religious studies departments to offer such courses today. It is the "state of the art" that religious studies scholars are divided on the nature and purpose of theology and religious studies and the relation between the two, and on the related issues discussed in this section, plus many more. That this state of affairs is not peculiar to religious studies scholars in Ontario, or in Canada generally, has been indicated at the beginning of this section. That disputes over the nature of a field, the methods appropriate to it, and the stance and involvement of scholars in the field are found in other, older academic fields — unless they are wholly stagnant — should not require demonstration. Nor does it require much effort to see that a number of the theoreticians' and methodologists' colleagues, in whatever field, would be wary — and at times a trifle weary — of what they might perceive as "method for method's sake" (C. J. Adams, 1974, 7) and would agree with Adams in urging them to get on with actually applying method to the data themselves (see, further, chap. 12.8.2 below). Or, though just as methodologically concerned, they may have shifted to other paradigms and distanced themselves from what they perceive as, by now, sterile wrangling over "theology-and-religious studies" — or, at the least, perceive as overblown, given that religion is studied in a number of academic fields other than theology and in ways that are helpful to religious studies scholars (see, further, chap. 12.2 and 12.8.1 below). That, too, is "the state of the art," in religious studies in general and in Ontario religious studies in particular.

2.4.4   Comparative Study of Religions

What was potentially of greater significance than any of the Christian-oriented study outlined in the preceding sections in gaining for religious studies a place in Canadian universities in a time of increasing religious pluralism and multiculturalism was a fundamental change both in attitude toward religions other than Christianity and in study devoted to them.[13] Beginning already with scholars such as H. S. Reimarus (1694-1768), professor of oriental languages at the University of Hamburg in the eighteenth century,[14] but coming into its own in the nineteenth century as such fields as philology, archaeology, anthropology, and ethnography emerged, a comparative study of religions developed that contrasted with the previous, invidious approach that viewed Christianity both as unique and as superior to the peoples and religions encountered by Europeans during the Crusades and the early modern explorations and conquests of the Americas, Asia, and Africa.[15]

The development of "comparative religions" has been abundantly documented (e.g., Tiele, 1893; Eliade, 1963; Ashby, 1965; Waardenburg, 1973, 1974; Smart, 1974; Sharpe, 1975; Long, 1977; Clebsch, 1981). Canada is often overlooked in these histories, both by Canadians and non-Canadians. *Prima facie*, this is not surprising. Even in countries with universities that enjoyed long and firmly established traditions of scholarship, academic recognition of expertise in the many religious traditions of the world came but slowly and often with difficulty (see Sharpe, 1975, 119-43). In a country like nineteenth- and early twentieth-century Canada, struggling to establish institutions of higher learning on a firm footing and often preoccupied, as was much of Canadian society generally, with Christian concerns and intra-Christian rivalry and strife, such study was not high on the agenda.

There are exceptions, however. One is the little volume *The Religions of the World in Relation to Christianity* by George M. Grant, Principal of Queen's University, which appeared in Fleming Revell's Guild Text Book series (n.d. [1894?]). The title may suggest that, breathing the Victorian *Zeitgeist*, this will be one of those invidious comparisons of Christianity and other religions mentioned above. In many ways Grant is indeed representative of the Victorian period generally and of Christians of that day in particular. He espouses evolutionary ideas about religions, postulating a development from "unsystematised" religions, with their "crude and incoherent notions by which savage tribes explain to themselves the problems of existence" (n.d., 2), through the Hebrew prophets, to Jesus (ibid., 7-11). Christianity is thus superior to other religions (ibid., 5), also to its ancestor, Judaism, which is portrayed in various stereotypes of the day (e.g., 8-9, 34).

However, and here Grant parts company with many of his Christian con-
temporaries, his book shows he sees Christianity as one species of a genus,
religion, and assertions of its superiority must rest on "a thorough and
impartial examination and comparison" with other species (5). Its forms
and scriptures are subject to the same rules of study one applies to those of
other religions (6). But Christian apologists, in replying to "a shallow
deism," have commonly focused solely on defending Christianity and were

> quite willing to toss all other religions to the wolves. The differences
> between Christianity and other religions were accentuated. To be a good
> Christian it was thought as necessary to believe that other religions were
> from the devil as to believe that ours was from God (4).

The Christian apologist in the present day, however, must strive "not to disparage any religion or to accentuate the differences between them" but,
rather, to consider "all religions" as "legitimate products of that faith in
the unseen which is recognised as an essential part of man's [sic] constitution" (5). Even the "Strange and horrible" religions of "savage tribes" (as
he describes them) "indicate man's [sic] nobleness, for they express his
gropings after God" (2). These "unsystematised" religions contrast with
the "systematised" ones, the "great historic religions," each of which
"has given birth to a civilisation" (2-3). These were all "blessings to the
peoples among whom they originated" and "marked a stage of progress in
their history" (3).

> They are professed by great and compact societies of industrious, intelli-
> gent men and women. They are identified in the affections of their
> votaries with venerated names. . . . if Christianity should succeed in
> absorbing and take the place of one of them, it would be a more crown-
> ing demonstration of its superiority than was its triumph over the reli-
> gions of Greece and Rome (3).

If the Christian student of religions brings "a genial and not a hostile spirit
to this study," then "Our religion will be seen to be the best friend of all the
others," and demonstrate its superiority by "vindicat[ing] the good that is
in them and their gropings after light," "offer[ing] a reconciling element to
bring completeness to each and harmony among all. This will be its noblest
Apology" (6).

Missionary work by members of a religious group must be conducted in
the same spirit, putting themselves in the place of the religion they are
approaching and standing "on the common platform of brotherhood" with
them (11). Christian missionaries must realize that

> we shall never gain those whom we hate or despise, or endeavour to
> bully or bribe. . . . [nor] the non-Christian nations until we treat their reli-
> gions with justice, and until courtesy, respect, and love take the place of
> the contempt which is now so general and the only excuse for which is
> that it is largely based upon ignorance (11).

Grant's chapters on the four religions he treats evince this same mingling of respectful study with (on the one hand) assessment based largely on comparison with a superior Christianity (and a superior Victorian civilization) and (on the other) with an eye to winning their adherents. His stance is probably closest to a "crown" theory of religions — Christianity as the consummating apex or fulfilment of all religions (thus especially Maurice, 1847 and Farquhar, 1913; more recently cf. Hocking, 1940, Part IV, chap. 2, e.g., 230-32, 238, 249; in general see Sharpe, 1977, 13-15 and his chap. 2) — and overall it is hardly the approach one would expect to find in a religious studies course. But Grant takes some of his cues from Max Müller (G. M. Grant, n.d. [1894], 3-4), one of the pioneers in the modern comparative study of religions, and in some respects he anticipates (in Robert Merton's sense, 1967, 9ff.) the approach of some of his Canadian successors in the comparative study of religions (see below).

Louis H. Jordan's works (see Clebsch, 1981, 17, n. 5) focus on the history of the comparative study of religion. Jordan (1855-1923) was a Presbyterian minister who had studied at Dalhousie in his native Halifax as well as at Edinburgh and Oxford and in Germany. After serving churches in Halifax, Montreal, and Toronto, he retired to a life of study and travel. At one time he served as a special lecturer in comparative religion at the University of Chicago. In what reads like a dutiful introduction by a luminary to a book by a lesser light, namely, Jordan's *Comparative Religion: Its Genesis and Growth* (1905), A. M. Fairbairn, Principal of Mansfield College, Oxford, describes Jordan as a man who

> has for years sundered many friendships, surrendered his pastoral ties, wandered and dwelt in lands remote from his delightful Canadian home, that he might with a freer and more unfettered mind pursue the studies which have taken shape in this book (Fairbairn, 1905, vii).

Judged to be Jordan's best treatment of the subject (Clebsch, 1981, 17, n. 5), the book seems deserving of Fairbairn's rather ambiguous characterization of Jordan as "an earnest and laborious student" (1905, vii). Almost 500 pages are devoted to an encyclopedic, somewhat meandering tracing of the roots of comparative study, in religion as well as other areas, from pre-Christian origins to the present. There follow 41 appendices on a melange of topics as well as four charts comparing world religions numerically, showing their geographical distribution, and tabulating replies to a questionnaire on the comparative study of religions in universities and colleges around the world. Even though Jordan includes an appreciative summary of Grant's little book, noting that an amplified version has been translated into Chinese and "several other languages" (1905, 205), his tabulation of Canadian institutions shows none with a chair or other provisions for instruction in comparative religions apart from that given in areas such as Oriental languages, Old Testament, church history, historical theology, and dogmatics (ibid., 580).

By the 1940s, however, as one Ontario professor reported to us, comparative religion was taught in at least one theological college in the Atlantic provinces—"fairly objectively but rather bloodlessly." And in the latter part of the twentieth century, when religious studies departments began to be established in North American colleges and universities and included in their curricula courses in religions besides Christianity, and studied them by the methods developed in the century preceding, Canadian scholars came to play a significant role in the conceptualization and institutionalization of such study, both in Canada and the U.S.A.

Robert L. Slater (1896-1984), sometime professor in Huron College, London, Ontario, and McGill University, was the founder of Harvard Divinity School's Center for the Study of World Religions and through his publications advocated "dialogue among religions through honest respect for differing positions" (McLelland, 1976-77, 483; cf. R. L. Slater, 1961; his publications are conveniently listed in *Studies in Religion/Sciences Religieuses* 6/5 [1976-77], 485-86). The Center embodied the title of Slater's address (1961) at the inauguration of the Center, "The Meeting of World Religions": professors and students came from various world religions and thus encountered these religions not simply through texts and artifacts but, daily, face to face in the classroom and common living quarters (Bloom, 1976-77).

This tradition continued at the Centre under Wilfred Cantwell Smith who, after study and teaching outside Canada, returned to his home country where he joined Slater at McGill and later succeeded him at Harvard. For Smith it is a guiding principle that knowledge of a religion other than one's own comes through encounter of persons or communities (W. C. Smith, 1959, 31-58; 1976, 139-57, 177-78), "in mutuality: in respect, trust, and equality, if not ultimately love" (ibid, 177).[16] This approach derives in part from his experience as a teacher in a college in India (W. C. Smith, 1972, 9-10), in part "from the unsettling experience of Muslim hostility towards [his book] *Modern Islam in India*" (C. J. Adams, 1983, 187). To arrive at an adequate understanding of (for example) what Smith calls "the faith of Buddhists" one looks not at "Buddhism" but "at the world, so far as possible through Buddhist eyes" (ibid., 171; similarly, 1972, 17).[17] Moreover the Buddhist—or Hindu or Muslim or whoever—must be able to recognize his or her faith in the scholar's description of it (W. C. Smith, 1959, 42-43, 52; 1957, vi; similarly, C. J. Adams, 1967, 189-90).[18]

These principles were given institutional embodiment in Canada when Smith established the Institute of Islamic Studies at McGill in 1952 (see the detailed account in C. J. Adams, 1983, 186-89); half the faculty and half the students were to be Muslims (W. C. Smith, 1959, 32-33; C. J. Adams, 1983, 187) who would engage in constructive encounter with the non-Muslims. Some such principles have guided the selection of faculty and determination of curricula in some religious studies departments in Canada, notably at McMaster University (2.4.7 below). Pursued blindly, they can lead to distortions and absurdities (Welch, 1971, 16-17). In Ontario, however, they have proved their worth (see G. P. Grant, 1968, 65-67; Coward, 1986, 284-86, 288), contributing to the legitimation of study of indigenous and world religions in Ontario universities.

This kind of study goes under various names, none of them undisputed: "comparative religion(s),"[19] *l'étude comparée de(s) religion(s), l'histoire de(s) religion(s), science de(s) religion(s), Religionsgeschichte, Religionswissenschaft,* "science of religion," "history of religions,"[20] "world religions"(see, e.g., W. C. Smith, 1959, 37, n. 14). Common to all of them would be an approach something like that outlined by Joseph M. Kitagawa (1959, 15):

> First is a sympathetic understanding of religions other than one's own; second is an attitude of self-criticism, or even skepticism, about one's own religious background. And third is the 'scientific' temper.

By whatever name, the fact that the study of religions besides Christianity was pursued in a responsible academic way, and had become a staple of the academic study of religion, meant that the establishing of departments of religious studies in Ontario universities could be defended against suspicions that they would turn out to be (partisan) departments of Christian theology or of Christianity (cf. chap. 8.2 below). Already in 1972 virtually all religious studies departments in Ontario offered courses in non-Western religions, though often only at the generalist level (see Anderson, 1972, 54-256). In looking at American and Canadian religious studies curricula in 1970, Claude Welch termed the relatively few non-Western courses "tokenism" (1971, 193), but went on to observe that such curricula were "not necessarily more Western-oriented than college curricula generally. European history and American history have tended to dominate the work of history departments," and there is point to "the argument that the Western religious traditions have a certain claim to prominence in our educational scheme" (ibid.). In the words of George P. Grant (1986, 68), "in Canadian universities the chief lingering is Christianity."

In religious studies departments, courses in "Western" religions had strong overtones of their seminary heritage, whether Protestant or Roman Catholic—not surprisingly since the majority of religious studies faculty had theological training prior to undertaking the graduate study that led to appointments in religious studies departments.[21] Van Harvey, writing at the same time as Claude Welch, lamented that a Protestant seminary ethos defined the field of religious studies and thus the departments and curricula (1970, 24-25).[22] In the academic study of Judaism similar-sounding complaints have been voiced by Jacob Neusner (1970, 1985).

Definition, or redefinition, of a field of study and reconception and restructuring of curricula are hardly confined to religious studies departments, as is evident to anyone who has ever sat on a university curriculum committee, faculty council, or senate. The general direction such discussions have taken in religious studies is toward a more pluralistic conception of religion, away from particularistic presuppositions and categories. This movement has been accelerated as new faculty are hired; these now come mainly from religious studies undergraduate and graduate departments of religious studies without having undergone professional theological education (cf. chaps. 4.2.2 and 5 below). Statistically, curricula in religious studies departments in Ontario universities reflect the constituencies of those universities: courses in Christianity predominate while those treating other religions (as well as atheism) are represented somewhat in proportion to their representation in the population (2.2 above). As the population changes, so also do curricula; whether sufficiently or not is a question deserving further discussion (see, further, chaps. 8 and 12 below).

2.4.5 Judaism

It is in large urban centres with significant Jewish populations—Montreal, Toronto, Winnipeg—that one finds a significant number of faculty and courses in Judaism, either in departments of Jewish studies or in religious studies departments. In the latter, once again, the way religion is studied has changed from traditional to university-informed methods. The scholarly study of Judaism is a long and diverse tradition, ranging from close textual study of rabbinical literature in synagogue and yeshiva to the critical and self-critical study of the nineteenth-century *Wissenschaft des Judentums* connected with Jewish emancipation and the desire of some Jews to apply university scholarship to the study of Judaism (Glatzer, 1964; Gilbert, 1969; Neusner, 1970; Dinur, 1971). It is this critical approach that has won acceptance for study of Judaism in North American universities.

"Semitics" chairs or departments had been established in a number of leading American universities in the late nineteenth century; the faculty were sometimes Christian, but many were Jewish (Remus, 1971, 123). Significant for the study of Judaism in its own right was the appointment at Harvard in 1915 of Harry A. Wolfson to the Semitics department and then, in 1926, as the first Nathan Littauer Professor of Jewish Literature and Philosophy; a similar chair was endowed at Columbia in 1929, followed by still others (Gilbert, 1969, 565; Schwartz, 1978). By 1966 Ph.D. programmes in Judaic studies existed in at least twenty-two North American universities.[23] Many of the scholars surveyed in a 1966 study were teaching in departments of religion—"a sign of our times: religion is studied as a historical phenomenon in these departments, and not as a truth to be propagated" (Band, 1966, 12). A few years later Jacob Neusner (1970) set forth a detailed prospectus for the study of Judaism in a university department of religious studies.

In Ontario one significant result of this kind of study has been the project on Jewish and Christian self-definition directed by professors in the Department of Religious Studies at McMaster University. Funded with a sizable grant from the Social Sciences and Humanities Research Council of Canada, it assembled international symposia of distinguished scholars. In addition to the three volumes resulting directly from the project (Sanders, 1980; Sanders, Baumgarten, and Mendelson, 1981; Meyer and Sanders, 1982), a number of articles and monographs derive from or are related to it (Meyer, 1988).

Another important undertaking has been the anti-Judaism and Torah-*nomos* seminars held at the annual meetings of the Canadian Society of Biblical Studies in the 1970s and 1980s. The scholarly context of the seminars was the reappraisals in recent decades of ancient Judaism, questioning or rejecting stereotypes of it as "late" (*Spätjudentum*), that is, fallen from a once venerable vitality into a moribund legalistic sterility (see Klein, 1978; Nickelsburg, 1978) or as in fact soon virtually extinct once Christianity gained ascendancy (contra, see Wilken, 1971, chap. 1; 1980, 467; 1983, especially chaps. 2-3; Remus, 1986, 72-74). Put another way: even as some Western students of non-Western religions have come to approach them as living religions (2.4.4 above), so, too, such revisionism treats ancient Judaism as a living religion, thanks in part to a fresh examination of the ancient sources, in part to new methods of study (2.4.9 below), in part to participation by Jewish scholars of ancient Judaism and of early Christianity. All these factors figured importantly in the seminars. A significant number of Ontario religious studies scholars took part in the seminars and contributed to the publications resulting from them (Baumgarten, 1985; Corbett, 1986; Desjardins, 1985; Fraikin, 1986; Granskou, 1986; Hurd, 1986; Reinhartz, 1986; Remus, 1984, 1986, 1987; Sanders, 1986; Shukster and Richardson, 1986; Westerholm, 1986; S. Wilson, 1986a,b).

2.4.6   Islam

In Western universities the critical scholarship that came to prevail in the study of religion came to be applied also to the study of Islam.[24] While, on the one hand, this assured such study a place in various university departments, including religious studies, it has, on the other hand, provoked Muslim critiques of "Orientalism" as a distorted understanding of Islam (indeed, of the whole of the East) that forced it into a procrustean Western bed and treated Muslims and other "Orientals" as subhuman, or as humans inferior to Westerners, as Edward Said (1978) has so acutely documented. In Hamid Algar's summary:

> It is scarcely an exaggeration to say that so radical is the disparity between the Islam of Orientalist description and the Islam known to Muslims from belief, experience, and practice that they appear to be two different phenomena, opposed to each other or even unrelated. The reasons for this are numerous. The persistence of traditional Judeo-Christian theological animus toward Islam should never be underestimated. Probably of greater significance, however, is the unwillingness of the quasi-

totality of scholars to accept the autonomy of the religious "fact" and
their insistence upon historicist or sociological reductionism (Algar,
1980, 85, reviewing the work of Henry Corbin, whom Algar exempted
from this charge; cf., similarly, Abdul-Rauf, 1985).

A past president of the Canadian Theological Society perhaps summarizes
the response of many religious studies scholars to such critiques when he
both acknowledges "the benefits of Said's work in laying bare the dynamics of our traditional [Western] intentionality vis-à-vis Islam" and at the
same time "eschew[s] the enthusiasts' passion for exposé and the tendency
toward self-righteous identification with as-yet-unspecified alternatives
which also appear in his work" (Stover, 1988, 27).

Insider-outsider conflict over religion has a long history (cf. Remus,
1987). Even when outsiders seek, as have two former directors of the Institute of Islamic Studies at McGill (2.4.4 above), to approach Islam as a living religion—not just by reference to "origins" and a "classical" period
and through texts but in personal encounters of respect and mutuality leading to presentations of Islam recognizable to Muslims as Islam and sometimes in fact appropriated into their tradition (C. J. Adams, 1967,
191-92)—insider and outsider views inevitably differ (W. C. Smith, 1976,
32-33; C. J. Adams, 1967, 188-89; 1983, 200-01).

In part, this is simply because the outsider is outside (see the essays
[1985] by two Muslim insiders, Islamics scholars Muhammad Abdul-Rauf
and Fazlur Rahman, who themselves present different insider views). But in
the case of Western students of Islam it is also owing to the responsibility
they feel to Western traditions of scholarship (C. J. Adams, 1967, 189;
1983, 200-01; Lawrence, 1990, 298-99)—leading to charges of historicism
and reductionism, as in the quotation by Hamid Algar cited above, or to
what Western scholars may well regard as anti-intellectualism and attacks
on academic freedom (C. J. Adams, 1983, 201).

These tensions are present, either explicitly or near the surface, in Ontario
departments of religious studies, and will continue to dog questions of new
faculty appointments and curricula (cf. chap. 5.2.3.1 below). The study of
Islam does not have a high priority in Ontario departments of religious studies, however, despite the importance of Islam in today's world and even
though Muslims in Canada now outnumber the memberships of quite a few
Christian denominations.[25] In 1974 Charles Adams, then Director of the
Institute of Islamic Studies at McGill, observed that when a religious studies
department finds it possible

> to add specialists to its staff in addition to individuals teaching general or
> survey or methodological courses, the first choice almost always goes to
> persons with competence in Hindu or Buddhist studies. While in princi-
> ple there is recognition that a balanced programme of studies should ide-
> ally include other elements, the pressure of budgets, of student demands
> and preferences, as well as the general academic climate, work strongly

to tip the scale toward the exotic traditions of the sub-continent and the
Farther East. In consequence there are numerous departments, centers
and theological schools that can offer work specialized to a greater or
lesser degree in Hinduism and Buddhism. Many even hold the possibility
for a student to do a major or a graduate degree in one of these religions,
and if they are not able to go so far can at least offer a range of courses,
seminars or guided study programs beyond the introductory level (C. J.
Adams, 1974, 3).

By contrast,

> In overwhelmingly the largest proportion of colleges and universities
> offering work in History of Religions, the only opportunities for
> acquaintance with the Islamic tradition are limited to introductory
> courses. . . . graduate opportunities in the Islamics field are limited to a
> very few specialized university centers and to departments of Religion
> located in universities that have the good fortune to possess such centers.
> Otherwise the facilities, both is [read: in] personnel and in libraries, do
> not exist for any level of significant or solid work in the Islamics field
> (ibid., 4).

A decade later the picture looked somewhat brighter to Adams (1983,
192; 1985). In introducing a volume on *Approaches to Islam in Religious
Studies,* he perceived in the 1980s a closing of the gap between traditional
Islamic studies, with its ''strong, indeed almost exclusive, textual and philological orientation,'' and religious studies, which looks beyond such
approaches and ''the ideal forms of a normative Islam'' to ''such subjects
as Islamic worship, popular religious practice, and the many-faceted significance of Qur'anic recitation in the daily lives of pious Muslims'' (1985,
vii-ix). Adams assessed this development as ''at least the beginning of a
breakthrough to a wider perspective on the study of Islam and to a more
mutually fructifying relation between those occupied with learning about
Islam and those who are principally interested in the phenomenon of religion'' (ibid., ix).

The Three Canadians were among the dozen scholars who contributed to the
volume Adams was commenting on, but none was from Ontario. Adams'
1974 observations cited above still apply for the most part in Ontario
departments of religious studies today. Islamic specialists are few (see the
faculty listings in Mills, 1987, 1988, 1989, 1990), and while the number of
courses has increased (see chap. 8.2 below), most are introductory or generalist. The Department of Middle East and Islamic studies at the University
of Toronto does not have Islamic religious traditions as its primary focus,
but some of its faculty have made major contributions to the field (e.g.,
Ahmad, 1967; Wickens, 1964; Savory, 1980).

A relatively recent development in Canada affecting the way religious
studies professors view the study and teaching of Islam is that Muslims are
beginning to take an interest in such study and teaching (C. J. Adams, 1983,

199). Not surprisingly, Muslim students who enrol (and persist) in religious studies courses in Islam sometimes challenge the instructors' presuppositions and methods; but some at least are also learning more about their tradition. In both these respects Muslim students resemble those of their elders who learn from Western scholarship (C. J. Adams, 1967, 191-92) as well as those students standing in other traditions who enrol in, and learn from, religious studies courses in their traditions.

2.4.7 Asian Religions

The approach to the study of religions outlined in section 2.4.4 of this chapter characterizes the way Asian religious traditions have come to be studied and taught in departments and programmes of religious studies in Ontario and in Canada generally. To come to understand the Asian world on its own terms has been the goal — through study of texts in the original languages, through first-hand encounter with adherents of Asian religions, and in general through seeking to overcome ethnocentrism or whatever else might hinder such understanding. The important role of Canadian scholars in pioneering such an approach and in seeking to give it institutional embodiment has been indicated in the same section.

In sheer numbers, religious studies scholars constitute a significant percentage of Canadian academics engaged in the study of Asia. In research on India, for example, almost a quarter of the Canadian scholars are working in religious studies, compared with 13% in political science and sociology, while in teaching the figure approaches two-thirds of the total (Coward, 1986, 281). For reasons developed earlier in this chapter, when religious studies departments began to be established in Ontario, professors and courses in Asian religions were given high priority, and today in Ontario such courses are standard items (chap. 8.2 below).

In his review of the study of South Asian religions in Canada, Harold Coward notes that the religious studies department at McMaster "quickly emerged as the leader" (1986, 284). Coward is himself one of a goodly number of religious studies professors who did their doctoral work in Asian religions at McMaster and are now teaching in Canadian religious studies departments. The M.A. and Ph.D. programmes were established soon after the Department came into being, and by the mid-1960s the first degrees had been awarded. This has been one of the important contributions of the Department to the study of Asian religions in Canada. In the period 1982-89, for example, 18 M.A. and 11 Ph.D. degrees were awarded in Asian religions.

Another important contribution is the way the Department conceived and structured the study of Asian religions and hired faculty to accord with its aims. As the Department describes its graduate programme today, the "main characteristic" is "the combination of Eastern and Western studies; all graduate students participate in seminars in both East and West, and

Ph.D. students write comprehensive examinations in both East and West''
(Mills, 1990, 390). This kind of approach was developed in the early years
of the Department.[26]

After provincialization of McMaster in 1957, the University underwent a
metamorphosis to public institution, from what had been a rather typical
church-related college (Baptist, in this case) in which all students were
required to take a course in the New Testament taught by the President,
George P. Gilmour, a Baptist minister and sometime professor in the school.
The earliest emphases of the department that came into being for the study
of religion reflected the concerns of the first two appointees. For Paul Clifford, the theology professor in the college who had been asked to form a
department, the rationale for a department was one noted at other places in
this chapter: a public university should attend to the religious dimension of
human experience. For George P. Grant, who came to McMaster from the
philosophy department at York University, the perennial questions of human
existence should occupy a central place in university education. Reductionism was to be avoided — religious traditions were to be allowed to speak in
their fulness (G. P. Grant, 1968, 60-61). Denominationalism and sectarian-
ism were likewise precluded, and ''religion'' was to be understood as
including both Eastern and Western manifestations of it. Faculty appointments in the early 1960s reflected such an understanding: Eugene Combs
(Hebrew Bible) and A. A. Stephenson (patristics) were hired in the Western
area and J. G. Arapura and Paul Younger in the Eastern.

A rationale for an even-handed treatment of Eastern and Western religions was given early on by George P. Grant, department chair at the time.
At the undergraduate level, students ''must acquire some knowledge of the
religious history of the West,'' but concurrently ''must investigate some
other great tradition,'' ''great'' being defined by Grant as exercising ''a
widespread and lasting influence on large areas of the world,'' in contrast
(as he phrased it) to ''some fairly parochial religion which makes little
claim to universality, such as, for example, that of the Ojibways'' (1968,
62-63). Specifically, Grant mentions Hinduism and Buddhism, and, at
McMaster, Hinduism, which must be approached without assumptions of
''Western superiority'' (ibid., 64).

At the graduate level, one needs to balance the need for specialization
against the need to think ''comprehensively about religion'' (ibid., 64-65).
For both purposes Grant stresses a principle mentioned earlier (2.4.4),
namely, first-hand contact with representatives of the religious traditions
one is studying (1968, 66). It follows that a ''balanced department should
make evident through its various members the manifold ways of responding
religiously'' (ibid.). The McMaster faculty, therefore, has over the years
included scholars of Asian religions from both East and West, graduate students from Asia have studied alongside graduate students from North
America, and the latter have frequently spent time in Asia doing field work.

For many years the foci of graduate teaching and research in Asian religions at McMaster were Indian philosophy, Indian religious history, and Buddhist religious history. At present, the categories are (1) Asian religion and society and (2) Asian textual traditions. The second category continues a focus that has characterized much of the work in the Department, while the first, the study of Asian religious traditions in their social settings past and present, is a more recent concern. The purview of the Department has also broadened to include East Asia as well as South Asia. For students working in the textual-traditions area, strong emphasis is placed on linguistic competence. Languages taught include Sanskrit, Pali, Chinese, and Japanese.

Grant inclined to the view that it is better for institutions to cooperate than to compete with one another (1968, 64-65). This was a factor in McMaster's decision to focus on Asian religions rather than, say, Islam, in view of the work in Islam already being done at McGill and Toronto (though the Department is now contemplating some graduate instruction in Islam to complement its work in its major areas of study). Also, the Department has established ties with other institutions where Asian religious traditions are being studied, for example, the philosophy department at Brock, the religious studies department at the University of Calgary, and a number of institutions in India (Coward, 1986, 284, 285).

The University of Toronto is the other place in Ontario where one can do both M.A. and Ph.D. work in Asian religions. It has been a principle of the Centre for Religious Studies since its inception in 1976 to draw on the rich resources of the University in mounting its graduate programmes (2.5 and 2.6 below). So, too, in Asian religions. To provide coverage of the three main cultural areas — South, East, and Southeast Asia — the Centre draws on faculty from religious studies but also from the East Asian department and the South Asian programme as well as from departments such as anthropology and sociology (Mills, 1990, 414-15.) Thus students can, for example, acquire the facility to work in South Asian languages such as Sanskrit, Hindi, and Pali as well as East Asian languages such as Chinese, Japanese, Mongolian, and Korean. Doctoral students are expected to work in more than one religious tradition.

At the M.A. level, graduate courses in Asian religions, or that include Asian religions in their purview, are also offered at Carleton, Wilfrid Laurier, and Windsor. Specialists in Asian religions are found in most religious studies departments and programmes in Ontario. They teach undergraduate and graduate courses, publish articles and books, and present papers at national and international meetings of learned societies (see chap. 7.5 below). Much research in the religions of India by graduate students and faculty has been facilitated by support from the Shastri Indo-Canadian Institute, founded in 1968 as a joint enterprise of the governments of India and Canada (see the Institute's brochure for 1990-91). Named after Lal Bahadur Shastri, sometime Prime Minister of India, it seeks to promote knowledge and understanding of India in Canada, and vice-versa. The Canadian office is at the University of Calgary. Ontario religious studies students and faculty have benefitted from the fellowships offered by the Institute and from the Indian publications acquired by university libraries thanks to the Institute. Ten Ontario universities are members of the Institute, including all those with a graduate programme in religions of India.

In Ontario and elsewhere, Asian religious traditions have been studied, and are being studied, in university venues other than religious studies — in area studies, philosophy, and comparative literature departments, for example — but the advent of religious studies departments has added a focus and approaches that complement, while continuing to draw on and learn from, the work of scholars in those other fields.

2.4.8   Native Religious Traditions

Western interest in the aboriginal peoples of the Americas, and recording and explication of their traditions, began with the Europeans' earliest encounters with them, the *Jesuit Relations* (Thwaites, 1869-1901) sent to France from New France being a notable example of the genre. Such records, as well as new collections of data, have long been the object of study in various university departments such as history, anthropology, and sociology. The questioning by many in the 1960s and 1970s of typical values and mores of Western culture and society awakened fresh interest in indigenous North American traditions (J. E. Brown, 1976, 25-28; Waugh, 1979, v-vii) as did the growth in native populations after World War II and their increased political awareness and activism since the 1960s (Trigger, 1988, 36-37). Study of aboriginal peoples also assumed greater importance in universities, with new approaches such as ethnohistory according much fuller recognition to the place of indigenous peoples in Canadian society and culture, past and present (Trigger, 1988, 25-40; in general, Fisher and Coates, 1988).

Religious studies scholars and departments were not unaffected. In the 1950s Åke Hultkrantz, drawing on a long tradition of Swedish and other scholarship in native American religions (Hultkrantz, 1976, 108, 88-106), had begun the work that would set him apart as the dean in this field (see the bibliographies and other works by Hultkrantz cited by Gill, 1979; see further Hultkrantz's history of *The Study of American Indian Religions*, 1983). Some years later, Sam Gill (1978), noting that "with but few exceptions" scholars trained in religious studies have not focused on native American religions, outlined an agenda for study.

Hultkrantz places such study in the framework of the history of religions, thus according "to the American heritage its rightful place among the great spiritual traditions of mankind [sic]" (Hultkrantz, 1976, 90, citing J. E. Brown, 1964, 27). The emphases are familiar, as are some of the problems discussed in the preceding sections. Indigenous North American religions are living religions which one studies not only with reference to origins or recorded data but through first-hand encounter (Hultkrantz, 1976, 90-91). If, as was indicated above (2.4.4), W. C. Smith urges students of Buddhism to try to see the world "through Buddhist eyes," so, too, students of indigenous traditions are to approach them "seeing with a native eye" (the title of Toelken's essay, 1976, and of the volume edited by W. Capps, 1976). Such a first-hand approach stands in the long tradition of anthropological field study, but now with emphasis "placed on religion as such" rather than viewing it functionally, as do "too many anthropologists," said Hultkrantz, "as a new mechanism for providing social and cultural values" (Hultkrantz, 1976, 93; repeated, Hultkrantz, 1983, 99). One thus hopes to avoid "the functionalistic fallacy":

> the use and function of a religious phenomenon is not the same as its explanation and meaning. The reductionist theory has to be abolished if we shall be able to arrive at a real understanding of American Indian religion as a value system and symbolic structure (1976, 93).

Similarly, Sam Gill, in articles published a few years later.[27]

Even so, once again insider and outsider views will inevitably differ, with natives often disputing non-natives' interpretations (W. Capps, 1976, 7; Toelken, 1976, 11-12; Sekaquaptewa, 1976; Sekaquaptewa, Brown, and Toelken in Capps, 1976, 113-15; Waugh, 1979, *passim*; Stover, 1981) or, sometimes, the secular conditions under which sacred, esoteric traditions are studied (Waugh, 1979, vi, x) or even the right of non-natives to study them at all (ibid, ix-x).

In fact, in Ontario religious studies departments indigenous religious traditions are not being studied much. Only a handful of courses are devoted explicitly to aboriginal (Indian and/or Inuit) traditions (chap. 8.2 below). For those few who teach them, theirs is a competence and an expertise acquired alongside their main expertise (cf. chap. 6.1 below). For doctoral study, students need to go outside Canada (see, further, chap. 12.5 below).

Nonetheless, there is a lively interest in indigenous North American religious traditions among Ontario (and Canadian) religious studies professors and students. Various courses—in methodology, religion and literature or art, religion in Canada, history of Christianity in Canada or North America—include such traditions in their syllabi. Courses in prehistoric Canadian archaeology are sometimes offered by religious studies departments, and excavations of prehistoric sites have been conducted by Ontario religious studies scholars (Wagner, Toombs, Riegert, 1973). Native religious traditions have often been studied in religious studies courses entitled "Primitive Religions." Such courses have now largely been given names such as "Prehistoric Religions," "Preliterate Religions," or "Indigenous Religions," and some have been redesigned to reflect new understandings of aboriginal religious traditions. Sometimes natives serve as resource persons in these various courses.

In connection with the Fourteenth International Congress of the International Association for the History of Religions in Winnipeg in 1980, *Studies in Religion/Sciences Religieuses* sponsored an essay contest on "the interaction between European and native religions in Canadian history" (Davis, 1980, 123); the journal then published the prize essays as well as other entries (vol. 9/2 and 9/3), several by Ontario religious studies professors. Sessions devoted to indigenous religious traditions appear regularly in the programme of the Canadian Society for the Study of Religion. In some cases, an Ontario religious studies scholar has been asked to serve as spokesperson for natives (Paper, 1983), or the work of such a person has been appropriated by them or has been directed to or affected government or museum policy toward them and their heritage (Grimes, 1986b).

2.4.9   New Subfields

If history is "a field-encompassing field" (Harvey, 1966, 54-59), so, too, religious studies. One of the characteristics of religious studies in recent decades has been the emergence of new subfields and the appropriation of methods and insights from other fields.

Psychology of religion, sociology of religion, and anthropology of religion were established subfields long before religious studies appeared on the academic scene. Their nature, history, and importance for the study of the complex phenomenon "religion" has been well documented (see the following and their bibliographies: Homans, 1968, 1987; Dittes, 1969; Smart, 1974, 617-22; Yinger, 1974; W. Capps, 1987; W. Davis, 1987; Nisbet, 1987; Stokes, 1978; Bregman, 1979; Heisig, 1987; M. D. Clifford, 1987; D. Capps, 1988). In recent decades even religious studies fields that have customarily shied away from social-scientific methodologies have begun to draw heavily on them (2.4.1 and 2.4.2 above). In part this is because traditional methods seemed to many to be threshing out more chaff than grain, but also, and especially, because religion was seen to be a more complex phenomenon than conventional textual, philological, philosophical, and theological approaches could encompass.

Whether or not they affirmed the aphorism by one of the theological luminaries of the twentieth century that "religion is the substance of culture and culture the form of religion" (Tillich, 1957, 57), students of religion came to understand "religion" as discernible not simply in such conventional manifestations as church, synagogue, and stupa, or *shema*, creed, and mantra, but also in what seemed to the modern West [28] to be areligious areas and activities: literature, art, sexuality, play, politics and patriotism — in short, religion and culture. In introducing a volume entitled *Religion and Culture in Canada/Religion et Culture au Canada*, the editor — at the time the chair of the religious studies department at Carleton University — characterized the pairing of the two words as a useful umbrella phrase for referring to ways of studying religion which leave aside questions of revelation and doctrinal purity and concentrate instead on the inevitable interpenetration in thought and practice between weekday and week-end patterns of action and concern (P. Slater, 1977, 3).

With reference to early Canadian history (see the lead essay in the volume, by J. W. Grant, 1977), the phrase could "denote primarily church-related topics and concerns," whereas "the religious connotations of Hockey Night in Canada [the contribution by Sinclair-Faulkner, 1977] may best be appreciated from a perspective which owes more to cultural anthropology than theology" (P. Slater, 1977, 2).

That the shoals of dilettantism lurk beneath the surface of subfields and courses bearing the rubrics "Religion and . . ." or ". . . of Religion" has not gone unnoticed, both in and outside religious studies. In older religious studies subfields such as biblical studies and history of Christianity, use of social-scientific methodology has generally been very self-consciously employed (e.g., J. Z. Smith, 1975, and bibliography; Elliott, 1986, and bibliography; Maier, 1991, and bibliography). Especially in the earlier stages of the newer subfields, such as religion and the arts, practitioners were also self-conscious about definition, identity, and rationale (e.g., Hopper, 1957; Wilder, 1958; Scott, 1968a,b; T. Driver, 1970; Turner, 1970; more recently, Scott, 1987; Yu, 1987; D. Adams and Apostolos-Cappadona, 1987). Subsequently, the proof of the pudding has been left to the eating — the generous portions of books and articles served up annually in those subfields, with periodic surveys assessing quality and plotting trends (e.g., Detweiler, 1978; D. Adams, 1985).

Some of the newer subfields are older than others, and in these the question in some universities has been, not so much whether they are legitimate as subfields, but rather whether they belong in a religious studies department or, instead, in older university departments such as psychology, sociology, and anthropology. Two new religious studies subfields, women and religion and ritual studies, draw on several of those mentioned above.

2.4.9.1   Women and Religion

The movers in the women's movement of the 1960s included religion scholars (e.g., Daly, 1968), leading to the formation (see Daly, 1973) of a women's caucus within the American Academy of Religion in 1971, a women's working group in the Academy in 1972, and at the International Congress of Learned Societies in the Field of Religion in Los Angeles in 1972 four sessions on women and religion. The volume of proceedings from the section included a contribution by a woman religious studies professor at the University of Manitoba (Washbourn, 1973) and was edited by a woman who was a member of the religious studies faculty at Sir George Williams University, Montreal (Plaskow Goldenberg, 1973). Sessions on women and religion have been a regular feature of the AAR's annual meetings since, and sessions such as "Women in the Biblical World" and "Female and Male in Gnosticism" now appear in the concurrent annual meetings of the Society of Biblical Literature. The literature in the field is now so voluminous that periodic reviews and assessments struggle to keep abreast of the tide (e.g., A. B. Driver, 1976; Christ, 1977; Falk, 1978; Kraemer, 1983, 1985; West, 1985; Knutson and O'Connor, 1986; d'Angelo, 1986). The *Journal of Feminist Studies in Religion* began appearing in 1984.

In Canada, work by women scholars or relating to women and religion appears regularly on the programmes of the annual meetings of the learned societies in religion, in the pages of *Studies in Religion/Sciences Religieuses* and *Toronto Journal of Theology*, and in publishers' catalogues. None of this is unusual on the academic scene, nor is the question whether women are adequately represented. Nonetheless, there are some distinctives in religious studies.

The policy on non-sexist language adopted by the Canadian Corporation for Studies in Religion/Corporation Canadienne des Sciences Religieuses in 1986 for its journal *Studies in Religion/Sciences Religieuses* (Sinclair-Faulkner, 1989) concerns human referents and occasioned little controversy.[29] But the question of what nouns and pronouns one uses in scholarly communication to refer to deity is still much *in statu disputationis* (ibid., 4; Clarkson, 1989; Landy, 1991). It is not unrelated to another issue that has occupied many feminist religious studies scholars, especially those reared in the Jewish and Christian traditions: how to interpret these traditions in the light of feminist scholarship. Various answers have been proposed. There is the thoroughgoing estrangement and/or the search for "a 'religious' view of life" beyond estrangement (Goldenberg, 1982, x) exemplified, for example, in books by Naomi Goldenberg, religious studies professor in the University of Ottawa: *Changing of the Gods: Feminism and the End of Traditional Religions* (1979), *The End of God* (1982), and *Returning Words to Flesh: Feminism, Psychoanalysis, and the Resurrection of the Body* (1990). There are reclaiming, feminist reconstructions of the canonical (New Testament) version of early Christianity, as in Elizabeth Schüssler Fiorenza's groundbreaking volume, *In Memory of Her: A Feminist Theological Reconstruction of Christian Origins* (1983). Some advocate a reformist, "paradoxical" hermeneutic that pits traditions within a sacred book like the Bible against one another so as to transform the dominant patriarchal paradigms of interpretation and practice (Tolbert, 1983; cf. Trible, 1978, 1984). Expanding sacred canons to accomplish a similar goal is still another approach (Ruether, 1985). More recently, Mieke Bal's works, which burst upon the English language scene in the late 1980s, have "put feminist study of the Bible in touch with critical currents in feminist study of literature generally" (Jobling, 1991, 1; see Bal, 1987, 1988a,b, and the review essay by Jobling, 1991 and other works by Bal cited there).

The areas in which feminist religious studies scholars are working also span a broad spectrum, from textual and historical studies, to philosophy-, psychology-, sociology-, and anthropology-of-religion, to art, literature, theology, and ethics. For example, Pamela Dickey Young, of Queen's Theological College and the Department of Religious Studies at Queen's, has recently developed a sustained argument for a Christian theology that is also feminist and, contrary to many Christian feminist theologies, takes as normative both the past (Christian tradition) and the present (women's experience) (1990, 20).

> If women's experience is not taken seriously, theology is incredible in its claims to be *adequate* Christian theology; if the tradition is not taken seriously, theology is inappropriate in its claims to be adequate *Christian* theology (ibid., 114).

The way religion is studied in academic settings, including Ontario universities and the departments of religious studies in those universities, is being affected significantly — though, for quite a few religious studies faculty and students, not sufficiently (see chaps. 3.2.4, 4.1.4, 4.2.6, 5.2, and 9.4 below) — by several factors: the work of feminist scholars, including those in religious studies departments in Ontario; the presence of women on previously all-male faculties of religious studies departments and at meetings of learned societies; and the presence, in significant numbers, of women students at both the undergraduate and graduate levels.[30]

2.4.9.2   Ritual Studies

Also interdisciplinary is the new subfield of ritual studies. This is but one of the ways it exemplifies changes in the study of religion discussed here and in which it is a microcosm both of new religious studies subfields and of the direction religious studies generally is tending. Like other new subfields, and like religious studies generally, ritual studies is methodologically self-conscious. Ronald Grimes, of Wilfrid Laurier University, one of its early theoreticians, in a succession of articles (e.g., 1975; 1976a; 1979a,b; 1982a; 1984a,b; 1986a,b; 1987; 1988a,b,c,d; 1989), books (1976b; 1982b; 1985; 1990a), and chapters in books (1982c; 1983) provided much of the impetus, formative definition and rationale, and bibliographic labours that helped to demarcate ritual studies as a distinct area of study and lead to institutional recognition. Beginning in 1977 the American Academy of Religion convened consultations on ritual studies at its annual meetings, leading in 1982 to establishing of the Ritual Studies Group within the Academy (Grimes, 1987, 422). In 1987 *The Journal of Ritual Studies* came into being, with Grimes as General Editor.

While ritual studies is not wedded to any one setting, the university was its original venue and will likely continue to be its most congenial academic home, for several reasons. It draws heavily on university fields of study such as symbolic anthropology; psychology- and sociology-of-religion; history of religions; literary, art, drama, and performance criticism; kinesics;

and various other subfields and specialties (Grimes, 1984b; 1987). In assessing the phenomena that ritual studies scholars observe in field study, or the texts, art, and artifacts they examine, their judgments would be based — and judged — not on religious premises and commitments but, as in literary, art, and drama criticism, on informed acquaintance with what is being studied, in this case, with a broad spectrum of ritual — from ritual behaviour of insects, to secular rituals, to rituals of various religious traditions (Grimes, 1982b, chap. 3; 1987). Although located in the university, ritual studies — like religious studies in general — nonetheless distinguishes itself from cognate university fields (details in Grimes, 1987). In contrast to much anthropological field study of ritual, for example, ritual studies scholars are less apt to draw a sharp line between the study and practice of ritual (ibid., 423). Rather, they "are developing a style of integrating participation, observation, and reflection" and are seeking to "maintain a balance between performing as insiders and watching as outsiders" and to explicate rather than bracket or deny "their involvement in the rituals they study" (ibid., 424; cf., further, Grimes, 1982b, 5-14).

Some ritual studies scholars focus primarily or exclusively on texts rather than combining textual with field study (J. Z. Smith, 1987), or reflect on fieldwork done by ethnographers (Zuesse, 1979), or collaborate with ethnographers (Tyson, Peacock, Patterson, 1988). Ritual in popular culture (Goethals, 1981), and the relation between myth and ritual (Doty, 1986) — long a disputed issue — have also been the subjects of investigation by ritual studies scholars; and historians of religion are recently paying more attention to ritual performance than heretofore (Clothey, 1983). A study that draws together women's studies and ritual studies is Bruce Lincoln's investigation (1981) of women's initiation rituals.

Liturgics, a cousin of ritual studies, shares some of the distinctives of ritual studies. It has, especially in Europe, a long history of substantial, often formidable scholarship.[31] Increasingly, liturgiologists are drawing on scholarship not traditionally associated with liturgics[32] and in the classroom sometimes include dance and the relation of worship to art in the syllabus. However, liturgics is still distinguished from ritual studies by reason of its venue (church and theological college rather than university), its focus on texts, traditionally in their ecclesiastical contexts (rather than gestures, in their social contexts), its methodology (still largely historical and theological), its audience and clientele (primarily those responsible for designing and leading Christian worship and shaping its physical settings), and its normative purpose (see, further, Grimes 1982b, 4-5, *et passim*; 1987). In Ontario, liturgics is well and long established in theological colleges; ritual studies is now in its adolescence and coming to maturity in the university. Ritual studies courses are few, but its emergence as a subfield is affecting the study of ritual not only in religious studies departments but in other university departments as well.

2.4.10   Then and Now

The thirteen volumes of the now classic *Encyclopaedia of Religion and Ethics* (*ERE*) edited by James Hastings appeared in the first quarter of the twentieth century (1908-26). The sixteen volumes of the *Encyclopedia of Religion* (*ER*) edited by Mircea Eliade appeared in the last quarter (1987); it will be a standard reference work for some time to come. Each epitomizes its time and the way religion was and is being studied—a Then and a Now—and a comparison of the two publications highlights the changes in the study of religion that underlie the emergence of religious studies as an academic field in the second half of the twentieth century.[33]

The *ERE* already reflects the explosion of knowledge in the modern period and especially in the Victorian era in which it came into being. Today, in the study of religion Ecclesiastes' dictum, that of the making of books there is no end, is truer than ever. In addition to *ER* and the proliferation of books and journals devoted to the study of religion noted earlier (chap. 1 above), recently there have appeared in North America alone reference works organized by geographical area (Hill, 1984; Lippy and Williams, 1988), by particular religion (*New Catholic Encyclopedia*, 1967-79; Ferguson et al., 1989) or covering religions generally (C. J. Adams, 1977; Crim, 1981), as well as the traditional multi-volume works devoted to one sacred book, the Bible (Buttrick, 1962 and Crim, 1976; Freedman and Herion, forthcoming). The aim of both *ERE* and *ER* was to cover all of "religion," and they do so more comprehensively than the seven-volume *Die Religion in Geschichte und Gegenwart* (Galling, 1957-65), which provide detailed coverage of Western religions but at the price of scanting others.

There are significant differences between *ERE* and *ER*, too, however. Though fewer in number, the *ERE*'s twelve non-index volumes have about twice the word-count of *ER*'s fifteen non-index volumes, which meant contributors could generally go into their subjects in greater depth. For that reason alone, the articles are still worth consulting, and some of the *ER* authors refer readers to them. *ERE* treated non-Christian religions of the West, but the contributors were more likely to do so in relation to the Christian Bible and Christianity than those writing in *ER*. *ER*'s coverage of Christianity itself is more evenhanded, with more articles on Eastern Christianity and by representatives of it. Articles by Jewish scholars and on Judaism appear in both encyclopedias, but the coverage in *ER* is more comprehensive and less oriented to ancient Judaism. In general, *ER* articles are less ethnocentric, and the evolutionary assumptions of *ERE* are eschewed in *ER*. There are more articles in *ER* on religion and culture in its various aspects, and more attention is given to religious practice, as opposed to religious thought.

Another significant difference is the smaller percentage of women contributors to *ERE*, approximately 5% to 6%, as compared with somewhere between 14% and 26% in *ER*.[34] About a third of the women contributing to

ERE held academic positions, all but three of which were at the lecturer or fellow level. Of the approximately 841 male contributors a little over 40% did not occupy academic positions (which says something about Victorian society; see n. 36 below). Of the 60% or so who did, these were commonly in the professorial stream. In *ER* about three-fourths of the contributors — women and men — hold academic positions.[35]

Still another noteworthy difference between the two works is the relative percentages of contributors serving in religious institutions (synagogue, church, mission, religious order): approximately 15% in *ERE* as compared with about 2% in *ER*.[36]

These various differences reflect the two encyclopedias' differing premises, which in turn bear the imprint of the times in which each came into being but also the differing backgrounds and careers of the two editors and the scholars they recruited. James Hastings (1852-1922) was a Scottish Presbyterian cleric and, with the help of others, a tireless editor of reference works (e.g., 1898-1904; 1906-08; 1915-18). There is no doubting their erudition, or their Victorian provenance:

> The world as it looked to British and especially Scottish moderately liberal Protestants at the turn of the century is what the older reference work [*ERE*] exudes: Western, Christian, evolutionary, committed to historical criticism and idealistic philosophy, it has a magisterial assurance about its assumptions (D. D. Wallace, 1988, 206).

One of these assumptions was that exposing the editor's and contributors' assumptions through articles on method in the study of religion was unnecessary. Their methods manifested themselves, instead, in the execution of their assignments.

By contrast, the articles in *ER* on the study of religion — history, theory, methods — are many and substantial, reflecting the coming into being of religious studies as a field self-conscious about its place in the university. A number of articles treat shapers of present-day study of religion. One of these is the editor himself, Mircea Eliade (1907-86). Even as *ERE* articles on minute aspects of Scottish Presbyterianism betray the editor's hand, so, too, various *ER* articles reflect Eliade's Romanian origins and his continental *savoir-faire* but also his erudition in many religions, Western and non-Western, and his interest in methodology.

Whether these various changes from *ERE* to *ER* go far enough, reflecting adequately the changes in the way religion is studied between Then and Now, is doubtful. ''Old Habits Die Hard,'' as one reviewer entitled his essay on *ER* (Green, 1989). Though recognizing that *ER* presupposes many of the changes in the study of religion in this century, a number of reviewers of *ER* have also pointed out how in various respects the work is plagued by antiquated or unexamined assumptions about religion and the study of it and is still in thrall to ethno- and Eurocentrism (see the extended critiques cited in n. 33 on p. 91 below and, further, chap. 12.8.1 below). Ursula King, a religious studies professor in the Department of Theology and Religious Studies, University of Bristol, has shown how underrepresented in *ER*'s articles are women scholars (only four of "the 142 significant 'scholars of religion'" accorded a separate article are women [King, 1990, 93]). Similarly neglected or overlooked are women generally, whether as "religious specialists" or "as ordinary practitioners of religion" (ibid., 95). With few exceptions, issues raised in recent feminist scholarship also do not figure significantly in the work (ibid., 95-96), and exclusivist "man" language still appears in many of the articles (ibid., 96-97).

The minuscule percentage of Ontario academics contributing to the two encyclopedias changed little from the earlier work to the later one.[37] But the changes in the way religion is studied during the six or more decades separating the publication of each work are reflected in their contributions, even as these changes are reflected in religious studies departments in Ontario universities. So, too, the problems and challenges. For example, even as the percentage of women contributors to *ER* is greater than to *ERE*, so, too, the number of women faculty in Ontario religious studies departments has increased. Nonetheless, they are still underrepresented (chap. 5.1.1.1 and 5.2.2 below). To take another example, covering the whole field of religion is an insuperable hurdle, even for encyclopedias with resources enabling them to draw on hundreds of scholars from all parts of the world, let alone for a single department of religious studies. Methodological concerns are prominent in *ER*, but moving into genuinely cross-cultural and multidisciplinary approaches to the study of religion, for example, was only partially achieved (Smart, 1988, 196-97). So, too, in Ontario religious studies departments. Prominent on the agenda of these departments also has to be the refocusing of study to include more than the intellectual aspects of religion that for so long were so central a part of education in the theological colleges which played such an important role in the origins and formation of religious studies departments in Ontario universities. To that development we now turn.

2.5   The Study of Religion in Universities: Religious Studies

Both the changes in the role of religion in Ontario society and culture and the changes in the conception and study of religion, as outlined in the preceding sections, are reflected in changes in the way universities viewed the study of religion within their walls. What resulted was the recognition of religious studies as a legitimate academic field and the establishment of programmes and departments of religious studies. There are distinctively Canadian aspects of this development, and it varied from one Canadian university to another; but similar developments were taking place elsewhere as well, as has been noted at several places in this study. Claude Welch's *Graduate Education in Religion* included reports by scholars from the European continent and Great Britain (Welch, 1971, chap. 8). But the establishing of religious studies departments in Canadian universities is more closely paralleled by what was happening in U.S. colleges and universities after World War II.[38]

The U.S. story is long and complex (see Remus, 1988). The upshot was the establishment of religious studies departments that accorded with the U.S. Supreme Court's ruling in the landmark Schempp case (1954) that prayer and devotional Bible readings in public schools were unconstitutional under the First Amendment to the U.S. Constitution. However, the Court also ruled that "the teaching *about* religion, as distinguished from the teaching of religion, in the public schools" was lawful under the Amendment. The Court's reasoning provided the basic rationale for the establishing of religious studies programmes and departments in public universities:

> It might well be said that one's education is not complete without a study of comparative religion or the history of religion and its relationship to the advancement of civilization. It certainly may be said that the Bible is worthy of study for its literary and historic qualities. Nothing we have said here indicates that such study of the Bible or of religion, when presented objectively as part of a secular programme of education, may not be effected consistently with the First Amendment.

The court's decision meant that in the postwar expansion of public higher education in the U.S. the study of religion was not left out. The graph charting the establishing of religious studies departments in four-year public institutions of higher education veers sharply upward in the 1960s (Welch, 1971, 171, Fig. 9-2), as though in belated response to questions posed in 1932 by Robert Sproul, president of the University of California:

> Is religion itself a legitimate field of learning in the university? Is it a specific experience of the race, a necessity for each growing citizen, and a way of cultural growth for the future, or is it only a vestigial activity, and an antiquated pre-scientific anachronism?

Concurrently, religious studies appointments to faculties of private colleges and universities with no religious ties also increased (Welch, 1971, 173, Table 9-5). And in those with religious affiliations, where the teaching of religion was traditional, required courses in religion were gradually replaced by electives (ibid., 176, Fig. 9-3). These were increasingly reconceived as religious studies courses, and the "Religion" and "Theology" departments and programmes that offered them were renamed "Religious Studies."

In Canada, as has been indicated earlier, the line between church and state, religion and education, has not been as sharply drawn — either *de jure* or *de facto* — as in the United States. As the boundary became increasingly distinct, however, the question of whether religion could be studied in provincial universities had to be addressed afresh. The old questions of which religion(s) was (were) to be studied, and how, also had to be asked anew.

In private, ecclesiastically-founded and -funded universities, it was changes in the conception and study of religion, rather than legal considerations, that led to renaming and transforming of religion departments and courses into religious studies departments and courses, with the latter becoming elective in nature. When such universities were provincialized in Ontario in the 1960s and 1970s, few structural changes needed to be made in those departments.

More important than legal considerations, however, were political and theoretical issues within the universities. As early as the 1950s scholars trained in the study of religion lamented that provincial universities did not include courses in the study of religion in their curricula and did not permit departments of religious studies to be established. John W. Wevers, then Assistant Professor of Oriental Languages in University College, University of Toronto, pointed out the irony of excluding courses in the study of Christianity from curricula of provincial universities that owed their founding to Christian denominations. Courses in other religions — "Islam, Hinduism and Buddhism" — were in fact "permitted and encouraged" while "Christianity, the unloved mother of our Western culture, is moved into the attic rooms of Oriental Literature and Medieval Philosophy, or consigned to the lonely rest home of the theological college" (Wevers, 1956, 161). When he reported that "The invidious misinterpretation of the original intent of a policy of separation of church and state has promoted an unwarranted secularization whereby religion has become the naughty word of our Senior Common Rooms" (ibid., 161), it seems that the "religion" he meant was Christianity. Although the focus of his argument is the exclusion of Christianity from university curricula, he also recognized that "a university serving and subsidized by a Canadian citizenry should be non-sectarian"; that was "a principle with which no one can quarrel" (ibid.).

Wevers' goal, which he termed an "imperative" rather than a "luxury," was the establishing of university departments of religious studies (ibid., 162; similarly, Conway, 1959), presumably not restricted to, but also not excluding, Christianity, in accord with the provincial universities' non-sectarian nature. A dozen years later, that goal was beginning to be realized. In an essay published in 1968 George P. Grant spoke from the vantage point of the religious studies department he chaired at McMaster University, but he also took cognizance of religious studies departments already established or coming into being at other Canadian universities (Grant, 1968, 61-62). From the 1920s to the 1960s Canadian universities had largely excluded "the study of one segment of what it has been and is to be human," namely, religion (ibid., 60). True, "the study of religion is in fact carried on in various departments," but it is not true "that there is no need of a specialized department of that name" (ibid.). "Religion must of course be studied in terms of psychology, sociology, philosophy, and political science," but to restrict its study to such departments, or to English and history departments, would lead, he feared, to methodological reductionism (ibid.).

Aside from observing that "An understanding of the works of Raphael, Shakespeare, and Mozart requires departments of fine art, literature, and music more than departments of sociology and psychology" (ibid.), he offered no detailed rationale for departments devoted specifically to the study of religion. At about the same time, however, in a chapter on "Why Religious Studies?," Claude Welch summarized the arguments for such departments. "The practical point is simply that in the university things grow only if they are tended, and that means being given an organizing center, a structure, a budget, some appointive control, and so on" (Welch, 1971, 55-56).[39] But there are also substantive arguments to be made, especially at the graduate level:

> If the phenomena of religion are to be responsibly investigated at the highest level, both kinds of study are essential: the sort that takes place in the context of other constellations of interest, and the kind that occurs when the range of religious phenomena is the primary focus. To say that religion can be studied significantly as part of a program in sociology or Near Eastern studies is not to say that it will be. The multiplicity of other disciplines that may involve the study of religion is both a problem for organizing this investigation and a reason for doing it. In other contexts religion is often not studied well, and sometimes not at all (ibid., 56).

In the 1960s and 1970s these kinds of arguments ultimately carried the day in Ontario universities. But there was a legacy that first had to be overcome. On the one hand, there were those whom the young Professor Wevers encountered in the commons room for whom religion was a naughty word. But there were also those who not only favoured the teaching *of* religion — inculcation — but also thought any other alternative was, in practice, impossible. There was good reason for these varying views. The study of religion in Ontario universities had not been of the kind outlined earlier in this chapter: theological and Christian in nature, it had been directed to moral uplift, indoctrination, and, sometimes, proselytizing; the teachers were often clergy, often lacking the kind of academic training other faculty had, and often unfamiliar with the newer, pluralistic, academic study of religion. Little wonder, then (as three consultants to the Ontario Council on Graduate Studies observed), that "The picture of religious studies held by many people, including educators, is derived from the theology model" and that they "often expect the study of religion to be *normative*" in nature (ACAP, 1974, A-3, para. 1.52).[40] "The main breakthrough" in this picture, wrote Charles Anderson in 1972, "was the acceptance by the university community of a distinction between the religious study of religion and its secular study" (1972, 8).

Several Ontario religious studies departments established in the 1960s exemplify some of these observations.

At McMaster University, an ecclesiastical institution (Baptist) turned provincial, the religious studies department's commitment to religious pluralism and to an even-handed approach to religious traditions—East and West—and its development of a graduate programme reflecting these emphases have been indicated earlier (2.4.7 above; see, further, 2.6.10 below). The religious studies department at the University of Ottawa likewise reflects a metamorphosis, from ecclesiastical (Roman Catholic) origins to provincial institution (2.6.10 below). As is evident from its publicity materials (quoted in chap. 6.2 below), the Department is self-consciously pluralistic in intention and conceives of its orientation as "Science of Religions" or *Religionswissenschaft*. The M.A. and Ph.D. programmes, which date to the time of the establishment of the University as a provincial institution in 1965, are designed to accord with this orientation, stressing "historical and psychological methods" while not "neglecting any other strict and scientific approach" (in Anderson, 1972, 155). Francophone academic traditions, reflecting the University's origins, are carried forward in the Department, but with anglophone traditions now represented as well by a number of faculty.

At the University of Toronto, where the role and study of religion had such a long and troubled history (2.1 above), an academic unit called the Combined Departments of Religious Studies was established in the Faculty of Arts and Sciences in 1969 by bringing together the departments of "Religious Knowledge" of the church-related colleges federated with the University and including representatives of Erindale College, of the Near Eastern Studies departments of University College and Victoria College, and of the University's Islamic Studies and East Asian Studies departments (Anderson, 1972, 216; Classen, 1978, 391). In 1975, the University and its colleges entered into a Memorandum of Agreement according to which all departments of the colleges became departments of the University. The Combined Departments of Religious Studies became simply the Department of Religious Studies of the University and the faculty of the Department received their salaries from the colleges with funds provided by the University. Decisions on hiring, tenure, and promotion came to reside, in effect, with the University. (See, further, 2.6.10 below.)

These moves did not automatically transform the *status quo ante* into a religious studies department, any more than changing the names of departments of "Religion" or "Theology" to "Religious Studies" in other Ontario universities (Anderson, 1972, 13) effected instant transmutations. The same individuals constituted most of the faculty of the renamed departments. In the ACAP report of 1974 the consultants observed that "the history of doctrines and institutions" still weighed heavily in Ontario religious studies departments "largely because of the[ir] previously denominational character" (ACAP, 1974, A-5, para., 1.74). Nonetheless, the name changes, or the new departmental status of religious studies in other universities, were significant steps, and the appointment of newer faculty—trained in religious studies—meant that the move toward religious studies in Ontario universities would proceed.

Once the academic legitimacy of religious studies had been recognized at the undergraduate level, and undergraduate departments had been established, the addition of M.A. programmes at a number of Ontario universities was based on the criteria commonly employed in universities. These programmes continued the undergraduate specialization in religious studies and either led to a terminal M.A. or prepared for doctoral study (see chap. 9.3 below). Ecclesiastical doctorates (the Th.D. and the D.D. in course) had been established by Emmanuel College in 1929 (Calendar, 1929-30) and the Th.D. by Knox College in 1965 (Welch, 1971, 231, Table 12-1). (The D.D. programme at Emmanuel was later dropped, but the Th.D. was continued and in the 1960s was put under the oversight of the Toronto Graduate School of Theological Studies.) The University of Ottawa established a Ph.D. programme in religious studies in 1960, while still a private university. In 1965 McMaster — eight years after provincialization of the University — followed suit (ibid.). To do so required approval by the Ontario Council on Graduate Studies (OCGS). McMaster and the University of Toronto, which was also seeking to begin a Ph.D. programme in religious studies, designed their respective programmes to avoid duplication of efforts, one of the Council's concerns.

The road to graduate degrees in religious studies at the University of Toronto was long and rocky. What had to become clear, both within the University and to the OCGS, was that the study of religion at the graduate level was a legitimate academic enterprise and that any institutional embodiment of such study would be distinct from the Toronto Graduate School of Theological Studies (TGSTS) founded in 1944 (succeeded in 1969 by the Toronto School of Theology), although some faculty from TGSTS might also serve as religious studies graduate faculty.

A Committee on the School of Graduate Studies appointed by the President of the University[41] reported in 1965 that one of the gaps that should be closed in the University's graduate education was religious studies (University of Toronto President's Committee, 1965, 41). Noting that "the University has a large and competent group of scholars who are willing and anxious to engage in a regular graduate programme but whose work has been confined so far to the professional theological degrees which, as such, are outside the University's jurisdiction" (ibid.), the committee explained the confinement as partly due to "the hypnotic effect of sections 7 and 112 of the University of Toronto Act, which, in effect, prohibit the teaching of religion in the University as such" (ibid., 41-42). The committee read these clauses as

> designed to avoid a situation in which academic credit might depend on a profession of faith in religion. In the opinion of this Committee, they cannot be interpreted as prohibiting the academic study of religion, at least at the graduate level. To interpret them in this way would be as foolish as to try to abolish the Department of Political Economy on the

ground that some students might get indoctrinated with Conservative or Liberal ideas (ibid., 42).

The committee drew attention to the Th.D. programme then being offered by the theological faculties of Emmanuel, Trinity, Wycliffe, and Knox colleges through the Toronto Graduate School of Theological Studies. These, plus the theological faculty of St. Michael's College, "could well form the nucleus of a regular M.A. and Ph.D. programme in Religious Studies" (ibid.). Scholars in other religions, as well as from departments such as philosophy, psychology, and anthropology, could also be included, thus constituting not a department, but a centre or an institute, "broad enough to encompass Comparative Religion" but not excluding students who might wish to work "in the academic fields now included in the Th.D. programme" (ibid.).

A decade later (July 1976) the Centre came into being, despite fears expressed by the ACAP consultants in 1974 that Christian studies, represented by strong faculty in the theological colleges, would outweigh the study of other religions (ACAP, 1974, A-21-22, paras. 5.45-47; C-21, para. 2.1; C-22-24, paras. 3.0-4.1, 4.12, 4.2-4.3) — an interesting reversal of the picture as Wevers saw it a couple of decades earlier. A "Prospectus" (February 1975) sets forth by now familiar arguments about the importance of the study of religion and the nature of religious studies, reviews areas of specialization, specifies the methodologies to be employed, and lists the fifty professors from various areas of the university who would form the faculty (Prospectus, 1975).

Writing ten years later, on the changing role of religion in Canadian culture, a member of the Centre faculty cites a dictum by several Marxist scholars that "Religion stubbornly refuses to sink away quietly into that dustbin of history that has recently been regarded as its proper resting place" (O'Toole, 1985, 107, quoting David Gross, Patrick Murray, and Paul Piccone, "Introduction" to special issue on religion and politics of *Telos* 58 [Winter 1983-84], 2). Religion, once so integral a part of Ontario university curricula and university life, but then relegated to various academic nooks and crannies "regarded as its proper resting place," re-emerged — transmuted as the academic study of religion in its own right — in the latter decades of the twentieth century in religious studies courses, programmes, and departments in those same universities. In the words of the Editor-in-Chief's valedictory in the final issue of the *Canadian Journal of Theology*,

> the academic world has changed [since the *Journal* was founded in 1955]. In 1970 a Canadian university which fails to provide for religious studies, Christian and non-Christian, invites the criticism that its curriculum is anachronistic and inadequate (Fairweather, 1970, 128).

2.6   A Taxonomy

As is evident at a number of places in this examination of the development
of religious studies in Ontario, the process was not uniform, nor were the
results. What has emerged is a variety and a mixture of formal or informal
arrangements for the study of religion at the post-secondary level, as set out
in Table 2-1.

The table is not intended to be hierarchical or evolutionary. Four classif-
iers are basic to the taxonomy: (1) Does an institution offer any religious
studies courses whatsoever? (2) If not, are religious studies courses available anywhere on or nearby the campus? (3) Is there a programme of religious studies? (4) Is there a department of religious studies? Graduate and
undergraduate components of programmes and departments as well as other
variables specified in the table and in the accompanying descriptions
account for the categories within these larger groupings. Excluded are Bible
colleges, the subject of Chapter 11 below.

The descriptions of individual institutions are brief, intended primarily as
background for reading the Table and as explication of it. Further background
or references to sundry aspects of the study of religion at various institutions
are found at a number of places in the study. Where that is not the case, as with
Type 1 (2.6.1 below), for example, the description is fuller. Readers should
bear in mind that this study is a review of religious studies as a whole in
Ontario, rather than of individual institutions (see Preface above).

2.6.1   Type 1: No Religious Studies Courses, Programme, or
Department (Brock, Guelph, Trent)

In both Canada and the United States, prior to the establishing of university
and college religious studies departments and programmes, departments of
English, history, philosophy, psychology, anthropology, and sociology
sometimes included courses such as "The Bible as Literature" or "The
Psychology [or Sociology] of Religion," or examined the religious aspects
of a writing, an historical event, or a philosophical issue.

At Brock, Guelph, and Trent universities this is still the pattern, as an
examination of their recent calendars shows.

2.6.1.1   Brock

At Brock a considerable number of courses in several departments treat religion in some way:
- Politics 2F90, "Political philosophy" (". . . Plato, *The Bible*");
- Classics 1P95, "Greek myths and religions"; 1P97, "Roman religions
  and myths" (including those of Christianity); 2P49, "The mystery religions and the background of early Christianity"; 3P48, "Religion and
  society in the ancient world"; 3P49, "Religion and the individual in the
  ancient world"; HebrlF00, "Hebrew language (introductory)";

Table 2-1[a]

A Taxonomy of the Study of Religion in Post-Secondary Institutions in Ontario

Name of Institution	Date of Founding of Institution	Agency Founding Institution	Provincialization	No. of Faculty	Majors/ Honours	M.A.	Ph.D.	Th.D.[b]
1. No Religious Studies Courses, Programme, or Department								
Brock	1964	Provincial	—	—	—	—	—	—
Guelph	1964 (Ontario Veterinary College, 1862; Ontario Agricultural College, 1874; MacDonald Institute, 1904)	Provincial	—	—	—	—	—	—
Trent	1963	Provincial	—	—	—	—	—	—
2. Religious Studies Courses in Church-Related Colleges Affiliated with a Provincial University								
Brescia	1919 (as Ursuline College; renamed, 1962)	Roman Catholic	—	2(p-t)[c]	1	—	—	—
Huron	1863 (as theological college); 1958 (as liberal arts college)	Anglican	—	4(p-t)[d]	—	—	—	—
Western	1878	Anglican	1982[e]	—	—	—	—	—
3. Religious Studies Programme in a Church-Related College Not Affiliated with a Provincial University								
Redeemer	1980	Christian Reformed	—	6[f]	10	—	—	—
4. Graduate Religious Studies Programme in a Church-Related College with a Theological Faculty and Federated with a Provincial University								
St. Michael's (Faculty of Theology, St. Michael's, University of Toronto [see, further, no. 11 and App. B below])	1852	Roman Catholic	—	31	—	24[g]	45[g]	—

Table 2-1 (continued)

Name of Institution	Date of Founding of Institution	Agency Founding Institution	Provincialization	No. of Faculty	Majors/Honours	M.A.	Ph.D.	Th.D.[b]
5. Religious Studies Programmes or Centre in a Provincial University								
Lakehead	1965 (Lakehead Technical Institute, 1946)	Provincial	—	2	—	—	—	—
Toronto (Centre for Religious Studies [graduate studies only]; cf. no. 10 below)	1827 (King's College)	Anglican	1850	57	—	21	50	—
York	1959	Provincial	—	35	55	—	—	—
6. Religious Studies Department in a Church-Related College Affiliated with a Provincial University and a Theological College								
King's	1954 (as Christ the King College; renamed 1966)	Roman Catholic	—	12	20	—	—	—
(St. Peter's Seminary)	(1920)	(Roman Catholic)						
7. University Religious Studies Department Constituted by Denominational Universities Federated with a Provincial University								
Laurentian	1960	Provincial	—	12	85	—	—	—
Huntington	1960	United Church of Canada	—	(4)	—	—	—	—
Sudbury	1913 (as Collège du Sacré Coeur; renamed, 1957)	Roman Catholic	—	(6)	—	—	—	—
Thorneloe	1961	Anglican	—	(2)	—	—	—	—
8. University Religious Studies Department Constituted by University and Church-Related College Faculties								
Waterloo	1957	Provincial	—	15[h]	68	—	—	—
Conrad Grebel	1961	Mennonite		(4)		—	—	—
Renison	1959	Anglican		(2)		—	—	—
St. Jerome's	1865[i]	Roman Catholic		(4)		—	—	—
St. Paul's	1962	United Church of Canada		(3)		—	—	—

Table 2-1 (continued)

Name of Institution	Date of Founding of Institution	Agency Founding Institution	Provincialization	No. of Faculty	Majors/Honours	M.A.	Ph.D.	Th.D.[b]
9. University Religious Studies Department with Theological School Connection								
Queen's	1841	Presbyterian	1912	12	51	—	—	—
(Queen's Theological College)	(1912)	(Presbyterian)						
Wilfrid Laurier	1911 (Waterloo Lutheran Seminary; 1925, Waterloo College; 1960, Waterloo Lutheran University)	Lutheran	1973	8[j]	24	32	—	—
(Waterloo Lutheran Seminary)	(1911)	(Lutheran)						
10. University Religious Studies Department with Little or No Connection to Colleges								
Carleton	1942 (Carleton College)	Private	1952	8	70	7	—	—
McMaster	1887	Baptist	1957	23	64	15	45	—
Ottawa	1849	Roman Catholic	1965	12	54	13	33	—
Toronto ([undergraduate] Department; cf. no. 5 above)	1827 (King's College)	Anglican	1850	17[k]	200	—	—	—
Windsor	1857 (Assumption)	Roman Catholic	1963	13	62	29	—	—
11. Graduate Theology Programmes in a Theological School								
Collège dominicain	1900	Roman Catholic	—	11[l]	—	15	7	—
Saint Paul	1849	Roman Catholic	—	25	—	187	43	—
Toronto School of Theology[m]	1969[m]	Christian Inter-denominational	—	70[n]	—			
Emmanuel	1928[m]	United Church of Canada	—		—	0	1	27
Knox	1844[m]	Presbyterian	—		—	1	1	4
Regis	1930[m]	Roman Catholic	—		—	2	10	11
St. Michael's (see also no. 4)	1852[m]	Roman Catholic	—		—	24	45	10
Trinity	1852[m]	Anglican	—		—	2	12	5
Wycliffe	1877[m]	Anglican	—		—	4	13	12

Table 2-1 (continued)

Name of Institution	Date of Founding of Institution	Agency Founding Institution	Provincialization	No. of Faculty	Majors/ Honours	M.A.	Ph.D.	Th.D.[b]
12. Graduate Christian Studies Programmes in an Institute								
Institute for Christian Studies	1967	Private	—	8	—	**M.Phil.F[o]** 15	12	
Pontifical Institute of Medieval Studies	1929	Roman Catholic	—	28[p]	—	**M.S.L.[q]** 35	**M.S.D.[q]** 1	

— = not applicable

a Data for this table and for the descriptions in the text derive from interviews, letters, and phone calls; current college, university, and seminary calendars; Mills, 1987, 1988, 1989, 1990; *Commonwealth Universities Yearbook 1988*, vol. 2; Marsh, 1988. The statistics are current within the range 1987-90 and should be regarded as close approximations of the data in the sources and of actual present figures; figures for the number of faculty generally do not include part-time faculty; annotations to the table call attention to significant discrepancies between sources. Additional sources are cited in the text and notes. For Bible colleges see Chapter 11 below.

b On the nature of Th.D. programmes and their relation to religious studies see chap. 9.1 below.

c Brescia employs two part-time faculty to teach religious studies but plans to make a full-time appointment. Students can major in religious studies by taking courses at King's College and Huron College.

d Huron employs several part-time faculty each term to teach religious studies courses; future appointment of full-time faculty is uncertain. A major in religious studies is not possible.

e 1908 is usually given as the date of "secularization" of the University, i.e., when control of the University and ultimate responsibility for financing passed to the City of London (Talman and Talman, 1953, 55-66; Gwynne-Timothy, 1978, 146-62), and thence in 1982 to the Province of Ontario (under the University of Western Ontario Act), though the Province had provided partial direct funding since 1914 (Gwynne-Timothy, 1978, 182).

f Includes one full-time faculty member and five persons who teach religious studies and theology courses part-time.

g St. Michael's confers the Th.D. through the Toronto School of Theology, but awards the M.A. and Ph.D. degrees on its own. The M.A. and Ph.D. degrees of students in the Toronto School of Theology are also conferred by St. Michael's. (See, further, no. 11 and App. B below.)

h This figure includes some part-time faculty.

i St. Jerome's traces its founding to a small school in St. Agatha (a village near Berlin, now Kitchener), which moved to Berlin in 1866; it provided elementary education, then also training of priests. Affiliated with the University of Ottawa in 1947, the College was granted university status in 1959. The next year it federated with the University of Waterloo.

j Not included in this figure are four adjunct faculty from Waterloo Lutheran Seminary who teach undergraduate and graduate courses and serve on thesis committees and seven adjunct faculty from the Department of Philosophy and the Department of Sociology and Anthropology who teach courses and

Table 2-1 (continued)

serve on thesis committees in the Humanities Option of the M.A. programme.

k This figure is taken from Mills, 1989, 394; the list of faculty in the 1990-91 undergraduate calendar of the University, which is more inclusive (e.g., Lecturers and Special Lecturers, many of whom teach only part-time in the Department, are listed), is more than twice as large. Some of the faculty in both lists are appointed only to the Department of Religious Studies, some to both the Department and the Centre for Religious Studies, while still others hold appointments both in the Department and in colleges or theological colleges affiliated with the University (see App. B) but teach courses in the Department.

l Professeurs réguliers; not included are professeurs assistants and chargés de cours (six persons in 1988-89).

m See, further, App. B below.

n Does not include those faculty who teach only in the basic theology degree programme or the nine adjunct faculty appointed to the advanced degree programmes.

o M. Phil. F. = Master of Philosophical Foundations.

p Does not include eight emeritus or non-supervisory staff.

q M.S.L. = Licentiate in Medieval Studies; M.S.D. = Doctorate in Medieval Studies.

- History 1F95, "A violent [i.e., the twentieth] century" ("... the Jewish Holocaust, Gandhi"); 1P92, "Early Medieval Europe" ("... the nature and roles of early Christianity and the ultimate survival and expansion of Christendom in the face of both pagan and Muslim challenges"); 1P93, "The high middle ages" ("... Ecclesiastical problems, religious beliefs, scholasticism"); 2F74, "Canada to 1864" ("... political, social, religious and economic growth"); 2F80, "The Thirteen Colonies" ("... the social and theological bases of Puritanism, Quakerism and witchcraft, political developments and commerce, slavery and warfare"); 2P21, "Early Modern Britain" ("... the impact of religious reformation"); 2P31, "Europe during the Reformation, 1480-1580" ("... the economic, demographic and political environment within which Luther, Calvin and other innovators attempted to reform Europe's religious life"); 2P34, "Europe during the Iron Century, 1560-1715" ("... the concurrent maintenance of antecedent religious and intellectual traditions"); 2P52, "Europe from ruin to recovery: 1914-1972" ("... the Holocaust"); 2P96, "Piety, religious dissent and reform in the Reformation";
- Philosophy 2F91 "Religion and philosophy: comparative studies"; 2F05, "Introduction to ethics"; 2F95, "Bioethics"; 2P15, "The beginnings of existential philosophy" ("Kierkegaard, Nietzsche and Dostoyevski"); 2P95, "Metaphysics"; 2P97, "Philosophy of religion"; 2P99, "Ethics and sexuality"; 3P19, "The rise of Christian philosophy"; 3P20, "Scholastic philosophy" ("the great Islamic, Jewish, and Christian philosophers of the 13th century"); 3P58 "Hegel and the 19th century" (includes Schleiermacher); 4P08, "Advanced studies in 19th century existential philosophy" (e.g. Kierkegaard, Nietzsche); Sans1F00, "Sanskrit" ("special emphasis on religious and philosophical literature"). Several courses are devoted to Asian philosophy: 2P12, "Indian philosophy: an introduction to Hindu thought"; 2P13 "Indian philosophy: an introduction to Buddhist thought"; 2F16, "Early Chinese philosophy"; 2P17, "Introduction to Chinese Buddhism."

In the English department there are courses on Milton and the seventeenth century (3F21) and on Victorian literature (3F30), which may, or may not, include attention to religion. In Liberal Studies, Great Book Seminars include study of the Old and New Testaments, Aquinas, Luther, and Calvin.

For a period of time beginning in the 1970s and extending into the late 1980s a religious studies programme leading to a BA in religious studies was in place, drawing on some of the courses listed above but also, and primarily, on courses in the part-time studies programme.

2.6.1.2 Guelph

At Guelph, courses treating religion or that would seem to bear on it in some way are offered in a number of departments:

- Classics, for example, 200, "Classical Mythology"; 310, "Religion in Greece and Rome";

- English, for example, 287, "The Bible as Literature," and courses in the Canterbury Tales (357), Spenser (319), Milton (323), English Romanticism (330, 332), Victorian Writers (334), and "American Literature before 1900" (354);
- History, for example, 235, "Ancient Near East"; 220, "Medieval Europe"; 470, "Medieval Institutions" (includes "the papacy"); 375, "The Reformation Era"; 313, "Folk-Belief," "Popular Culture and the Witch Hunt, 1500-1700"; 360, "The History of Modern Quebec, 1850-1970" (includes "the role of the church"); 226, "Religion and Society in the Modern World";
- Philosophy, for example, 212 and 414, "Ethics"; 213,"Philosophy of Religion"; 291, "Indian Philosophy"; 292, "Chinese Philosophy"; 306, "Medieval Philosophy"; 380, "Contemporary Christian Philosophy";
- Sociology and Anthropology (311, "Sociology of Religion").

In the M.A. and Ph.D. programmes in the history and philosophy departments, students may do work in Reformation studies and philosophy of religion.

2.6.1.3   Trent

At Trent, courses in the English department might, or might not, include in their purview religious dimensions of the authors, movements, and periods treated, for example, Milton (English 201), the Romantics (210, including Blake, Coleridge, and Wordsworth), "The American Renaissance" (231, including Emerson, Thoreau, Hawthorne, Melville), "Elizabethan and Jacobean literature" (253, including Spenser, Marlowe, Shakespeare, Donne, Bacon), "London" (302, including Johnson), Chaucer (331), and English Canadian prose (including Morley Callaghan, Robertson Davies, Margaret Laurence).

Classics courses are more explicit in their descriptions: Classical Literature 200, "Mythological themes in Greek and Latin literature," examines "gods and demi-gods" and "Modern Theories . . . [of] the nature and function of myth." Course 202b is Roman religion, and 211, on "Belief and ritual in Greek society," includes study of "funeral procedures, superstitious beliefs, mythology, worship . . . some Athenian festivals."

Similarly, various courses in the philosophy department treat religion specifically. In addition to "Philosophy of Religion" (275), there are courses that include study of ethics and "the existence of God" (101), "Christian thinkers of late antiquity" (210), medieval philosophy (311), Kierkegaard (214), Oriental philosophy (282), and moral philosophy (330). Sociology of Religion (347) in 1988-89 focused on "the religious life of early Christianity and Hindu India."

Anthropology of Religion (320) examines "Cross-cultural generalizations concerning magico-religious systems in various societies, including Christianity." The anthropology courses in African "peoples and cultures" (301), "Cultures of the Pacific" (302), and native studies (201, 311, 450) would presumably include religious aspects of culture.

Of the fifty-five Canadian Studies courses, only that on "La civilization québécoise" (250) mentions religion. The Native Studies course on "Iroquois culture and traditions" (220) covers "political, economic, kinship and religious institutions of traditional Iroquois society" and "longhouse religion."

2.6.1.4   Conclusions

If nothing else, courses such as these, not only at these three universities but in Ontario universities generally, show that considerable resources exist at the tertiary level for the study of religion. Faculty teaching them may object that what they are teaching is not "religion," as happened when Anderson and Nosanchuk (1967, 1) included in their *Guide to Religious Studies in Canada* a course on "The History of the Early Church" offered in a history department. And indeed it was not "religion," in the traditional sense of inculcation. But such a course would probably have fit comfortably into a religious studies department of the time.

Some of the faculty teaching such courses hold undergraduate or graduate degrees in religious studies or theology. Most do not. Both those who do and those who do not sometimes present papers at the annual meetings of the Canadian learned societies in religious studies, for example, in patristics or religion and literature. In two of the three cases these courses are offered at relatively small universities that are similar to liberal arts colleges, with an emphasis on the humanities and teaching and less specialization than in larger schools. In all three universities it seems that many of those who teach such courses do so out of a personal interest in religion, which often means Western religion and, more specifically, Christianity. Without questioning the credentials and competence of the instructors of such courses, persons in religious studies departments might still wonder how religion is treated and studied in them, even as a psychology or sociology professor might wonder what happens in a psychology- or sociology-of-religion course in a religious studies department.

Where there is in fact such a department in a university, professors in that department and other departments can ask such questions of one another, and learn from one another, as happens in Ontario universities — more in some cases, less in others. As was noted earlier (2.5 above), where there is no religious studies department or programme the study of religion is, for the most part, incidental. Students may include a fair number of courses in religion in their programmes, but a major or concentration is difficult, though at a university like Trent it would be facilitated by the stress on crossing disciplinary boundaries (*Calendar*, 1988-89, 10). Graduate study would, of course, have to be done at a university with a graduate programme in religious studies. At none of these three universities are there any plans, it seems, for establishing (or, in the case of Brock, for re-establishing) either a programme or a department of religious studies.

2.6.2 Type 2: Religious Studies Courses in Church-Related Colleges Affiliated with a Provincial University (Brescia, Huron, Western)

At the *University of Western Ontario* and its affiliated colleges several courses relating to religion are offered, for example, the literature of the Bible (English departments at Western and at Huron), the psychology of religion (King's), philosophy of religion and related subjects in philosophy (Western, Huron, Brescia, King's, St. Peter's Seminary), and Hebrew (Huron College Faculty of Theology). In addition, however, Brescia and Huron offer religious studies courses that are open to Western students. Brescia, Huron, and Western students may also take courses in the religious studies department of King's College and, through King's, at St. Peter's Seminary (2.6.6 below).

These arrangements are deliberate: having delegated the study of religion to its affiliated colleges, Western has no plans to establish a department or programme of its own.

2.6.3 Type 3: Religious Studies Programmes in a Church-Related College Not Affiliated with a Provincial University (Redeemer)

Like the Institute for Christian Studies (2.6.12 below), *Redeemer College* in Ancaster stands in the Reformed tradition of Protestant Christianity, was established to provide university education from a Christian (in this case, Reformed) perspective, and is privately governed and funded. General and honours majors are offered in the religion and theology programme, leading to the Bachelor of Christian Studies, a degree authorized under the provincial charter granted in 1980. Except for a course in "The Contemporary Religious Situation" and one in world religions, and courses in philosophy of religion and sociology of religion offered in the philosophy and sociology programmes, all courses are in the Christian area. A year of New Testament Greek is offered in classics and of Hebrew in religion and theology. Two courses (or three, depending on previous education) in religion and theology are part of the core requirements for every student. Apart from Bible colleges, this is the only instance in Ontario colleges and universities of what was once a standard requirement in the Province. In addition, the College has a three-year pre-seminary programme and, in cooperation with Calvin Theological Seminary in Michigan, a four-year pre-seminary programme.

2.6.4 Type 4: Graduate Religious Studies Programme in a Church-Related College with a Theological Faculty and Federated with a Provincial University (St. Michael's)

St. Michael's College Theological Faculty, like other members of the Toronto School of Theology, awards the Th.D. degree through the School (2.6.11 below). In addition, however, St. Michael's in 1966 instituted M.A. and Ph.D. degree programmes within its Faculty of Theology and by virtue of the College's university status (conferred by the Province of Ontario in 1958) grants both the M.A. and the Ph.D. in its own right. In 1979 the Faculty of Theology also assumed responsibility for the M.A. and Ph.D. programmes of the Institute of Christian Thought at St. Michael's. Faculty size and enrolments are considerable (see Table 2-1). The focus of the programmes is Christian studies.

2.6.5 Type 5: Religious Studies Programmes or Centre in a Provincial University (Lakehead, Toronto [Graduate], York)

These programmes resemble those in large state universities in the U.S.A., for example, in the University of California system or in the Big Ten universities (e.g., Illinois, Michigan). The U.S. programmes are headed by a director or chairperson, draw on faculty from a variety of fields, stress ''an interdisciplinary and cross-cultural approach'' (Illinois, in Watson, 1990, 141) looking to ''a sympathetic understanding of a wide range of religious traditions'' (Michigan, ibid., 188), and offer majors with various foci (Illinois, ibid., 141): ''religion and culture, Asian religions, biblical studies, Judaica, philosophy of religion, and Western religion'').

The Interdisciplinary Religious Studies Programme at *Lakehead University* was established in 1972; an Interdisciplinary Committee on Religious Studies oversees the Programme (Rabb, 1983, ix, xv). In 1989-90 the faculty were drawn from the departments of philosophy, psychology, and sociology plus an occasional sessional instructor. Some of the courses are specifically religious studies offerings; others such as philosophy of religion, psychology of religion, and sociology of religion are cross-listed from those departments. There is a double major in religious studies and a related discipline, a double major in religious studies and philosophy, and a minor in religious studies.

The Religious Studies Programme at *York University* describes itself as reflecting the ''conviction that religious phenomena are open to inspection by the entire range of academic disciplines'' (in Remus, 1985, 328). In recent years 35 faculty have participated in the Programme (ibid., 328-30; Mills, 1989, 407-08). The largest component is drawn from the Humanities and Social Sciences divisions of the Faculty of Arts; others come from Fine Arts, Atkinson College, and Glendon College (Remus, 1985, 328). Nine departments are represented: Anthropology, English, History, Languages,

Music, Philosophy, Psychology, Sociology, Visual Arts (ibid.). Students may major in "Religion and Culture, Biblical Studies, Christian Studies, and Judaic Studies" (Mills, 1989, 407). York majors include three-year concentrations ("ordinary" majors) and various four-year honours options. In 1987-88 there were 55 majors (ibid.) plus students in combined honours programmes. There is a co-ordinator, the offices of many of the faculty are located close to one another, and the Programme looks and functions in many respects like a department.

Although there is no M.A. programme in religious studies as such, in the Interdisciplinary Studies M.A. programme in the Faculty of Graduate Studies some of the M.A. theses bear close resemblances to those in religious studies graduate programmes. At Atkinson College, it is the Department of Humanities that is involved in the Programme. The Department itself, however, also has an interdisciplinary religious studies programme which (according to the Department brochure) includes a major as well as a combined honours degree and courses in the Religious Studies, History of Ideas, and Comparative Literature streams. Glendon College offers some religious studies courses; these are open also to students in the Faculty of Arts and in Atkinson College.

At the graduate level there is the *Centre for Religious Studies at the University of Toronto.* Its origins and founding have been examined earlier (2.5 above). It has both a director and an associate director as well as an administrative assistant. The 57 faculty are drawn from the Centre and the undergraduate Department of Religious Studies as well as from 14 other University departments and the Toronto School of Theology (Mills, 1990, 414-15). In addition, it is expected that students will take a considerable number of their courses outside the Centre. Enrolments have grown to the point where they are comparable to those in the somewhat older graduate programmes at Ottawa and McMaster (see Table 2.1)

2.6.6   Type 6: Religious Studies Department in a Church-Related College Affiliated with a Provincial University and a Theological College (King's)

The Roman Catholic diocese of London established *King's College* (originally called Christ the King College) in 1954 as an extension of the College of Arts of St. Peter's Seminary, which was affiliated with Western. The Seminary relinquished this affiliation to the College in 1966 but retained an affiliation with the University through King's. Philosophy and religious studies constitute a single department of fair size (Table 2-1). In addition to courses at King's, religious studies majors and other students can take courses at St. Peter's as well as at Brescia and Huron, and students from these institutions and from Western may enrol in courses at King's (see 2.6.2 above). King's religious studies courses are "concerned primarily with the Western Judaeo-Christian heritage, the Catholic tradition and the relationship of Christianity to contemporary culture," for example, "Christian approaches to such matters as marriage, war, and technology" (Calendar, 1988-89, 51).

2.6.7   Type 7: University Religious Studies Department Constituted by Denominational Universities Federated with a Provincial University (Laurentian [Huntington, Sudbury, Thorneloe])

The joint Department of Religious Studies at *Laurentian University*, a provincial institution, is staffed by faculty from the three denominational universities federated with the University: *Huntington* (United Church of Canada), *Sudbury* (Roman Catholic), and *Thorneloe* (Anglican). There are no faculty from Laurentian itself, and funding comes from the three denominational schools. The pattern is thus a continuation of "the old" (churchrelated colleges traditionally taught religion) combined with "the new": the department is a joint undertaking, and the courses are religious studies courses.

Of the three church-related universities, Sudbury is the oldest, having been established in 1913 as Collège du Sacré Coeur, a francophone institution standing in the Roman Catholic francophone academic tradition. Renamed the University of Sudbury College/Le Collège de l'Université de Sudbury in 1957, it federated with Laurentian in 1960 and is now a bilingual institution. Huntington owes its establishment in 1960 largely to the financial contributions of United Church members in mid-northern Ontario presbyteries who wanted a university to serve people in that area. Thorneloe, founded in 1961 by the Algoma diocese of the Anglican Church of Canada, federated with Laurentian in 1963. Like Laurentian generally, the Department is devoted to regional (i.e., northern Ontario) education; distance education is therefore an important component of the curriculum.

2.6.8   Type 8: University Religious Studies Department Constituted by University and Church-Related College Faculties (Waterloo [Conrad Grebel, Renison, St. Jerome's, St. Paul's])

The *University of Waterloo* was a provincial creation (1957) that developed out of Waterloo College, an ecclesiastical institution (see University of Waterloo, 1990; and below, 2.6.9, Wilfrid Laurier University). The churchrelated colleges affiliated with the University soon began to offer Religious Knowledge courses: *Renison* (Anglican) and *St. Jerome's* (Roman Catholic) in 1960; *St. Paul's* (United Church) in 1962; *Conrad Grebel* (Mennonite) in 1964. After a Faculty of Arts was established in 1964, it was decided to appoint religious studies faculty, the first such in 1969, when a religious studies programme was established, and two more shortly thereafter. Although no further appointments were made in the Arts faculty, religious studies appointments continued to be made in the colleges. In 1977 a University department was formed that included the three University professors plus the religious studies faculty now in place in the four church-related colleges. The result is a department of considerable size (see Table 2-1).

2.6.9 Type 9: University Religious Studies Departments with Theological School Connection (Queen's, Wilfrid Laurier)

These departments are in universities which were founded by Christian denominations and in which both the study of religion and theological education were, until provincialization, intrinsic components of the curriculum. As was indicated earlier (2.5 above), even before provincialization religion requirements were being dropped and religion or theology departments were being reconceived as religious studies departments and generally renamed as such (exceptions in Ontario: "Department of Religion" at Carleton; "Department of Religion and Culture" at Wilfrid Laurier). At the time of provincialization the theological colleges were legally and formally separated from the universities. However, some connection between department and college persists; for example, the two may cooperate in academic or professional graduate degree programs, or faculty from the college may teach courses in the department, or vice-versa.

At *Queen's University* the relation between the Department of Religious Studies and Queen's Theological College is close, but the two are distinct, and increasingly so, as the change of name from "Religion" to "Religious Studies" in 1990 suggests. Both are housed in the College building, and until July 1, 1990 the Principal of the College headed the Department. Since then the Department has had its own chair. As at Western, the University has delegated responsibility for religious studies to the Department, but unlike Western, the University assumes the costs (e.g., salaries and some overload compensation and fringe benefits). Most of the faculty—both in the Department and the College—teach both religious studies and theology courses. The ratio varies from year to year and for each person.

One effect of the College's federation with a university is that its appointment, tenure, and promotion policies are now very close to University policies. Religious studies faculty are viewed as University faculty; they serve, for example, on thesis committees in other departments and on University committees generally. Another effect is that the library resources of the College are fully integrated into the University library system and are thus readily available for religious studies research and teaching, and vice versa. These observations apply generally also at the other Ontario universities

where religious studies departments or programmes and theological colleges are located on the same campus or have some institutional affiliation
even though they may be geographically separate.

Wilfrid Laurier University traces its origins to the founding in 1911 of
Waterloo Lutheran Seminary, whence grew Waterloo College in 1924 with
a baccalaureate programme, which in 1925 affiliated with the University of
Western Ontario (which actually granted the degrees), followed by Waterloo
Lutheran University (1960) and, finally, provincialization as Wilfrid Laurier
University (1973). The Department of Religious Knowledge (established
1959) was succeeded in 1964 by a Department of Religious Studies and, in
1968, a School of Religion and Culture with faculty and library resources
from the Religious Studies and Ancient Near Eastern departments and
Waterloo Lutheran Seminary. With provincialization of the University and
the constituting of the Seminary as a legally separate institution, the School
gradually became a Department, and the faculty, which had functioned in
great part as one, now became two. What continues is that faculty from the
Department teach some Seminary courses, Seminary faculty teach some
Religion and Culture undergraduate and graduate courses, Religion and
Culture M.A. courses are open to Seminary students, and some Seminary
courses may be taken by M.A. students.

2.6.10   Type 10: University Religious Studies Departments with Little or No Connection to Colleges (Carleton, McMaster, Ottawa, Toronto [Undergraduate], Windsor)

These are like the religious studies programme at York, but with departmental status: either no theological college is associated with the university (thus
the departments at Carleton and Windsor), or else there is little or no connection between the university religious studies department and a theological college affiliated with the university (thus the departments at McMaster and
Ottawa), or there is a historical connection between the religious studies
department and colleges affiliated with the university but the connection is
now only residual (thus the department at the University of Toronto).

Carleton College, founded in 1942 as a private institution, was provincialized in 1952 and acquired university status in 1957. Although it was not
in its origins a provincial creation *de novo*, as are Brock, Lakehead, Trent,
Waterloo, and York, like them it represents a departure from the traditional
pattern of ecclesiastical founding. Like them, too, it shared in the Ontario
university expansion of the late 1950s and the 1960s. St. Patrick's College,
a Roman Catholic institution, was incorporated into the Division of Arts in
1967, but there is no theological college on campus or connected with the
Department.

The religious studies department at the *University of Windsor* has no connection with a theological college, but it differs from the department at

Carleton inasmuch as Windsor developed out of an ecclesiastical university (Assumption) with affiliated denominational colleges. This had an effect on the way the first appointments were made in religious studies. When Assumption became a provincial university, a department of theology was established (later renamed religious studies). The University made the appointments to the Department, but in consultation with four affiliated church-related colleges: Assumption (Roman Catholic), Holy Redeemer (then a Roman Catholic seminary), Canterbury (Anglican), and Iona (United Church). Subsequent appointments have been made by the University without such consultation. There is today no formal or direct relation between the Department and the four colleges.

McMaster University has some formal similarities to the University of Windsor: an ecclesiastical (Baptist) institution in origin, it was provincialized in 1957, and McMaster Divinity College was established as a distinct but affiliated institution in that same year. There are no formal ties between the religious studies department and the Divinity College. A Divinity College professor occasionally teaches (or teaches in) a course in the religious studies department, and Divinity students have sometimes taken Hebrew there, or religious studies students take Greek or Hebrew at the College. Some idea of the considerable size of the Department may be gained from Table 2-1. (On the history and significance of the Department in the development of religious studies in Ontario see 2.4.7 and 2.5 above.)

The origins of the *University of Ottawa/Université d'Ottawa* need to be considered in relation to those of St. Paul University/Université Saint-Paul. The latter is descended from the College of Bytown founded in 1849 by Bishop Joseph-Eugene Guigues, who in 1856 placed it in the hands of the Oblates of Mary Immaculate. Renamed the College of Ottawa in 1861, it was granted university status by the government in 1866 and a pontifical charter in 1889. Under a revised civil charter it became Université d'Ottawa in 1933. On July 1, 1965 it became St. Paul University/Université Saint-Paul, a Roman Catholic institution that retained the civil and canonical charters of the Université d'Ottawa but conceded the majority of its holdings to a new institution, the University of Ottawa/Université d'Ottawa, established by the Province of Ontario on the same date. The religious studies department in the new university set itself apart from ecclesiastical ties through its "Science-of-Religions" orientation. The francophone academic tradition continues in the Department, but now alongside the anglophone. The language of instruction is French in some classes, English in others, but both faculty and students are expected to be bilingual. The Department has both undergraduate and graduate (M.A. and Ph.D.) programmes and considerable numbers of students enrolled in each (see Table 2-1). Ottawa faculty sometimes teach at St. Paul, and vice versa. Graduate students at St. Paul may pursue civil degrees (M.A. and Ph.D. in theology), but these are conferred by Ottawa (2.6.11 below). (On Ottawa, see, further, 2.5 above.)

The background and antecedents of the present (undergraduate) *Department of Religious Studies at the University of Toronto* have been delineated at a number of places in this chapter (see especially 2.5 above). It is a university department, with its own university office and administrative officers. However, some of the faculty teach only in the Department, some are appointed both to the Department and the Centre for Religious Studies (the two are distinct; see 2.6.5 above), while still others are appointed to colleges (church-related and otherwise) or to theological colleges affiliated with the University but are also cross-appointed to the Department or teach courses in the Department. Prior to 1975 (when the Combined Departments of Religious Studies became the Department of Religious Studies [see 2.5 above]), faculty were drawn from colleges affiliated with the University. Subsequently, all appointments to the Department have been made by the University. When those faculty appointed prior to 1975 retire, all faculty will be University-appointed. Some idea of the considerable size of the Department can be gained from Table 2-1.

2.6.11   Type 11: Graduate Theology Programmes in a Theological School (Collège dominicain, Saint Paul, Toronto School of Theology [Emmanuel, Knox, Regis, St. Michael's, Trinity, Wycliffe])

The bachelor of theology and master of divinity programmes offered at the institutions considered in this section are excluded from consideration here, but their M.A., Ph.D., and Th.D. programmes are included, for the reasons given in Chapter 9.1 below.

The *Collège dominicain de philosophie et de théologie* in Ottawa dates its founding to 1900 and its recognition by the Dominican order as a seminary to 1909. In 1965 Rome constituted it as a theological faculty with university (degree-granting) status. In 1967 the Province of Ontario granted it a university charter with power to confer the M.A. and Ph.D. degrees.

The origins of *St. Paul University/Université Saint Paul* have been outlined in 2.6.10 above. On July 1, 1965, when what was then the Université d'Ottawa became St. Paul University/Université Saint Paul, it retained the civil and canonical charters of the Université d'Ottawa but also federated with the newly created provincial institution, the University of Ottawa/Université d'Ottawa. St. Paul restricts its teaching to faculties of theology, philosophy, and canon law and various institutes related to these. The ecclesiastical doctorate in theology (D.Th.) is conferred by St. Paul and the civil degrees — the M.A. and Ph.D. in theology — are conferred by the University of Ottawa. As in the latter, the academic traditions are both francophone and anglophone, and instruction is bilingual.

Prior to the formation of the *Toronto School of Theology* (TST) in 1969 (see App. B), two of the constituting schools had instituted doctoral programmes, Emmanuel College the Th.D. and the D.D. in course in 1929 and Knox College in 1965 (2.5 above; on the Th.D. degree see chap. 9.1 below). In the period 1952-69 Emmanuel (which had discontinued the D.D. programme but retained the Th.D.) awarded 39 Th.D. degrees (Welch, 1971, 236, Table 12-6b). In the year that TST was formed, 12 students were enrolled in the Th.D. programme at Emmanuel and four in that of Knox (ibid., 241, Table 12-9). After 1944 these and other advanced degree programmes in theology of the theological colleges and faculties associated with the University of Toronto were cooperative in nature, through the Toronto Graduate School of Theological Studies. The advanced degree programme of TST is a continuation of this cooperative venture. The faculty are drawn from the federated colleges. The colleges have been empowered by the Province to grant degrees in theology; since 1979 these have been conferred jointly with the University of Toronto through TST. However, any M.A. and Ph.D. degrees of the member schools are awarded by the University of St. Michael's College (see 2.6.4 above and App. B below). The Advanced Degree Council of TST handles admissions to the programme. Some idea of the size of the programme can be gained from Table 2-1. Further information on the member colleges of TST is given in Appendix B.

2.6.12   Type 12: Graduate Christian Studies Programmes in an Institute (Institute for Christian Studies, Pontifical Institute of Mediaeval Studies)

The *Institute for Christian Studies* in Toronto stands in the Reformed tradition of Protestant Christianity and was established by the Association for the Advancement of Christian Scholarship in 1967. The aim of the four Dutch immigrants who in 1956 founded the Association (originally named the Association for Reformed Scientific Scholarship) was a Christian university. In accord with this original goal, the Institute's degree programmes are non-clerical, intended "to help people in almost any field of study to understand their field in a Christian way" by focusing "on the fundamental points in a field where theological, philosophical, and methodological questions naturally arise" (*Calendar*, 1990-92, 4). The Master of Philosophical Foundations programme (M.Phil.F.), accredited by the Province in 1983, is a two- to three-year course of study that includes a thesis. The foci of the degree are "Biblical Foundations" and "Philosophical Foundations" (ibid., 6). Accreditation is being sought for the Master's programmes in world-view studies and in education. The Institute's Ph.D. programme, offered in cooperation with the Free University of Amsterdam and also not provincially accredited, is offered in the fields of history of philosophy, systematic philosophy, and "the Philosophy of some Discipline" (ibid., 13-14). It normally follows upon the M.Phil.F. degree and requires two years of residence at the Institute, a comprehensive examination, and writing of a dissertation under the supervision of a Free University professor with an Institute faculty member as joint supervisor. The Institute is privately funded and governed by a Board of Trustees and a Senate. Over half the approximately 100 full- and part-time students in the various programmes and courses at the Institute are from outside Canada.

The *Pontifical Institute of Medieval Studies* in Toronto was established in 1929 under the auspices of St. Michael's College, Toronto, and a Roman Catholic religious order, the Congregation of the Priests of St. Basil, with the aim of furthering research on the Middle Ages and, secondarily, to offer graduate academic programmes for a limited number of students. Ten years later Rome granted it pontifical status and a charter empowering it to confer the pontifical Licentiate in Medieval Studies (M.S.L.) and Doctorate in Medieval Studies (M.S.D.) The number of students is small (see Table 2-1), the original focus on research remaining primary. It characterizes itself as "a small autonomous academic community with no departmental divisions" (*Syllabus*, 1988, 4), governed by a council and various committees composed of the Institute's scholars and students (called, variously, Senior Fellows, Junior Fellows, Research Associates, Junior Associates, etc.) The Committee on Publications oversees the Pontifical Institute of Medieval Studies Press, which publishes texts, translations, and monographs as well as the journal *Medieval Studies*.

In addition to these institutes that offer degrees alongside the research carried on by the faculty, there are those devoted solely to research and public education such as the *Institute of Anabaptist-Mennonite Studies* and the *Institute of Peace and Conflict Studies* at Conrad Grebel College, University of Waterloo; the *Institute for Christian Ethics* at Waterloo Lutheran Seminary; and the *Westminster Institute for Ethics and Human Values* at the University of Western Ontario. The Westminster Institute was established in 1979 by Western and its affiliate, Westminster College; foci of recent research include bioethics, environmental ethics, business and professional ethics, and values and the law. The two institutes at Conrad Grebel sponsor research, conferences, and publications. Waterloo Lutheran's Institute for Christian Ethics provides a research base for studying current social problems, issues study papers, and offers continuing education programmes.

2.6.13   Diversity and Commonality

Taxonomies attempt to do what William James saw as the "first thing the intellect does with an object," namely, "to class it along with something else." And like the crab that might "be filled with personal outrage if it could hear us class it without ado or apology as a crustacean" (William James, 1958, 26), the individuals thus classified might protest their classification to the classifier, as a smoothing away of differences and distinctives. Moreover, the rudimentary taxonomy of Table 2-1 and the accompanying bare-bones exegesis do not convey the "flavour" of an institution or a department—in what ways the inclusion of St. Patrick's College theological faculty in Carleton's religion department affected that department, for example; or the interaction between religious studies departments and theological faculty at Queen's or Toronto or Wilfrid Laurier; or the disparity between ideal (a department's self-description) and actuality (how it really works, or doesn't work, or how slippage or infighting clogs the works). Nor does the Table or the commentary on it take much account of another kind of teaching that is a not insignificant component of instruction in several religious studies departments in Ontario, namely, distance education, through correspondence, cassette, radio, television, or combinations of these.

However, if the taxonomy and exegesis are "thin descriptions"—and they do not even include Bible colleges (chap. 11 below)—they are "thick" (Geertz, 1973) in that they do in fact point to differences and distinctives, to the complexity—and the reticulateness—of arrangements for the post-secondary study of religion in Ontario. There is a plurality—some might say a plethora—of courses, programmes, departments, and degrees within the provincial system of higher education, alongside it, and outside it.

In the Ontario vernacular, it is a "schmozzle." Tidiness is not necessarily a virtue, of course, or attainable. The "schmozzle," as the preceding pages have indicated, is the result of diverse historical, social, and cultural factors representing persons, interests, and institutions that interacted and changed over a period of two centuries. At the post-secondary level, there are Christian schools, schools Christian in origin but now provincial, schools provincial from the start, and various combinations of these. There are anglophone schools, francophone schools, and bilingual schools. There are schools that stand in the francophone academic tradition, both European and Canadian, and others whose faculty and traditions are more British, or American, in origin, and reflect those beginnings—and various combinations of these.

The ways and means for studying religion in Upper-Canada-become-Ontario reflect this diversity amid a commonality described in Chapter 1 and in preceding sections of the present chapter. The wry characterization of one of the Ontario religious studies programmes by one faculty member we interviewed—"It may work in practice but it'll never work in theory"—would seem to apply to arrangements for the post-secondary study of religion in Ontario as a whole.

2.7 Toward Maturity

A number of differentia characterize religious studies in Ontario at the end of the twentieth century. Some are peculiar to it, most are not—they are the common property of academia, whether in Ontario, in Canada, or in North America generally. That in itself is one of the most evident characteristics of religious studies in Ontario: it has come to take its place alongside other branches of learning in the Province's universities, with programmes or departments staffed by faculty chosen on the basis of academic expertise, rather than religious profession, and committed to the professional goals of teaching, research, and publication, and the development of indigenous graduate education in their field.

Underlying the development of religious studies in Ontario are the changes outlined earlier in this chapter — changes in the population of the Province and the nation, in the role of religion in the life of the Province and the nation, and in the way religion is conceived and studied. What persists from Ontario's past is a perduring — now perhaps increasingly vestigial — religiosity, broadened and enlivened, however, by the infusion of diverse religious traditions brought by immigrants and by the revival of indigenous religious traditions — a religiosity that gives substance to the claim that religion, as a significant and persisting element of human experience, deserves to be studied in the Province's universities. As John Webster Grant expressed it a decade and a half ago, it is a time in Canada when establishing of religious studies departments signals "the end of a period when religion represented a heavyhanded pressure to be resisted and the beginning of one when it offers an exciting field to be explored" (1977, 20).

The characteristics of religious studies in Ontario today were seen to be foreshadowed in various ways in the Department of Oriental Languages at the University of Toronto at the end of the last century (2.1.3 above). That some of them remain as goals only partially realized or persist as contentious issues is evident from this and subsequent chapters. Such a situation is not peculiar to religious studies. But as a young field, religious studies is still self-conscious about its youth and how it moves from adolescence to maturity, without succumbing to senescence.

One of the steps it has taken toward maturity — one distinctive, if not unique, among academic fields in Canada — is the facilitating of scholarly publication. In the late 1960s and early 1970s, religious studies scholars in North America were increasingly frustrated by the limited capacity of university presses and by commercial publishers' eagerness to publish their textbooks and popularizations but reluctance to issue their scholarly works. Religious studies scholars decided that in their learned societies, whose numbers had swelled thanks to the expansion of religious studies and a large infusion of young scholars, they had the expertise to referee manuscripts and the financial resources to publish them. They acquired typesetting equipment and began publishing both books and journals.

This development was outlined in an article in *Scholarly Publishing* in 1976 by Norman Wagner, then professor of religious studies, graduate dean and director of research at Wilfrid Laurier University and director of Wilfrid Laurier University Press as well as executive officer of the Council on the Study of Religion, a federation of North American professional societies in religious studies whose office was then located at Wilfrid Laurier. The Council, either in cooperation with or on behalf of its constituent societies, began publishing scholarly books and a number of religious studies journals, including its own publication *Religious Studies Review*, inaugurated in 1975 and devoted solely to reviews of works in religious studies (Shriver, 1988).

Much of the rationale for the emergence of learned societies as publishers was provided in a small volume published by the Council in 1972, *Scholarly Communication and Publication* (MacRae, 1972), in Wagner's article (1976), and in two articles in the 1977-78 volume of *Scholarly Publishing* by Robert Funk, then professor of religious studies at the University of Montana and the first director of Scholars Press, which had been established at the University in the early 1970s by several constituent societies of the Council on the Study of Religion. The Council's publishing ventures served as precedent and model for Scholars Press, for Wilfrid Laurier University Press (established in 1974), and for the publishing programme of the Canadian Corporation for Studies in Religion/Corporation Canadienne des Sciences Religieuses established by religious studies learned societies in 1970 (see Wagner, 1976; Coward and Chagnon, 1988, 1850; Canadian Federation for the Humanities, 1987c, 12). The Corporation began publishing *Studies in Religion/Sciences Religieuses* in 1971, as a successor to the *Canadian Journal of Theology*. The Corporation is currently publishing, through Wilfrid Laurier University Press, five series of volumes and recently announced publication of the first volume in a dissertation series (see *Studies in Religion/Sciences Religieuses* 18/3 [1989], 364-65). Ontario religious studies scholars have played prominent roles in these developments.

A recent, significant development is the appearance of a Canadian journal based in the Toronto School of Theology and devoted specifically to theology rather than religious studies. In the editorial introducing the *Toronto Journal of Theology*, Jean-Marc Laporte observed that when "the *Canadian Journal of Theology* ceased publishing in favour of . . . a fine periodical of more general scope, *Studies in Religion/Sciences Religieuses*,"

> Canadian scholars of many denominational affiliations lost a forum of more specific theological character in which they could converse with each other and with the educated public of the Canadian Churches. Moreover in the intervening years the Canadian theological scene has expanded considerably. With the *Toronto Journal of Theology* we intend to provide an additional opportunity for serious theological discourse within Canada, and thus fill a real need (Laporte, 1985, i.; cf. Fennell, 1985, 412).

Many of the articles that have appeared in the *Journal* might well have appeared in *Studies in Religion/Sciences Religieuses*, and vice versa, suggesting, once again, that at least in the realm of scholarship the line between "theology" and "religious studies" is not easily or neatly drawn. Still another recent arrival is a journal edited by graduate students in the Centre for Religious Studies at the University of Toronto. Launched in 1989, it grew out of a course required of all Centre students and took its name from the title of that course, *Method & Theory in the Study of Religion*.

Basic not only to much of the publication efforts of Canadian religious studies, but also to the development of Canadian religious studies in general, have been the various learned societies established to advance the scholarly study of religion (chap. 1 above). Again, Ontario religious studies scholars have played important roles in their founding and functioning (cf. 2.4.1 above). The emergence of these societies was part of ''the academic revolution'' in North America—leading to meritocracy in universities and professionalization of university faculty—documented by Jencks and Riesman (1969, 13 ff., *et passim*; in Canada cf. McKillop, 1987 [chap. 6] and chap. 3.1.1 below). These concerns are evident in the societies' statements of purpose (see CFH, 1987c, 13-16, which also gives brief histories, as do Moir, 1982, 66-71 [Canadian Society of Biblical Studies/Société Canadienne des Études Bibliques]; Combs, 1976-77 [Canadian Society for the Study of Religion/Société Canadienne pour l'Étude de la Religion]; N.K. Clifford, 1969, 521 [Canadian Society of Church History]; Fennell, 1985 [Canadian Theological Society]). Junior scholars are encouraged to participate through annual awards to students for outstanding research papers and through travel grants to society meetings.

The commitment of the societies to bilingualism has been, at best, imperfectly realized. On the one hand, their journal, *Studies in Religion/Sciences Religieuses*, publishes articles and reviews in both French and English; the series published by the Canadian Corporation for Studies in Religion/Corporation Canadienne des Science Religieuses include titles by both franco- and anglophone scholars; official communications are often in both languages; and officers and editors are chosen to achieve representation of both languages. On the other hand, English predominates in the societies, especially at the annual meetings of most of them.

As the authors of the state-of-the-art-review of religious studies in Quebec observe, the aims of the Canadian Society for the Study of Religion/Société Canadienne pour l'Étude de la Religion (CSSR/SCÉR) are praiseworthy, and its structure and official policies as well as the good will of many of its members are directed toward inclusion and participation of francophone scholars. Nonetheless, these efforts have foundered on ''le fait brutal de l'unilinguisme de la majorité des universitaires anglophones,'' so that the Society ''n'a pas réussi depuis sa fondation à offrir aux francophones un espace de communication satisfaisant'' (Rousseau and Despland, 1988, 141). The established place of English in scholarly communication makes mastery of French unnecessary for anglophones; on the other hand, it is absurd for francophone religious studies scholars to limit their scholarly encounters with one another to the annual meetings of the CSSR/CSÉR (ibid.). Rousseau and Despland therefore proposed formation of a Société québécoise pour l'étude de la religion, without prejudice to individual membership in the CSSR/SCÉR (ibid., 141-42).

In a response, Bruce Alton, President of the CSSR/SCÉR, acknowledged the legitimacy of the proposal, even while noting hopeful signs of bilingualism; moreover, more than language is involved:

> Religious experience and behaviour in a francophone context has unique dimensions, the details of which must be sounded with scholars who work primarily in that domain before they can be offered to the larger academic community (Alton, 1988, 7).

At its May 1989 meeting the Section des sciences religieuses of the Association canadienne-française pour l'avancement des sciences (ACFAS) voted to proceed to the creation of a Société québécoise pour l'étude de la religion (SQÉR) that would meet annually within the framework of the ACFAS, bringing together

> tous les Québécois partageant ses objectifs, francophone et anglophones et tous les francophones canadiens qui souhaitent se relier ainsi avec se foyer distinct de l'espace scientifico-culturel au sein du grand ensemble canadien (Rousseau, 1989, 1).

A provisional executive committee was elected and plans were laid to draw up a constitution and enter into discussions with the CSSR/SCÉR regarding representation of religious studies in Canadian and international scholarly and government forums (Assemblée générale de la section des sciences religieuses de l'ACFAS, May 18, 1989).

Since then, the SQÉR has held its first annual meeting, at which a constitution was adopted (CSSR/SCÉR *Bulletin* 14/1 [Oct. 1990], 17). At the meeting of the International Association for the History of Religions in Rome in September 1990, the new society was received into membership (ibid., 5; see also Rousseau, 1990, 31). It has also applied for membership in the Corporation Canadienne des Sciences Religieuses/Canadian Corporation for Studies in Religion. In addition, it has established a liaison committee to discuss areas of common concern with the CSSR/SCÉR and has begun publication of a biannual bulletin (CSSR/SQÉR *Bulletin* 14/1 [Oct. 1990], 17). About 60 persons are members (ibid.).[42]

The formation of a specifically Quebec learned society and of specifically Canadian learned societies in religious studies have been in part acts of distancing—attempts to preserve and enhance cultural independence, integrity, and distinctiveness, in other words, indigenization. The factors Keith Clifford cites as important in the founding of the Canadian Society of Church History figured into the formation of other religious studies societies in Canada as well: "a search for a national identity," apprehension about cultural domination from the outside, and concern about academic identity (N.K. Clifford, 1969, 521). "It was natural therefore that a young discipline in the process of defining its identity would begin by defining its boundaries and by guarding its frontiers" through the formation of a Canadian learned society (ibid.).

Indigenization has also been an important issue in Ontario universities beginning in the late nineteenth century (Wallace, 1927, 141; Clark, 1976, chaps. 8, 9; McKillop, 1987, 81ff.). As was noted earlier (chap. 2.1.3 and 2.5 above), indigenous graduate study began to alter the pattern of graduate study outside of Canada that had been customary for future professors of theology and religious studies. Today an Ontario student in religious studies can obtain her or his entire education, undergraduate and graduate, within the Province's university system; the financial advantages — scholarships and lower tuition rates for Canadians — offer an incentive to do so. Such indigenization is a sign of maturity; provincialism is the risk attending it (see, further, chaps. 5, 9, and 12.10.1 below). At present there is no Canadian organization devoted specifically to graduate religious studies. The need for a Canadian equivalent of the Council on Graduate Studies in Religion was expressed at the 1990 meetings of the religious studies learned societies in Victoria, BC, where Harold Coward, then President of the Canadian Corporation for Studies in Religion/Corporation Canadienne des Science Religieuses brought together a number of scholars to discuss the possibility of a conference on graduate religious studies the following year. Although initial interest was substantial and planning commenced, it proved impossible to hold a conference in 1991 on such short notice. Instead, a special session on the subject was planned for the 1991 meeting of the Learneds at Queen's University (see, further, chap. 12.10.2 below).

That religious studies in Ontario universities has kept pace with the development of religious studies generally, at both the undergraduate and graduate levels, was indicated by early external appraisals (Welch, 1972b, 100; 1971, 92-93). The periodic internal appraisals by the universities and the Province are directed to the same end. That the status quo, come weal or woe, is not the desideratum is evident at various places in this volume (see especially chap. 12 below).

Notes

1 In the 1830s Methodists had received government money for work among the natives and for educational purposes, but when the Canadian Methodists broke with the British Conference in 1840 the money was withheld because the government was unwilling to choose between the two factions.
2 Although the term "pluralism" has been labelled "essentially American" (J. W. Grant, 1972-73, 340), nonetheless, both in Canada and the United States "the equality of denominations in the eyes both of the law and of the public was generally admitted. Religious pluralism is thus apparently as much a Canadian as an American phenomenon" (ibid., 341). Canadians "take for granted the existence of a plurality of religious groups but have never found it necessary to articulate a consistent theory of religious pluralism" (346); it is an "informal plurality" (347). In place of the sharp American distinction, in theory and generally in practice, between church and state, Canadians seem to "assume the existence of an unwritten separation of the things of Caesar from the things of God, but equally they assume without definition an essential connection between religious principles and national life," resulting in "an attitude of legally

disestablished religiosity'' (Moir, 1968, 247). Religious pluralism is a recurrent term and theme in the writings of Wilfred Cantwell Smith, who early in his career came to see it as characteristic of the modern world and, then, increasingly, of Canada as well (W.C. Smith, 1972 [originally published 1963], 9-12; cf. further W.C. Smith, 1976, chaps. 1, 8, *et passim*).

3 Regiopolis College was first solely a seminary, but in 1866 it received university powers; when the Ontario legislature withdrew its annual grant in 1869, the college closed ("Regiopolis," in W. S. Wallace, 1937). A secondary school in Kingston now bears the name.

4 J. W. Grant, 1977, 13-16, groups Roman Catholic and non-Anglican Christians together as "missionary" churches, quite distinct in aims and outlook but sharing the common goal of Christianization without the benefit of establishment.

5 The separation of undergraduate and theology students was connected, on the part of religious studies, with the dissociation of religious studies from theological education. In the classroom this meant focussing on the study of religion apart from the professional and confessional concerns of theological education. Pedagogically, having undergraduates and theology students in the same class made teaching difficult, both for religious studies and theology professors. The Association of Theological Schools (ATS) has had as one of its criteria for accreditation the restricting of undergraduate students in theology courses to a small percentage of enrolments. The concern of the ATS was to protect the academic integrity of theological education. Its recent decision (summer 1990) to allow theological schools affiliated with a university (which is the case in most theological colleges in Ontario [see App. B below]) to admit undergraduates at the university into theological courses when these courses are part of the undergraduate curriculum suggests that the ATS does not now see that as endangering the integrity of those courses. It is too early to tell what effects this decision will have in Ontario. It could help avoid duplication of courses (e.g., teaching of biblical languages) and increase the options both for religious studies and theology students. However, courses designed for theology students may not be suitable for religious studies students, and vice versa.

6 The divinity students mentioned were taking their arts courses in University College (Sheraton et al., 1906, 106, 194; Moir, 1982, 3).

7 In 1849 Toronto Jews had purchased land for a cemetery from John Beverly Robinson, the prominent Anglican mentioned earlier in this chapter (Wrong, 1959, 45-46).

8 As percentages of the Canadian population: Buddhists, 0.22%; Hindus, 0.29%; Jews 1.23% Muslims, 0.41%; Sikhs, 0.28% (computed from 1981 Census of Canada, *Population: Religion*, Table 1). 72.78% of Buddhists live in cities of 500,000 or more; Hindus 80.15%; Jews, 92.35%; Muslims, 82.12%; Sikhs, 63.60% (computed from ibid., Table 2). In Toronto Buddhists constitute 0.40% of the population; Hindus, 1.05%; Jews, 4.16%; Muslims, 1.24%; Sikhs, 0.39% (computed from 1981 Census of Canada, *Population: Ontario: Religion*, Table 6).

9 Such a situation would not seem to be unique, if one accepts Stark and Bainbridge's thesis (1985) that secularization is countered by religious revival and religious innovation, so that, while the specifics of religious institutions may change, religiosity persists. "What organizational secularization has produced," the authors write, "is a large population of unchurched people who retain their acceptance of the existence of the supernatural. They seem only to have lost their faith in the ability of the conventional churches to interpret and serve their belief in the supernatural. Hence, . . . many of these unchurched believers are willing, perhaps eager, to examine new religions, to find a faith that can offer an active and rigorous conception of the supernatural that is compatible with modern culture" (444). See, further, the chapter "Church and Cult in Canada" (ibid., 457-73) and, earlier, Andrew Greeley's *Unsecular Man: The Persistence of Religion* (1972).

10 On the impact of these in Anglo-Canada, see McKillop, 1979, 1987.

11 Jewish theologians *qua* theologians in religious studies departments in Canada, and in Ontario, in particular are a rarity; Emil Fackenheim, sometime professor in the Department of Philosophy in the University of Toronto and member of the faculty of the University's Centre for Religious Studies, would be an example (see, e.g., Fackenheim, 1967, 1968, 1970, 1978, 1982, 1987 and Oppenheim, 1987 and Shapiro, 1987). One does find a sprinkling of courses in Jewish theology, or Jewish thought or Jewish philosophy (some of which may include what Christian theologians might call theology), in religious studies and Jewish studies department and programs in Canadian universities (see Anderson, 1972, 53-256, *passim,* and current calendars).

12 Wiebe's later essays are in part an attempt to clarify latent confusions in his earlier work and perhaps to exorcise their source, namely, "my earlier and predominant (Christian) apologetic concerns" (1984, 422), which he says (n. 128) were "the primary focus of my doctoral work at the University of Lancaster." Cf., too, a statement in his 1978 essay (15) that seems closer to Davis' position than his later views: "To define religious studies as a science so as to exclude all theological 'elements,' it seems to me, is no more justifiable than the positivist attempt to define philosophy so as to exclude all metaphysics. Just as the latter itself implies a metaphysic, so the former involves, although perhaps only implicitly so, a religious (or religiously significant) *Weltanschauung.*" Cf., further, Stoesz's examination (1988) of the question, "Don Wiebe: A Shift in His Method?"

13 Cf. the comment by Wilfred Cantwell Smith that adding Asian Studies to university curricula in the West "may turn out in the end to be as transforming as was the addition of the sciences" (cited in Klostermaier, 1976-77, 561).

14 Cf. the title of Reimarus' essay published by G.E. Lessing in 1777, "Unmoglichkeit einer Offenbarung die alle Menschen auf eine gegrundete Art glauben kannten," and his remarks (p. 335 of the 1897 ed.): "Ein jeder stelle sich unpartheyisch in die Stelle der Heyden, und urtheile denn, ob es wohl moglich sey, dass die durch gegründete Ueberführung zum Christemthume zu bringen sind. Sie sind erstlich von ihrer väterlichen Religion, so wie wir, von Jugend auf so eingenommen, dass sie sich um andere zu bekümmern so unnothig als gefährlich halten. Wer ihnen dieses verargen wollte, der mag mir zuvor antworten, ob er den Talmud, die Misna und Gemara, den Alcoran, den Zendavesta des Zerduscht, den Sad-der der Destur, den Con-fu-zu und andere dergleichen Bücher gelesen? ob er Volker Religionen so genau zu kennen und so unpartheyisch zu untersuchen jemals Lust, Fähigkeit oder Zeit gehabt? ob er nicht glaube, die Religion, darin er erzogen worden, sey die einige wahre und seligmachende? ob er nicht daher unnothig zu seyn glaube, sich um andere Religionen viel zu bekümmern? ja ob er es nicht fast für sündlich erachtet hätte, sich nach andern, als bessern, umzusehen, und aus Reizung zu denselben ihre Bücher zu lesen und nach ihren Lehrern zu laufen?"

15 C. P. Tiele's interesting characterization (1888, 358) of the study of religion prior to the nineteenth century is still apt: "With the exception of a few good books containing useful information on some ancient religions and on the religious customs of uncivilized nations, nothing written on this subject [religions] in former centuries can be said to possess any scientific value. It is not that the old books are antiquated, as all works of learning must become with the lapse of time: they were worth nothing even when published. There were huge collections, containing descriptions of all the religions in the world, so far as they were known, laboriously compiled, but without any critical acumen, and without the least suspicion that unbiblical religions are not mere curiosities. There was a philosophy of religion, but it was all but purely speculative, and it could not be otherwise, as then it had but scanty means to work with, and was obliged to draw the facts it required from very troubled and insufficient sources. Attempts were made to explain the mythologies of the Greeks and the Romans, and even of some Oriental

nations, but for the same reason they could not but fail. Then there was the theological bias, which caused all religions except one to be regarded as utterly false; the philosophical bias, which caused all religions, except the arbitrary abstraction then called natural religion, to be decried as mere superstitions, invented by shrewd priests and tyrants for selfish ends; and, finally, the total lack of a sound method in historical investigation, which was one of the prominent characteristics of the 18th century. It was only after the brilliant discoveries which marked the end of that century and the first half of this, and after the not less brilliant researches to which they gave rise; after the sacred writings of the Chinese, the Indians, the Persians, and some other ancient nations could be studied in the original; after the finding of the key to the Egyptian hieroglyphics and the Assyrian and Babylonian cuneiform writing had lifted the veil which for many centuries had covered the history of these most ancient civilizations—it was then only that a history of religion could be thought of and that something like a science of religion could be aimed at, if not yet founded.''

16 Cf. further W. C. Smith, 1959, 34: "The traditional form of Western scholarship in the study of other men's [sic] religion was that of an impersonal presentation of an 'it.' The first great innovation in recent times has been the personalization of the faiths observed, so that one finds a discussion of a 'they.' Presently the observer becomes personally involved, so that the situation is one of a 'we' talking about a 'they.' The next step is a dialogue, where 'we' talk to 'you.' If there is listening and mutuality, this may become that 'we' talk *with* 'you.' The culmination of this progress is when 'we all' are talking *with* each other about 'us.'" Similarly, Smith's successor as Director of the Institute of Islamic Studies, Charles J. Adams (1967, 188-92). For critical reviews of several of Smith's major works see Gilkey, 1981 and H. Smith, 1981.

17 "To be an historian," writes W. C. Smith (1976, 172), "or indeed a rational student in any humane field, is to stand imaginatively in the shoes of other men [sic]. This is possible, in principle, because we are persons, and because they are persons."

18 W. C. Smith does not assume that just any such description acceptable to a representative of a religion "is *ipso facto* true: one can flatter or beguile" (1976, 147); in the kind of mutual encounter he envisages there would be mutual growth in knowledge and understanding, so that "in a sense all members of the encounter are in effect expected *ipso facto* to end up as in some sort comparative religionists; presumably some of them might well start so," e.g., as a "well-qualified Buddhist student of comparative religion" (151). So also C. J. Adams, 1967, 190-91.

19 W. C. Smith (e.g., 1957, vi; 1976, chap. 8) uses this term (and refers to such an approach as "comparativist," e.g., 1976, 49) as well as "history of religions" (1978, 143). Ashby (1965, 7, n. 2) states that in the U.S.A. the latter is generally preferred to the former (see n. 20 below); "comparative religion" still persists, however (Ashby, 1965, 29, 39; Clebsch, 1981), also in Canada as a designation of a field and of courses (see, *passim*: Anderson, 1972, 53-256; Remus, 1978, 1981, 1985; Mills, 1987, 1988, 1989, 1990; and current Canadian university calendars). George P. Grant, writing on the study of "other great religions" (i.e., other than Christianity) at McMaster University, was convinced that it was "necessary as soon as possible to give up the term 'Comparative Religion' " because it had "been so abused as to be no longer of any use"; specifically, courses with this title were "generally taught within the assumption of western superiority, either the superiority of Christianity or (more recently) of the progressive West" (Grant, 1968, 64). W. Holsten (1961b, 1040-41) remarks that as long as *Religionswissenschaft* restricted itself to data, ideas, and systems, the comparativist approach enjoyed "uneingeschränkte Gültigkeit. Hat man es aber mit Personen zu tun [Holsten cites W. C. Smith], tritt das Vergleichen genauso an die zweite Stelle wie die Systeme," for human life is unrepeatable and analogy is more appropriate to it than comparison in the strict sense, such as one finds in the natural sciences.

20 "History of Religions" often appears alongside or as a translation of *Religionswissen-schaft* (thus Wach, 1967, 1; Kitagawa, 1959, 1, and 1967, 40), though it would more literally (and perhaps more properly) translate *Religionsgeschichte*; on the distinctions and relations between *Religionsgeschichte* and *Religionswissenschaft*, see Holsten, 1961a, 1961b, and cf. C. J. Adams, 1974, 7: "immersion in the historical material must precede all else; *Religionsgeschichte* continues to be fundamental and indispensable for a *Religionswissenschaft*." Also used interchangeably are "history of religion(s)" and "science of religion(s)," both of these as a translation of *Religionswissenschaft* or *science de(s) religion(s)*; thus Ashby, 1965, 29, 49. The profusion (and confusion) of terminology would seem to be related to the inadequacy of "historical," "comparative," or "science" to describe what scholars in the field attempt to do (cf. ibid., 39-49).

21 In the Welch survey of nearly 2,000 doctoral students in the 1969-70 academic year, two-thirds held professional (seminary or equivalent) degrees prior to entering their doctoral programmes; but the percentage was declining among entering students (Welch, 1971, 204-05); see, further, chap. 4.2.1 below.

22 "Departments of religion were obviously making exceedingly fine distinctions within one religious tradition by offering courses in Christian ethics, the history of Christianity (early, medieval, and modern), theology, and Bible (the very term is Christian) and then adding one or two catch-all survey courses into which Hinduism, Buddhism, Taoism and everything else must fit. It is as though a history of science department were to offer a number of courses within the history of chemistry and then, as an afterthought, to add one or two entitled 'the Non-chemical Sciences' " (Harvey, 1970, 25). Similarly, Holbrook, 1963, 159-60; J. Wilson, 1970, 10-11.

23 Band, 1966, 14; "Judaic studies" here is used in the broad sense employed by Band, 1966, 5: "the discipline which deals with the historical experiences, in the intellectual, religious, and social spheres, of the Jewish people in all centuries and countries."

24 Some critical, relatively non-technical reviews of some important modern Western scholarship on Islam: Waldman, 1976; Lawrence, 1978, 1990; Algar, 1980. On "The Development of Islamic Studies in Canada," see the essay with that title by C. J. Adams, 1983.

25 *Census of Canada 1981: Population*, Table 5-1: Islam, 98,165; Brethren in Christ, 22,565; Canadian Reformed Church, 10,560; Christian Reformed Church, 77,370; Christian and Missionary Alliance, 33,895; Churches of Christ, Disciples, 15,350; etc.

26 I am grateful to David Kinsley, Chair, Department of Religious Studies, McMaster University, for information on various details in the next paragraph, as reported in interviews with early faculty members in the Department publication *R. in R.* 5/1 (Dec. 1975) and 6/1 (Sept. 1976).

27 Gill, 1979, 253: "Although much can be learned from such [social-scientific] studies, religion students cannot be fully satisfied with them because of their functionalism and because, in the end, they are not really concerned with religion. As students of religion we must take seriously the potential truth of religious language and attempt to understand and describe the criteria of truth and meaning in the context in which religious statements are made. We must seek a much fuller context in order to obtain an appreciation of the deeper sense in which religious statements are true and meaningful. The interests and assumptions of social scientists will never lead them to such concerns, and herein lies the mandate for the student of religion as well as the agenda for developing appropriate methods of study. The question of truth can no longer either be simply ignored or left to social scientists." And 1978, 127: "A major area for research involves the relationship between religion and healing or health. It has become a major concern in the social sciences, but as I examine these studies, they are usually based on the presupposition that all cures are explainable only in terms of Western medicine. Their approach involves a search through native medical practices, which are typically

of a ritual character, for some correspondence with scientific medicine. What remains unexplained is attributed to native beliefs in magic. An implicit assumption in this approach is that religion is incapable of affecting the world. Or, to put it more crudely, that the native American gods ain't there. We must, it seems to me, reject this notion. If we assume that the gods are not there, or, little better, that they are ineffective, we find ourselves in a rather peculiar situation as students of religion.''

28 Yu, 1987, 559, points out how in India religion and literature have, until relatively recently, been so interwoven as to be indistinguishable; he also notes the close association of religious and literary history in the pre-modern West (ibid., 560-66).

29 A paper presented to the annual meeting of the Canadian Society of Biblical Studies by Pamela Milne of the religious studies department, University of Windsor, and subsequently published (Milne, 1989) played an important role in achieving consensus on the policy among the constituent societies of the Corporation (Sinclair-Faulkner, 1989, 3).

30 Similar observations apply to Ontario theological colleges (see chap. 3.3 below).

31 See the encyclopedic textbooks such as Jungman, 1941; Dix, 1945; Rietschl and Graff, 1951-52; Jones et al., 1978; historical studies such as Jungman, 1949, 1960, 1962; Klauser, 1974; Wegman, 1985; Jasper, 1989; Koenker's monograph (1954) on liturgical renewal in Roman Catholicism; and serial publications such as *Worship* (1926ff; originally titled *Orate Fratres*), *Studia Liturgica* (1964ff.), *Liturgical Review* (1971ff.), *Liturgy* (1980ff.), *North American Academy of Liturgy Proceedings* (1988ff.), *Jahrbuch für Liturgiewissenschaft* (1921ff.), *Liturgisches Jahrbuch* (1951ff.), *Archiv für Liturgiewissenschaft* (1950ff.), *Leiturgia: Handbuch des evangelischen Gottesdienstes* (1954ff.).

32 E.g., Collins, 1987; Zimmerman, 1988; cf. the comment by the General Editor of *Worship* (Seasoltz, 1987, 81) that the editors ''want our authors to mine the resources of the modern behavioral sciences and arts. . . .''

33 This comparison draws in part on Smart, 1988 and D.D. Wallace, 1988, which may be consulted for some of the details cited here. For further details and critiques of *ER* (and some comparisons with *ERE*) see the extended reviews by McMullin, 1989 and (in *Critical Review of Books in Religion 1989*) by Penner, 1989c; Green, 1989; Duke, 1989; McAuliffe, 1989; Brooks, 1989; Eckel, 1989.

34 The statistics in the text are based on an examination of the lists of contributors in the index volumes of the two encyclopedias. Determination of gender was based on first names, a much surer indicator in *ERE* with its full names and predominantly Western contingent of contributors (with the occasional ''Mrs.'' attached) than in *ER* with its polyglot list of contributors and initials sometimes appearing in place of full names. The variance in the percentages given in the text result from those instances where first names give no clue to gender. If all such persons were male, the lower percentage of women contributors cited in my text would be valid; if they were women, the higher percentage would be correct. The actual percentage in *ER* is probably somewhere in between the two figures cited. The counts:

> *ERE*: 41 of 882 names appeared to be women; 11 names uncertain;
>
> *ER*: 190 of 1,357 names appeared to be women; 163 names uncertain.

The *ER* calculation was done independently of that made by Ursula King who, also acknowledging the difficulty of distinguishing women from men contributors in the work, counted ''about 175 women'' in the list of contributors, or ''somewhat less than 13%'' of the total (U. King, 1990, 92).

35 Precise comparisons between the two works are not feasible. The detailed information on vocations of contributors provided in *ERE* made it much easier to determine whether or not they held an academic position and what it was. In *ER* it was possible to determine only whether or not the person was associated with an academic institution. Thus, non-academics such as students and administrators, who were excluded from the statistics compiled from *ERE*, may have been included in those gleaned from *ER*'s list of

contributors. Also, whereas *ER* gives only the present position of contributors, *ERE* lists present, past, and multiple positions, which made it possible to include in our count former academics or academics holding non-academic positions as well. The counts:

> *ERE*: 13 of the 41(?) women contributors were associated in some way with an academic institution, compared with 492(?) men; 4 uncertain;
>
> *ER*: 145(?) of the women contributors were associated with an academic institution, compared with 882(?) of the men; 133 uncertain.

36 These various data do not lend themselves to quick generalizations or precise comparisons. In the Victorian-era British Empire, which accounted for so many of *ERE*'s contributors, individuals moved back and forth between academic and ecclesiastical positions, and the clergy generally were literate, often with scholarly attainments. Many of the contributors who were serving in religious institutions when the list of contributors was published had held academic positions, and vice-versa, and some occupied positions in both at the same time. Moreover, for most contributors *ERE* supplied information on academic degrees, past and present employment, membership in learned societies, and publications, whereas *ER* gives only the person's name and academic institution or other employment or place of residence. Given these qualifications, the counts are as follows:

> *ERE*: 136 out of 882 contributors were serving in religious institutions;
>
> *ER*: 29 out of 1,357 were thus engaged.

37 In *ERE*, about 1.4% (12 out of 882) were from Ontario, half of whom were from the University of Toronto and its affiliated theological colleges; in *ER*, about 1.7% (24 out of 1,357) were from Ontario, about two-thirds (15 of 24) of whom were from the University of Toronto and its associated colleges. Canadians generally constituted about 2.4% (21 out of 882) of *ERE*'s contributors and about 3.5% (48 out of 1,357) of *ER*'s.

38 Developments in the U.S. are cited, or appealed to, by various Canadian writers advocating or reporting on the establishment of religious studies departments in Canadian universities (e.g., Wevers, 1956, 162; Classen, 1978, 392).

39 Welch cites Richard Schlatter, then Provost of Rutgers University, who concedes that having departments can lead to departmentalization, which "fosters more and more specialization, more and more pedantry, and more and more triviality" (Schlatter, 1967, 18). Yet, he continues, "Without departments, the intellectual establishment would be disordered and amateurish. The organization by discipline fosters a needed specialization and a concentration of intellectual efforts.... In spite of the limitations which we all recognize, the organization of our intellectual establishment of higher learning along disciplinary lines has been a success and continues to be a success. We should break down the fences at some points; we should redraw the boundaries from time to time; and we may want to recreate new disciplines. But we need the disciplines all the same.... Unless such a subject [as religious studies] has the status and dignity of a departmental organization, students will conclude that the subject is of little intellectual importance. Without a department and without a major program which a department makes possible, the teacher of religion is reduced to a general service function which derogates his [sic] dignity and deadens his [sic] own intellectual growth" (ibid., 19).

40 The consultants were Henry E. Duckworth, President, University of Winnipeg, and religious studies professors Van A. Harvey, University of Pennsylvania, and Ninian Smart, University of Lancaster.

41 Chaired by Bora Laskin (later Chief Justice of Canada), the committee included Northrop Frye and future Nobel Prize winner John Polanyi.

42 The draft agreement prepared by the liaison committee was published in the CSSR/SQÉR *Bulletin* 14/2 (April 1991), 3-5 and in the first issue of the *Bulletin* of the Société québécoise pour l'étude de la religion.

3

Perceptions: Administrators and Faculty

Harold Remus

How is religious studies in Ontario universities perceived, both from within and without? In our interviews various questions relating to perceptions of religious studies were asked of university administrators, of religious studies and theological college faculty, of religious studies students, both undergraduate and graduate, and of students in theological colleges. This chapter and the next report on these interviews, sometimes briefly — since other chapters are devoted to some of the issues raised — but more fully when that is not the case.

3.1 Administrators

The efforts of Ontario religious studies scholars and departments to achieve academic legitimacy and respectability have been largely successful, judging from the comments of the university administrators interviewed — deans of undergraduate faculties, college principals, and, at institutions with graduate programmes in religious studies, deans of graduate faculties. They view religious studies departments as formally little different from other departments in the university, as measured by the common criteria.

3.1.1   Hiring, Tenure, Promotion

In the provincial universities of Ontario, the factors that enter into decisions of hiring, granting of tenure, and promotion of religious studies professors were seen by the university administrators we interviewed as no different from those in other departments, namely graduate preparation, teaching

---

Notes to Chapter 3 can be found on pages 115-18.

experience, publications, and "fit" between the person's field and the position.

That is what one would expect of the system of meritocracy — the professionalization, one might say — that came to dominate North American academic institutions (Jencks and Riesman, 1969) and repudiated the non-academic factors that used to enter into such decisions and the special pleading and political lobbying that sometimes accompanied them in Ontario institutions of higher education (McKillop, 1987, chap. 6). But in the study of religion, where confessional commitment was considered important or essential, meritocracy was longer in coming. That confessional commitment as a factor in hiring, tenure, and promotion would now seem to be a thing of the past in Ontario's provincial universities is illustrated by the genuinely puzzled reaction of one dean to the question whether it entered into such decisions: "Should I be concerned about that?"

In at least some church-related colleges the situation may be somewhat different. Administrators and faculty expect the usual academic qualifications, but some also look for confessional commitment, either to Christianity or to a particular denomination. An administrator at one such college saw such a commitment as essential, given the "faith dimension"[1] of the college, which he contrasted with religious studies, which he characterized as closed to that dimension. Substantiating such a view would be that of the university administrator who said the church-related colleges on his campus made tenure and promotion decisions "according to their own lights" and who perceived their approach to religious studies as more confessionally oriented than in the university's religious studies courses.

That that would not necessarily be the case in church-related colleges generally is clear from our interviews.[2] Nonetheless, these observations point to a tension between past and present, and sometimes an uncertainty of purpose and identity in church-related colleges, as a result of the secularization and professionalization of higher education in North America. In what sense, it has been asked, are Christian colleges still Christian, or Roman Catholic, or Protestant, or United Church, or Presbyterian, or Lutheran (Masters, 1966; Greeley, van Cleve, Carroll, 1967; Greeley, 1969; McCluskey, 1970; Commission of Inquiry, 1970; Shook, 1971; Gamelin, 1975; Wade, 1978; Solberg and Strommen, 1980; Ringenberg, 1984)?

In the United States, church-related colleges of the Protestant mainstream have gone the furthest in assimilating the academic ethos (Jencks and Riesman, 1969, 322-28). D. C. Masters' history of Protestant church-related colleges in Canada concluded, similarly, that the nineteenth-century idea of university and church-related college as institutions "to which the Christian faith gave unity" had given way by the 1960s to "an intellectual *mélange*, an epitome of the university world in Canada as a whole" (Masters, 1966, 211). The establishing of Bible colleges might be viewed as partial confirmation of Masters' conclusion (chap. 11 below). The statements of mission and purpose by some Protestant church-related colleges in Ontario would seem, however, to belie or to qualify it, at least in intent,[3] and the recent conference on church-related colleges, Protestant and Catholic, hosted by St. Jerome's College and Conrad Grebel College in Waterloo (May 1-2, 1990) suggests that perhaps some Protestant colleges in Canada may be seeking (to borrow from the title of a recent book) new directions and to reclaim a mission (DeJong, 1990; cf. B. Fisher, 1989).

A 1970 study of Roman Catholic colleges and universities in Canada saw considerable loosening or dilution of the factors that fifty years earlier were deemed essential to a Roman Catholic institution of higher education (Commission of Inquiry, 1970, 31-33). The study also pointed, however, to principles or practices that persisted as "essential marks" of Roman Catholic institutions of higher education (ibid., 36). One such "mark" was a faculty "'intellectually Catholic,'" namely, "scholars committed to pursue the totality of truth and to relate intellectual truths and human values (religious and moral, including civic) within a Christian context" (ibid.). They "need not be members of the Catholic Church, though in normal circumstances most will be" (ibid.).

This "mark" would seem to be one aspect of a "faith dimension" like that mentioned by the college administrator cited above. With it may go, in many Roman Catholic universities and colleges, conceptions of academic freedom somewhat different from the usual definitions.

A fairly representative view of what "academic" might mean in a Roman Catholic context is that of William Sullivan, a Jesuit theologian (1972). He distinguishes (43) between "commitment courses" and "description courses"; both make truth claims, but commitment courses base these on "the faith position" of the teacher. A department of theology need not

> offer only descriptive courses in order to be academic. It is perfectly legitimate to offer commitment courses in one's own or in other traditions, provided they are acknowledged and identified as such. A department does not have to be "neutral" in order to be academic. A department in a Catholic institution may and I think should offer both types of courses (ibid.).

Commitment courses accord with the Catholic university's responsiblity for teaching and research in the Catholic tradition, while descriptive courses such as history or philosophy of religion "offer another mode of approach to the whole dimension of religion" that is important (and attractive) to the educated Catholic (ibid.).

According to a Canadian study, academic freedom in Roman Catholic contexts would, on the one hand, mean something other than "rejection of the notion of absolute truth and by implication all religious dogmas" and, on the other hand, a view of Roman Catholic tertiary schools "as mere instruments of the official *magisterium* of the Church through which the teaching authority of the Church is exercised" and therefore entailing limits on teaching and research (Commission of Inquiry, 1970, 192-93). Roman Catholic colleges and universities are, rather, "'the Church learning,'" and limits on freedom are those intrinsic to "academic competence and accepted professional responsibilities" (ibid., 193).[4]

This Canadian study (ibid. 194-97) as well as Andrew Greeley's studies of Roman Catholic colleges and universities in the U.S.A. (1967, 109-15, 164; 1969, 114-20) found that, both *de jure* and *de facto*, academic freedom in Roman Catholic schools differed little from, and in some cases was better safeguarded than, that in non-Catholic schools. Greeley concluded that one should "suspend generalizations and be prepared to evaluate each Catholic institution on its own merits rather than dismissing on a priori grounds the possibility that it might be, in fact, a free institution" (1969, 120). Greeley did in fact cite one notorious case of dismissal, without due process, of twenty-some faculty members at one Roman Catholic university midway in the academic year (1969, 38n.). He also pointed to the right of superiors of religious orders to transfer from, or parachute into, a department a faculty member who is also a member of a religious order; on the other hand, he cited cases where an order failed to protect several of its members (1967, 131-32).

More recently, the cases of prominent Roman Catholic theologians censured or silenced by the Vatican,[5] and the "Oath of Fidelity" required of Roman Catholic academics since February 25, 1989,[6] show that particularly in the areas of theology and religious studies academic freedom can at times be cause for concern on Roman Catholic campuses and especially for Roman Catholic theologians.[7] A case in point in Ontario is the forced resignations of two faculty members at St. Augustine's Seminary in Toronto in 1984, which led the University of Toronto to sever ties with the Seminary in 1988 and thus to revocation of University privileges of the Seminary's students.[8] It should be noted that this was at a seminary, not a Roman Catholic college or a religious studies department, and the Seminary's association with the Toronto School of Theology and the University and the desirability of university privileges were presumably important factors in restoring something approximating the *status quo ante*.

These various cases illustrate the question posed by Jencks and Riesman two decades ago: Could Roman Catholic colleges and universities assimilate the standards of higher education generally — that is, become "academically respectable" — and still remain in any significant sense Roman Catholic (1967, 398-405)? Greeley suggested that there were resources in the long Catholic tradition for doing so, and cited several examples of places where it was happening (1969, 158-63).

That non-Roman Catholic church-related colleges in Ontario also aspire to distinctiveness in the educational spectrum is clear from their calendar statements (see n. 3 of this chapter). Important in achieving distinctiveness is the hiring of faculty who, if they are not loyal members of the denomination with which the college is affiliated, at least are in sympathy with the institution's distinctive aims. The variety in these aims, as set forth in calendar statements and expressed in our interviews, suggests that the way loyalty and sympathy are assessed will also vary widely. When denominational loyalty and convictions figure into the hiring of religious studies faculty in these colleges, the *kind* of convictions and loyalties will also be assessed: there are, after all, Anglicans and Anglicans, Mennonites and Mennonites, etc. One might ask how different such assessments would be from the overt, or often covert, criteria sometimes applied to prospective professors in other departments of a university: What "school" (or faction) do they belong to, or what are their methodological loyalties? Whatever the denominational tests applied to prospective religious studies faculty in Ontario church-related colleges, they all must also pass through the gate of professional qualifications.

Andrew Greeley's observation that for younger faculty at Roman Catholic colleges and universities loyalty to their profession and its standards and expectations takes precedence over the loyalty to school (and denomination?) that used to characterize faculty there (1967, 106-09) applies, *mutatis mutandis*, to religious studies faculty in Ontario church-related colleges at the end of the twentieth century. The tension between these two kinds of loyalties is somewhat similar to that experienced by religion scholars who must balance their commitment to modern religious studies scholarship against their attempts to enter empathically into the study of a religion so as to describe it in a way recognizable to its adherents (above, chap. 2.4.4).

(On hiring of religious studies faculty see the fuller treatment in chap. 5.2 as well as chap. 12.2.)

3.1.2   Religious Studies Courses and Teaching

University administrators are necessarily concerned about statistics and "bottom lines." A common observation by those we interviewed was that enrolments in undergraduate religious studies courses were healthy, sometimes large, which meant, at the least, that the religious studies departments on their campus were seen as institutionally viable. The enrolments were variously attributed to good teaching, good reputation of the faculty, and the reputation of certain offerings with large enrolments as "bird" or "decorative" courses. In some such courses efforts were being made to upgrade them by limiting enrolments so as to monitor the instructor more closely, or through retirements: the faculty members offering them were holdovers from an earlier period when the offerings were still conceived of as "religion" or "religious knowledge" rather than religious studies, were predominantly Christian in content and approach, were taught by theological faculty, and, in the view of one dean, were "a joke." "Bird" courses were mentioned only as exceptions, and, where they were, certainly not as a phenomenon unique to religious studies departments. One dean, who cited an example, saw the problem not as the course itself but the person teaching it.

Another dean pointed to the cross-listing of religious studies courses by other departments and other faculties as indications of the respectability of the courses.

At the graduate level, one dean expressed concern about thematic courses (on which see chap. 8 below): In what way are they specifically religious studies courses? At another place a graduate dean raised a similar query about thesis topics: they seemed diffuse and unfocussed. If this was the "religious studies" approach, it seemed applicable to any subject matter. Implicit in such observations is the question, much discussed within religious studies, whether, or in what ways, religious studies is a "discipline" with its own distinctive methodology and data, or, rather, a field (see chap. 2.4.3 above).

(See, further, the chapters devoted to teaching [chap. 6] and curricula [chap. 8].)

3.1.3 Religious Studies Faculty and Departments

Several themes emerged in administrators' comments on religious studies faculty and departments.

One, already noted (3.1.1 above), was that hiring, tenure, and promotion decisions in religious studies departments in universities accord with general university policies and practices.

Also noted earlier (chap. 2.2 above) was that religious studies faculty participate fully in the life of the university, serving on and sometimes chairing committees, and sometimes as administrators—principal, dean, assistant dean, etc. A third theme was that religious studies departments and the composition of the faculty are in a state of transition. In one respect, this is distinctive of the field of religious studies as it has evolved, and continues to evolve, from "religion" or "religious knowledge" to religious studies (chap. 2 above). It is a relative distinction, however, inasmuch as all university fields and departments in the 1990s are quite different from what they were prior to World War II. In the postwar decades, Ontario universities, like North American universities generally, have participated in the shift of focus from undergraduate education and teaching to graduate education and faculty research and publication.[9]

In religious studies one manifestation of this shift is the gradual passing from the scene—through death and retirement—of the pioneers in establishing religious studies departments and religious studies as a field. Some leave having achieved notable scholarly reputations, sometimes acquired without the benefit of an earned doctorate, which was not the union card it has come to be or the only road, or even the high road, to the realm of scholarly research and publication. For others who never achieved doctoral degrees, however, their focus—in accord with the ethos of the day—was on teaching, often of many and large classes, with little published research. Still others set aside their doctoral programmes under pressures to assume administrative duties or to fight administration battles to establish a religious studies department. Faculty in these last two categories are apt to be looked at askance by newer faculty who, having gone the full graduate route, are productive scholars and teach the new mysteries of religious studies — in departments established through the labours of their predecessors.[10]

These circumstances account in part for the scanty publication records, pointed out by administrators, of some of these older faculty. Another factor, as one dean pointed out, is now discarded tenure and promotion policies based more on years in service than on scholarly achievement. A resulting irony, not lost on newer faculty with a string of articles and a book or two on their c.v., is that they are often assessed for tenure and promotion by older faculty with perhaps an article or two and not a single book to their credit.

A glance at other university departments reveals similar marks of transition. Not peculiar to religious studies either is the typical cross-section that deans draw of research and publication in religious studies departments: a few highly productive scholars, at least one or two unproductive ones, and the rest somewhere in between. Deans tended to rate research and publication by religious studies faculty in graduate programmes somewhat higher. The newer, more stringent tenure and promotion policies now in place, imperfect instruments, to be sure, can improve the picture, in religious studies departments as well as in other departments, provided they are taken seriously (see chap. 12.2 below).

(See, further, chap. 7 below, ''Faculty: Research and Publication.'')

3.1.4 Retrospect

It became evident in our interviews that the deans were weighing their statements carefully. Even though they had been informed that we would be reporting on religious studies in Ontario as a whole, rather than on specific institutions and departments, as representatives of their institutions and faculties they were wary of washing dirty linen in front of outsiders. Observations tended to be restrained; and as seasoned academics and administrators they strove for balanced judgements. Nonetheless, at times they were very frank.

In a few cases a lingering suspicion of religious studies as a field, or of a particular department, seemed to lurk beneath the surface — as though an unspoken question was whether religious studies had really moved beyond instruction-in-religion (indoctrination) and whether faculty were serious academics and their courses seriously academic. In one such case the dean said he would give stronger support to the department at his institution if it were more serious — that is, more pluralistic and more dedicated to research and publication. Other deans characterized the departments at their institutions as having precisely those qualities. In no case was there talk of singling religious studies out for cuts, or dissolution, because of criticisms voiced. Problems would be dealt with in the normal way, as they were in other departments.

With rare exceptions the deans interviewed were well informed about the departments on their campuses and, sometimes, on the nature of religious studies as a field. When asked how representative of the campus their judgments of the local religious studies department or programme were, answers ranged (to paraphrase) from "Others think as I do" to "Others don't think about religious studies at all" to "Others don't know that religious studies has changed from what it used to be."

This last view concurs with other data gathered in our study: in Ontario universities there is much ignorance or misunderstanding of religious studies as a field, of how religious studies faculty approach what they study, and of what and how they teach. To many, "religious studies" still means "teaching religion" — that is, indoctrination and proselytizing, especially for one religion, Christianity.

It is somewhat surprising, though also instructive for outsiders' perceptions of religious studies, that even persons knowledgeable in the study of religion may still see fit to characterize religious studies departments and programmes as "at least slightly removed from denominational control and exclusively ministerial concerns" (Laperrière and Westfall, 1990, 43). While some within religious studies may see it as not sufficiently distinct and distant from "theology" and not immune to covert "theologizing" (chap. 2.4.3), that is still something different from "denominational control and exclusively ministerial concerns." One might suggest that religious studies departments should mount P.R. campaigns to try to bring their colleagues in other departments up to date. But it is more likely that sound practice of their craft and full participation in the life of their universities will do more to convey what religious studies professors do, and what religious studies is, than any efforts at P.R.

3.2   Religious Studies Faculty

In selecting faculty to be interviewed at universities with religious studies departments and programmes, we aimed for a representative cross-section that included both women and men, long-time members as well as those newly hired, and some in between, and persons in the different areas of religious studies and/or in the streams or divisions into which the particular department or programme divided its faculty and courses of study. In writing department chairs and programme co-ordinators, we requested these persons by name, with the understanding that if they were unavailable, individuals of comparable characteristics would be interviewed in their stead. Usually our original requests were honoured. We also interviewed department chairs and programme co-ordinators. Where a department or programme drew on faculty from a university and federated colleges, we sought individuals from those components. In addition to these interviews with individuals, we asked to meet other faculty members over lunch and were thus able to get other viewpoints and to follow up questions that arose in the interviews. Response by administrators and faculty to our requests was gratifying (though there were the occasional inevitable schedule conflicts or other miscues), and the interviews provided many useful data.[11]

At a number of points the views of faculty members interviewed in university departments of religious studies were similar to those expressed by administrators. Hiring, tenure, and promotion are to be based on merit, not seniority or (with some qualifications in church-related colleges) on religious and denominational commitments. The "bird" courses cited by administrators were also pointed out by faculty. Religious studies departments are in a state of transition.

There were also differences, however. And issues were discussed that were not raised with, or by, administrators.

3.2.1 Research and Teaching

Faculty at some institutions tended to rate their research and publication higher than administrators did. The now dominant emphasis on research was seen as healthy, though some worries were expressed about a possible slighting of teaching as a result. Faculty in church-related colleges sometimes stressed their school's attention to teaching as a strong point.

(See, further, chaps. 6, "Faculty: Teaching," and 7, "Faculty: Research and Publication.")

3.2.2 Transition

As persons directly involved in religious studies departments faculty were more apt than administrators to perceive the affective, "human" side of change and transition — the sense of loss and grief (and, sometimes, relief) as the first generation of religious studies professors passes from the scene, but also anticipation of what new faces would bring. On the other hand, since the majority of departments consist of faculty who will reach retirement age in the 1990s, there was in the meantime a feeling of *déjà vu* — these people on my floor have been around here a *long* time — and a desire to see new faces and the fresh ideas and learning they would bring. A common view was that the new faces one might like to see would be female and/or from an indigenous or other minority group; born in Canada and educated, at least at the undergraduate level, in Canada; and solidly grounded in religious studies alongside a specialization.

As to specializations, a number of faculty expressed a desire to move even further away from the still-lingering "Protestant seminary" curriculum and methods to ones more distinctive of religious studies. One professor offered examples. Courses in "Bible" or "Scripture" would include not only the Hebrew and Christian Bibles as well as the scriptures of the ancient Near East generally, but, in addition, sacred texts of religions of other peoples and other parts of the world. "Ethics" courses would cover more than Christian or Western ethics and would include business and medical ethics. At the same time, faculty expressed concerns similar to those of some administrators about religious studies courses and curricula that were too diffuse and unstructured. That none was as sweeping as Peter Slater's resounding call for academic discipline and integrity in religious studies nearly two decades ago (Slater, 1972) suggests that some tightening up has occurred. Nor is religious studies the only academic field in which integration and cohesion are concerns (see W. C. James, forthcoming).

(See, further, chap. 7.6, "Directions of Research," and chap. 8, "Undergraduate Curricula.")

3.2.3   Religious Studies as an Academic Field

Faculty generally said they would teach a seminary course differently than a religious studies course. Theological students, like religious studies students, should be taught to think critically; but the training-for-ministry dimension present in the seminary course would be lacking in the religious studies course; so, too, would the confessional aspect — one would not assume religious commitment on the part of students and professor. Opinions divided on whether, or how, one could teach theology in a religious studies department (cf. chaps. 2.4.3 above and 12.5 below). More than one faculty member who said yes, however, saw such teaching as part of a humanistic, liberal arts education, and not as a means of indoctrination or proselytizing.

Several faculty made a point of emphasizing that proselytizing was not an aim in their teaching. Others remarked that "preaching" to students is less apt to be found in religious studies departments than in other departments. They might be apt to agree with the judgment expressed some years ago by Peter Slater (then teaching in the religious studies department at Carleton) that "it is an irony of the times that philosophers and historians tend to preach at will to their students, while religion professors are supposed to remain scrupulously noncommittal" (1972, 33). Just recently, in his Presidential Address to the American Academy of Religion, Robert Wilken (1989) has argued that religious scholars should not shy away from showing publicly — in the classroom and elsewhere — that they care "for" as well as teach "about" religious traditions. One of our interviewees said he has a "missionary" stance in that — through what he teaches and through students' seeing how he, as a confessedly religious person, thinks and teaches — he seeks to get students to think critically about religion and to take it seriously as a major influence in society and as a legitimate world view; that entails moving beyond the parochial understandings of religion that most students bring to class.

One might compare these perceptions of teaching and the stance of the teacher, as seen from the inside of religious studies, with those of an outsider, the late Hans George Classen, an Ottawa writer who published a mini state-of-the-art study of the field in the *Queen's Quarterly* a dozen years ago. After interviewing "some sixteen" religious studies professors across Canada, including seven in Ontario universities (1978, 390), he puzzled at some length over the apparent anomaly that professors in other fields often make no secret of their personal views and commitments and give what amount to believing interpretations of their subject matter, while the religious studies professors he interviewed were very reluctant to do either.

> It is considered academically acceptable, and is no doubt fairly common practice, for history professors holding Marxist views to explain the course of history as obeying the laws of dialectical and historical materialism, but it is *not* acceptable for a RS professor to explain the course of history as obeying the design of God. Again, it is acceptable to explain beliefs as a product of economic relationships, but it is *not* acceptable to explain economic relationships as part of God's design. In short, one can be a spokesman [sic] for almost any cosmic force or principle in today's universe, as long as one does not call it God (Classen, 1978, 395).

The distinctions our own interviewees drew between teaching a religious studies course and teaching a course in a theological college suggest that, for them, the sort of thing Classen saw as excluded from the university classroom would be permissible in a seminary classroom, where (as in the nineteenth century [cf. chap. 2.4.2 above]) religious commitment can be assumed and expressed. Underlying that exclusion is religious pluralism, and the long history behind it, which premise religious studies (chap. 2 above) and which Classen briefly notes earlier (ibid., 392) but seems to forget in his subsequent reflections. It might also be pointed out that even in a theological college Classen's view of what it might mean to be a "spokesman [sic] for . . . God" would likely be seen by many faculty as too constrictive.

Classen did report some chinks in his interviewees' professional armour. For some of them, who cited the example of history and political science professors, "this bending-over-backwards approach [to teaching] is yielding to a let-your-commitments-show approach" (ibid., 394). Classen cites one professor who "said she made no 'testimonials' in class, but whether she let her own religious views enter into the discussion depended on the situation." (ibid., 396). Another, Norman Pagé of the University of Ottawa, "said he might give his personal views to a student after class," and another "thought it depended on the person" (ibid.).

But do students really care whether or not a religious studies professor emerges from behind those texts and data and theories to disclose her or his commitments or personal opinions? They don't, asserted one Ontario religious studies professor, Millard Schumaker of Queen's — any more than they care "about the personal opinions of a biology teacher" (ibid., 396-97). "Is this true?" asked Classen.

> What if a biology teacher believed that the theory of evolution was a lot of nonsense? What if a teacher of astronomy believed that the positions of the planets had profound effects on the lives of men [sic]? (ibid., 397).

Classen's opinion was

> that if the personal beliefs of the modern RS teacher evoke little interest on the part of his [sic] students it is because in most cases these beliefs are so attenuated and so hedged about with explanations and qualifications that they bear hardly any relation to the fundamental dogmas of the major religions (ibid.).

This judgment, itself a leap of faith on Classen's part, is tempered by his report that none of his interviewees was prepared simply "to declare that he or she teaches religion as if it were a purely human phenomenon because he [or she] *believes* it to be a purely human phenomenon" (ibid., 395).

Classen's observations and reflections are valuable because they hold up to religious studies professors a picture of themselves as seen from the outside. Some of the features are familiar, as is evident in various places in this volume. But those on the inside may be inclined to regret the omission of some of the hues and shadings that are part of life in the classroom — more sophisticated understandings of the nature and role of myth, for example, or a more capacious understanding of "belief" as comprehending more than cognition and assent — and to see Classen's picture as a "thin" description (Geertz, 1973), perhaps inevitable in a journal article and by someone not an adept in the field.

Those who have had to struggle to establish and maintain religious studies departments in Ontario universities — as many of our interviewees have — are still close enough to the earlier "religious knowledge" and confessional-indoctrinational-proselytizing approach to the study of religion — which, some insist, still persists (cf. chap. 2.4.3 above) — to know the continuing importance of the descriptive "teaching-about-religion" ethos premised on pluralism and the kind of scholarship described in Chapter 2. The empathy that is part of that ethos and makes it possible to teach responsibly a religion to which one is an outsider is illustrated by Wilfred Cantwell Smith's view, as reported by Classen (ibid., 398):

> Instead of having to hide, or declare, his or her belief in a number of fundamental religious tenets, most of which the student with a modern secular outlook must find unbelievable, the teacher need only affirm that he or she can *enter into the feelings* (what the Germans call *Nachfühlen*) of, say, a Muslim or a Hindu.

One of our interviewees reported to us that when he is teaching Buddhism his students are convinced that he is a Buddhist, and when Christianity a Christian—which he is, and makes no secret of if asked by them. To Classen's example of the biology teacher he might respond that such a person might indeed be able to teach the theory of evolution responsibly by bracketing his personal view that evolution is "a lot of nonsense" and then entering empathically into the theory. It is highly unlikely, however, that a biologist such as Classen describes would be at all inclined to do so, or would in fact be hired in the biology department of a provincial university. Even as it is unlikely that the hypothetical fundamentalist Classen adduces in the same context would be hired by the religious studies professors we interviewed, or that the fundamentalist would want to be hired if it meant keeping "his beliefs to himself" (ibid., 397) and subscribing to the teaching-about-religion ethos.

That ethos does not preclude expressing personal opinions in the classroom—faculty in other fields do so, and our interviewees offered no disclaimers about doing the same, if it were germane to what was happening in the class. Nor, it has been argued in recent years, does the ethos, which aims for "objectivity" as well as empathy, necessarily preclude passion and personal involvement; these may in fact improve understanding and enhance teaching and research (Whittaker, 1981; Wilken, 1989; cf. Remus, 1988, 1664). Whether religious studies professors should go further—pass judgment on the ultimate truth of the religious traditions they are treating, that is, disclose their own beliefs—is still a subject of some debate in religious studies (chap. 2.4.3 above). But, to judge from our interviews and our general acquaintance with the field, many—perhaps most—religious studies professors in Ontario and elsewhere would fit Classen's portrayal of them as generally reluctant to come out of the closet—certainly not to give "testimonials." They might note that they have more than enough to do simply to lead students toward some understanding of the beliefs, practices, social patterns, and various other facets of the complex phenomenon "religion."

There is, moreover, what Classen (ibid., 401) labels a "pedagogical device": "the refusal of the RS teacher to proclaim in class what, if anything, he himself [sic] holds to be true in religion." For religious studies professors this can, indeed, be a serious pedagogical concern. Disclosure of one's commitments may vitiate teaching by allowing students to put the instructor in predetermined, stereotyping boxes, and thus hinder learning, as if they were to say to themselves:

> If you are a Jew, what business do you have teaching the letters of (my very Christian) Paul [overlooking the expertise of the professor in Christian origins and the fact that Paul was Jew]?
>
> Or, if you are a Roman Catholic, with Catholicism's well-known emphasis on salvation through works, how can you possibly teach me the letters of Paul, with his (and my) Protestant emphasis on grace and faith [overlooking, again, the professor's expertise as well as the stress on grace and faith in Roman Catholicism and the essential place of "works" in Paul and in Protestantism]?

Or, if you are a committed Christian, how can you give me the objective view of Paul and his letters that I expect in a university [overlooking the way religious professors are trained and the rites of entry to a religious studies faculty]?

An example is that of a course in Islam offered in one Ontario department. A Muslim student in the class was so taken with the instructor and the instructor's approach and with what he was learning about his religion that he was convinced the instructor would be converting to Islam at the end of the course. What would have happened had he learned, or known beforehand, that the instructor would have been able to confess the student's creed, "There is no god but God," only as far as the word "god"?
(See, further, chap. 6, "Faculty: Teaching.")

3.2.4 Morale

Many of the feelings faculty had about "life in the trenches" came out in responses to our question about morale in their department. "Good" was a common characterization, based on such (predictable) factors as mutual respect and good relations between colleagues, favourable conditions for research and publication, reasonable teaching loads, capable department chairs and administrators, and, in some cases, new faculty.

Where morale was rated poor or not good, the same factors were cited, but negatively, as well as others. One was infrequent contact between professors and a lack of collegiality because the department or other administrative unit was scattered among or drew from various institutions of the university. In one place faculty saw themselves as the workhorses of their institution because high enrolments in their courses were essential to financial viability and job security; the attendant emphasis on teaching, even in the summer, left little time for research.

Also affecting morale were what one might call ideological conflicts over the theory and methodology of religious studies, sometimes rooting in deep-seated cultural differences. Another factor producing tensions within a department was hiring and tenure decisions, some of which had to do with the relation between men and women faculty in a department. Tensions, and conflicts, were apt to arise where women perceived themselves as numerically or psychologically outnumbered, or felt that their concerns were being ignored, or that the men in the department were insensitive to discriminatory language, unacquainted with or unsympathetic to feminist studies and approaches, or were covertly or openly biassed to the point of blocking tenure and promotion.

In a recent tenure case in the Trinity College (Toronto) Faculty of Divinity a women professor successfully appealed a negative decision on grounds of sexual discrimination by the dean. Although the venue was a theological college rather than a department of religious studies, the case (as reported in the daily press [*Globe and Mail*, February 7, 1990, A13; Canadian Press dispatch, *Kitchener-Waterloo Record*, February 7, 1990, F8]) has implications for university life as a whole, as the special grievance panel of the University of Toronto pointed out. It is "improper [said the panel] for any supervisor . . . to impose a dress or behavior code drawn from a stereotype of the male academic." The University should "establish a set of measures that recognizes the demands of combining work and active parenting." It should not expect professors with young children to be involved in extra-curricular activities to the same extent as was common when male professors had wives at home looking after their children. It is unreasonable for the university to expect staff members with children to be "supermothers or superfathers" doing extensive research, counseling students, serving on university committees as well as caring for their families. The case led to institution of a grievance procedure for staff at Trinity College.

In most of the departments we visited, although men outnumbered women, tensions and problems like those indicated were not evident. One woman, asked whether being a woman gave her any particular insights into religious texts, said that in her scholarly work, she perceives herself as a professional — "I don't think with my genitals" — and that any discrimination she had experienced had come from other women: "Why do you need a job? Your husband works." Not surprisingly, at any one institution opposite viewpoints were often expressed, not only on gender issues, but on other questions as well.

Grievance procedures and policies on sexual harassment are slowly being instituted in Ontario universities and theological colleges. "None too soon" would be a safe guess. In our interviews we did not ask explicitly about sexual harassment, and none was mentioned. Outside the interviews, however, women graduate students cited incidents (chap. 4.2.6 below). Statistics on harassment and anecdotal evidence suggest that it is not unknown among religious studies and theological faculty and that there would be cases where the victim, usually a woman, endures in silence, nagged by doubts and anxieties. Do others know, and if so, do they think she invites the advances or acquiesces in them — or just what do they think? Is she, after all, perhaps "overreacting"?

If she is a faculty member and does nothing by way of formal protest or grievance, will her career be jeopardized by rumours or by the harasser's maligning of her for resisting his advances. And if she does something, will that have the same effect — because the harasser, for whatever reasons, seeks to hinder it, or because the whole business undoes her concentration on her work and undermines her confidence? And if her institution has no grievance procedures or published policy on harassment, how should she proceed, and what are the chances of a fair hearing?

Male faculty members are much less likely to be troubled by harassment. There is, however, the possibility of unprovoked charges of harassment by colleagues or students, as has been reported in Ontario primary and secondary schools. None such came to light in our visits, but, here again, a published harassment policy is important – for the protection of all concerned.

(On gender issues see, further, chaps. 4, 5.2, 9.4, and 12 below.)

With several exceptions, we did not interview part-time faculty. They were mentioned, however, both by administrators and full-time faculty because of the important role they play in Ontario universities generally and religious studies departments in particular. The exceptions were graduate students who were also employed as part-time instructors and a woman who specifically asked to be interviewed. A Ph.D. with publications (including a book) to her credit, she had been teaching part-time in a department for a decade but evidently with only nebulous promises of full-time employment. Judging from these interviews and from contacts with other part-time faculty, morale among part-timers is not good. Nor is it likely to improve since part-time instruction has become a way of life in a time of budgetary restraints. In some places, as in the case just cited, long-term employment of part-time instructors has meant perpetual part-timers – persons sometimes superior in teaching and research to full-time faculty, as some of the latter readily admit. On the other hand, where a faculty union contract limits the number of terms a part-time instructor can be employed, but full-time faculty appointments are not forthcoming as replacements, consistency in curriculum and teaching standards can be difficult to maintain, which would affect morale all around.

The Canada Research Fellowships offered in recent years by the Social Sciences and Humanities Research Council were designed to facilitate movement of unemployed or underemployed Ph.D.s into teaching positions by funding the first year of a successful applicant's employment, with the university expected to pick up the costs for two more years, by which time, it was hoped, university funding for the position would have acquired a regular line in the university's budget. The programme has now been discontinued, and current projections envisage faculty shortages, especially in the humanities, as faculty retire in large numbers in the 1990s (Bowen and Sosa, 1989; for Ontario, OCUFA, 1990a; see, further, chap. 5.1.1.2 and 5.3 below).

3.2.5   Learned Societies

Data on faculty membership in learned societies, and faculty views on learned societies, are reported in some detail in the context of research and publication in Chapter 7.7 below. A summary account of faculty perceptions and opinions of learned societies, of membership in them, and of attendance at their annual meetings will suffice here therefore. They cover a broad spectrum.

At one end are those persons who see them as extremely valuable. Generally, these are persons who attend the annual meetings regularly, presenting papers, presiding over sessions, and serving on committees and as officers.

These regular attenders would probably agree with Martin Marty (1986, 244) that what attracts them to these annual get-togethers is not only the lectures and seminars but also the publishers' book displays and the reunions — often connected with "elbow-bending" — with old friends, alumni/ae, and former colleagues.

Some perceive the Canadian societies as too small a pond, in contrast to the large or prestigious international bodies. A few see the Canadian societies as not sufficiently specialized, and instead of — or in addition to — membership in them they find kindred scholars in the continuing seminars and groupings in the American Academy of Religion and the Society of Biblical Literature or in other, more narrowly-focused societies. A variation of this is the professor for whom research trips abroad function as a substitute for attendance at learned society meetings.

A number of persons expressed strong loyalty to Canadian religious studies societies. Their meetings are an annual highlight in the lives of many religious studies professors (at the least, one gets to see the country); especially is this true of those who see themselves as overburdened with teaching or labouring in geographically or psychologically lonely outposts.

One professor, a young scholar, is probably a harbinger of the future. An active participant in a computer-linked network of scholars in his field, he weighs the merits of learned society meetings against electronic exchange, which brings him into contact with scholars not only in Canada but also in the U.S.A., Europe (now both East and West), the Middle East, Australia, and Asia. Moreover, these contacts are more frequent — often daily — than learned society meetings as well as cheaper, an important factor, especially now when society dues are steadily increasing and travel funds are tight. He might be inclined to save his money for conferences where he and his BIT-NET colleagues can continue, *viva voce*, their on-line exchanges of scholarly lore and gossip.

Several faculty we interviewed said they not only do not attend the AAR-SBL annual meetings, they stay away from them, preferring the smaller scope and the collegiality of the Canadian Learneds (from which many francophones have felt excluded, however; see chaps. 2.7, 7.7, and 12.9). A few alternate their attendance between the AAR-SBL and the Canadian annual meetings.

At the other end of the spectrum are persons who said they find little or no satisfaction in membership in Canadian learned societies or in attending their annual meetings. For some this was a "left out" feeling. They don't present papers or get involved in the operation of the societies, which some perceive to be in the hands of a few. The societies don't sponsor sessions on matters close to their hearts or their day-to-day concerns, such as teaching. Other professors are lone wolves — productive scholars who may attend professional society meetings from time to time but, at bottom, perceive them as distracting and a waste of time. Another professed loner said that he keeps abreast of research through journals, correspondence, and visits to his campus by scholars in his field. This kind of scholarly *modus operandi* presupposes a milieu with good library resources and a significant community of scholars. In Ontario universities generally, however, religious studies departments sponsor colloquia and symposia at which local or outside scholars present papers and which offer, on a small scale, scholarly exchange of the kind provided by the annual meetings of learned societies.

Somewhere in between are persons who would be inclined to attend the meetings, or to attend more often than they do, but feel hindered by teaching or administrative responsibilities or by inadequate department funds for travel, especially for those who don't give papers. Others see advantages to belonging to learned societies or to attending the annual meetings, and say they want to do so, but don't get around to it. Their lives at their institution, and/or their personal lives, fill up their days.

(See, further, chaps. 7.7 and 12.8.)

3.3   Theological College Faculty[12]

As is noted at a number of places in this volume, although theological colleges and religious studies departments and programmes are distinct enterprises, there are various ties — historical and continuing, institutional and personal — between them and their respective faculties. Some theological college faculty are directly involved in religious studies degree programmes. How they view themselves, religious studies, and the relation between religious studies and theological education bears, therefore, on religious studies. Other theological faculty are not thus involved in religious studies. Their perceptions are important inasmuch as, formally at least, they stand outside the field and provide still another perspective on it.

The procedures for selecting faculty members for interviews at theological colleges were very similar to those for religious studies departments and programmes (3.3 above). In a few cases we left the selection up to the college dean or principal, requesting that those chosen would represent the various areas of theology and a spectrum of age and experience and (where applicable) both men and women. We also interviewed the dean or principal and, where the college was federated with a university, with the graduate dean, schedules permitting. Lunch provided opportunity to meet other faculty members as well. At smaller colleges we were sometimes able to interview all, or virtually all, the full-time faculty. As with religious studies faculty, the response was gratifying, and the interviews proved fruitful.

Both for those professors directly involved in religious studies and for those who are not, their views on hiring, promotion and tenure generally corresponded — with some qualifiers — with those indicated earlier for university administrators and religious studies faculty. The qualifiers have to do with denominational requirements of theological colleges and the weight often attached, alongside research and publication, to service rendered to the religious bodies that own and govern the colleges. Giving merit credit for such service, as one administrator noted, could lead to morale problems among those with significant publication records who considered publication more important than service. Nonetheless, as in the interviews with religious studies professors, the importance of research and publication was a common thread in the interviews, bearing out the prediction of Gilles Langevin (speaking a couple decades ago of theological education in francophone Quebec) that theological professors would in future devote themselves more to those two aspects of academic life (1968, 170). Also similar to religious studies (see 3.2.5 above) is that membership in learned societies is a mixed bag: some faculty are firmly committed to membership and regular attendance, others not at all, and others are somewhere in between; some prefer Canadian to American and international societies, and others the reverse.

The views of theological faculty on these matters reflect the professionalization of academia noted earlier (3.1.1 above), which made significant inroads into theological education in the 1920s and subsequently through the Conference of Theological Seminaries and its successor, the American Association of Theological Schools (AATS), later renamed the Association of Theological Schools (ATS) (Remus, 1971, 125-27, and the literature cited there), and in the case of Roman Catholic seminaries through papal, conciliar, and episcopal directives (e.g., *Providentissimus Deus* [1893-94]; *Divino Afflante Spiritu* [1943]; *Optatam Totius* from the Second Vatican Council). In recent years the increasing association of theological colleges with universities has also contributed to academic professionalization.

The comprehensive AATS study of theological education in North America by Charles Feilding (1966a) of Trinity College, Toronto, resulted in a sharp critique of Canadian theological colleges (1966b) which, inter alia, contrasted them unfavourably with the burgeoning religious studies departments:

> it will not be possible to tolerate for long a developing caste system based on good standards, good libraries, and good scholarship in university departments of religion, and poor standards, poor libraries, and underpaid teachers in weak seminaries (1966b, 237).

A few years later when the *Canadian Journal of Theology* ceased publication in favour of a religious studies journal, *Studies in Religion/Sciences Religieuses*, the farewell editorial predicted that with the advent of religious studies in Canadian universities "the Canadian theological faculty or seminary" that isolated itself from current "theological and religious scholarship" would end up "underprivileged" (Fairweather, 1970, 128).

That Canadian theological colleges have taken these kinds of judgments seriously is clear from the gradual accreditation of Canadian theological colleges in the last two decades by the AATS/ATS (see App. B below). In our interviews, theological professors involved in graduate programmes in theology generally did not think their standards were inferior to those of religious studies; some involved in doctoral programmes in theology maintained that admission as well as other requirements were stricter than those in religious studies doctoral programmes.

Since a number of the faculty in Ontario's theological colleges have received their graduate education in religious studies programmes, and/or rub shoulders with religious studies scholars on their campus or at learned society meetings, and/or sometimes teach religious studies courses, it is not surprising that quite a few of those interviewed showed themselves to be informed on religious studies and in various ways bring its concerns and approaches to their research and teaching. They were able, for example, to specify, in ways similar to those outlined by religious studies professors interviewed, how they would teach a religious studies course compared with how they teach their seminary courses. One such professor observed that theological students who had taken religious studies courses had learned to ask adult questions about religion and brought to their seminary courses a familiarity with content and methodology; and that it was in religious studies courses that some students had acquired their interest in theology. Another, at a Roman Catholic theological college, perceived a brain drain from Roman Catholic seminaries to religious studies departments where, it was thought, there was greater freedom to think and to teach. A professor at a Protestant theological college, on the other hand, saw greener grass in the Roman Catholic pasture: he believed there was a greater percentage of lay people enrolled in Roman Catholic than in Protestant seminaries and that this served as an incentive to diversify curricula to include courses of a more academic nature alongside those geared to professional ends.

In general, our interviews of theological professors would seem to confirm what various Canadian and American theological educators have said over the past twenty-five years on the importance of religious studies. Noting that "university departments of religion are growing," Feilding maintained that

> It would be impossible to consider the location of theological schools apart from the growth of departments of religion in the universities. Not everyone who wants to study religion or Christian theology wants to enter the ministry. In fact the tendency to make theology into a subject of exclusively masculine and clerical interest has done it much harm (1966b, 236).

A couple of years later, Norman Wagner of Waterloo Lutheran University and Aarne Siirala of Waterloo Lutheran Seminary, urging interdisciplinary theological education, stated that "such a programme would assume that a new impetus from growing departments of religion in this country had led to more teaching in this area at the B.A. level" (1968, 159).

More sweeping were the statements by George Lindbeck of Yale Divinity School in a 1976 study[13]: "the expansion of religious studies," he wrote, "has had a pervasive influence" on theological education, so that "Religious studies increasingly set the tone for all academic work in religion'' (1976, 17). Moreover, "the ethos of the graduate school profoundly affects professional training. . . . And this ethos [in the case of theological education] . . . is increasingly that of religious studies, not theology'' (ibid., 38). More specifically, "the traditional disciplines of bible, church history, etc., are more and more dominated quantitatively and often qualitatively by religious studies approaches'' (ibid).

Similar views were expressed a decade later by Claude Welch, then Dean of Graduate Theological Union:

> With respect to the quantity, at least, one may observe that over the past two decades the center of gravity for scholarship in Bible, in the history of Christianity and Christian thought, and perhaps even in constructive theology has shifted from the theological schools to the university and college departments of religion (Welch, 1985, 65).

Recent statements by an American theological professor and seminary president (Sweet, 1990), an American religious studies professor and past president of the North American Patristics Society and the American Academy of Religion (Wilken, 1989), and a Canadian religious studies scholar and past president of the Canadian Society of Church History, the late Keith Clifford (1990), accord with these assessments by Lindbeck and Welch.[14]

However, one point on which the professors interviewed would seem to take issue with Lindbeck is his assertion that "Before learning to think like a Barth or a Tillich, one [i.e., a theologian] compares them to a Ramanuja or a Shankara'' (Lindbeck et al., 17). Our interviews suggest that the study of religions other than Christianity and (ancient) Judaism — study pursued in varying degrees in religious studies (chap. 2.4.4-6 above; chaps. 8.2 and 9.2.2.1 and 9.3.3 below) — seems to have had little effect on theological education in Ontario. Some theological faculty expressed regret about this. One said that these religions were being treated in some theological schools, but in a traditional, apologetic (refutational) way. Another noted the common practice of contrasting Christianity and other religions, the latter serving as background in order to see Christianity more clearly. Others noted that some theological students do in fact take advantage of religious studies offerings in world religions, mostly because (interestingly) they know someone from a religion other than Christianity, but that the majority of those enrolled in such courses are from the Third World. One Third World student from an area where Muslims and Christians are in conflict had wanted to take a course in Islam and lamented the fact that his college offered none — nor, evidently, was he advised to take one in a nearby university religious studies department.

These examples bring home the pluralism of today's world indicated earlier (chap. 2.1-2.3 above), which Feilding's study had already noted — "older religious divisions are cut across by newer ones of greater significance'' (1966b, 234) — and which theological educators have, more recently, drawn attention to: "pluralism of nations and national ideologies, pluralism of world religions, and pluralism within each religion, including of course our own [Christian religion]" (Suchocki, 1985, 68; cf. Welch, 1985, 66).

This is an issue that affects both religious studies and theological education. Religious studies developed in part in response to an increasingly pluralistic society and culture (chap. 2 above), and its continued musings and debates over its identity and rationale, methodologies and curriculum, represent further points along that path. As for theological colleges, Douglas John Hall of the McGill University Faculty of Religious Studies has argued in various publications (e.g., 1985a, 1985b, 1989) that theology must be contextual in order to be effective, and that its context today is a post-Constantinian, pluralistic world in which Christianity is once again a minority religion. Theological education would seem to have to be concerned, as Claude Welch insists, with "non-Western religions and Native American religion" (1985, 66). Not in an apologetic way, assessing them "as merely error," or "passed over in silence or relegated to the category of the unconscious or crypto-Christian" (ibid.). Welch's own version of contextuality is "the historical consciousness, with the consequence of recognizing the limited and sociohistorically conditioned nature of the theological enterprise," and "the striking growth in the understanding of non-Christian religious phenomena," which means that "Christian theological investigation simply cannot be carried on except in relation to other traditions than our own" (ibid.; cf., similarly, Tracy and Cobb, 1983; Tracy, 1991). But Welch suspects (and objects to) "A kind of division of territory, in which theological schools do the Christian thing and religious studies departments do the other things" (ibid.).

Charles Feilding, in his 1966 study of Canadian theological colleges, proposed that students in those colleges "should be in *working* encounter with theological students in other religious traditions" (1966b, 236), by which he may have meant students in other Christian traditions. But the approach is similar to that of religious studies departments and scholars that follow the dialogue approach pioneered by Robert Slater and Wilfred Cantwell Smith for study of religions generally (chap. 2.4.4 above). For professors and students in Christian theological colleges, dialogue with religious studies professors and students knowledgeable in, and sometimes practising, non-Western and indigenous religions could provide some "working encounters" of the kind Fielding suggested. The experience Christian theologians have acquired in their working encounters in the Christian ecumenical movement over the course of this century would stand them in good stead for similar encounters in the new, pan-religious ecumenism of the next century.

More than one theological professor we interviewed thought that theological and religious studies professors and students need something more than the rubbing of shoulders that for quite a number is often the only contact between them: without significant contact with a cognate field like religious studies theological education tends to complacency and parochialism; and without contact with the actual practice of religion such as a theological college or some other locus of religious practice provides, religious studies runs the risk of abstraction — cut off (in Martin Marty's words) from "the warm bodies and communities in which sacred texts are engendered, where symbols are celebrated, and myths retold," and without which "religious studies would soon be for archaeologists, nothing more" (1986, 248).[15]

Notes

1 A fuller statement of the ideal of a "faith dimension" is given in Wade, 1978, referring to Roman Catholic universities but presumably applicable, with changes in terminology and concepts, to other church-related colleges and universities: the "essential role of faith . . . is to keep mystery vitally alive in Christian intellectual life" and the role of such a university in academia is "to keep mystery alive in the world of intellect" (39). The role of a department of theology (as religious studies departments are often called in Roman Catholic colleges and universities) or of religious studies is to provide

> those having the faith . . . the opportunity of studying their faith at the level of disciplined intellectual competence.
> Along with growth in their knowledge of the arts and sciences their faith can be more precisely and fully articulated.
> Consequently, they are not caught in the impossible bind of trying to unify their advancing knowledge in other fields with a static and simplistic knowledge of their faith (42).

2 Cf. the emphatic statement in the Victoria College Calendar (1990-91, i): "Rooted firmly in the Non-Conformist tradition of nineteenth century Methodism, Victoria has always defended the right of its members to pursue the truth unhampered by real or implicit tests of orthodoxy."

3 In the role they allot to religion the self-descriptions of Protestant church-related colleges in Ontario cover a considerable spectrum. Some do not mention religion as one of the characteristics setting them apart from other colleges and from the university context as a whole. Trinity (Anglican) in Toronto focuses on the advantages to students of "a community of limited size" (Calendar, 1990-91, 2). Huron College (Anglican) in London is "committed to providing the setting that makes excellent undergraduate learning possible," with "Highly trained faculty committed to undergraduate education, small classes, and a strong sense of community" (Calendar, 1990-91, ii).

Other colleges mention their religious connection as one of a number of distinctives. The description of Huntington College on the Laurentian University campus notes that it is named after a Methodist missionary to northern Ontario and "is affiliated with the United Church of Canada" (Laurentian University Calendar, 1990-91, 14). Thorneloe on the same campus cites "As part of its Anglican origin" its "small, beautifully designed, separate chapel," and points out that though it is "Anglican in foundation and affiliation," it "is open to all" (brochure, 1990). Victoria College (United Church) in Toronto sees its roots in "the Non-Conformist tradition of nineteenth century Methodism" as a warrant of academic freedom in the College (Calendar, 1990-91, i; see above, n. 2 of this chapter). Renison College (Anglican) in Waterloo offers (in the words of the Principal) "a small college setting in which students can follow their studies while enjoying all the benefits of the resources of a major university and a Christian atmosphere in which students of any religious persuasion may live and study" (Calendar, 1990-91, 2). The Principal's message to students of St. Paul's College (United Church) in Waterloo includes a "strong affirmation of university life and our United Church affiliation. . . . Freedom is a treasured gift and we celebrate it here. But we also know that absolute freedom does not exist and that we live within the freedom of our commitments" (Handbook [i.e., Calendar], 1989-90, 1).

Conrad Grebel College (Mennonite), affiliated with the University of Waterloo, is more explicit and detailed on the role of religion in the *raison* of the College. Its statement of mission describes the College as

> a learning community of teachers, students, and staff who seek to further knowledge and wisdom; to integrate knowledge, faith and action; and to nurture persons who, in their diverse vocations, will contribute to the well-being of the church and society (Calendar, 1988-89, 3).
>
> The college seeks to be a Christian presence in the university community, reflecting the vision and values of the Mennonite church. As a mediating institution between the university and the church, Conrad Grebel College challenges the church with the insights of the university and the university with the understandings of the church (Calendar, 1990-91, 5)

Redeemer College in Ancaster, which is not affiliated with a provincial university, is quite emphatic regarding its Christian and denominational character and purpose. It describes itself as

> a Christian university offering Scripturally-directed, liberal arts and sciences education which explores the relation of faith, learning and living from a Reformed Christian perspective and which enables students to gain a deeper understanding of God's creation, equipping them for a life of service and leadership under the Lordship of Christ (Calendar, 1989-90, 1).

(For further information on these schools see chap. 2.6 above.)
4 Cf. the statement by Archbishop Rembert Weakland of Milwaukee:

> Major American Catholic universities . . . long ago adopted the standard American guarantees of academic freedom. This was done not as a compromise of ideal to secular reality, but as a way to make those institutions more effective in service to the church. They would be more effective because they could attract to their work more competent faculty and staff, and thereby enhance the cultural impact of their Catholic witness.
>
> Academic freedom must not be interpreted to mean that truth and falsehood are the same, nor does it mean that one does not have a grave obligation to search for and teach the truth. Academic freedom in our Catholic universities has made them stronger and is a heritage that must not be jeopardized.
>
> The risks of this are also clear. . . . But the risks were taken for the greater good that could accrue to the church in America. Seeing, as I do, the immense contributions of . . . the assembly of American Catholic universities, and seeing around the world no collection of Catholic universities to compare with the American, I believe it was a risk well taken. (Cited from *The Catholic Herald*, March 21, 1985, 6, by Boyle, 1985, 175, who edited out local references.)

5 See the statements and studies on academic freedom and due process by the Catholic Theological Society of America (e.g., *Council on the Study of Religion Bulletin* 10/4 [Oct.1974], 114; CTSA *Proceedings* 32 [1977], 261; CTSA, 1980) and the committees established by the CTSA to study the issues (*Council on the Study of Religion Bulletin*

11/5 [Dec.1980], 148; 14/4 [Oct.1983], 116; 15/5 [Dec.1984], 150-51; CTSA, 1980). The Vatican's withdrawal of Charles Curran's right ("canonical mission") to teach at Catholic University of America in Washington, D.C. resulted, ultimately, in the University trustees' decision to respect his tenured status and allow him to teach in an "area of his professional competence" but not in the graduate school of theology; Curran regarded the trustees' decision as a "vindication of academic freedom in Catholic education" (*Time*, April 25, 1988, 85) but, nonetheless, later departed the University. The foil to the trustees' decision is the dismissal or forced resignation of faculty at Catholic University in the early twentieth century for failing to teach according to Roman Catholic doctrine (Remus, 1971, 122).

6 *L'Osservatore Romano*, Feb. 25, 1989; *New York Times*, March 25, 1989, sec.1, p.22.

7 See the actions taken by the Catholic Theological Society of America, reported in *Council of Societies for the Study of Religion Bulletin* 19/1 (Feb. 1990), 13; 19/2 (April 1990), 43, 46; 19/3 (Sept. 1990), 69.

8 *Globe and Mail*, June 24 and 25, 1989. The technical point that led to the University's severing of ties with the Seminary was Emmett Cardinal Carter's refusal to sign a document, presented to him by the University after the resignations, committing the Seminary to University policies promoting academic freedom and freedom of speech (ibid., June 24, 1989).

9 Jencks and Riesman, 1969: The undergraduate college is "a downward extension of the various graduate professional schools for which it prepares, and more especially of the academic graduate schools" (244). "The graduate schools are by far the most important shapers of undergraduate education. It is, indeed, only a small exaggeration to say that undergraduate education in most universities and university colleges is simply a cut-rate, mass-produced version of graduate education" (247-48).

10 Cf. the observation by Philip Gleason (cited in Greeley, 1967, 22) of "the disposition sometimes manifested to treat the earlier efforts of Catholic educators with condescension or scorn because they are not what we are doing or trying to do today."

11 One department did not respond to our request. Two programmes were not visited for budgetary reasons. Also excluded were two graduate degree programmes that do not conceive of themselves as religious studies in aim and orientation. Various data from these institutions, derived from published sources and phone calls, are presented in other places in this study (see, especially, chap. 2.6).

12 Since the theological college administrators interviewed were also active in teaching, and their views generally corresponded with those of their faculty, they are included here with faculty, except as noted. Of the theological colleges listed in Appendix B below, we conducted interviews with faculty at about half.

13 Lindbeck prepared the report in consultation with Karl Deutsch, a political scientist, and Nathan Glazer, a sociologist, "but [writes Lindbeck] responsibility for the report rests entirely with the principal author" (Lindbeck et al., 1976, vii).

14 Leonard I. Sweet (1990, 160), Professor of Church History and President, United Theological Seminary, Dayton, OH:

> Why has theological education been taking its cues from everyone else, with no significant voice to speak for itself, no equivalent to what religious studies departments and scholars have in the American Academy of Religion? Why, indeed, does a religious studies piety, not a church piety, dominate the theological scene?

Robert L. Wilken, Professor, Department of Religious Studies, University of Virginia, in his Presidential Address to the American Academy of Religion, Anaheim, CA, 1989:

> Until a generation ago most religious scholarship took place within institutions affiliated with the religious traditions, in seminaries and divinity schools, in rabbinical schools and yeshivas, and in madresehs. Within a very short time, in this country, and to a growing extent elsewhere in the world, scholarship in the field of religion has shifted to the colleges and universities (Wilken, 1989, 713).

N. Keith Clifford (1990, 3-4):

> Prior to the 1960s the theological colleges in Canada had no competition in the study of religion, but since then a larger proportion of the academic study of religion is taking place in undergraduate and graduate departments of religion. . . . The traditional theological disciplines of bible, church history and historical theology are increasingly dominated by religious studies approaches. Again, whereas thirty years ago scholarly work in religion assumed the church as the proper context for its intellectual activity and as the affirming background for its publication, today the church is viewed less and less as providing the readership for publications of theological educators. Indeed promotion and tenure committees in the theological colleges, like those in the religious studies departments, are making careful distinctions between material published in refereed academic journals and articles appearing in church publications, and they tend to discount the latter in favour of the former. As Leon Pacala has noted, another aspect of this change is that while in the 1950s 35 [sic; Pacala: 34] percent of the articles published in the *Journal of Religion* were written by seminary professors, in 1979-80 there were none [Pacala, 1981, 23]. Consequently, it has become clear in the 1980s that the seminaries are no longer the main institutional locus within higher education for the study of religion. They no longer set the agenda or the standards in the academic area and the trends in the scholarly study of religion no longer originate in the seminaries.

15 See, further, chaps. 4 and 12 below.

4

Perceptions: Students

Harold Remus

The students we interviewed included religious studies undergraduate and graduate students as well as students in theological colleges. They were selected by department chairs and theological college administrators in response to our request for a representative cross-section that would include, at the undergraduate level, majors/concentrators, minors, and honours students in religious studies; both women and men; full- and part-time students; and persons from different age groups. At the graduate level we requested persons from different areas of study, from M.A. and doctoral levels, and at different stages in their graduate careers. The representativeness of the undergraduates interviewed was affected at a few institutions by the fact that we had to schedule our visits there during exam periods. At one place that seemed to work in our favour, however: a full contingent showed up.[1]

4.1 Undergraduates

The undergraduates selected (and who showed up) for interviews were, we found, typical of students who sit in our own classes and end up, some of them, working toward a religious studies degree. They included the once "typical" young undergraduates who head straight for university after high school as well as the mature students, often second- and third-career persons, increasingly seen in universities at both the undergraduate and graduate levels and in professional degree programmes in theological colleges. These ranged in age from "thirtysomething" on up — though not as far up as some of those in religious studies courses who are well beyond the current age of retirement in Ontario. Also similar to the student population in religious studies courses was the sizable proportion of women among the

Notes to Chapter 4 can be found on pages 143-44.

119

interviewees; they were enrolled in university and specifically in religious studies in order to pursue academic or personal interests or, more commonly, looking to careers outside the home — either launching into one, or testing the waters, or trying to get deflected or "put-on-hold" careers back on course.

As will become evident in what follows, the religious backgrounds and commitments of the undergraduates interviewed often surfaced in the interviews and are therefore worth noting here. Not surprisingly, they reflected those of the population of Ontario and Canada generally (see chap. 2.3 above). Mainline Christian denominations predominated, with a sprinkling of atheists and persons of non-traditional allegiances, one of whom saw his drinking buddies as his religious community. The one Buddhist interviewed was on study leave from his job in Asia. Of those with Christian backgrounds, some are active in churches; more seem not to be.

Religious backgrounds, preferences, and commitments of the students interviewed and (we learned) of students enrolled in religious studies courses at their universities seemed, again not surprisingly, to reflect the locality or region in which the universities were situated. According to one student at a university located in a metropolitan region, those enrolled in religious studies courses with him ranged from Christian fundamentalists to persons with loose attachment to a religious group to those with none. In another, somewhat less metropolitan area a student reported that committed Christians in a seminar of a dozen or so students fluctuated from one year to the next, from 25 to 100 per cent. In areas with large Roman Catholic populations and where the student body comes largely from the surrounding region, Roman Catholics show up in large numbers in religious studies classes, according to professors we interviewed. One might expect this, but it is also interesting: many Roman Catholic students don't steer clear of religious studies courses, as might well have happened prior to the Second Vatican Council in 1962-65 and the new directions it imparted to the denomination — had such courses been available then. A professor in a religious studies department in one such geographical area observed that, alongside the predominantly Roman Catholic enrolments, those of Pentecostal and evangelical Christians were increasing, which suggests changes in those traditions as well.

4.1.1   Religious Studies as a Degree Choice

Why do students decide to work toward a religious studies degree? Or, why do students even enrol in religious studies courses?

These are questions that religious studies professors have puzzled over and to which they have given various answers. One professor we interviewed offered a list based on his observations of students over the years. Parents' religiousness provokes curiosity. Some students from religiously affiliated tertiary-level institutions that lack provincial accreditation may want a university degree and gravitate to religious studies courses. Persons wanting to teach religion in separate schools take religious studies courses to satisfy board requirements. A large, and growing, group that has sought out exotic forms of religion or has an existential but unschooled interest in religion is looking for ways to talk about God in a secular and atheistic environment without getting jeered at.

To this list may be added, from our own experience, students standing in a religious tradition — to which they are committed in varying degrees, or not at all — who want to learn more about it. Or students curious about the religions, manifestations of religion, and religious persons they see around them or that they encounter in reading, films, or other ways.

Then there are the other, more mundane motivations, ones common to students in university departments generally: filling an empty time slot; picking up a needed credit and maybe at the same time meeting a distribution requirement; "looking for a snap elective," as one religious studies professor, Keith Clifford of the University of British Columbia, put it in Hans George Classen's survey (1978, 400) cited in Chapter 3 above — and often getting a jolt when the first test or the first paper is returned. More specific to religious studies is the burgeoning interest in the Pacific Rim among business students that has led them to swell enrolments recently in Asian religions courses.

These various observations are confirmed, in varying degrees, as well as supplemented by those gained in our interviews with students when we asked why and when they decided to concentrate their work in religious studies. Only rarely did our interviewees come to university intending to major in religious studies. These were persons for whom religion was important in their lives, personally and/or professionally: a parent was a minister; the student was committed to a particular religion and wanted to learn more about it, or more about it in relation to other religions; he or she had gone to separate schools and wanted to gain a better understanding of Roman Catholicism — more "objective," less parochial — or a religious studies degree was a step on the way to teaching in a separate school, although, as one student put it, she didn't know if she would still be acceptable with the kind of perspective she had acquired in religious studies. Other, related professional interests entered into decisions to concentrate in religious studies: it was a step on the way to the M.A. and the Ph.D. in religious studies, or in preparation for the Master of Divinity degree in a theological college, or an M.A. in pastoral studies in a theological college, or it would enable a nurse to relate to people better.

More commonly, students first learned of or became interested in religious studies when enrolled in an introductory course — which is one reason religious studies professors, departments, and learned society meetings spend so much time agonizing over Religious Studies 100-101. This path to a religious studies degree might intersect with one frequently cited in the interviews, namely, *away from* another academic field or department. Religious studies students as "refugees" from other departments have been cited frequently in recent decades to account for the great interest in religious studies among students that contributed to the formation of religious studies departments by supplying the numbers of warm bodies that impress university administrators. Writing in 1968 Robert Spivey, sometime Executive Director of the American Academy of Religion, saw as important to this interest the disinterest of many students in "the educational model adopted by much of the university" which "avoids the 'big questions' in the interest of solving littler ones" (1968, 1). Moreover,

> The scientific model, which stresses precision and exactness, [and] has invaded such traditionally humanistic areas of study as literature and philosophy so that often the only place where students can ask and ponder the "big questions" is the religion department (1968, 1).

Comments by two Ontario religious studies professors cited in Classen's survey of Canadian religious studies professors (1978, 393) echoed Spivey's observations. After the Second World War, said Peter Slater (then department chair at Carleton), "there was a vacuum created by the swing of philosophy to linguistic analysis and loss of interest in metaphysical questions." Eugene Combs of McMaster mentioned a "yearning of students for ultimate answers."

Writing some years earlier, Claude Welch cited polls of students and reports by religious studies faculty in the U.S.A. showing that, alongside the desire to fulfill an academic requirement, students were moved to take religious studies courses by intellectual curiosity, search for meaning in life, and wanting to know more about their particular religious tradition. Welch related these motivations to "the serious-minded and deeply troubled character of the undergraduate generation of the 1960's and 1970's" (1971, 179). What the mood will be of young people in the 1990s is a subject that occupies those who study the "twentysomethings." Alexander Austin, of the Higher Education Research Institute, which has been monitoring attitudes among first-year students in American colleges and universities for the past quarter-century, finds that the current crop lacks "the quest to understand things, to understand themselves," and that for them higher education is a means to middle-class bliss (*Time*, July 16, 1990, 48). That motivation, it turned out, was latent in the 'sixties and 'seventies students Welch observed as well. And it is not absent from the 1980s students we interviewed. Nonetheless, for many of them the motivations Welch cites were present in marked degree and brought them to religious studies, often via — and away from — another department.

One student found English literature "very dry," dominated by critics who had decided how it was to be approached. Having moved away from her Roman Catholic upbringing, she found religious studies enabled her to pursue answers to intellectual questions she had about religion. Another student in the same department chose religious studies over history and women's studies because she found it interesting personally and academically. A recent religious studies graduate of the same institution deserted the life sciences and tried a variety of majors before turning to religious studies which, he said, went to the roots of personal questions he had, dissipated his cynicism, and helped him "get rid of [his] petty rebellion against religion" — whereupon he returned to the life sciences. Elsewhere a student who interspersed some years of full-time employment with two years as a math and physics major finally returned to university with an interest in psychology, especially Jung and Freud; finding psychology courses too experimentally oriented, he turned to religious studies where, he said, he could pursue "a personal quest" through psychology of religion and other religious studies courses. Yet another student forsook a fine arts major in acting because she wanted more intellectual stimulation and found religious studies offered it in a way that also allowed for introspection. Further, similar examples could be cited from the interviews of refugees from English, history, psychology, sociology, and the natural sciences.

What did these students discover in religious studies that they said they did not find in other departments? A variety of things, as has already been indicated. None mentioned easy grades, though religious studies departments are hardly immune to that infection and our interviewees certainly knew about bird courses (cf. chap. 3.1.2 above). One interviewee said that students who enroll in religious studies courses think the professors will be a soft touch for extensions on paper deadlines. This is a dubious surmise, judging from our acquaintance with religious studies professors over the years, but of course there are exceptions, as there are in other departments; insofar as lenience and easy grading are found in religious studies departments, those are not phenomena peculiar to religious studies: a recent year-end issue of a student newspaper on one campus gave thanks for arts professors generally for being "softies." For students actually concentrating in religious studies, however, as our interviewees were, the reasons for doing so were more serious. Some are obvious. In order to teach religion in a separate school or religious studies in a university, a religious studies degree is important or essential. A religious studies degree is not required for entry to a theological college, but a major study of Protestant pre-seminary education conducted a few decades ago in the U.S.A. and Canada recommended it as the undergraduate degree of choice (Bridston and Culver, 1965). Students who enter university planning to continue on to theological college often agree, with some paying special heed to courses not apt to appear in a seminary calendar, for example, in religious traditions other than Christianity or thematic and dialogic courses that cover more than one religious tradition (chap. 8.2 below). A religious studies degree may enhance other professional pursuits as well, especially the caring, "people" professions.

For a significant number of our interviewees, however, religious studies was a path to a career in a different, more oblique way: they had to find their way through personal problems or religious questions before they wanted to think — or could begin to think — about looking for a job. In various ways religious studies gave them the opportunity to do so. They could (in the words of one student) get at the "roots" of questions. One woman whose parents died shortly after one another when she was still a teenager was troubled by the problem of evil, and after a year as a psychology major, followed by marriage and four children, returned to school "searching for God and the idea of God." The breadth of religious studies offerings — which sometimes worries deans and religious studies departments (see chap. 7.1 and 7.7 below) — enabled some students to approach the questions troubling them from different angles.

Some of these students labelled the kind of education they were able to get in religious studies "a liberal education." That is the way religious studies was commonly conceived and promoted in its formative days (Holbrook, 1963), and it is one of the ways religious studies departments in Ontario and generally see themselves (see the eloquent and remarkably concise statement of the case in Crites, 1990). It is also a tradition with deep roots in Anglo-Canadian universities (McKillop, 1979, chap. 1). It stands in tension with the professionalization of university education indicated earlier and evident in interviews with religious studies professors (chaps. 2 and 3 above). Important as the professionalization of the study of religion has been to establishing religious studies departments and religious studies as a field, our interviews with undergraduate students strongly suggest that the maintaining of religious studies as "a liberal education" is also essential in Ontario universities and to the continued credibility and survival of religious studies departments.

If the students interviewed didn't turn to other university departments for answers to personal and religious questions, why didn't they, on the other hand, turn to religious institutions, the traditional locus of such concerns? The answer would seem to be that for many these institutions are no longer fulfilling that function. In explaining why students enroll in religious studies courses, Robert Spivey observed that

> in the present rapidly changing world where traditional values and institutions, such as the church and the home, are losing their influence, then it is natural that the university should become a place where values, meaning, and purpose are both questioned and pursued. . . . the study of religion thrives best when religious life falters. When the church and synagogue are weak, then religion study will be strong because people will be questioning and thinking about their traditional religious roots (1968, 9-10).

Such generalizations need qualification. Students quite committed to a religious tradition also show up in religious studies courses, as was indicated in the introduction to this chapter. Sometimes they are (in the words of the late Peter Craigie of the University of Calgary religious studies department) looking for "a forum . . . free from the dogmatic authority of religious establishments'' (cited in Classen, 1978, 392). Spivey's comments are not so wide of the mark, however, given the current state of religious institutions, sometimes rocked by scandal and seen by many as irrelevant and moribund. That one critically *studies* religion rather than (or in addition to) practising it says something about the nature and role of religion in the modern Western world (cf. chap. 2 above). Hans George Classen's opinion (1978, 392), expressed as an outsider to religious studies and a layperson with ''only the general intellectual climate to go on,'' was that

> the major genetically related religions – Christianity, Judaism and Islam . . . became a fit subject for critical study because they ceased to be a subject of awe. Was not the lack of awe the reason why the religions of classical antiquity and ''primitive'' religions had long formed part of the arts curricula?

In some non-Western countries, as those who keep an eye and an ear on the news today know, one does not, in fact, study religion critically. In Western countries some groups and individuals also reject or shy away from doing so (cf. chap. 2.4.6 and 2.4.7 above). But many in mainstream religious traditions, both of Western and non-Western origin, are not thus inhibited and, like a number of our interviewees, turn up in religious studies classes wanting to broaden their understanding of their religious tradition, whether or not they intend to continue in it. Some have little intention of doing so, and ''when they are done,'' says Spivey (1968, 10), ''they are likely to be no more committed than before; yet they will have a better understanding of the nature of commitment.''

Another kind of commitment was expressed by a self-professed atheist among our interviewees who said she was in religious studies because atheists are ''so interested in religion.'' Though it was not much in evidence in our interviews, our own acquaintance with religious studies majors and honours students over the years shows that for a fair number religion is more an intellectual interest than an existential concern. The same is true of many students who elect religious studies courses. As well there are those who belong to what Martin Marty calls ''the 'anti'-side'' of organized religion who enroll in religious studies courses because religion, or a particular religion, ''haunt[s], bewilder[s], or tantalize[s] them'' (1989, 8). They, too, are ''interested in religion.''

4.1.2   Religious Studies as an Academic Field

From these and other comments by our interviewees, one observes that students in religious studies degree programmes view religious studies in ways similar to those of their professors as reported in the preceding chapter. Another way of putting this is to say that they have been socialized into religious studies.

They see it as an academic field. Study of a religion, they said, does not necessarily relate to practice of it, though such study can — and does — affect some students' practice. One student said that when he first enrolled in religious studies courses he expected his professors to be sort of all-wise, wisdom-dispensing gurus, embodying what they taught. Now older and wiser himself, he saw that as a misperception, even as many students on his campus misconceive religious studies majors as all headed for theological college. He and the interviewees generally did not expect their religious studies professors to be practitioners of the religious traditions in which they offer courses, nor did they see that as necessary to fair and balanced treatment in class. Neither did they expect their professors to pass judgment on the "truth" of a religious tradition — though students were concerned about such truth questions. Their comments about how, in religious studies, they had learned to analyze religious traditions as they sought to understand them suggest that their studies had not left them wholly clueless on how to approach the question of the "truth" of those traditions.

What counts in religious studies professors is mastery of their subject. This was the common opinion of the students interviewed. An important element in such mastery, some said, might well be first-hand acquaintance with the practice and practitioners of a religion. However, as more than one student pointed out, overt expression of religious commitment by a professor, or inability to distance oneself from personal religious commitment, could get in the way of full and fair treatment of a religious tradition — one that didn't "put down" other traditions. The nature of religion and religious commitment made these concerns more important in religious studies than in political science or literature, was the view of one student.

For the most part, the religious commitments of professors were not known to their students. If they were, it might be from knowledge gleaned outside the classroom. Expressions of commitment sometimes surfaced in class discussion but (a number of students pointed out) with no attempt to impose religious beliefs. In a certain religious studies course offered in a church-related college, however, one student found that it was taught from the perspective of that church. A student at another university complained that courses often focused on Christianity, even though they were not designated as such in the calendar. On another campus, interestingly, the students looked with favour on the fact that the religious studies department is related to a theological college: they perceived the connection as giving the department moral credibility, and they found that having theological students in class (see chap. 2, n. 5 above) was valuable in that it provided direct contact with practitioners of a religion.

Though not generally aware of their professors' religious commitments, students were quite aware, as students generally are, of the academic slant in their courses, usually reflecting the instructors' current research interests. One welcomes evidence of research bearing fruit in the classroom and one expects professors to teach from their strengths. But one wonders whether, in introductory courses, it sometimes overshadows, or neglects, the basics of the subject at hand. That is not a concern peculiar to religious studies, of course.

4.1.3   Religious Studies as Preparation for Vocation

Whether vocational opportunities for religious studies graduates are better or worse than for graduates in other areas of the humanities would be difficult to judge from our interviews.

Some fell in the camp of those who see liberal arts degrees generally, religious studies among them, as professional in that they prepare one for a number of careers. They might agree with those observers of academia who argue that an honours degree from a particular institution is more important than the particular field of the humanities in which the degree is earned. Recognition of the market value of a humanities degree is not a recent phenomenon. Three decades ago a book entitled *Toward the Liberally Educated Executive* contained calls by business executives, echoed frequently since, for ''broadly educated executives'' with ''a really firm grounding in the humanities or liberal arts'' (Baltzell, 1957, 11, 12) and spoke of ''Liberal Arts as Training for Executives'' (Pamp, 1957; similarly, Peckham, 1960). Technical professional education, in the opinion of one educator of such professionals, leaves most students ''at graduation mentally clumsy, relatively narrow in interest and perspective, and awkward in writing and speech'' as well as ''practically incapable of analyzing problems and situations in terms of general principles. They think narrowly in terms of special formulae and specific cases'' (Doherty, 1950, 10). Some of our interviewees saw religious studies as providing the kinds of skills the educator lamented as lacking (cf. Crites, 1990, 19-20). As one of them put it, religious studies prepares one to approach many different situations objectively and understand them better. She also thought that a religious studies degree suggests honesty and moral integrity to a employer — not a necessary inference, she added, but useful when looking for a job.

Then there were those students, mentioned earlier, who saw their religious studies degree as a professional degree, a step on the path to teaching the study of religion at various levels or to entering the ranks of the clergy or other jobs related to religious institutions. For other students, however, a religious studies degree had no direct vocational payoff. ''I haven't had a bad course in this department,'' said one, but ''I don't feel I have any expertise in anything.'' Millard Schumaker of Queen's, one of the religious studies professors interviewed by Classen, is quoted by Classen as saying that ''he sometimes discouraged students from concentrating on RS — their youthful enthusiasm made them overlook the poor job prospects awaiting them'' (1978, 400). Other religious studies professors have, alongside such warnings, sometimes handed students, undergraduate and graduate, a booklet published (subsequent to Schumaker's remarks) by the Council on the

Study of Religion, *Career Guide for Graduate Students in Religion* (Campbell, 1980, 1981). One of our interviewees thought that graduates in English literature are taken more seriously than those in religious studies, perhaps unaware that English professors may counsel their students despairing about entry into The Real World by calling to their attention Dorothy Bestor's book *Aside from Teaching English, What in the World Can You Do?* (1977).

Falling somewhere in the middle of this spectrum of opinion were those students who thought the understanding one gained in religious studies of self, and of peoples and religious traditions other than one's own, would fit one for "people"-type jobs. One student, for example, was planning to work with geriatic and terminally ill patients — having herself now worked through personal problems in her religious studies courses.

For a number of students, as is clear from much of the foregoing, such coming to terms with oneself came first, career second. Put another way, it was an inescapable preliminary to job and career — education preceded vocation. They might agree with the sociology professor involved in a programme inducting business executives into the liberal arts that "A real education is an emotional as well as an intellectual experience" (Baltzell, 1957, 16). One might characterize that as one of the marks of a liberal arts education. As a liberal education, religious studies was liberating for one student who said she came to university having been "taught only one way of life, which isn't right." For such students the task of the religious studies professor might be, as Wilfred Cantwell Smith phrased it to Classen (1978, 398), "getting the students to see that all faiths are reasonable ways of being human, to make students more fully human."

4.1.4 Morale

If, judging from our interviews, religious studies professors and the students in their undergraduate degree programmes seem *en rapport* about the nature of religious studies and what they expect of each other, what did they have to say about morale? Various criticisms of their programmes and professors have been reported in the foregoing. Others were voiced as well. One student, for example, who was planning to continue on to Ph.D. study said the only way he had been able to pursue his interest in biblical studies was through directed studies courses. He felt there should be greater commitment in the department to languages for biblical studies and that persons headed for graduate school should be advised to study modern languages. On the other hand, he thought the undergraduate degree programme catered to the graduate programme (cf. chap. 3.1.3 and chap. 3, n. 9, above). For him the ideal would be two years of liberal arts followed by two years of skills and methodology courses. Despite all, his morale seemed good, he seemed to respect various professors, and he had stuck with the department and his degree programme, which he characterized as more comprehensive and rigorous than the one in which he began at an American university.

Generally, our interviewees expressed few or only muted criticisms and complaints. Some were quite complimentary of their programmes, professors, and courses, or even waxed enthusiastic about them. Various such comments have been reported along the way in this chapter, suggesting that morale among these students was generally good.

That is what one might expect, since we were interviewing a lot selected by their departments for interviews. They were also self-selected through agreeing to show up and, more basically, by choosing to work toward a religious studies degree, often for very fundamental reasons and after test runs in other fields, and then by persisting in their choice. They had a vested interest in seeing their choice, and the departments in which they were pursuing them, in a favourable light. On the other hand, students are not noted for shying away from criticism of professors and anyone and anything connected with the educational institution they are attending. Maybe now, some of our interviewees are having second thoughts — especially when looking for employment. But in the interviews even those few who voiced the criticisms reported at various points in this chapter expressed no regrets about their choice.

Even the fairly lengthy critique delivered by one student went together with a fairly positive view of her education as a whole. Why that was so bears examination, along with the critique itself. She found her department very androcentric. The history of Christianity was treated as though men and women had had the same experience of it. For example, an early church father's negative statements about women were not explored for the implications they might have for the restricted role women played in the decision-making process in early Christianity. Nor was the question in what way masculine images of deity were culturally conditioned, or how such images affect the way one relates to deity and conducts one's life, or how they can function to sanction subordinate roles assigned to women in a religious tradition. More time should have been devoted to the role of women in religion. And more books and articles by feminist religious studies scholars should have been assigned for reading.

That these desiderata were not satisfied for her the student attributed to her professors' failing to take feminist scholarship and women's issues seriously. One professor, a woman, did, however; and this would seem to provide a partial explanation of why, despite all, the student spoke well of the opportunity that religious studies provided to pursue her interests in an intellectually and personally fulfilling way. If one purpose of religious studies, and of a university education generally, is to lead students to think critically, this student was a prize example. She owed much, it seemed, to the woman professor in whose classes critical questions about religious studies were raised and who provided an alternative way of approaching the study of religion that proved enlightening and gratifying.

And if one mark of a good religious studies professor is that she or he doesn't "put down" religious traditions they stand outside of (4.1.2 above), then another would be that he or she doesn't put down students who stand outside — or who have placed themselves outside — current scholarly traditions. That is not only good pedagogy, it is intrinsic to education in the humanities and to the notion of pluralism so central to religious studies.

4.2   Graduate Students

One section of Chapter 9, on graduate education, is devoted to graduate students. The present section prepares for and supplements what is said there.

4.2.1   Two Profiles

In the Welch report on graduate education in religious studies at the end of the 1960s, the chapter on doctoral students sketched two profiles: one of the "typical" student, the other of a new, more atypical kind. The profiles, expanded and explicated in subsequent pages of the chapter, were based on responses to questionnaires received in 1969-70 from nearly 2,000 of the 3,000-plus doctoral students in almost all of the 75 doctoral programmes for the academic study of religion at 69 institutions in the U.S.A. and Canada (Welch, 1971, 203, 204); in addition interviews were conducted at nine of the graduate schools, chosen for "representative variety and geographical distribution" (ibid., x). A sketch of these two profiles will be followed, in 4.2.2 and 4.3.2, by a comparison with the graduate students we interviewed.

4.2.1.1   Profile One: Graduate Students with Professional Degrees

In the first profile the students, by a ratio of at least two to one, came to doctoral study after completing a professional degree; for those studying for the so-called theological degrees — Th.D., S.T.D., D.H.L. (on degree nomenclature see Welch, 1971, 33-34, and chap. 9.1 below) — the ratio was even higher. They were virtually all male: 98% among Ph.D. students, 97% among the Th.D., S.T.D., D.H.L. students (Welch, 1971, 207, Table 10-4). For most, the decision to undertake doctoral study came while working toward their professional degree or while employed (208, Table 10-5), presumably by a religious institution. Their commitment to an institutional form of religion was fairly strong, judging from their frequent attendance at weekly services of worship (215, Table 10-10). Related to these factors is that, in comparison with other doctoral students in the humanities, they were apt to be considerably older and married (205-06).

4.2.1.2   Profile Two: Graduate Students without
a Professional Degree

Alongside this profile the Welch report observed another, quite different one among students who came to Ph.D. study without first having acquired a professional degree (summarized, ibid., 203, 209-10). In this group, which included students with B.A. degrees only as well as those with both the

B.A. and the M.A., the median age was 28.2; for those holding only the B.A. it was 25 (206, Table 10-3). Many in this group were attracted to universities connected with theological faculties — the prestigious, "grand-father [sic] institutions" (90) — but even more were enrolled in the newer doctoral programmes in religious studies departments with no such connection (205, Table 10-2). For almost two-thirds of those holding only the B.A. the decision to do doctoral work came during their undergraduate years (208, Table 10-5); that is, like doctoral students in other fields, an undergraduate degree was the preparation they brought to graduate study (208, Table 10-5; 209-10). In their commitment to institutional religion, they were also unlike their colleagues with professional degrees: though identifying in some way with traditional religious institutions, less than half of those under the average age of 28 worshipped weekly (215, Table 10-10). What the Welch report saw as perhaps "symptomatic" of the future was the small subgroup who "reported no religious preference," two-thirds of whom were under 30 and had not gone the professional degree route, and 79% of whom took part in institutional worship little or never — "even though three-fourths of the 79 percent attended church or synagogue weekly or almost weekly as children and some attended parochial schools as well" (216, n. 21).

Fields of study chosen by students in this second profile reflected these various data, tending away from the traditional, Christian areas that continued to attract the students with professional degrees (Welch, 1971, 203). Not having as many of the responsibilities that go with older years and outside employment as did the students with professional degrees, they were more apt to be enrolled full-time, present on campus, and in regular contact with faculty and student colleagues (203; 211, n. 11). Women were outnumbered three to one, but even this figure contrasts dramatically with the minuscule percentages of women among students with the professional degree (207, Table 10-4).

In short, the face of the doctoral student population at the time of the Welch report seemed to be changing as graduates of religious studies departments entered doctoral programmes, whether the new ones in religious studies departments or the older ones connected with theological faculties, an impression that seems to be confirmed by the present study: it is this second profile rather than the first that fits those of our interviewees enrolled in graduate programmes in religious studies. What the Welch report saw as "an interesting change" (209) would seem to have come to full flower in them.

4.2.2   Graduate Students in Ontario Religious Studies Departments and Programmes: Profile Two

The budget for our study and the time we were able to devote to it did not, unfortunately, permit the kind of data gathering the Welch investigators could afford. We sent out no questionnaires to students, and the number of students interviewed was small in comparison with the total population of students enrolled in graduate programmes for the academic study of religion in Ontario.[2] However, as was noted at the beginning of this chapter, the manner of their selection was intended to provide a representative sample, and the interviews indicated that the aim was not wide of the mark, confirming our day-to-day and year-to-year impressions of the kinds of students enrolled in such programmes in Ontario. The faculty involved in those programmes will probably not be surprised, or need to be told, that the profile of students in theological college graduate programmes is closer to the first than the second profile outlined above (see 4.2.3 below) whereas students enrolled in religious studies graduate programmes fit the second more closely.[3] In Roman Catholic theological college graduate programmes, however, the majority of students are lay people who come to graduate study lacking a professional degree. They would seem to fall somewhere between the first and second profiles. It is this second group especially that reflects the changes, treated in various places in this volume, in the role and in the study of religion in Ontario.

Graduate religious studies programmes in Ontario are an institutional manifestation of those changes. Some students still do come to them with what was once the standard preparation for academic study of religion at the graduate level, that is, a professional degree; but they are a distinct minority. Our interview sample of students in these programmes was perhaps unrepresentative in that it included only one person with a professional degree, acquired after a religious studies undergraduate degree; her subsequent education and employment, however, had been largely in religious studies. It is possible that for others with professional degrees who may have been asked to sit for the interviews the demands of full-time employment as professionals, or family responsibilities, kept them away. Nonetheless, their almost virtual absence among the students interviewed in these programmes was striking.

The students interviewed were predominantly in their twenties. In religious studies it seems to be the case that the undergraduate population is graying whereas at the graduate level there is a larger percentage of younger students. This is not surprising since so many religious studies graduate students bypass professional degree programmes on their way to graduate study whereas persons with professional degrees gravitate more to graduate theology programmes, which may suit their interests and vocational goals better and where their professional degrees stand them in good stead.

Those of our interviewees in M.A. programmes came with an undergraduate religious studies degree or, in the case of a few, another humanities degree supplemented by qualifying courses in religious studies. The Ph.D. students had completed their M.A. in religious studies, usually at the same institution where they were currently enrolled. Virtually all the students had done their undergraduate work in Canadian universities, in a variety of provinces, east and west. The rest were persons originally from other countries.

The students' specializations represented the traditional, Christian fields of study in which the professional degree holders in the Welch study were likely to concentrate — "Bible, theology, or history of Christianity" (203) — but also, in significant numbers, the relatively new areas common in religious studies such as Asian religions, psychology of religion, and methodology (on which see, further, chaps. 2.4.7 and 2.4.9 above and 9.2.2.2 and 12.8.2 below.)

Since the scope of our study was much narrower than that of the Welch report, we did not ask questions pertaining to religious background and commitment. The fact that students volunteered very little such information suggests that for students in religious studies graduate programmes it is not an overt concern in their studies. It would not seem too much to assume that their earlier decisions to pursue an undergraduate religious studies degree were similar to those reported for the undergraduates we interviewed and that, like many of them, some at least had worked through various religious questions during undergraduate (or even M.A.) study (4.1.1 above). The generalizations in the Welch report about personal beliefs and how they entered into students' study would probably apply also to our interviewees. One would not expect them to fall on the conforming end of sociologists' "orthodoxy scales" (Welch, 1971, 215-16). As to how personal beliefs affect their scholarship and teaching, they would probably agree with the Welch interviewees that (of course) such beliefs would, "both positively and negatively, but that this was not peculiar to the field of religion" (216). Some might agree further that "Commitment to a narrow belief system, however, would very likely impair one's work as a scholar or teacher since it was apt to be a species of ignorance and of limited experience" (216).

Common to all of these profiled groups were concerns about finances. For the professional degree holders in the Welch report, who were older and with considerable family responsibilities, this was a serious concern: though employment as religious professionals could put bread on the table, it could also distract from study. Those students without professional degrees were apt to have fewer such responsibilities, and this plus scholarships or assistantships and a spouse's income made full-time study possible (ibid., 203). Among the students we interviewed the variables of support differed considerably from person to person and institution to institution. Some were doing quite well, others definitely not — with predictable effects on morale. (See, further, 4.2.6, 4.3.2, and chap. 9.4 below.)

A significant difference between our interviewees and both of the Welch profiles is the much higher proportion of women students. In our interviews they outnumbered men students two to one. (Further data on gender are reported and analyzed in chaps. 5.1.1.1 and 9.4 below.)

4.2.3   Preparation for Graduate Study

Most of the students we interviewed in religious studies graduate programmes had undergraduate religious studies degrees and therefore brought
to graduate study an acquaintance with the field. For some it meant that the
courses in methodology that are a standard fixture in religious studies graduate programmes were old hat. For the few that came from other fields, via
qualifying work in religious studies, they were not. One student with an
undergraduate religious studies degree found that undergraduate courses
had not been comparative or methodologically diverse. A common observation was that coverage of religious traditions in their undergraduate programmes had been good, though for one student this meant having to get
some courses in another, nearby religious studies department. Another common observation was the lack of preparation in the languages of sources,
which meant adding language study on to regular course loads. It was a lack
accepted rather stoically, it seemed, perhaps in recognition of the difficulty
of crowding it into already crowded undergraduate years, or because the
decision to study a religious tradition requiring special language skills was
made late in an undergraduate career or only after beginning graduate study.
(On language preparation see, further, chaps. 8.3, 9.2.1.2, 9.3.2, 11.4, and
12.13 below.)

In general the students spoke well of their undergraduate work in religious studies and, for those in Ph.D. programmes, of their M.A. work, an
impression confirmed by the fact that graduates of Ontario M.A. programmes regularly go on to doctoral study not only in doctoral programmes
in Ontario but in the U.S.A. and Europe as well. In one university, out of a
total of 117 M.A. graduates in the period 1982-89 nearly a quarter went on
to doctoral study at thirteen different graduate schools in Canada, the
U.S.A., and the United Kingdom.

4.2.4   Vocational Goals and Preparation for Them

Vocational goals and how well graduate studies prepare students for them
are discussed in detail in Chapter 9.4 and 9.5 below. Some general observations and reflections will suffice here, therefore.

For some of the students we interviewed, M.A. study was a continuation
of liberal arts undergraduate study, undertaken for the love of learning with
vocational payoff of little or no concern. Others saw it as the kind of liberal
education in preparation for a variety of careers in the way that the undergraduate religious studies can be (chap. 4.1.3 above). For still others it provided specific, employable skills or was a step on the path to a Ph.D. and a
teaching job.

For this last group doctoral study is professional training (see chap.
9.2.2.3 below) and includes not only the academic requirements of course
work but also apprenticing in teaching and learning the ropes of publication

of research and giving of papers at learned society meetings. Predictably, students' perceptions of how well their doctoral programmes were preparing them in these various areas varied with the individual and the programme in which each was enrolled. Some had acquired or were acquiring considerable experience in teaching. Some reported that professors took pains to initiate students into the mysteries of learned societies, giving of papers, and getting research published; a fair number of our interviewees belonged to learned societies, had presented papers, won prize essay contests, and published articles in journals. Those not receiving such guidance from faculty expressed a desire for it and, lacking it, will have to find their own way.

The socialization into religious studies that these various aspects of doctoral studies represent is of vital importance. It is a process that begins, as was indicated earlier (4.1 above), while students are enrolled in an undergraduate religious studies degree programme, where they are apt to be exposed to a variety of religious traditions and, having achieved some perspective on religious commitment (their own and others'), move beyond what Paul Ricoeur has called ''a primitive naïveté'' to ''a second naïveté'' that follows after critical reflection on the original immediacy of belief (Ricoeur, 1969, 351). For persons lacking such socialization, whether in undergraduate or graduate study or both, there is the distinct possibility that, if hired by a religious studies department (perhaps out of an understandable desire to invite interdisciplinary work) they will — overtly or covertly, wittingly or unwittingly — be teachers of religion rather than of religious studies. Put another way, persons not trained specifically in religious studies, though expert in their fields, if hired by a religious studies department or programme, may work at odds with the aims of those who hired them. A religious studies department programme would be foolish to look askance at a Victor Turner or a Northrop Frye on these grounds. But with more ordinary mortals, a concern for the integrity of a religious studies department or programme would suggest paying careful attention to socialization into religious studies as one of the qualifications for employment (see, further, chap. 5.1.1.5 below).

4.2.5 Choice of Graduate School

Why did students choose to study where they did? Not surprisingly, for a mixture of academic and non-academic reasons. The reputation of a certain professor, or professors — only to find, in one student's case, that the chosen had departed by the time of her arrival on the scene. The recommendation of someone who had studied there before. The opportunity to study in a particular academic area or areas, or to combine that with the language training requisite to it.

As with the undergraduates we interviewed, there were also refugees from other departments. One student who had wanted to study a certain subject found that neither of two departments of philosophy where she might reasonably have expected to pursue it were interested, and so she turned to religious studies. In the same vein, "openness" and "flexibility" were cited by students in one graduate programme as among the reasons for enrolling there while other students cited accessibility to faculty in other departments, or the opportunity to do interdisciplinary work. The possibility of working in lesser plowed fields influenced one student in making her choice, while the opportunity to study abroad as part of the graduate programme appealed to students at another place.

Students with specific desiderata did not hesitate to travel long distances to find what they were seeking. But convenience was also an important factor: the programme was close by and did not require re-locating. That was particularly true of students pursuing a terminal M.A. degree or undecided about study beyond the M.A. One such mentioned a combination of personal, academic, and vocational reasons for her choice: she wanted to study "god concepts"; in religious studies she was able to do so using a variety of approaches; and an M.A. would give her better credentials in the local world of work.

Weighing heavily in students' decisions about place was financial aid. The promise of aid was a deciding factor for a number of students, to the point in some instances where they chose to forego or redefine what they really wanted to study, but couldn't afford, at the institution of their choice, in order to be able to study at all — at an institution of their second or third choice. It did not deter other students, however, who managed, somehow, in the less endowed and less generous graduate programmes because that was where they found what and whom they were looking for.

4.2.6 Morale

As with the undergraduate students we interviewed (4.1.4 above), the graduate students interviewed were a selected and self-selected group, which meant that we were not apt to hear a great deal about the down side of religious studies graduate programmes. Students at one institution spoke of a high dropout rate there. If so, we were interviewing the survivors, there as well as elsewhere.

That did not mean they were all Candides living in the best of all possible worlds. The transition in which Ontario religious studies departments find themselves (chap. 3.2.2 above) was felt by some students, especially at one institution where the composition of the faculty had undergone significant changes, producing some uncertainty and anxiety. Inadequate financial aid was a prominent topic among students at another place, standing in marked contrast to the mood at institutions where assistantships and scholarships were readily available. Computer literacy seemed to be assumed by the students, but inadequate facilities concerned students at one institution. Undertones were also audible. There was distress caused students by faculty infighting, forcing students to assume some of the faculty's burdens as well as their own. Irresponsible teaching was mentioned, as was a seminar that three weeks into the term had still to get underway, and another (hardly a seminar) where the professor simply lectured, from notes dating, at least in content, from two or three decades earlier.

Concern about issues raised at various places in this volume was also expressed. Students at one institution perceived their department as crypto-Christian, belying professions to the contrary. At another, students said problems of inclusive language were not being addressed, and at yet another that more stress on feminist hermeneutics was needed. Complaints (or reports of complaints) of sexual advances and innuendo by male faculty came up in talk with women students outside the interviews. Several male doctoral students voiced concern about finding jobs as affirmative action and employment equity policies begin to be implemented (see chap. 12.11 below). As is pointed out in Chapter 9.4, where there is only an M.A. pro-gramme, graduate students are apt to find it difficult to establish a group identity distinct from undergraduate degree students. Students at one such institution expressed a desire for colloquia that would bring them together, also with faculty.

Nonetheless, morale among the students seemed reasonably good. The desires and expectations that had brought them to their respective graduate programmes were generally being met. They seemed to be studying what they wanted to study, often with professors of their preference. At the Ph.D. level especially, some at least were being guided into full participation in the field by being encouraged to join learned societies, to present papers, and to publish their research. Various interviewees mentioned collegiality among students, often germinated in core courses required of entering stu-dents. The diverse religious backgrounds of students in one such course meant that interesting questions were raised, said one student, with discus-sion spilling over into after-class gatherings. A religious studies graduate students' association exists in at least one large university. In one of the smaller ones there is a general graduate students' association. But ties with students in one's field and at one's own level were preferred. None of the students mentioned a buddy or mentor system linking incoming students with those already in the programme. Nor did any cite the day-to-day advice and guidance we observed being offered by the uncanonized saints of grad-uate study, the administrative assistant or department secretary who inter-prets the canons and spikes the canards of the local scene, or drops hints about who to see about what or where to go for that, and generally helps students feel "at home."

Graduate study, like a terminal illness, one might say, is a career, and the students we interviewed seemed to be advancing in it without devastating pain and with reasonable hopes of attaining the eschaton. Nonetheless, one wonders if religious studies graduate students in Ontario might find some of their academic aches and pains alleviated were they to gather regionally or province-wide once a year, apart from faculty, to compare symptoms from one academic environment to another, to address causes, and, in general, to look for ways to improve the quality of life in religious studies graduate programmes.

4.3   Students in Theological Degree Programmes

4.3.1   Students in Professional Degree Programmes

These degree programmes and the students enrolled in them are not of direct concern in this study (see chap. 9.1 below; Welch, 1971, 32-33). But in view of the origins of religious studies in theological colleges (chaps. 1 and 2 above), the persisting ties of various sorts between religious studies and theological colleges (chap. 3.3 above), and the significant effect religious studies seems to have had on theological colleges (ibid.), comparison of students in professional degree programmes with those enrolled in religious studies degree programmes is important to the "state of the art."

The contrasts with religious studies students, both undergraduate and graduate, are the most evident aspect of such comparison. For students enrolled in professional degree programmes in theological colleges, that is, the Master of Divinity (M.Div.), the Master of Theology (Th.M., M.Th.), and the Doctor of Ministry (D.Min.) (see chap. 9.1 below), the college is a professional school, and of a very specific kind: it is preparing them for careers in Christian ministry (future rabbis generally go outside Ontario to study), usually in a parish setting but sometimes in another kind of pastoral role such as hospital or military chaplaincy, or, in the case of some Roman Catholic students, for teaching in a separate school. Christian commitment is presupposed, the curriculum and ethos are directed to fostering it, and probing and testing of it — informally by professors and administrators and formally by church authorities and agencies — are part of the process. Like students in other professional schools, those in professional degree programmes in theological colleges are career oriented therefore.

This was true of the students we interviewed.[4] But unlike students in religious studies graduate programmes, who are also preparing themselves for a career (teaching, in their case), these professional degree students are required to take many more courses in the "practical" or "functional" or "contextual" area (the terminology varies) — courses directed toward their roles as preachers or liturgists or counsellors. Some of the students at one college complained about the heavy requirements in the practical area, which made it difficult for them to pursue academic interests. Some students with good undergraduate records observed that preparation for ministry and the socialization it entailed led them to abandon early in their theological studies their previous dedication to "academic" excellence. A graduate of the college told one of the interviewers that the courses he found most "practical" were the so-called academic ones, and that much of what was supposed to be taught in those designated "practical" could only be learned in practice, that is, in field placements, internships, or upon graduation while serving in a clergy position. For other interviewees, however, it was the nuts and bolts of seminary education and of their future careers that interested them, rather than courses in what some of them labelled "abstract" (i.e., academic) subjects.

Like many of today's students, those in theological colleges are very often there because of a career change (cf. 4.1.1 above). It is not surprising, therefore, that very few of our interviewees had a religious studies degree: they had not entered university intending to go to theological college afterward (see 4.1.3 above). A fair number, however, had taken a course or courses in religious studies in university. Students in colleges where there was a close connection with a religious studies department were more knowledgeable about religious studies than those with a loose connection or none at all.[5] A professor at a theological college with significant formal connections with a religious studies graduate programme noted that few students in the college enrolled in the religious studies courses offered in that programme. Were the courses, or the professors teaching them, suspect? Or was the home environment simply more comfortable? Would the pluralistic environment in which pastoral ministry is carried on today bring these students back to university departments of religious studies some day to take courses in world religions (cf. chap. 3.3 above)?

One marked change since Charles Feilding's observation that "much harm" had been done to theological education by the tendency to restrict it to males (1966b, 236; chap. 3.3 above) is the large percentage of women now enrolled in Ontario theological colleges. In the entering classes of some colleges they outnumber men students, sometimes considerably. Some are preparing for ordination, some have other, often related vocational goals, and some are studying primarily to satisfy personal interests.

Quite a number of those in the these last two groups are enrolled in Master of Theological Studies (M.T.S.) programmes. As is indicated in Chapter 9 (see n. 3 there), this is conceived of as an "academic" rather than a professional degree: students take many of the same academic courses as the professional degree students but few or none of the practical ones. These are students who have a university degree, have decided they want to study religion, and choose to do so in a theological college rather than in a religious studies graduate programme (or in some cases perhaps because a religious studies graduate programme is not available in the university nearest to them). Some of these students were among those we interviewed.

Generally, they are increasing in numbers in theological colleges. This is not universally so in Ontario. In one college we visited the M.T.S. programme seemed to be marginal to the school's main enterprise, the M.Div. programme. At another place, however, quite the opposite is true, if statistics are any criterion. In the rather considerable student body, M.T.S. students in 1989-90 constituted about eight percent of the full-time students but virtually one-third of those enrolled part-time. A professor at the college reported that his class of thirty-some in introduction to theology was divided almost equally between M.Div. and M.T.S. students. These kinds of statistics would seem to support his view that more and more students are turning to theological colleges to pursue an interest in religion. This sets them apart from persons with a similar interest who, lacking a university degree, enrol in an undergraduate religious studies degree programme to pursue it, or those with a university degree who do so in a religious studies graduate programme. That so many of the M.T.S. students in the examples cited above are part-time suggests that their motivations are similar to those in religious studies programmes: they are exploring a subject of new or renewed interest to them, or perhaps a possible career or career change, or may be seeking to increase their competence in their present career.

Why did they choose a theological college rather than a religious studies programme? Several reasons suggest themselves, based on our observations of these students and on conversations with theological college professors. Many of the students are active in church, and study in an institution of the church seems logical. This does not mean that they are simply unquestioning, status-quo Christians — many are quite critical of their churches. But they are apt to see the critical questions they have as better pursued on territory perceived as more familiar — and perhaps more friendly — than the *terra incognita* of a religious studies department in a university. Or, if they do have some acquaintance with religious studies, they may prefer a setting where open expression of Christian commitment and beliefs is likely to one where it is less so (see chap. 3.2.3 above). Denominational loyalty also brings some to the theological college of their particular denomination. A professor at one college, however, drew attention to a new M.T.S. student with no religious background who had become interested in Christian ethics through religious studies courses she had taken as an undergraduate and had then enrolled in the college because it had Christian ethics courses whereas religious studies departments in her geographical area, at least as she perceived them, did not.

Whatever the specific motivations, it seems that both religious studies departments and programmes and theological colleges are attracting and serving, each in their own way, a significant portion of the Ontario population at the end of the twentieth century.

4.3.2   Students in M.A., Th.D., and Ph.D. Programmes

The M.A. programmes in Ontario theological colleges are construed as academic rather than professional in nature, and the Th.D. and Ph.D. programmes as research and teaching degrees (see chap. 9.1 below; cf. Welch, 1971, 33-34). They relate to religious studies more directly therefore than do those treated in the preceding section.

The large number of students enrolled in these programmes (see chap. 2.6, Table 2-1, above and chap. 9.1 below) indicates the continuing vitality of this traditional mode of graduate study of religion. Those we interviewed were fairly typical in that many of them came to graduate studies after completing the M.Div. or the equivalent. As was pointed out earlier, however (4.2.2 above), students in Roman Catholic graduate theological programmes diverge from that general pattern. In recent years students in M.Div. and other professional theological degree programmes have come increasingly from the thirty-and-above end of the population spectrum. This change will be reflected in a corresponding graying of students enrolled in M.A., Th.D., and Ph.D. programmes in Ontario theological colleges. In these, as in some of the other respects indicated in section 4.2.1 above, students in these programmes fit the first of the two profiles in the Welch study more than they do the second (4.2.2 above). One variation from that pattern, students in Roman Catholic graduate theological programmes, has been noted above. Another is that more students with M.T.S. degrees (see 4.3.1 above) – i.e., persons lacking or not seeking ordination – are showing up in these programmes. In graduate programmes in Roman Catholic institutions, for example, laity, including women, are now apt to outnumber clergy.

A professional theological degree was once the standard way station enroute to graduate study of religion. It provided solid grounding in the pertinent ancient languages and in the traditional subfields for the study of Judaism and Christianity. The move from that pattern to the one followed by students in the second of the Welch profiles was one facet of what Welch called an "identity crisis in the study of religion": "What is to take the place of the theological degree as the base on which advanced studies in religion are built?" (1971, 21).

The years since have provided some answers to that question as the religious studies graduate programmes the Welch investigators studied have matured. At the same time, the research and teaching graduate programmes also continued in theological institutions, many of them the well-known prestigious graduate schools (Welch's "grandfather institutions" [1971, 90]), while newer ones developed and matured (also in Ontario) as part of the professionalization of theological education (chaps. 2.6.11 and 3.3 above; cf. Welch, 1971, 92-93). Given the long tradition of this pattern of graduate study of religion, it is perhaps not surprising that some professors in Ontario theological colleges see their graduate programmes as in some respects superior to religious studies graduate programmes (cf. chap. 3.3 above). However, they would probably not go so far as to echo the opinion of then-nascent religious studies implicit in a remark attributed to a noted biblical scholar at an American theological college regarding the newly formed American Academy of Religion: "They'll never make it an academy!"

The students we interviewed were, like their professors and the students interviewed in religious studies graduate programmes, concerned about the academic and professional side of graduate study today: research, publication, their fields and subfields. Like the students in the first of the Welch profiles, theirs were predominantly the traditional fields of Christian studies — biblical studies, history of Christianity, theology, liturgy, etc. — along with some newer ones such as pastoral theology and counselling. There was little concern expressed for the kind of comparativist approach, attendant on pluralism, advocated by the theological educators cited in Chapter 3.3 above; nor, many reported, was a world religion or a religious studies methodology course required. However, since most of these students were in theological colleges connected with religious studies graduate programmes, in their classes they might sit alongside religious studies graduate students and be exposed to religious studies approaches.

Like their religious studies classmates, they were concerned about such things as finances, availability of computer facilities, and jobs upon graduation. Some were also concerned about the distinctiveness — or lack thereof — of their programmes from the professional degree programmes of their colleges, measured by such criteria as separate classes and study and meeting facilities. They differed from most religious studies graduate students in the greater varieties of jobs open to them thanks to the combination of professional and post-professional degrees they would hold upon graduation. Students at one institution mentioned jobs as chaplains or in ethics departments of denominational offices or in religious education in separate schools. These students also mentioned the assistance their school provided in job placement.

Aside from the concerns expressed above, morale seemed good. "Networking" was going on. Students at one institution reported how they listened in on the grapevine to hear who would and who would not make a good thesis advisor. At another, students mentioned efforts to welcome new students and bring them into the academic community there. Students at a couple of institutions reported faculty assistance in writing of grant proposals or encouragement to attend learned societies meetings or to publish research of high quality.

For these students, as for those in religious studies graduate programmes, graduate study was a career, but generally from a different starting point and often with different termini. They reflect the development of religious studies, but not to the degree that students in religious studies graduate programmes do.

4.4 Concluding Observations

Students who choose to make religious studies their undergraduate concentration are not unlike those concentrating in other areas of the humanities. Vocational goals are important but not paramount; learning about the world and themselves takes precedence.. Whatever label is attached to it — liberal, liberal arts, humanities — they value a degree programme that makes such learning possible. Their reasons for choosing religious studies vary but are related to that basic concern.

Insofar as the students we interviewed are representative of religious studies concentrators generally, it seems that Ontario undergraduate religious studies departments and programmes must be doing something right: students have a pretty fair understanding of the field, and morale is relatively good. Not surprisingly, however, there are concerns that need to be attended to (4.1.4). Faculty would also do well to take note of the reasons students give for choosing a religious studies concentration (4.1.1) and to weigh these in relation to their own perceptions of religious studies and their goals for majors and honours students (cf. chap. 12 below).

The composition of the graduate student population in religious studies reflects changes in religious studies in Ontario and North America generally over the past two decades (4.2.1 and 4.2.2), distinguishing them especially from students in both professional and graduate theology programmes (4.3). As religious studies looks ahead to the next millennium (chap. 12), further changes in graduate programmes may be required (see, further, chaps. 9 and 12.10).

Some of the concerns raised by religious studies graduate students (4.2.6), for example, financial support, are familiar and are already on the agenda of graduate officers and graduate faculty. Some, one suspects, are not and require attention (see, further, chap. 12.10 and 12.11). One specific recommendation at this point is that students in Ontario religious studies graduate programmes think about annual gatherings, formal or informal, to discuss common concerns (4.2.6). If these were held at the Learneds, where a fair number of students now give papers and where students from other provinces could also take part, they could be a counterpart to any council-to-be on graduate religious studies (chap. 12.10.2) with a place on the programme of the Canadian Society for the Study of Religion. Perhaps, as well, the time is ripe for students to form an Ontario religious studies graduate students' association.

Notes

1 See chap. 3, n. 10, on religious studies departments and programmes not visited. At two others we were unable to schedule interviews with undergraduate students. With one exception, undergraduate students were interviewed in groups.

   We conducted interviews, all but one in groups, with students in all M.A. and Ph.D. programmes in provincial universities and with students in about half of the M.A., Th.D., and Ph.D. programmes in Ontario theological colleges or faculties.

   Interviews, mostly in groups, were also conducted with students in professional degree programmes at about a third of the theological colleges in Ontario.

2 See the preceding note.

3 So that the data from the second profile in the Welch report would be more comparable with those for the M.A. and Ph.D. students we interviewed in religious studies graduate programmes only the data on the Ph.D. students in the Welch study are included but not those on the Th.D., S.T.D., and D.H.L. students.

4 On their selection see n. 1 of this chapter.
5 At the one theological college where time permitted asking specifically "religious studies" questions, the answers were very similar to those reported for undergraduate religious studies students in Chapter 4.1.2 above; this was a college connected with a religious studies department.

5

Faculty: Preparation and Hiring

William Closson James

5.1 Preparation and Background of Faculty in Religious Studies

Through the distribution of questionnaires, the examination of curricula vitarum, and on-site interviews with faculty and administrators we sought to discover what graduate school preparation Ontario professors in religious studies have, especially in comparison with faculty in other university departments and in theological colleges. Do religious studies faculty usually hold degrees associated with training for professional ministry (that is, the Master of Divinity degree [M.Div.] or its equivalent)? We also wondered whether recent appointees have graduate school preparation differing from that of their older colleagues, with less likelihood, for instance, of having a professional theological degree.

Although advocacy of a religion is typically avoided with rigour in university departments of religious studies the question still arises whether a particular tradition is better taught by an insider or outsider. Therefore we wanted to determine what consideration, if any, was given in the hiring process to the personal stance of a candidate towards a tradition. Do religious studies departments want Christians to teach Christianity, Jews to teach Judaism, Hindus to teach Hinduism, and so on? Another aspect of academic preparation and hiring practices is whether Ph.D. graduates from certain universities are over-represented in religious studies departments in the province. Does one find across the province, or at a given institution, faculty members with similar graduate school background? These specific fac-

---

Notes to Chapter 5 can be found on page 170.

tors — along with questions of average age, gender, highest degree, years of university teaching experience, and academic rank — all contribute to a profile of the religious studies professoriate, especially when compared with colleagues in other humanities departments on the one side, and colleagues in theological colleges on the other.

5.1.1   Profile of the Religious Studies Professoriate

In 1986 the Canadian Federation for the Humanities conducted a survey of approximately 3,000 humanities scholars (CFH, 1987b). With a return rate of 43% of those surveyed, the results provide data from about 20% of the total population of humanists teaching full-time in Canadian universities. From this survey the CFH derived a "Profile of Canadian Humanists" (see Table 5-1) showing, among other things, the following:

- they are middle-aged;
- most are men;
- most have the Ph.D. degree;
- on average, they began teaching full-time at about age 30, achieved tenure at age 35, and had been teaching for 20 years;
- most are at the rank of either full or associate professor, with a fairly even split between the two ranks;
- 8.4% of Canadian humanists are in religious studies (as compared, e.g., with 10.8% in philosophy, 7.4% in music and theatre, and 3.7% in classics).

Table 5-1
Profile of Canadian Humanists, 1986*

Average Age	50
Gender	Males, 82.8%
	Females 17.2%
Highest Degree	Ph.D. 91.1%
	M.A. 8.3%
Average Career Length	Teaching for 20 years; tenured for 15 years
Rank	Full Professor 45.3%
	Associate Professor 41.9%
	Assistant Professor 9.5%
	Other 3.3%

* Source: CFH, 1987b

The profile of religious studies faculty for the same time period is fairly similar, though with a few important differences. The profile is based on data gathered in 1987 for this Ontario State-of-the-Art Review on some 364 faculty members: 206 in departments of religious studies, 133 in theological colleges, and 25 having a joint appointment in a religious studies department and theological college (see Table 5-2 below). Like Canadian humanists generally, religious studies faculty are middle-aged. On average, they had held their appointment since 1972, or 15 years.[1] Over three-quarters are at the rank of either full or associate professor (41% and 37% respectively). Three out of four hold the Ph.D. degree, about one in ten have the Th.D., and slightly less than one in ten have an M.A. as their highest degree. Overwhelmingly they are male.

Table 5-2
Profile of Ontario Religious Studies Faculty, 1987

Average Age	52
Gender	Males, 92.2%
	Females, 9.8%
Average Age	Males, 53 years
by Gender	Female, 47 years
Highest Degree	Ph.D. 75.7%
	Th.D. 10.7%
	M.A. 8.3%
Years in Most Recent Appointment	15
Rank	Full Professor 41.2%
	Associate Professor 36.8%
	Assistant Professor 9.3%
	Lecturer 4.9%

As compared with other colleagues in humanities, then, faculty in religious studies are on average two years older, include significantly fewer women, have been in their positions four or five years less, and fewer have achieved the higher ranks: a lower percentage of the religious studies faculty in our survey is at the level of full or associate professor, while about the same number are at the assistant professor rank (9.3% as compared with 9.5% among humanists generally). Further, a slightly lower percentage of faculty in religious studies has an earned doctorate (87% as compared with 91%).

Probably it is unwise to attempt too many generalizations based on these differences. In comparison with the CFH survey, ours includes more part-time and adjunct faculty and recent appointments (5% of the religious studies faculty surveyed were at the rank of lecturer). Furthermore, the route to the doctorate for religious studies faculty has typically taken more years of post-graduate study than in other areas of the humanities, in part because an M.Div or its equivalent was for a long time customarily acquired en route (see chap. 4.2.2.1 above). Max von Zur-Muehlen, a research professor in the Faculty of Administration at the University of Ottawa and Executive Director of the Canadian Higher Education Research Network, reports in a working paper that the length of time Canadians spent acquiring the doctorate in religious studies was six years on average (1987, 20-21, Table 2; see, further, chap. 9.2.2.1 below). (Though von Zur-Muehlen is not specific at this point, presumably the years of study are counted from receipt of the master's degree to the granting of the doctorate.) By way of comparison, the time required for the doctorate in religious studies was the same as in history, both falling at the upper end of the estimated range of four to six years taken in other areas of study in the humanities and social sciences.

5.1.1.1   Women Faculty

A report on women students in Ontario universities prepared by the Council of Ontario Universities Committee on the Status of Women shows significant increases in the percentage of women enrolled and graduating at both the undergraduate and graduate levels in the 20 years between 1968-69 and 1988-89 (see Table 5-3).

Table 5-3
Proportion of Women Students and Graduates,
Ontario Universities, 1968-69 to 1988-89*

	1968-69		1988-89	
	Total Number	% Women	Total Number	% Women
Enrolments				
Undergraduate				
Full-time	81,091	34.0	178,248	51.1
Part-time	32,871	41.4	85,599	65.4
Graduate				
Full-time	11,498	17.4	22,940	40.6
Part-time	4,047	17.9	11,924	49.3
Degrees Awarded				
Baccalaureate and				
First Prof. Degrees	17,660	37.8	43,998	55.0
Master's	3,268	18.6	7,011	45.5
Doctorate	504	6.4	1,038	32.8

* Source: CAUT, 1990b.

One of every two full-time undergraduate students in Ontario universities is now female as compared to one in three two decades ago. Among part-time students, the four-out-of-ten figure of 20 years ago has become two out of three. At the graduate level, less than one in four students was female two decades ago. Now, among full-time students that figure has increased to four out of ten; among part-time students, the percentage is one out of two. Of degrees awarded at the first level the proportion of women recipients has grown from something more than one in three to more than one in two. Among master's graduates, the proportion has increased from less than one in five to almost one in two, and at the doctoral level from less than one out of 16 to one in three.

In some cases these percentages approximate the ratio of women to men in the general population; in others they lag far behind it. Generally, they might be seen as encouraging for religious studies departments looking to a more equitable balance of women and men. However, the statistics for religious studies are somewhat less encouraging. A study by Max von Zur-Muehlen (1986, 19, Table 4a) shows that between 1970 and 1983 the proportion of doctoral degrees obtained by Canadian women in Canada and elsewhere in religious studies averaged 9.5% over that fourteen-year period. The fluctuations range from 0% in 1975 to 20.7% in 1977. The overall average of 9.5% is the lowest among the disciplines in humanities, contrasting with 37% in English, 18% in history, 20% in philosophy, and more than 40% in French and other modern languages. Whereas the overall proportion of doctoral degrees awarded to women in humanities is 28.5%, the figure of 9.5% for religious studies is closer to the proportion for mathematics and physical sciences (7.1%), or such social sciences as economics (9.8%) and geography (7.8%).

Our own data for Ontario doctoral programmes in religious studies (see chap. 9.4 below and Table 9-3 there) show much higher percentages of women receiving graduate degrees in religious studies, and percentage increases comparable to the increases in the percentage of master's and doctoral degrees awarded to women in all fields in Ontario in the two decades since 1968-69 (Table 5-3 above). It is likely the case that women would not be well represented among the significant numbers of Canadian scholars who, especially in the 1960s and 1970s, earned their doctoral degrees in the United States and Europe (see 5.1.1.4 below).

Turning to religious studies faculty in Ontario, according to a Statistics Canada data-set (in an unpublished report to the Ontario Council on University Affairs) covering all Ontario university staff who in 1985 were tenured or in a position leading to tenure, there were 127 men and 12 women in religious studies with an average age of 50. The percentage distribution of 91% men to 9% women matches exactly our own statistics (see Table 5-2 above) and corresponds closely with the men-to-women ratio for doctoral degrees in religious studies from 1970 to 1983. By way of contrast, the percentage of men in tenure or tenure-track positions in Ontario universities is 78% in English, but the 91% figure for religious studies is close to the percentages in history (90%) and philosophy (92%) in Ontario.

Though the situation in religious studies has been improving recently, these measurements show how badly women are under-represented in the field as compared with some other areas of the humanities, both as holders of doctoral degrees and as university staff in tenured or tenure-track positions. The results are both expected and surprising.

They are expected because of the historical exclusion of women from ecclesiastical positions, an exclusion that persisted in colleges and universities where the academic study of religion was founded or influenced by a church or theological college. Although more women are now enrolled in doctoral studies in religion and theology, according to Statistics Canada data for 1988 (as reported and calculated by the Ontario Confederation of University Faculty Associations [OCUFA, 1990b]), the percentage of women still remains among the lowest in the humanities — 31.1%, slightly higher than the field of philosophy at 28.1% but considerably less than the average for the humanities as a whole (45.5%) and for the social sciences (43.3%).

In 1989-90, according to Statistics Canada (reported in CAUT, 1991b, 12-13), the 82 women enrolled, on either a full- or part-time basis, in Canadian Ph.D. programmes in religious studies constituted 24.3% of the total enrolment in the field. The three women who in 1989 received doctorates in religious studies were 12% of the total number of doctoral recipients in the field that year. For theology the figures are also low: 70 women enrolled in doctoral programmes in 1989-90 (27.5% of the total for the field), and five women receiving doctorates (24.9% of the total for the field). The 1989-90 figures for enrolments in doctoral programmes show some fluctuation from those reported for 1988 in the preceding paragraph (not entirely explained by the combining of religious studies with theology in the earlier figures). Overall, though, the message is the same: among all the fields in the humanities, religious studies continues to have among the fewest number of women enrolled in, and graduating from, doctoral programmes.

Though expected, these kinds of data are nonetheless somewhat surprising in light of the upsurge of interest and demand for courses in the area of Women and Religion. In a number of institutions the religious studies department is closely allied with the area of women's studies. Furthermore, in several religious studies departments in Ontario the most recent appointment has been a woman and in several more the promise is made that the next appointment will be a woman. Since our data do not permit a distinction between tenured and non-tenured appointments, it may be that recent appointments of women are to positions not leading to tenure.

If women have been appointed to untenured positions the cause may be tokenism, or else women may simply be sharing the uncertain fate of male colleagues recently at a time when new tenure-track positions have become scarce. Von Zur-Muehlen (1987, 19) describes many doctoral recipients as being in a "holding pattern," in which they may take term or sessional appointments, or engage in post-doctoral research. He suggests, though, that women are disproportionately affected. While women have in the past decade or so increased their share of the doctoral degrees earned from one in ten to one in four, only 16% are employed in full-time university teaching, concentrated in education, health sciences, and languages and literature.

Recent statistics show the changing status of women in Ontario universities. Whereas in 1970-71 they constituted 11.8% of full-time faculty, by 1989-90, when more than one-third of new full-time appointees were women, their proportion had reached 20.2% (CAUT, 1991a). These figures show how slowly, with a replacement rate of only 8%, the percentage of women faculty members changes even when many new appointments go to women. Against this background, and keeping in mind the small numbers involved, in Ontario women with doctorates in religious studies are now doing better than they were in obtaining academic employment. The data collected for our study show that of 204 faculty members in religious studies departments and programmes in Ontario 90% are men and 10% are women (see Table 5-2 above). Of 190 faculty, both male and female, for whom we have data, 56 (29%) were appointed during the half-decade from 1965 to 1969, 54 (28%) were appointed in the period 1970-74, 27 (14%) in the period 1975-79, and 19 (10%) in the period 1980-84 (see Table 5-4).

Table 5-4
Female-Male Faculty Appointments
in Religious Studies in Ontario,
by Half-Decades, 1955-87

Years	Female		Male	
1955-59	0		5	
1960-64	1		19	
1965-69	5		51	
1970-74	2		52	
1975-79	4		23	
1980-84	3		16	
1985-87	4		5	
Totals	19	(10%)	171	(90%)

But during this twenty-year period there has been a steady increase in the ratio of women to men appointed, from the first half of the seventies when women were appointed to only 3.7% of the positions available (that is, 2 out of 54 openings), to the period between 1975 and 1984 when 15% of appointments went to women (7 out of 46 appointments). And, though the numbers are small, the trend may be accelerating, considering that in the three years from 1985 to 1987 almost half (4 out of 9) of the appointments went to women. Expressed slightly differently, the fact that most women have come comparatively recently to their positions stands out more clearly: considering women currently teaching in religious studies in Ontario, 11 out of 19 (or approximately 58%) have been appointed since 1975. By comparison, roughly 39% (or 44 out of 171) of men have come to their positions since 1975. Though the statistics for recent years suggest a trend to increasing appointments of women faculty in religious studies, it is evident from Table 5-4 that the relative stability of religious studies departments and programmes in those years and therefore the small numbers of appointments overall — both of men and women — have done little to offset the continuing imbalance — currently ten to one — of men to women in Ontario departments and programmes of religious studies.

A fuller picture of the opportunities for women as academics in religious studies would have to consider earlier stages than the point at which a doctorate is granted or employment offered. Whether or not the playing field is level for players of both sexes in the hiring game, one should look into the special difficulties women have in getting a chance to play the game at all. What is the proportion of women to men completing honours degrees as undergraduates in religious studies as compared with the proportion of women to men entering graduate school and as compared with the proportion of women to men who actually receive the doctorate? If, as is surely likely, that proportion steadily drops (see Table 5-3 above), then we should be examining such matters as who gets encouragement and financial assistance to continue their studies and whether (or, more precisely, how) practices of "mentoring" favour male graduate students. Not only unofficial "gatekeeping" practices but the difficulties in religious studies for a woman to challenge the traditionally androcentric bias may diminish the will to persevere in graduate school. One woman in religious studies suggested to us that the higher ratio of women Ph.D.s in economics may be because in such a "scientific" field there is, at least as far as subject matter is concerned, less need or opportunity to confront an overt male bias; Keynes or GNP calculations, for example, do not bring gender issues to the fore in the manner of many of the texts in traditional religious studies canons.

In an essay published in 1978 Karen McCarthy Brown describes the experience of dislocation that leads women in the academic world to gravitate to the margins of their disciplines, if not to drop out altogether: "Because academic women are workers in a system that, not only is not designed for us, but at times is positively antagonistic to us, we cannot operate in that system in a simple and direct way" (Brown, 1978, 285). Women, declares Brown, "are the heretics and pagans in the academic world" (286). One example of a possible corrective measure is the recommendation by the Canadian Association of University Teachers' Status of Women Committee to the CAUT Council that academic journals "be encouraged to institute a system of 'blind reviewing'" (i.e., not revealing authors' names to referees) in order to preclude possible discrimination against women authors (CAUT, 1990c). The unresolved problem, of course, is that a (male) "blind" reviewer might still "see" the method, approach, and content to be heretical or marginal according to the received canons of a male-oriented academic field.

Referring perhaps to the effects of conformity in a male-dominated academic world, Anne C. Hall, Dean of the Faculty of Music at Wilfrid Laurier University, laments that she — and many of her female colleagues — are plagued with the unfair label of being a "conscientious and unoriginal, uncreative woman academic" (Hall, 1980, 40). She laments, too, that the women students she teaches, shaped as they are by many of the same forces and frequently stereotyped with the same labels, "often seem less determined to do well" in comparison with men:

> They seem not to believe they can do well, not to believe it important
> that they do well, not to be sure they should do well. They hesitate to
> seek help when they need it, which makes it more likely they will not do
> well. They do not envisage themselves in a career, and do not act as if
> they are headed for one (ibid., 39).

Hall also suggests that religion may contribute to these differences between
men and women students, which are perhaps less pronounced in a large
American metropolis but "depressingly persistent here, in a smaller Canadian community influenced by conservative religion"(ibid., 39).

Even considering the case of a talented student who does do well, and
acknowledging too "the demoralizing effect on women students of the scarcity of women on university faculties" (40), Hall claims that such a gifted
student "has not emerged unscarred from her socialization to be a good little
girl" (40). What Hall calls the "wilfulness" requisite to a musician has been
"socialized away," making it difficult to trust and act on one's feelings as a
basis for creative work. In such instances the passage from obedience to wilfulness may best be assisted by someone who has recognized (and escaped)
her own socialization into the same role. The presence of women academics
in greater numbers could do much to counteract the special difficulties
women students have in functioning within the academic world.

Whether, in the 1990s, as retirements open up faculty positions, more
women will be hired to fill them would seem to depend not only on affirmative action and employment equity policies on the part of universities and
faculty associations (see OCUFA, 1990c) and the good intentions of those
doing the hiring but also on these other, less visible factors. Also, if as the
1990s wear on, a faculty shortage develops as the result of large-scale
retirements (see 5.2.4 below), and the percentage of women in religious
studies doctoral programmes does not increase or even hold steady, finding
qualified women candidates may become a serious problem. The experience
of a psychology department at one Ontario university may portend what is
to come. Its efforts to hire women were frustrated by a variety of factors,
according to a letter by a department member to the university paper
(Bowers, 1990):

> Since 1980, the department has made 21 job offers to applicants for full-
> time, tenure-track positions. Whereas 25% of the applicants were
> women, they received 75% of first offers for a faculty position, and 62%
> of all offers. Of the 13 women who received offers, 7 did not accept. Of
> these 7 women, at least 4 indicated a strong desire to come to UW, but
> could not do so because of spousal considerations. Of the 6 women who
> accepted apppointments, 3 of them have since left; spousal consider-
> ations were again the main issue. About half the time, spousal concerns
> involved men who were also academics seeking faculty appointment. It
> is thus no accident that of the 7 full or part-time tenured women in the
> department of psychology, 5 of them have husbands who also have fac-
> ulty appointments.

One lesson drawn by the writer of the letter is that success in hiring of women "is much more likely if qualified husbands can also be hired," but, ironically, the addition of more males to the faculty by this means would hinder the achieving of equity (ibid.).

5.1.1.2   Degrees Held and Average Age

In 1967 only 45% of those teaching religious studies in Canada had an earned doctorate, a figure which had increased to 70% by 1972 (Anderson, 1972, 14). Claude Welch reported that in 1970 63% of faculty in North American religious studies departments had doctorates (1971, 185). In 1987, of 203 faculty in Ontario religious studies departments, 154 held the Ph.D. degree and 22 the Th.D. — a total of 87% with an earned doctorate (see Table 5-2 above). Clearly, the pattern has been to expect the doctorate as the normal qualification for assuming a university teaching position, a trend as manifest in religious studies as elsewhere. Those faculty without either a Ph.D. or Th.D. are mostly those hired before 1970 or are young appointees in the 1980s with dissertations not yet completed. (For the 18 individuals lacking an earned doctorate on whom we have data, eight were appointed before 1970 and six after 1980.)

It should be pointed out that the difference between the Ph.D. and the Th.D. is now largely a matter of nomenclature — many Th.D degrees have been converted to Ph.D.s (see, further, chap. 9.1 below). Similarly, the degree formerly known as the B.D. (Bachelor of Divinity) has almost universally become the M.Div. (Master of Divinity) in recent years. In Ontario departments and programmes of religious studies 41% of faculty have the M.Div. or its equivalent (interpreted as meaning post-secondary training to be a member of the Christian clergy or Jewish rabbinate), whereas 48% do not (the data do not show whether the remaining 11% have the M.Div. or its equivalent).[2] A trend, already faintly discernible in 1971 among doctoral students in religious studies (Welch, 1971, 204-05, Table 10), is clearly evident today: students planning to teach in religious studies departments are by-passing seminaries and entering religious studies graduate programs directly after receiving their baccalaureate degrees (see, further, chap. 4.2.1 and 4.2.2 above).

Whereas those Ontario religious studies faculty who held the M.Div. averaged 55 years of age in 1987, those who did not have that degree or its equivalent were, on average, age 49. The trend away from the M.Div. among younger faculty, with the corresponding reduction of the time spent in university studies, means that they are entering the profession three or four years earlier than their older colleagues did. Only two women among the faculty surveyed held the M.Div., as contrasted with almost two-thirds (61%) of the men. Another comparison shows that those holding the Ph.D. earned it about a year later on average (1970) than those holding the Th.D. and that 44% of those with a Th.D. received it during the 1960s, whereas only a third of the current holders of the Ph.D. obtained their degree in that decade. Although the retroactive conversion of Th.D. degrees to the Ph.D. by some graduate institutions complicates the picture somewhat, these figures nonetheless indicate a trend away from the Th.D. as the highest degree held by faculty in religious studies, as well as suggesting a decline in the popularity of that degree generally in relation to the Ph.D.

Whereas in 1974-75 over two-thirds (69%) of full-time university teachers in Canada were 35 or older, by 1982-83 the percentage had reached 86% (CFH, 1984, 5). In 1987 almost 60% of religious studies faculty in Ontario were in their forties; of the rest, a third were 50 years of age or under, and only 8.8% were under forty. Claude Welch's study of departments of religious studies provides contrasting data for the United States and Canada in the early 1970s. Welch (1971, 184, Table 9-11), surveying 3,762 individuals at 633 institutions in 1970, found only 7% of faculty over 60. The median age for all faculty in religious studies, Welch found, was "just over 40." The median age was even lower in Canada, where 58% of the religious studies faculty were 40 or under (contrasted with 49% in the U.S.). Of course, those religious studies faculty who were teaching in the early 1970s were almost twenty years older in the late 1980s. But comparing statistics for median and average ages over the past two decades points up how a hiatus in hiring has resulted in a faculty now past the middle stage of middle age. An uneven distribution of faculty in terms of age has meant a lack of new blood in the religious studies professoriate, and may mean in future greater numbers of vacancies occurring at once if the usual retirement age of 65 continues to be the norm (see Von Zur-Muehlen, 1987). However, a fair number of early or late retirements could mean a more gradual rate of retirement (see 5.3 below).

In 1990 the Ontario Confederation of University Faculty Associations (OCUFA, 1990a) made a submission to the Ontario Council on University Affairs projecting a "bleak picture" with respect to future staffing in Ontario universities. Considering about eleven thousand faculty who in 1988 were tenured or in positions leading to tenure, OCUFA predicted more than a quarter of them would be eligible for retirement by 1999, a situation that would worsen in the succeeding few years: "By the year 2002, more than a third will be in that position, and over 50% will reach retirement age by the year 2006" (OCUFA, 1990a, 3). The OCUFA submission spoke of "striking" differences between fields, predicting that "in the next 15 years, without replacement, Humanities would be virtually wiped out" (ibid.). Considering the higher average age for the professoriate in religious studies as compared with the humanities in general, these projections become even more dire when applied to Ontario faculty in religious studies. In fact, our own data show that, if current patterns hold, more than two-thirds of present faculty in religious studies in Ontario will be retired within fifteen years.

5.1.1.3   Faculty in Theological Colleges: Some Comparisons

Faculty in departments of religious studies in Ontario universities may also be compared with their colleagues in theological colleges in the province with whom they are often associated in various ways. Also available for comparison are the profiles prepared by the Association of Theological Schools (ATS) of more than 2,000 faculty teaching in its member institutions in the U.S.A. and Canada in 1971 and 1981 (Taylor, 1982).

In age, Ontario theological faculty and Ontario religious studies faculty are approximately the same, theological faculty averaging 50 years of age, slightly younger than their colleagues in religious studies (Table 5-2 above). Marvin Taylor's ATS data show that during the period 1971-81 the median age of faculty in Canadian theological colleges had dropped from 53 to 49; the percentage of those over 60 had decreased from 22% to 13%. These figures indicate that there have been more faculty replacements in Canadian theological colleges than in Canadian religious studies departments and programmes: religious studies faculties have been getting older and theological faculties younger.

Between 1971 and 1981, the proportion of male faculty in American and Canadian theological schools dropped from 96.9% to 91.6% in non-Roman Catholic seminaries and from 98.1% to 88.1% in Roman Catholic institutions (Taylor, 1982). It would appear that special efforts have been made, especially in Roman Catholic seminaries, to redress the male-female imbalance. In Ontario in 1987, of 130 faculty in theological colleges 15% (19) were women, compared with slightly more than 10% (19 out of 189) in religious studies (Table 5-4 above). The average age of women in Ontario theological colleges at that time – 49 – was slightly less than that of their male colleagues, namely, 51 years. In comparison with women faculty in Ontario religious studies departments and programmes, those in Ontario theological colleges averaged three years older.

In the 1970s, faculty holding an academic doctorate in Canadian and American theological schools rose from 71.6% in 1971 to 81% in 1981 (Taylor, 1982). The proportion of those with Ph.D.s increased by 41.7%, chiefly the result of a decline in the number holding the Th.D. degree. Our data for Ontario theological colleges show a similar picture. Eighty percent of the faculty held an earned doctorate in 1987. This compares with an 87% figure for Ontario religious studies faculty (Table 5-2 above). Ontario theological faculty holding the Ph.D. (74) far outnumbered those with the Th.D. (33), a ratio of 2.3 to 1. Among an additional 25 theological faculty teaching in both a theological college and in religious studies the ratio was the same, with 16 persons holding the Ph.D. and seven the Th.D. Putting these two groups together, the proportion of theological college faculty with earned doctorates was 92%.

Another comparison shows that while a quarter of theological college faculty had the Th.D. as their highest degree in 1987, only 11% of religious studies faculty held that degree. Moreover, not surprisingly, 83% of theological faculty had the M.Div. or its equivalent, that is, had graduated from theological college, more than double the percentage in religious studies (see 5.1.1 above). Of the women teaching in Ontario theological colleges, about half (10 of 19) held the M.Div. or its equivalent. This contrasts with the small number of women in religious studies (2 out of 19) with that degree.

There are no big surprises in these comparisons. Like religious studies, theological colleges in Ontario have been swimming with the main currents of academia, moving to meritocracy and professionalization (see chap. 3.3 above), hiring faculty with better academic credentials, and making an effort to hire more women. Where religious studies departments or programmes and theological colleges are connected or work together in some way, these changes should prove to be mutually beneficial.

5.1.1.4   Source of Highest Degree

Previous studies of sources of graduate degrees held by religious studies and theology faculty have given some attention to four institutions, sometimes referred to as "the big four," which have been the sources of many of the doctoral degrees for professors in religious studies and theology in North America: Columbia University (including Union Theological Seminary), Yale University, the University of Chicago, and Harvard University (see Welch, 1971, 186, Table 9-14; Taylor, 1982). Surveys done for the Association of Theological Schools (ATS) showed that these universities accounted for about 30% in 1971, and 25% in 1981, of the doctorates held by faculty in American and Canadian Protestant seminaries (Taylor, 1982). But a comparison with statistics for the source of highest degrees for North American graduate faculty in religious studies in 1971 revealed that only 18% of them came from these "big four" institutions.[3]

Turning to the Ontario data one finds that in 1987 these four universities accounted for only 14% of the highest degrees held by religious studies faculty in Ontario: 18 doctorates from Harvard, 13 from each of Columbia/Union and Yale, and 9 from Chicago. This proportion corresponds almost exactly with the percentage of Ontario religious studies faculty whose doctorates came from universities within the province, suggesting that holders of Ontario doctorates are finding positions within the province in religious studies and creating a small but significant component of Canadian graduate degrees within some departments at least.

In Ontario roughly one-third of the religious studies faculty took their highest degree outside North America (whereas more than half the doctorates for Ontario theological faculty are from outside North America). It has been suggested by Walter Ong (1981, chap. 4) that the European model of higher education, implying a more magisterial role for the professor, has more of the aspect of "contest" about it than the "collegial" American model. Until the 1960s, says Ong, Western education was a ritual contest of ceremonial enmity between teacher and (male) pupil (ibid., 120). An agonistic structure stressing orality, Latin, an all-male environment, and the thesis method of instruction continued in Roman Catholic theological education until the late 1960s (ibid., 139). Yeshiva study undoubtedly leads to another distinctive style of pedagogy. Rather than an agonistic model, the pattern is more a dialogical relationship between a rabbi and disciples. Or, if one thinks of the Talmudic style of debate, the nature of the literature being studied sets up a pattern of argument between disciples with the result that that becomes the method of pedagogy.

While only the most tentative speculations can be offered about how the academic culture of a department is shaped by the national origin or religious environment of its professors' highest degrees, perhaps it can be ventured that there are bound to be differences between a department whose professors are mostly American-trained and one whose faculty studied in continental Europe (or in Rome rather than Germany) or between faculty with rabbinic training and faculty whose teaching style is influenced by a Protestant pastoralism. How these differences may be reflected in the way a department characterizes its own aims in the study of religion is discussed in Chapter 6 below.

5.1.1.5 Other Issues Related to Academic Preparation

An important question for this study, though not susceptible to statistical analysis from our survey data, is whether religious studies faculty are themselves trained in religious studies, either at the undergraduate or graduate level. It becomes apparent that many of those teaching in the area of religious studies, especially where there is a programme but no department, have come from some other area, and not necessarily theology, but fields such as philosophy, sociology, anthropology, or history. Since religious studies tends to be interdisciplinary, this is not surprising. Still, what is the effect on students' academic formation if their professors have not themselves been socialized in the field, have few professional contacts with colleagues in religious studies, do not attend conferences or subscribe to journals in the area, or perhaps lack a commitment to its viability or significance?

Such breadth and inclusiveness may be beneficial in various ways in allowing students and faculty to pursue wide-ranging interests in cognate fields loosely clustered around religious studies, but the price of diversity may be the lack of definable core. Further, one notices with some alarm that in Ontario institutions graduating Ph.D.s in religious studies a number of the faculty (sometimes most of the faculty) have been drawn from outside religious studies, or else (we were told) the next appointment was to be a specialist in some other field, perhaps in order to ensure enhanced credibility in a cognate field. (See, further, chap. 4.2.4 above.)

Another, somewhat related, concern is the lack of Canadian background of some faculty teaching in religious studies in Ontario, especially when most members of one department are in that situation. It has been reported, for instance, that for academics appointed nation-wide ''75% of those hired in 1972 were neither Canadian citizens nor landed immigrants'' (CAUT, 1990a, 7). But does it matter in the 1990s if someone received a Ph.D., say, from an American university when they have been living and teaching in Canada for twenty years? Perhaps not, if the first or second degree is from a Canadian university, or, even if American-born and trained, they have become Canadian citizens (significant as an indication of some degree of commitment to the Canadian milieu), or have been using Canadian materials in their courses regularly. The concern becomes acute if most members of a department were born, raised, and entirely educated outside Canada and if their courses showed little effort to contextualize their teaching. Students might then be unaware of the significant connections between their studies and their own cultural environment. Perhaps, on one level, it might not make any difference whether one studies, say, Augustine's *Confessions* or the religions of India in Toronto rather than Syracuse. Yet, no subject is studied in a historical or cultural vacuum. At least the instructor's own background and kind of intellectual formation become apparent to students (so they report) through the content and nature of anecdotal or illustrative material, or the kinds of examples and allusions given.

Precisely the opposite problem may be emerging today. Because graduate education in the United States has become expensive, and because several universities in Ontario now grant the Ph.D. in religious studies, students having their B.A. from an Ontario university may be inclined to stay in the province for their graduate work — and, if possible, to stay here after receiving the Ph.D. (cf. chap. 9.5 below). The result may be, at some point in the future, too great a concentration of religious studies faculty in Ontario having most of their academic preparation within the province. However, there may also be a chance of Canadian candidates' being displaced if restrictions on hiring foreign academics are removed, a possibility should universities begin to hire significant numbers of new staff once again in a tight market (CAUT, 1990a, 7). (See, further, chap. 12.10.1 below.)

5.2   Hiring of Religious Studies Faculty

5.2.1   Factors in Hiring of Religious Studies Faculty

Deans and administrators were asked whether the factors that enter into the hiring and promotion of faculty in religious studies were any different from those for other humanities faculty. Where the department of religious studies exists as a regular, fully integrated department within an arts faculty, existing alongside other departments such as history, philosophy, classics, and English, the answer was universally ''No'' (see, further, chap. 3.1.1 above).

But that negative answer may need some qualification in a few situations where vestiges of past practices still linger, especially where religious studies courses and departments grew out of earlier courses in religious knowledge, or where a denominational college became a provincial university, or where federated church-related colleges make up a religious studies department or programme. Or, there may be occasional discrepancies between present policies and past practices, or differences in the basis on which earlier and present appointments were made. Such situations are worth paying special attention to here because of the ways they may differ from standard university practice or for insight into possible continuing effects within a university department of religious studies whose origins are ecclesiastical.

To supplement responses from the dean or departmental chair individual faculty members were often asked similar questions about factors in hiring and promotion. More specifically, some faculty members were asked to comment on the relative importance in hiring or promoting faculty of such factors as graduate school preparation, match of expertise or competence with the department's needs and expectations, publications, teaching experience, and other factors (gender, collegiality, confessional commitment, and denominational affiliation). Because the question did not provide the person being interviewed with equally weighted choices, frequently the interviewer had to push beyond the initial obvious response to a consideration of secondary factors. As might have been expected, faculty members usually answered that the most important factor in hiring was the match of the applicant's expertise or competence with departmental needs and expectations. This option to some extent incorporated various aspects of all of the other possibilities such as graduate school preparation, publications, teaching experience, etc. Typically, most would respond that the first principle in hiring was to obtain the best person for the job.

5.2.2   Issues in the Hiring of Women in Religious Studies

The assumption that ''the best person gets the job'' needs to be challenged at a time when feminists (among others) question ''the myth of academia as a meritocracy in which individuals rise and fall based solely on their own performance'' (Simeone, 1987, 42). Angela Simeone, in *Academic Women: Working Towards Equality*, has shown how ''Informal Relationships'' (chap. 4) and ''Sponsors and Proteges'' (chap. 5) operate within the academic world such that both an informal ''old-boy'' network and the ''mentor/protege'' relationship (where the mentor's recommendations further the protege's career) work against women in colleges and universities. In the academic world as elsewhere it tends to be the case that people hire people like themselves. A department of religious studies hires someone not only to teach courses and conduct research, but someone who is expected to be a suitable colleague to the department's present members.

In the past, especially in institutions where most of the faculty had the same religious affiliation, networks and relationships were restricted or favoured members of one's own community or tradition. When Canadian universities were not graduating any significant numbers of Ph.D.s in religious studies, frequently ecclesiastical bodies kept lists of members of their denomination who were studying abroad or in the United States, or else American co-religionists were sought to fill Canadian vacancies. When theologically trained faculty were responsible for staffing newly formed departments of religious studies they often turned to colleagues in their own denomination, or contacted a friend teaching in a graduate department for recommendations about new Ph.D.s. A look at some departmental rosters of faculty reveals some instances where several graduates from the same doctoral programme were hired in successive years. In the early years of the growing separation of religious studies from theological studies many faculty, under the pressure of heavy teaching duties and with responsibilities to their churches, lacked time for research and attendance at learned societies meetings. They also lacked the kind of contacts in the field of religious studies that are the norm today. In the 1960s and early 1970s, appointments were sometimes made under these conditions, in the absence of the more formal procedures for advertising a position and conducting a search that are accepted practice today. Such a situation did not favour the hiring of women, since most stood outside the picture, even had there been a significant number available for academic employment (see 5.1.1.1 above).

Today it is generally the case that one's religious affiliation does little or nothing to enhance prospects of employment in religious studies. The only exceptions might be instances where a department is seeking to diversify and might favour a candidate of different background; for instance, a department whose religious background was predominantly Christian might seek a scholar of Jewish or Hindu origins (see 5.2.3.1 below). Thus the ecclesiastical ties that once worked against the hiring of women should in theory do so no longer, but that does not preclude the necessity of clear, non-discriminatory hiring policies that are published and visibly public.

Among the factors most often cited by women as institutional barriers to their progress are the "absence of objective hiring and promotion criteria," the "use of informal, shifting hiring and promotion procedures and criteria," and the "use of 'crony-based' decision-making systems for hiring and promotion" (Simeone, 1987, 38). In several instances in Ontario religious departments or theological colleges where disputes have arisen about appointments — of men as well as of women — clear procedures and criteria have been lacking. Sometimes policies have been developed only after a crisis occurred within a religious studies department or theological college (see chap. 3.2.4 above). Further, it is probable that more problems will arise unless appointment procedures are fair, up-to-date, and clearly stated. Where a religious studies department or programme has an ecclesiastical connection or an affiliation with a theological college, such policy statements, reflecting current academic practice in universities, are especially important.

On the positive side, a number of women faculty we interviewed or have had contact with during the course of this study reported general acceptance in their departments and universities. One recent religious studies appointee, commenting on the interview that resulted in her being hired, reported that the question of female "role model" was raised. During the discussion that followed she objected to being stereotyped as a *female* scholar. Subsequently, however, she found, to her surprise, that her presence in the department turned out to be a source of inspiration for women students. They were enrolling in her classes, coming to her for academic counselling, applying for graduate study, and asking her for references. This is an instructive example, confirming some of the things feminist scholars and others have been saying for some time about the importance of hiring women.

5.2.3   Other Issues in Hiring of Religious Studies Faculty

5.2.3.1   Diversity

In addition to matters related to the appointment of women there are other issues in hiring practices such as ensuring faculty renewal by having a spectrum of ages and ranks represented throughout the department or better representation of minorities. Some formerly homogeneous departments have begun to diversify by making their most recent appointment a person different from the previously prevailing norm. Yet such diversity has not always been without stress, least of all for the lone new member. In more than one place relationships between older male faculty and a younger feminist colleague have been strained, even bitter. Or, someone whose religious background differs from that of colleagues — Jewish or Muslim, say, rather than Christian — may experience isolation. As more such appointments are made, however, so that the new appointees do not feel outnumbered, these kinds of situations should improve (see, further, 5.2.2 above).

The familiar "insider-outsider" question (see chap. 2.4.6 above) has some relevance to questions of hiring. Is a particular religious tradition better taught by someone from within or by a person who stands outside it, thus guaranteeing by virtue of detachment — or so it is hoped — a measure of objectivity? "The ant cannot study the ant-hill" might sum up the case for preferring the outsider. One of our Ontario colleagues in religious studies has proposed, informally and partially in jest, a scheme to explain how a department of religious studies decides whether to hire an insider or outsider for a vacancy. This proposal, we might add, occasioned some groans and head-shaking, as well as chuckles of recognition and angry denials, when proposed at a conference on religious studies. Depending on the tradition to be taught, it was suggested that the choice is determined by the balance of the "love-hate" relationship between Christianity and the tradition in which there is the vacancy. If in Islamic studies, then a non-Islamic scholar is sought rather than a practising Muslim, who might be regarded as lacking in perspective on Islam. When there is an opening in Judaic studies, then the department wants an Orthodox rabbi, someone religiously observant who learned the Talmud in infancy and who will be unavailable for meetings on Friday afternoons. For a position in some aspect of Christian studies, though, the ideal is a former member of the clergy, perhaps an ex-priest, or an evangelical who has lost his or her faith.

More than a whiff of the outmoded surrounds this scheme, especially in its judgments of religious traditions and of their practitioners, or in its suggestion that some kind of Christian hegemony wields power in hiring that would outweigh other factors, let alone the fact that a search committee may be able to detect little from a c.v. or interview about a candidate's religious affiliation or practice. In some respects this scheme is another variation of what has been called the "zoo" theory for staffing a religious studies department — you try to install one representative of each species in the available cages (Welch, 1971, 16). Aside from factors relating to collegiality or stemming from religious prejudice though, whether or not an insider is preferred to teach a particular religious tradition may be determined by availability. Not all religious traditions have produced scholars qualified to teach in a Western university according to critical and historical canons of interpretation accepted in the field.

5.2.3.2 Canadianization

The issue of giving preference to Canadian applicants for positions, required by the federal Department of Employment and Immigration, has caused problems too. A few years ago the Canadian Society for the Study of Religion (CSSR) was asked to intervene in one case in which a department of religious studies in an Ontario university had allegedly violated the policy requiring that Canadians be examined for a vacancy before considering foreigners. The CSSR's response was to decline making a judgment with respect to the particular case at issue, while at the same time offering to advise about the availability of prospective Canadian applicants when future vacancies occurred, thus attempting to ensure that Canadians were given consideration before foreign academics were sought. In January 1989 the "two-tier" hiring policy was reportedly under review by the government. Though favoured by the Canadian Association of University Teachers, most members of the Council of Ontario Universities were against the policy as cumbersome in highly competitive areas. It was reported that of 919 new university appointments in Ontario in 1986, 91.2% were Canadian citizens or landed immigrants, an increase from 83.6% a decade earlier (*Globe and Mail*, January 10, 1989, A4). With massive faculty retirements looming in the 1990s and beyond, the Canadians-first policy will be difficult to maintain.[4]

5.2.4   Hiring in Theological Colleges: Some Comparisons

5.2.4.1   Hiring Policies and Procedures in Theological Colleges

As our "taxonomy" indicates (chap. 2.6 above), close links continue to be maintained on several Ontario campuses between a department or programme in religious studies and a church-related college or a theological college. Hiring practices in church-related colleges have been discussed in Chapter 3.1.1 above. Insofar as some positions in religious studies may be affected by links with theological colleges and thus effectively under the jurisdiction of ecclesiastical bodies, it is important to devote some attention to policies and procedures governing appointments in theological colleges. There the situation has historically been different from that within universities. Of special concern is the extent to which religious affiliation takes precedence over other factors in hiring, whether a faith commitment is a condition of continued employment, and what redress exists in the case of disputes. Underlying many of these issues is the place of academic freedom in the university and, within religious studies, whether the usual guarantees of such freedom can be subordinated to ecclesiastical concerns, as sometimes happens in theological colleges.

In theological colleges providing courses in religious studies, factors in hiring frequently conform closely to the procedures customary in a university setting. That is, academic qualifications are the foremost consideration, especially if the college or seminary has an affiliation with a university. Furthermore, if departments or programmes in religious studies are in any way affected by hiring procedures in theological colleges, it must be emphasized that such procedures are changing at a rapid rate, approximating in many places the procedures customary in a university setting (cf. 5.1.1.3 above).

Frequently such institutions have moved away from informal and local procedures, often exercised by the head of the college or seminary (and with reference to a governing board rather than to the collegial approval of other faculty members), toward adopting the hiring procedures of the university at large. Where such a transition is taking place in a theological college, it is often voluntary, involving a wide range of possibilities, from formal ratification of written procedures already in place in the university, to an informal agreement to follow such procedures (where applicable and possible), to using them as guidelines against which to measure and check their own procedures. The Association of Theological Schools, to which over half of Ontario theological colleges belong (see App. B below), states in its "Procedures, Standards, and Criteria for Membership" (ATS, 1986, 20):

> Institutional policies with respect to all conditions of employment (appointments, promotion, tenure, retirement, leaves of absence, responsibility for teaching, advising, governance and other duties, etc.) shall be available to all affected persons. These policies shall be in a faculty handbook or other public document.

Though this directive requires an openness with regard to procedures, no uniform model for seminary hiring and promotion practices is proposed by ATS nor is one evident within Ontario theological colleges. In some of these colleges a rigorous academic model stressing graduate school preparation and potential for research and teaching is used in appointment procedures, while clear policies for promotion may be informal or non-existent. In a few places where the faculty in theological studies are not ranked, the status of "professor" is granted after a trial period of several years. Elsewhere, university procedures in hiring and promotion are supposed to be followed, whereas in fact the theological college continues to operate according to its past practices and traditions, usually implemented by the head or principal. Pressure to follow university practice may occur when personnel from the college are cross-appointed within the university, especially at the graduate level. At such points tensions may arise as faculty become aware of discrepancies between practices in the theological college and the university.

Moreover, appointments in theological colleges frequently involve factors different from those within religious studies departments. In some seminaries the ability to participate in the spiritual formation of students or to assist in their preparation for professional ministry is an important consideration. Then, ordination, pastoral experience, the possession of an M.Div. degree or its equivalent, or, increasingly in cases where a woman is sought to fill a vacancy (and where ordination cannot be required), evidence of significant activity in the life of the church as a lay person may be a requirement. While sometimes all professors within a theological college must be ordained within a particular denomination or belong to a certain order, often it is sufficient to be simply Protestant or Roman Catholic. Because theological education is usually professional training for Christian ministry, and because theological colleges almost always are identified with one particular Christian denomination, these special kinds of criteria are important in that context. However, it is difficult to imagine any reasons why they should apply to undergraduate or graduate departments in religious studies; indeed, there the factors important in hiring are derived from the standard pattern of other humanities departments within the university. In fact, from the point of view of theological educators, religious studies is recognized to be undertaking a task distinct from education for ministry, and identified with the university model from which theological colleges distinguish themselves in various respects.

5.2.4.2   Confessional Requirements in Theological Colleges

The teaching of religious studies has frequently been differentiated from theological studies on the basis of its claim to be non-confessional (see chaps. 2.4.3. above and 6 below). In this light, it is worth examining what confessional requirements govern the appointment of staff within theological colleges. The ATS recognizes, in its discussion of academic freedom, that a theological college may insist that its faculty subscribe to a doctrinal or confessional standard, but it also requires that a challenge to the doctrinal regularity of a faculty member be in an open hearing and that there be appropriate safeguards for academic freedom (ATS, 1986, Part 5.4).

A wide spectrum of policies on the issue of confessional requirements exists in the published materials of theological colleges in Ontario. Some calendars include a detailed affirmation of faith voluntarily subscribed to by the faculty (e.g., McMaster Divinity College) or a statement of the theological position of the institution. At the other end of the spectrum there may be no more than a stated, though general, commitment by the college both to "faith in Jesus Christ" and to "free inquiry about the Christian faith" (Emmanuel College). A precisely worded statement of faith commonly appears at the beginning of the calendar of a theologically conservative Protestant seminary (or of the calendar of a Bible college; see chap. 11 below). The statements to be found in the calendars of mainline Protestant theological colleges tend to be general and brief. Among Anglican and Roman Catholic theological colleges the practice appears to be to assume — rather than test for — ecclesiastical membership or affiliation on the part of faculty and students as the basis of doctrinal integrity. That is, it is the role of the church rather than of the theological institution to deal with doctrinal conformity. Within the theological college the concentration is then on spiritual formation as an aspect of the school's curriculum and the means by which socialization occurs within the community.

Some faculty handbooks for theological schools in Ontario state that faculty must "maintain acceptable doctrinal integrity," while in others failure "to maintain good standing in a local congregation" of the institution's denomination may be cause for dismissal. Sometimes, if one has clerical status at the time of the appointment, it is required that that status be preserved in order to continue the teaching function. A few institutions explicitly subordinate academic freedom to principles of faith or state that freedom to pursue the inquiry for truth must remain within "the accepted constitutional and confessional basis" of the institution, but these schools have few if any ties to religious studies departments.

In a lecture given in 1988, Schubert M. Ogden, a professor in Perkins School of Theology in Southern Methodist University and a past president of the American Academy of Religion, addressed this issue of whether academic freedom can be restricted because of the religious aims of an institution. Ogden confronted the specific question of theology's right to be in a university, stating that theology must be on the same basis as any other discipline, department, or institution of higher education:

> Either theology is an academic discipline like every other and, therefore, bound by identical principles of academic freedom and institutional autonomy; or else, being an exception to these principles, theology has

no moral right to be reckoned an academic discipline on a par with every other and, therefore, is not an integral part of the university (1988, 6).

Ogden maintained that the integrity of theology depends upon its being subjected to the "principles of academic freedom and institutional autonomy . . . definitive of the university" (8). Even a "free-standing seminary" or non-university school of theology, Ogden contends, is increasingly determined by the culture of the university to the extent that subscription to articles of faith is already a compromise of academic freedom and the autonomy of the institution.

In this connection it may be noted that in May 1989 the Academic Board of the University of Toronto approved a memorandum of agreement between the University and the seven theological institutions making up the Toronto School of Theology. The theological schools agreed to afford their teaching staffs the same guarantees that protect University of Toronto faculty (see *University of Toronto Bulletin* 18, May 15, 1989). While such guarantees became formalized only after a problem had arisen in one of the theological institutions, and while it has been suggested that the agreement merely recognized the existence of procedures already in place, at least in some of the theological schools, the agreement signifies the growing conformity of theological institutions with university practices, along the lines urged by Ogden. For faculty and students in religious studies, who will often be working alongside or with faculty in theological studies, the protection of theological teaching staff puts them on the same basis as faculty in religious studies, affirming the integrity of the theological enterprise. Especially in situations where theological faculty might be used to teach courses in religious studies, or perhaps where a cross-appointment is being considered, the guarantee of academic freedom helps to dispel some of the suspicion that theological institutions impose constraints upon their faculty, preventing them from functioning in the normal way in a university context.

(See, further, chaps. 2.4.3 and 3.1.1 above.)

5.2.4.3   Other Issues in Hiring of Theological College Faculty

The matter of faculty diversity (see 5.2.3.1 above) is, if anything, more acute in theological colleges than in departments of religious studies. Whereas in religious studies there has been an impetus to include representatives from a variety of religious traditions as faculty members, in theological colleges there has frequently been pressure to maintain a core of faculty representative of the college's denominational tradition, giving rise to the perception that there are factors which override academic credentials in theological college appointments. Recently some Canadian theological colleges have been urged by clergy and lay people within the college's denomination to diversify their theologically "liberal" uniformity by appointing more theologically "conservative" faculty members, on the grounds that current faculty do not represent the theological views of the church constituency. At the same time, however, guidelines provided by the ATS urge another kind of diversity through the appointment of women, members of minority groups, and young faculty members (ATS, 1986, 5). And there is some evidence that in these respects a few theological colleges in Ontario have surpassed some departments of religious studies in their efforts to dirsify, perhaps because opportunities for hiring arose there, or else motivated by a theological imperative to rectify inequities and seek justice.

In some theological colleges, moreover, deliberate attempts at broader denominational representation or even at religious pluralism have been made, the result perhaps of an attempt to redress past injustices or to create greater diversity. Roman Catholic colleges have hired Protestants, Protestant colleges have deliberately sought denominational breadth or have hired Roman Catholics or Jews. In such circumstances it has been sufficient for a particular college to retain a certain "critical mass" of faculty members representative of its own tradition (though frequently the board of the institution or the ecclesiastical governing body becomes concerned about the appointments of faculty from outside the tradition). In general, though, denominational affiliation or confessional allegiance has been a decisive factor in hiring in theological colleges, even to the extent of overriding the factor of the candidate's area of specialization. That is, an institution might appoint a Canadian member of the clergy in its own tradition—this might be especially important in a denomination with strong American or European ties whose present faculty had largely come from outside Canada—even if that person did not have quite the specialization sought, in preference to hiring an "outsider" to the denomination who might nonetheless have precisely the graduate school credentials required for the position.

Alternatively, at least one theological college has found it necessary, in the absence of a pool of suitable applicants from within its own tradition, to single out a promising candidate from among its own current students or recent graduates, and then to finance the person's post-graduate training. While such a procedure ensures that the institution gets the precise qualifications and academic credentials it needs, as well as ensuring that faculty will come from within the tradition, the school may eventually become too "in-grown." Against this concern about provincialism it has been argued that study at outside institutions provides breadth and guards against narrowness.

In many instances, furthermore, openings within theological colleges are not advertised at a national level in publications such as *University Affairs*. While the Association of Theological Schools requires that faculty participation and consultation with students be part of the appointment process, there are no ATS statements about the criteria for appointments within theological schools, nor any recommendations about advertising in conjunction with the search process.

A review of the picture with respect to hiring practices within theological colleges sugges that no standard model exists. Many different factors have a role in determining how a vacancy is filled in a theological institution. Whereas hiring policies and practices increasingly resemble those of universities — which should facilitate working relationships between religious studies departments and theological colleges in places where there are such — all of them, at least in some respects, differ from customary university patterns.

5.3   Conclusions and Future Prospects

A 1986 study by Max Von Zur-Muehlen was pessimistic about the possibility of a greatly increasing demand for professors in Canada during the decade of the 1990s. His projection was that, as faculty take early retirements or continue to work past the age of sixty-five, vacancies would occur at a regular rate for many more years instead of occurring all at once. This projection, though, pre-dated a recent Supreme Court decision upholding mandatory retirement in Ontario universities, the result of which may be many retirements at one time instead of staggered over a longer period (see 5.1.1.2 above). Von Zur-Muehlen calculated that in the 1990s twenty-three Canadian citizens and permanent residents of Canada would be awarded Ph.D.s in religious studies each year, roughly fourteen of whom would be available for employment in university teaching. For these fourteen or so persons only about seven academic positions would be available. This projection of a 50% placement rate (half as many positions as job-seekers) was not expected to change for some years (Von Zur-Muehlen, 1987, 24).

On the other side, there is a growing expectation that severe shortages of new faculty will occur over the next decade or so as current professors reach what has been the normal retirement age (cf. 5.1.1.2 above). In the meantime, after so many years of a tight job market in universities various adjustments have taken place, either as recent graduates lowered their expectations about openings and employment and so dropped out of the academic job market, or as universities have introduced new measures to provide places for unemployed Ph.D.s through bridging appointments, postdoctoral fellowships, or other means. The general situation within humanities applies to religious studies too, but with the added complications indicated above (5.1.1.1).

The traditional association of religious studies with theological studies has sometimes created the suspicion that religious studies appointments have been governed by procedures for hiring used within theological colleges and church-related colleges. This association has sometimes resulted in conscious and deliberate attempts on the part of religious studies to differentiate itself from theological studies with respect to hiring.

At universities where religious studies developed from required "religion" or "religious knowledge" courses in a denominational setting, or where the academic study of religion emerged under the auspices of a theological seminary, frequently there have been efforts to differentiate it from the study of theology informed by ecclesiastical influence or confessional concerns. Distinguishing religious studies from the study of theology has sometimes meant a high degree of refinement on methodological issues, in the effort to remove any suspicion or taint of bias, to the extent that religious studies has sometimes achieved a greater fulfilment of the university's aims of objectivity or scholarly neutrality or academic freedom than in areas not pushed to much introspection on these matters (see chap. 3.2.3 above). Some undergraduates in one Ontario religious studies department stated that the department of film studies was more ''ideologically biassed'' than religious studies, suggesting that it was necessary for students to assent to a ''party line'' in order to feel at home in certain film courses. Elsewhere students felt that such programmes as native studies or women's studies exerted greater pressure to conform to the assumptions and organizing principles of particular courses — to demonstrate ''political correctness'' — than did religious studies.

Overall, it would be fair to say that religious studies departments have followed the university model in hiring, rather than the patterns of theological colleges. But it should also be pointed out that in recent years theological colleges have themselves endeavoured to move closer to standard academic procedures for hiring common throughout universities. Though in a few instances changes have been belated, or effected only after painful difficulties arose, we also found that in most religious studies departments and programmes in Ontario smooth and effective transitions were taking place as new faculty were appointed.

Notes

1 Because our study uses the year of appointment at the individual's present institution, the actual career would be longer if there had been an earlier appointment elsewhere, though not many would fall in this category.

2 It was frequently difficult to determine from a person's curriculum vitae, especially in the case of some religious studies faculty members, whether they in fact had had professional training for the rabbinate, ministry, or priesthood. Some c.v.s appeared to downplay, perhaps conceal, or even to omit such information.

3 Welch (1971, 186, Table 9-14) found that in the early 1970s Catholic University of America was, after Yale and Chicago, the third-largest source of highest degrees held by faculty in religious studies. Since one might have expected holders of degrees from Catholic University to show up in theological colleges in even greater numbers than in religious studies departments, this discrepancy is explained in part by the fact that at that time the ATS statistics did not include Roman Catholic institutions.

4 A recent review of the Canadianization question is to be found in CAUT, 1990a. An ad hoc committee of three members formed to review the CAUT Council's policy of 1977 was soliciting views of its members on the question.

6

Faculty: Teaching

William Closson James

6.1 Relationship of Graduate Preparation to Present Teaching

Do academics in religious studies in Ontario teach courses and carry on research in areas they studied as a part of their own graduate education? The answers to such a question might point to the shifts that have occurred within religious studies over the past few decades as scholars change direction, as well as indicate the adequacy of past graduate preparation for current teaching.

In the interviews conducted at each institution visited (see chap. 3.2 and n. 11 there) faculty were asked whether their present teaching and research were in the same area(s) as their graduate school preparation. In the documentation sought from faculty no request was made for information about their area of graduate study; the database, therefore, did not allow a statistical analysis of this question. Occasionally an individual's curriculum vitae contained the thesis title or other information enabling a general determination of the area in which they did their graduate work. The returned questionnaires did show, however, whether research and teaching are in similar areas, and the extent of that overlap (see App. A).

Initially the rationale was to discover whether scholars had shifted areas or moved into new fields since the completion of the doctorate. It would be useful and interesting to know whether, for instance, people trained in biblical studies continue to teach principally or solely in that field, while scholars trained in systematic theology end up teaching, for example, something like ethics as well. Are people teaching in areas in which they had not been trained in graduate school, and if so, how had they been prepared for these new areas?

Most of those interviewed affirmed identity—or at least continuity—between their graduate school training and their present teaching and research interests. However, many of these qualified their responses somewhat, speaking of acquiring "a new perspective," of the "evolution" of their current interests, of "developments" from past training, of having "broadened" from a previously narrow focus, of "continuity" with their earlier work, or of adding "other areas." Others indicated that while the subject of their specialization remained the same, the method by which they approached that subject had changed. A typical example might be a biblical scholar who in recent years had begun to employ a literary-critical or a socio-historical method.

One senior professor, a philosopher who had moved into the academic study of religion some time ago, claims that he is as close to his "original interests as one can be after thirty years." His summary comment: "My interests remain at bottom the same." The point is an important one: To what extent should we expect continuity in the teaching of religious studies from the 1950s to the present? Frequently the responses seemed as much a comment on the narrow focus of graduate school training—or on the breadth of the current demands of one's institution—as indicative of a personal change in direction. For instance, a person who maintained that their teaching was in the area in which they had been trained might go on to explain that they were widely educated. Another colleague, however, might attribute a change of direction to a narrow graduate education, perhaps because their graduate work was specialized in a theological area now seen to be restrictive in relation to the needs of religious studies.

Further, whether a person's graduate education was perceived as broad or narrow might depend in other ways on the nature of the current academic context. Someone trained in Christian studies might see their training as broad if their present teaching did not require a comparative approach encompassing several religious traditions. Those teaching principally at the graduate level might be able to give courses directly related to their research interests, whereas student demands and curriculum needs in an undergraduate program might require teaching courses in areas one had never formally studied at graduate school. A medievalist teaching in an undergraduate department might have to use that specialization as background for teaching courses in contemporary thought, where there is more student interest and demand. Even some undergraduate faculty, however, reported that they were able to organize what they taught around what they themselves had studied in graduate school. The flexibility of a curriculum and its capacity to incorporate new courses; whether people are able to teach courses related directly to their own specialization(s), or whether they are expected to branch out beyond; the personnel available and their diversity; whether a department has a sizeable component of majors or exists chiefly as a "service" department; the disciplinary self-consciousness or methodological "slant" of a department — all these factors affect the possibility of continuing to give courses in one's particular area of specialization.

Sometimes beginning faculty in junior appointments complained of being required to teach in areas for which they had not been trained. Underlying this complaint might be unrealistic expectations about being able to remain within one's (perhaps somewhat narrow) specialization while teaching undergraduates; or it could arise from a department's expectation that junior faculty would have to demonstrate versatility and adaptability in order to retain a position. Several faculty recounted stories of being pressured to teach, at the outset of their careers, courses totally unrelated to their own preparation and background, while senior colleagues had more freedom to select their own courses. Other beginning instructors, however, had experienced the comparative luxury of being able to teach exclusively in areas in which they themselves had studied in graduate school.

When asked how they had equipped themselves to teach in areas in which they had had no graduate school training, people mostly responded that their own subsequent reading and research had provided the necessary preparation. But many had made deliberate attempts to provide the necessary background for branching out into new areas. Some had taken courses or workshops on particular topics offered during the summer months, or used a sabbatical year to "retool." Others had joined an ongoing seminar in one of the learned societies (e.g., the Canadian Society for Biblical Studies) focussed on a particular topic and meeting regularly over a period of years. Frequently this was a means to bring new methods and approaches to bear on a particular area of religious studies. Several individuals found the opportunity to attend conferences where they would hear papers from outside their own area a useful way of expanding their horizons. Others learned from colleagues within their own department or in cognate fields within their university. In this instance, the opportunity for team teaching or to share instruction in a course often provided the occasion for colleagues to learn from one another. One individual who had begun to apply social-scientific methods to his field said he "tested" himself by publishing several articles in social-scientific journals.

In religious studies one sometimes encounters the distinction between those who regard themselves as historians of a particular religious tradition, and thus in that sense specialists, and those who see themselves as phenomenologists of religion, or generalists. The question has often been raised whether there is a religious studies "approach" or "method" (or better, group of approaches or methods) characteristic of the field, providing some sense of its boundaries and establishing its core (cf. chap. 2.4.3 above). A specialist of a particular religious tradition might have the closest professional associations, not with colleagues in religious studies, but with scholars from cognate fields working in that same tradition. Someone, for instance, who teaches courses in the religions of Japan might affiliate more closely with experts in Japanese language and history than with colleagues in religious studies. A scholar teaching courses in Judaism as an historical, political, or social phenomenon might have but little interest in its specifically religious (or "spiritual") dimensions. Alternatively, someone trained in, say, Buddhism in a graduate department of religious studies might be a comparativist who could handle large parts of an introductory course in world religions or teach thematic courses relating to several religious traditions. Here, once again (see chaps. 4.2.3 and 5.1 above), the nature of the graduate education scholars bring to their profession raises the issue of the place within religious studies of those whose own intellectual and academic formation was in some other area.

Occasionally the links between graduate training and one's present teaching and research are shaped by the vicissitudes of career development. Here one thinks not only of personal and family commitments and age, but more of opportunities for employment and for continuing study beyond the doctorate. Someone who received the doctorate in the 1950s would likely have shifted more than someone whose graduate work was done in the 1970s or 1980s. Further, a person who at an early stage of a career helped to establish a new department might devote much time and energy to its administration and development, to the detriment of their own growth as a scholar and teacher. Such a person might have relatively few publications a decade or two later, especially in comparison with junior colleagues who joined an established department at a point where there was greater emphasis on research (cf. chap. 3.1.3 above.). A tight employment market might also provide a young Ph.D. with the opportunity for post-doctoral work and with it the opportunity to acquire more academic breadth and flexibility, or at least more research and publications.

Overall, the various interviews suggest that scholars in religious studies remain conscious of the connections between their own graduate school training and their present teaching and research. They consistently demonstrate a responsible awareness of how they have moved and changed. Many could document precisely the shifts in their interests, approaches, and thinking and could correlate those shifts with changing demands on them within their institutions or with changes within their own fields. For some, the development of new subfields in religious studies, for example, women and religion or native religions, meant having to teach in areas they had not formally studied in graduate school. For many — perhaps most — shifts and changes in interests resulted simply from the necessities of keeping abreast of current thinking in their own area, and in religious studies generally. This could be no more than a normal aspect of career development. Still, there were, inevitably, concerns expressed about individuals becoming too fragmented, being spread too thinly across many fields (perhaps as the result of changing teaching assignments), to the extent that their research and teaching lack direction and focus. Deans — and especially perhaps graduate deans — seemed more positive about the work of a scholar who had a specific area of expertise than about a person whose work proceeded on several fronts.

Perhaps an even greater concern than a change in direction is the absence of any change, sometimes signalled in the claim to be teaching, some years later, exactly in the areas one had studied in graduate school. What of those who stated that they had not moved at all, and were teaching exactly in the areas in which they themselves had studied? Frequently one suspects that the scholar who claims not to have changed in method or area is the academically stagnant individual. One of the strongest claims to continuity from graduate study to present teaching came from a religious studies professor who reportedly was spending significant time in private business enterprises and who, colleagues suggested, had lost interest in the academic study of religion. Considering the multi-disciplinary character and relative newness of departments of religious studies, stagnation may not loom large as an occupational hazard, notwithstanding Ralph Waldo Emerson's comment in *Self-Reliance*: "A foolish consistency is the hobgoblin of little minds, adored by little statesmen and philosophers and divines." Few of the divines (or their academic successors) interviewed were obsessed with "a foolish consistency" in regard to their own development academically.

Considering the last two decades, probably it would be fair to say that the degree of continuity between graduate school and teaching in religious studies is about the same as that in other areas of the humanities. In other academic fields as well there have been shifts in interest on the part of faculty and students; and in other fields, too, some professors are teaching more or less the same courses today that they did in 1970. Perhaps as a recently developing field religious studies has been better placed to take account of and adjust to these new areas. (For discussion of how curricula in religious studies have changed, see chap. 8 below.)

6.2 Aims in Teaching

The differentiation of "aims" in teaching from "methodologies" in teaching (the subject of the next section) rests largely on a distinction of "ends" from "means," of principles and purposes from procedures. Sometimes departmental materials specify the understanding of the academic study of religion within an institution, perhaps indicating as well how teaching aims and methods within the department are shaped by that understanding. It is difficult, of course, to judge whether stated aims are being carried out in practice, either throughout the curriculum or by an individual faculty member (whose personal agenda might not coincide with departmental aims). The investigation of the aims governing the teaching of religious studies in a particular department was conducted in several ways, therefore. In addition to consulting materials published and distributed by departments in which goals were set down, we asked in our interviews of faculty members how the role of the professor in religious studies was understood in relation to that of professors in other departments of the university, or how they saw their own role within the department, or whether they would teach their courses differently if they were offering them within the context of a theological college. This procedure helped to build up a picture of how particular individuals saw their task, both in relation to their department and in comparison with the theological college professor. While this method provides both general (or institutional) as well as individual reflections on the goals in the teaching of religious studies, there will understandably be some overlap here with the discussion of "perceptions" of religious studies from those within the field (see chap. 3.2 above).

A departmental handbook of programmes and courses from the University of Waterloo endorses six goals set forth by the Canadian Society for the Study of Religion on the academic pursuit of religious studies, including such matters as factual and objective teaching, the use of various methodologies, the encouragement of intellectual honesty, developing the capacity to express one's own convictions in an informed and responsible manner, respect for the religious convictions of others, and development of research in the academic study of religion. In a similar vein, the Graduate Student Handbook prepared by the religious studies department at McMaster University states that the goal of the graduate programme "might be expressed by reference to three habits":

> openness both to the great religious traditions and to modern resources and methods of understanding them; independence of judgment, which bespeaks a critical mind; and reflection by which one who is critical within a particular horizon learns to become critical also of that selfsame horizon (1982-83, 1).

At the University of Toronto a handbook prepared for undergraduates indicates that, while there are a number of ways in which religions can be studied, the department "identifies itself with a model in which the major religious traditions (e.g. Buddhism, Christianity, Hinduism, Islam, Judaism) are studied within the context of comparative study," using a variety of approaches and methods (Handbook, 1987-88, 4).

The approach at the University of Ottawa to the study of religions is clearly and consciously set forth in the calendar, on posters, and elsewhere. The statement reads in part:

> The orientation of the Department of Religious Studies is that of the "Science of Religions" or Religionswissenschaft. The Department thus pursues the study of the religious phenomenon through teaching and research in the same manner and on the same level as any other category of facts accessible to human experience and observation.

It is explained further that the chief disciplines employed in religious studies are "of a historical, sociological and psychological nature." (In another statement "literary studies" are added to the list.) Further, the approach is "multidisciplinary" and "the Department does not consider any tradition as normative." McMaster's Graduate Student Handbook is similarly explicit, though alluding to the North American context of religious studies rather than to European methods:

> The Department as such has no confessional ties, nor does it aim at providing a theological education. It does not systematically presuppose a divine revelation. It is allied, rather, with those pioneer programmes established for the most part in contemporary North America, which set their sights on understanding religion and religious experience from the related standpoints of philosophy, history and the social sciences (1).

Frequently, as in this statement, a department of religious studies might consciously differentiate itself from theological studies, often reflecting its own history or the continuing proximity of a theological college. In other contexts, though, there is no hesitation in affirming the place of theology within religious studies. The head of one church-related college complained that religious studies was too much like a social science, treating religion empirically without being open to the dimension of faith. On that particular campus, it was argued, the church-related colleges had a distinctive role, and were looked to for leadership. This individual wondered whether academic freedom allowed one to be a person of faith, declaring that this dimension was important for people being hired in religious studies in that particular college — though only after their c.v.s and research records passed muster (cf. Welch, 1971, 193 and chap. 3.1.1 above). A similar view is expressed in some of the materials from Ottawa's Saint Paul University, an institution which also offers undergraduate courses toward a degree, though in theology rather than religious studies. The St. Paul's calendar (1985-86, 5) declares its awareness of "its special mission and possibilities," referring to factors which "contribute to the quality of the academic training and the Christian culture which it endeavours to guarantee."

Occasionally, the approach to the academic study of religion means a deliberate alignment with the social sciences, though it may be difficult to find what in practice that identification amounts to. Invoking social-scientific methods may simply be a way of declaring the "objectivity" of the study of religion in its concentration on the human aspects of religious phenomena. Yet, in spite of an occasional avowal of a "social-scientific" approach to the study of religion, religious studies is almost always conducted in the context of the study of humanities rather than of the social sciences. Even when situated in a social-sciences division of a university, that alignment seems not to make much practical difference in the way religious studies is conducted. One faculty member, clarifying the terminology of a department that represents itself as studying religion from a social-scientific standpoint, explained that there "social-scientific" simply meant "not theological," as if these were the (only) two approaches available. To say that you were studying religion "scientifically" meant that you were *not* studying it "theologically."

At one institution a senior member of the religious studies department had seen the milieu change, over 25 years, from an earlier confessional approach within a church-related institution to the present situation of the academic study of religion in a provincially funded university. The school's church affiliation had formerly meant a confessional or "theological" approach. Now the department's approach to teaching religious studies was characterized as "objective," and his own teaching, for instance, as "comparative and historical." At another university, one with no theological college on campus, someone commented similarly on changes from the 1960s, under the leadership of some academic clergy who founded the department, to the present: there was a shift from an early "sense of mission," with "theological objectives," to more "academic" aims today. Further, faculty here agreed that their teaching in religious studies was no different from that in other departments, or at least, "not really different."

One faculty member with experience teaching in both university religious studies departments and in theological colleges separates the two tasks according to their differing responsibilities. In a university setting the task is to advance the understanding of the human enterprise and to develop the student's intellect, whereas in theology Christianity has to be taken with radical seriousness, along with the Christian commitment of the students and their orientation to professional ministry. In such a situation, while recognizing that complete objectivity is impossible, students must learn to be self-conscious about their own biasses, understanding why one remains a Christian and accepting the role of doubt in criticism.

Sometimes faculty at institutions with no theological college on campus stated that their teaching would be no different if they were in a theological college rather than a religious studies department. (Except one said it would be more "existential," while another thought that the requirements of a faith test or of character formation in theological colleges created a different context of instruction.) Perhaps religious studies faculty lacking actual experience in a theological college would claim there was no difference in principle between teaching in either setting. Often that claim was based on the view that teaching should always be "objective" whatever the context. In a few cases, however, some of these instructors in religious studies maintained that the task was identical in either context because they themselves wanted to incorporate the dimension of faith into the academic study of religion.

In several instances it appeared that the backgrounds and requirements of the students determined to some extent what the aims in teaching religious studies were (see chap. 4.1 above). One religious studies department tried to take account of the fact that a majority of the students came from Roman Catholic families. These students had had required courses in religion in secondary school that led them to expect that religious studies would be boring, moralistic, and irrelevant to their concerns and careers. Elsewhere a faculty member suggested that theological students' professional aspirations and attitudes differentiated the approach of a theological college from that in a religious studies department: because theological students are being educated for a particular professional role in society one does not try to "stimulate their imaginations or get them to ask questions" (an interesting view of professions, one might add). Another said that theological college teaching, in contrast to teaching in religious studies, would require more student-tailored projects of a pastoral nature. One professor of theology, asked if undergraduate religious studies prepared students for theological studies, said the main benefit of such studies was that students "asked adult questions about religion" (cf. chap. 3.3 above).

Some religious studies departments deliberately address the relationship between the student's religious faith and the academic study of religion. A University of Waterloo publicity folder appears to assume that students are religious, speaking of the opportunity afforded them "to learn about religious beliefs other than their own," while the departmental handbook (1987-88, 5) states that "Our goal is not to destroy individual conviction and faith, but to deepen understanding so that whatever faith the student has can be enriched." At Queen's University, where the Theological College provides the staff for the department of religious studies, the College's calendar states that "the academic study of religion is independent of any specific doctrine or confessional commitment, and none is required of either teachers or students" (2). Yet this statement is not very different from the description of the school of theology as "ecumenical and pluralistic," where "everyone interested in theological study, with or without a professional or personal religious commmitment, is welcome in the community" (ibid.). A departmental brochure, *Studying Religion at Queen's*, asks, "Who studies religion?," and declares in partial answer: "Certainly not just the 'religious'!" A little further on, the same publication acknowledges that "many students accept no religion at all."

One professor perceived religious studies as differing from academic domains such as the natural sciences, where he believed competences, skills, and the field generally to be well defined, while in religious studies there is a wider spectrum of concerns and interests, some of these coming from students. Whereas this individual thought that an historian, for example, can be almost totally descriptive, a religious studies professor would have to be concerned with meaning. Thus, a successful course gets the student to like the subject, know the issues, and learn where to go to get material.

Some departmental materials set the academic study of religion in the context of the humanities or of a liberal arts education. For instance, the *Supplemental Calendar* of York University's religious studies programme begins with the observation that "religious experience is one of the master keys to the understanding of human behaviour and thought." At Laurentian University a brochure from the University of Sudbury discusses the nature of religious experience as the response to fundamental questions of the kind engaged by religious studies, confronting people "in search of meaning." Religious studies, then, attempts to "introduce the student to the method of analysis and the formation required to effectively pursue that search." Questions about the role of the student's religious commitments in the study of religion, and whether that ought to be addressed or considered or otherwise taken account of in a university classroom, touches upon a central and ongoing debate within the academic study of religion (cf. chaps. 3.2.3 and 4.1.1 above).

At some institutions the department of religious studies is consciously oriented in the direction of teaching, regarded as more important than research. One heard remarks about being a "teaching department," or, sometimes, a "service department," referring to the role of the department within the institution to provide elective courses for students from other departments and faculties. Especially where few students were taking a major in religious studies, offset by large numbers of students taking one or two courses in religious studies as electives, teaching would get a lot of attention, particularly in the designing and delivering of courses to serve as electives. In a situation where the religious studies courses provide the major basis of funding support for a church-related college, attracting students into classes becomes a matter of survival. In some places the department of religious studies appeared to have a strong role in providing courses off-campus, by television or correspondence ("distance education"), in summer school, or during the evening.

While the goals governing the teaching of religious studies courses in a particular department may be in part determined by its history, the relationship to a particular context, the clientele, and the training of the faculty, departmental literature at the same time manifests a high degree of awareness of the nature of the field. Frequently statements about methods and approaches to religious studies are carefully worked out, reflecting either a good deal of discussion within the department about such matters, a grasp of how these issues are addressed at learned society meetings or in books and academic journals, or the need to clarify the aims of religious studies in a manner appropriate to an academic context.

6.3   Teaching Methods

Given the autonomy of professors (perhaps a correlate of the cultivation of independent habits of mind), the methods employed in the study of religion, and in the teaching of courses in religious studies, derive more from individuals' preferences than from an institutional stance. In a typical department — even one where all of the members had offices in the same building or on the same corridor — a plurality of methods is employed, with little discussion or exchange about such matters except in an occasional colloquium. While a particular department often cannot be characterized as to approach, except in the broadest and most general terms (e.g., "non-confessional"), individual professors are usually exact about their own methods.

One individual, admittedly "methodologically oriented," achieved a high degree of precision in self-description: "a comparative phenomenological approach to the theology of religions." Another, a philosopher of religion, employed what was termed an "evolutionary" understanding of religion, differentiated from a biological, sociological, or phenomenological understanding. A third was able to chart three phases of development in his study and teaching of religion, from an initial use of structuralism and phenomenology, to structuralism, to the present method of bringing a philosophical approach to religious phenomena. This last approach, which asks what a particular mythology is saying, reportedly takes religious phenomena with greater seriousness than the previous two, since a mythology is not prejudged on the basis of a particular theory.

But even given a highly developed methodological precision, professors did not always exemplify their own theoretical approach in their teaching or endeavour to impart it to students. A few faculty members felt it was a mistake to advocate or demonstrate one specific method, especially in their own undergraduate teaching. Some made the point that discussing methods was less valuable than training students in the use of methods. Their teaching, rather than focussing on second-order methodological reflection, might demonstrate, through example, how various methods could be used on particular materials. Even apart from courses dealing specifically with methods employed in the academic study of religion, some professors used a course in an area such as Bible (for instance) as the occasion to survey a wide range of possible approaches to the biblical materials for the sake of enabling students to learn something of the multiple interpretations of the text available. One person made the point that talk about method "turns students off." Others spoke of "playing by ear," leaving themselves room to adapt to the needs of the students.

The nature of a subject area within religious studies, its own characteristic methods, or the instructor's graduate school training might determine the approach used in teaching. When asked about their own methods, religious studies faculty frequently invoked the name of someone they had studied with, or otherwise admired. One person's method was modelled on the work of Mircea Eliade; another spelled out a "history-of-religions" approach following Ninian Smart and R. C. Zaehner. Someone trained in philosophy might use a philosophical method; in the social sciences, a social-scientific; in history, an historical; and so on. Otherwise, the nature of the material being taught in a particular course might suggest a particular method: one professor employed a phenomenological and historical method when teaching world religions, a more philosophical and epistemological approach for a course on mysticism, and a more descriptive one for Buddhism. Or, the concerns and level of students being taught may determine the approach to be used. One professor endeavoured to have beginning undergraduates address fundamental questions about human life ("philo-sophical questions"), while at a more advanced level and with majors the approach was that of systematic theology understood as an academic disci-pline.

In some departments a broad spectrum of approaches, sometimes a repre-sentation in miniature of what one would find at the Canadian Society for the Study of Religion or the American Academy of Religion, appears within a group of just a few colleagues. One individual, attempting to look at other religious traditions empathically, endeavours to be objective, comparative, and multi-disiplinary, studying a variety of phenomena to see how a tradi-tion defines itself. Down the hall, meanwhile, is a biblical scholar whose methodological self-description results in the claim to be "historical-critical without exception." A third's teaching is "philosophical, especially with regard to the nature of religious knowledge." This last person mentioned the interesting dimensions epistemology takes on when seen from a Bud-dhist point of view, perhaps affecting the student in a way similar to anthro-pology or the sociology of knowledge, where examination of another's worldview, shown to be informed or conditioned by social and cultural milieu and ideological bias, frequently becomes the impetus for self-criti-cism about one's own Western assumptions. These three individuals, inter-viewed from a random selection within a single department, are typical of what one finds in religious studies with respect to method in teaching: each was clear about what was being done in terms of method, and yet together their respective approaches suggest diversity rather than uniformity.

One professor spoke of a departmental split between those who regarded themselves as historians of a particular religious tradition and those who looked at religion more generally, from a phenomenological point of view. While such a division has been commented on already from another per-spective (6.1 above), here it might be ventured that those most attuned to methodological questions are likely to come from among the phenomenolo-gists of religion. Questions of method in religious studies are perhaps con-sidered least pertinent by those whose teaching is principally in the area of languages, some of whom described their work as enabling students in the straightforward task of language acquisition. Though acquiring a language can become no more than an end in itself, the same instructors usually teach other courses in which the languages are in fact used. They frequently exhibit considerable concern about teaching methods in their courses, even if they may be less interested in pedagogical questions pertaining to other subfields in religious studies.

In one department the breadth of methods is represented at one extreme by a biblical scholar whose approach to the texts is quite narrowly defined as exegetical. A colleague in the same area puts such textual study in a much larger context, bringing in political, economic, and social factors. A third colleague, again having primary training in the biblical area, now mostly does social ethics using that background. Further along the spectrum one finds a more methodologically self-conscious scholar whose work draws upon a social-scientific discipline such as anthropology, relating this to the study of religion. And at the furthest extremity is a generalist whose teaching is principally thematic and dialogical, engaging the implicit (rather than explicit) religious aspects of secular culture.

While many professors want to emphasize that the teaching of religious studies in the university should be "critical" or "objective" or "academic" rather than "apologetic" — stressing that they were teaching "about" religion rather than "teaching religion" — others react to such an approach when it became too critical, or else felt that teaching should be constructive rather than critical in a destructive sense. Not only recognizing the possibility of bias in themselves, they felt it necessary to offer an approach different from that of colleagues in, say, philosophy or psychology where a negative or sceptical view of religion prevailed. While not necessarily apologetic, their approach to the study of religion would be more sympathetic, seeing religious world views as viable or legitimate. For some, this approach was a deliberate attempt to take seriously the concerns of students, many of whom are self-consciously religious.

Typically, individuals described their teaching methods in religious studies courses as involving a "phenomenological" or "historical" or "literary-critical" or "comparative" or "history-of-religions" (*Religionswissenschaft*) approach. One department chair commented that the teaching in the department followed a "standard humanities model." Some faculty were more precise: one claimed to use a "history-of-ideas" approach; another was characterized as a philosopher-theologian using a psychological approach. At other times individuals were able to chart, in remarkable detail, the methodological shifts they had gone through in their teaching. However, there was not always a common understanding of what these terms meant; for instance, people who maintained their method was that of the psychology of religion did not always appear to be doing similar things. Frequently these differing understandings of what was at the cutting edge of a particular subfield within religious studies emerged when individuals were asked to comment on the recent developments in their area.

Teaching methods employed by religious studies faculty thus vary considerably. Whether this variation was according to the background and training of the individual scholars, or due to the nature of the subject matter of the subfield within religious studies, or in keeping with the level and concerns of the students, professors we interviewed generally displayed a high degree of awareness about their own methods. In religious studies, as in other university departments in the social sciences and humanities, there is a diversity of teaching methods and occasional (sometimes frequent) methodological disputes. One can imagine a similar variety of methods of teaching and learning exhibited in a typical history or English department as well.

An important distinction in religious studies, in contrast to other departments, comes from the relationship of the student or professor to the subject being studied, namely, religious traditions, practices, beliefs, myths, and symbols. Generally it was taken for granted that teaching in religious studies is to be non-confessional, pluralistic, and "objective." Similarly, students we interviewed all seem to be distinctly aware of the differences between religious studies and "theology" (especially as related to ecclesiastical and personal issues), that is, between discourse on religion and discourse at the service of faith (cf. chap. 4.1.2 above). They often resent the intrusion of confessional concerns in a class discussion when some of the participants are committed Christians who do not adopt the "objective" perspective of religious studies.

While there are differences as to whether a course is better taught by an "insider" or an "outsider," there is a consensus that students should be acquainted with a variety of methods. Many students speak positively of the freedom they have in exploring other religions or investigating their own in other ways than the traditional ones. It is a requirement of Ph.D. students at the Centre for Religious Studies at the University of Toronto, for example, that they select courses such that they work "with more than one method of study" (Handbook, p. 9). A diversity of approaches within a department was in general not only tolerated, but considered to be a desirable thing.

6.4 Course Loads

The traditional course load for teachers of undergraduates in Ontario universities was three courses extending over the entire academic year, each meeting for three hour-long periods per week. In some undergraduate departments, the old pattern of three full courses per academic year (the equivalent of three half-courses in each of two terms) still prevails. At some institutions, though, the teaching load has been reduced from three to two-and-one-half courses, often to compensate for increasing class sizes with attendant heavier work loads. In a graduate department the nominal teaching load might be reduced from three to two-and-one-half courses in recognition of faculty research or the directed study courses or thesis supervision provided by faculty to graduate students. Another variation is in the amount of the "contact time" in a particular course: a class might meet for only two hours (rather than three) each week. In some cases, both in religious studies and in other departments, new faculty may have a reduced teaching load for the first one or two years in recognition of the heavy course preparation they face.

In at least one university, where the faculty in the department of religious studies was reduced in numbers by one-third over a period of several years, the trend toward a reduction in teaching hours has been reversed. There, the teaching load increased from two-and-a-half courses to three. Usually the number of courses taught is reduced by one or two for those having major administrative duties within the department. At some places, though the practice still appears to be rare, faculty may apply for a course remission to enable them to have more time for a research project. With very few exceptions the normal practice is for an instructor to teach between two and three courses in an academic year.

The exceptions to this norm are worth noting. At one Roman Catholic theological college with high expectations for faculty research, the teaching load consists of one course per year, plus thesis supervision. The normal theological college pattern appears to be less standardized than that in religious studies departments. In some theological colleges where small classes are the rule two or two-and-a-half courses appear to be a normal load. In theological colleges where in the 1960s faculty might have taught up to five year-long courses the load has been reduced to three, perhaps in conformity with the practice in universities. At the other extreme might be a church-related college participating in a joint religious studies department. There, maintaining enrolments becomes essential for funding purposes because the provincial Basic Income Unit (BIU) depends on enrolment. When such a college is heavily involved in teaching off-campus (distance education) and in summer school, faculty may teach ''overload'' courses (i.e., for an additional stipend rather than as a part of their usual teaching assignment) both to maintain enrolments at their institution and to compensate for low salaries. One individual reported having taught between four and five courses each year for a period of seven years.

Teaching loads are both difficult to compare and difficult to measure. How does one compare the workload of someone lecturing to two sections of more than 100 students each in a large introductory undergraduate course, where the marking and tutorial work may be provided by markers or teaching assistants, with someone giving a graduate seminar in his or her specialty to two or three students? Which is more demanding, to prepare a formal lecture to be delivered to a class, or to preside over a seminar in which papers are delivered by students each week? Some courses might have a very labour-intensive style of pedagogy requiring a great deal of work from a conscientious professor, whereas instructors who are especially demanding may be blessed in return with small classes. Again, someone teaching a course in a language might have (or do) very little preparation for classes, whereas someone teaching a course in contemporary issues might have to do extensive reading in order to design the course or select textbooks and other readings each year.

6.5   Creative Approaches

In interviews at various campuses individual faculty members were asked if they or their colleagues were using any new or creative approaches to their teaching. To ensure that a such activities within a department were covered, department heads were asked a similar question. This part of the study had as its focus pedagogy, a skill, it is often alleged, neglected at the level of university teaching (see chap. 9.2.2.3).

Some departmental administrators, faculty, and students interviewed suggested that good teaching is more important in departments of religious studies than elsewhere because of its humanistic context, perhaps with a concomitant ''person-centred'' approach. Alternatively, because many faculty had themselves studied to be members of the clergy, they are likely to have had training and experience in communication in public. In one religious studies department two faculty, both members of the clergy, had received their university's outstanding teaching award. Even given a change in emphasis in many Ontario universities from undergraduate teaching to research, many departments resist such a trend, or claim to continue to emphasize high-quality teaching while increasing efforts in the area of research.

Issues related to pedagogy have long occupied religious studies scholars (e.g., Johnson, 1973; Chernus and Linenthal, 1984). At the annual meetings of the American Academy of Religion a section devoted to ''Academic Teaching and Study of Religion'' attracts wide interest. Diversity and divergences characterize these various discussions, so that generalizations about teaching methods in religious studies are bound to be precarious. For example, at a panel on ''Helping New Colleagues in Teaching'' convened at a recent AAR annual meeting, one of the authors of this study gave a presentation entitled ''Old Tricks for New Dogs'' and discovered that some of the other ''old dogs'' on the panel came from different kennels than he did, while some of the ''new colleagues'' were performing in arenas where his ''old tricks'' might not apply.

Within courses in religious studies were there any new ventures representing departures from the traditional classroom format of lectures and seminars, or evaluation by other means than the writing of essays or examinations? Among the trends repeated from one institution to another were an increasing use of audio-video materials, especially slides and films, but also more frequent use of overhead projectors; provision for field trips to visit religious communities, or to study buildings or ritual space, or for other purposes; adaptation to student needs in courses once underway through active consultation with members of the class; the use of comparative approaches in thematic courses; more team-teaching, especially in courses such as those using specialists from both East and West; teaching methods such as role-playing, learning cells, and laboratory work to encourage more active learning on the part of students.

Some of the creative approaches used in the teaching of religious studies derive from the nature of the field itself. Increasingly, religious studies faculty are convinced of the necessity of being comparative in their work in thematic courses. Thus, courses such as Death and Dying, Ethics, Sacred Space, Myth and Symbol are today more likely to be cross-cultural, including materials from different religious traditions, rather than staying solely within Western traditions or restricted to Christianity, as was commonly the case previously. While a comparative approach might not lead inevitably to creativity, it at least raises questions about what is to be compared and how that comparison is to be done. Related to these questions of method, issues involving the selection of texts and the presentation of material will come into play.

In the same vein, professors have become increasingly aware that the study of religions entails studying behaviour and practice, and not just thought (cf. chaps. 2.4.9 above and 12.8.1 below). The result has been that they draw on the resources of such traditional collateral disciplines as philosophy, history, and literature, as well as more recent allies in sociology, anthropology, art, and music. The social sciences have proved useful in facilitating access to people's behaviour in rituals and other religious practices as central to what happens in their religious lives. While the basic medium of education within the university continues to be the book, new approaches have become necessary within religious studies as the object of such studies has become broader.

Not just prehistoric religions, but all manner of contemporary indigenous religions (or the religions of native or nonliterate peoples) have demanded of scholars oriented towards texts that they find new approaches. Within a classroom setting, then, faculty report a greater use of art and ritual objects, field trips to museums or art galleries (e.g., in courses in religion and art) or sacred sites (and in courses in archaeology, to the Middle East or China), an emphasis upon the visual (perhaps resulting in something so simple as more use of overheads), participant/observer methods in the study of New Religious Movements, and in all a generally more active, "hands-on" approach to learning. Even the use of films such as the BBC series *The Long Search* in courses in world religions attests to how much of religion is conveyed through symbols and images beyond discursive thought. The study of the religions of India might employ cuisine, dance, art, music, and architecture, as well as history and textual study. In the study of ritual, laboratory work provides fresh insights both for teachers and students.

Some scholars in Ontario have worked hard at developing films and video tapes for educational purposes in religious studies. Such efforts have ranged from making instructional films for distance education (perhaps involving no more than videotaped lectures), to the use of interview materials with experts and authors and religious leaders, all the way to the production of films on specific traditions of a calibre intended for public distribution. The interests of individuals have sometimes led to these developments; otherwise, some institutions have become heavily involved in off-campus instruction and distance education employing video cassettes for home learning or television courses. It appears, in keeping with its occasional role as a service department, that religious studies has become active in such ventures where they exist. Many departments report involvement in extension courses, in evening programmes, and in work with mature and part-time students. One professor was developing computer software for use in a course in world religions, and biblical scholars have been using computers in language instruction and the study of texts for some time now.

While lectures and seminars, essays and examinations undoubtedly still prevail in university classes in religious studies, even these age-old methods have their modern variations. The take-home exam is regularly used, perhaps combining the best (or worst) aspects of the essay and the examination. Some faculty have experimented with oral exams as an alternative to the usual written format. In lieu of essays, students have sometimes been encouraged to maintain "learning journals," or to write a series of short papers or book reviews as an alternative to a single lengthy research paper. Student involvement in courses ranges from prepared group presentations to courses based on self-directed study.

Classroom instruction has sometimes made use of a question-and-answer, tutorial-style format, occasionally involving students in leading the tutorial discussions. Various means of using teaching assistants (TAs) were reported, from giving the TA complete charge of one or more lectures, or a segment of a course, to having students select questions to be addressed, while using the TA as a resource person. At a few institutions attention had been given to helping faculty develop teaching skills, by establishing a teaching resource centre, or giving workshops on teaching methods. Regrettably, though, few graduate students reported being given much help or direction in equipping themselves for their role as teachers (cf. chap. 9.2.2.3 below). However, in one instance, a young faculty member had taken the initiative and enrolled in courses in teaching methods and skills while still in graduate school.

Some courses in religious studies stress the importance of a personal or an experiential approach, usually when the subject was something like religion and psychology (e.g., on dreams) or ritual studies (where a lab course was used; cf. chap. 2.4.9 above). Several spoke of employing a case-study method in their teaching, using the approach as developed through the Association of Theological Schools summer workshops, including at least one held in Toronto. Originally developed for use in business, medicine, law, and social work courses, the case method has been extended to ethics, philosophy, Bible, and theology as "a teaching method [that] encourages creative dialogue between theological reflection and real life situations," to quote from an advertisement for a May 1988 workshop held in Toronto. Others employed role-playing (in one example, one student was a reporter from a European newspaper questioning another playing the role of Wellhausen). Perhaps because of the proximity of a theological school, or the influence of theological education's field-work model, occasionally one saw various instances of an "action-reflection" approach to learning gaining ground. One could also reasonably speculate that approaches to learning regarded as distinctively feminist and anti-patriarchal will become more influential.

At one institution, "learning cells," an approach developed at McGill University, were being used (see Milne and Crowley, 1984). It requires students to prepare questions on assigned material in advance of a class period. In the class itself students in "learning cells" composed of two or three students discuss these questions, with provision at the end for each group to report. The approach requires a high degree of involvement from students and great demands on the instructor — more for either party than the usual seminar discussion — and accordingly has met some resistance. It is reportedly suited better to more advanced instruction than to beginning-level classes. In the study of ritual, fieldwork projects provide fresh insights for both teachers and students, with data gathered through interviews, tape-recorded oral histories, and the methods of participant-observer study, and engaging such varied topics as funeral rites and wedding customs, near-death experiences, aspects of contemporary popular culture, diverse processes in play and education, and the adaptation of certain religious groups (or individuals) to crises in their lives.

The overall picture of creative approaches to teaching in religious studies, then, differs from that in other humanities subjects in its greater use of interdisciplinary resources, an emphasis on experiential involvement, a focus on behaviour as well as on thought, and employment of learning methods from other fields of study.

7

Faculty: Research and Publication

William Closson James

7.1　What Is "Research"?

Respondents to a survey conducted by the Canadian Federation for the Humanities reported that between May 1985 and April 1986 they spent 28% of their time in research (as compared with 46.9% in teaching, including preparation; 14% in administration within the university and 5.7% outside; and 5.4% in thesis supervision) (CFH, 1987a, 10). Presumably faculty in Ontario departments of religious studies are occupied in research to about the same extent (i.e., more than one-quarter of their time) as their colleagues in other fields within humanities across the country. In fact, among the 1,095 scholars responding to the CFH survey 92 of them, or 8.4%, were from religious studies. Universities tend to value research highly, considering that the formula used for evaluating faculty for promotion, tenure, or merit-pay increases typically involves a scale in which an individual's workload is considered to be 40% teaching, 40% research, and 20% administration. The CFH survey, which suggests a division more like 50-30-20 than the common 40-40-20 formula, indicates that in practice academics in the humanities spend more time on activities related to teaching and less on those connected with research.

The nature of research in religious studies does not differ greatly from that in other areas of the humanities and social sciences. The exception might be, once again, in certain understandings of the responsibility of theology — and specifically within the context of theological or church-related colleges — to an ecclesiastical body. Perhaps such a distinction as that made in the sciences between "pure" and "applied" research might be useful, when applied research refers to work done under contract to an outside

191

agency. By analogy the "applied" research in theology (and less frequently in religious studies) might be work done for a religious institution, for instance, when professors prepare documents for church commissions or sit on task forces.

Still, the questions arise: Exactly what is academic research? And, when is one doing it? Reading related specifically to course preparation would normally be considered to be time devoted to teaching rather than research. But what about reading a book or article in an area common to both teaching and research yet without the reading being specifically geared toward either activity? If academic reading is not directly related either to a course being taught or a book, article, or paper being prepared, is it part of research or teaching responsibilities? At institutions where undergraduate teaching is considered of primary importance some scholars in our survey considered as "research" many of the activities related to course preparation, even to the extent of including in their curriculum vitae under the heading of "Publications" the manuals they prepared for use in correspondence versions of courses. Within theological colleges some professors counted as research and publications their work on church committees resulting in briefs or position papers or leading to the publication of study guides for laity.

One of the familiar distinctions between the two main tasks of the university, teaching and research, has it that teaching involves the transmission of knowledge whereas research involves the discovery of new knowledge (see this distinction as reflected in the titles of chapters two and three of the Quebec volume for this state-of-the-art review on the study of religion in Canada: "La transmission du savoir" and "De nouvelles connaissances," in Rousseau and Despland, 1988). But many scholars in religious studies might find it pretentious to describe what they do in their research activities as the "discovery" of new knowledge, especially if what they hope for, for example, is to shed some new light on an ancient text. Many have complained that such an understanding of research makes normative within religious studies an understanding of the meaning of research derived from the natural sciences. Some humanities scholars find that for colleagues from other divisions of the university what really counts as "research" is work done under grant or contract for an outside agency: that is, funded research comes to be regarded as the only legitimate research activity (see 7.2 below).

Perhaps a more useful determination of a research-related (as distinct from a teaching-related) activity is to consider the audience to which it is directed. Thus, one might decide whether a book or article is an academic publication by using the criterion of its intended or actual readership (a test used to some extent in deciding which books and articles were to be counted from c.v.s submitted for this study). Clearly an academic work deriving from research is one adjudicated by peers and intended for an audience of one's peers. An academic paper delivered in the context of a learned society meeting can thus be distinguished from a talk to a high school graduation class, an address to a group of professionals in a related field, or a lecture in a series sponsored by a church. Lectures and writings addressed to audiences other than one's peers are more akin to forms of teaching (where the speaker is assumed to be more knowledgeable than those addressed) than to presentation of the results of one's research.

Of course, such distinctions are not capable of settling all questions about the work's importance or quality, nor about the amount of effort entailed in producing it. A scholar in religious studies might labour hard over an hour-long lecture in biomedical ethics to be delivered before health-care professionals who might not share the same assumptions and methods and approach as the speaker. That assignment would be considerably more demanding than a twenty-minute paper read to a half-dozen people at one of a number of concurrent sessions of a regional meeting or workshop of a learned society. Stepping outside the boundaries of one's own field, or presenting research to scholars in cognate disciplines, might require more plain hard work than the preparation of a paper for delivery before peers in one's own area.

Another problem arises in the evaluation of the relative worth of different kinds of research. In several institutions it appeared that a department head might judge there were a half-dozen strong researchers in the department of religious studies whereas the dean of the faculty might comment there were only two or three (cf. chap. 3.1.3 above). Sometimes, when a disparity was evident, the tendency was for the department to rate itself more highly than the dean. Frequently, these differences occurred because a graduate dean, for instance, especially one from the sciences, might consider the most valid kind of research endeavour to be that supported by outside grants. Alternatively, someone who had published in many different areas was sometimes regarded as suspect, especially in comparison with a specialist whose expertise was recognized within a fairly restricted field of research. Generally, to command a relatively small area seemed to be prized more highly, especially in the view of those outside religious studies, than to have ventured into several areas.

In a typical case, a department of six to eight members, there might be two or three individuals widely recognized as strong researchers and excellent scholars in their areas. Another two or three individuals might be seen as average to good, or else the usefulness and validity of their work would be difficult to assess, while the remaining two or three would be poor or weak to average. Those at the extremes may be identified readily and with little dissent; those in the middle group are more problematic in that their work might be well known within religious studies or in the context of learned societies meetings, but little known outside the field. But probably similar comments could be made of the members of almost any department in a university.

The field of religious studies, then, shares with other fields in the humanities many of the difficulties of deciding what research is, how much time is or should be devoted to it, and assessing its worth. Drawing on interviews and on documents submitted by faculty, the remainder of this chapter will focus on resources for research, changes in scholarly productivity and emphases, new directions for research, and the role of learned societies.

7.2   Financial Resources for Research

John Thorp, Executive Director for the Canadian Federation for the Humanities, summed up the disparity in research budgets when university professors in humanities and social sciences are compared with their colleagues in the natural sciences:

> On average, 80-90% of professors in experimental sciences apply for research grants, and 70% of those who apply get them; in the humanities and social sciences roughly 10% apply for grants, and only 50% of those who apply are successful in getting them. In other words a humanities professor with a research grant is a relative rarity; a science professor with a research grant is the norm. The research expenses of hard scientists are paid by the federal government; the research expenses of humanists are, for the most part, paid out of the humanist's pocket, or out of university funds (Thorp, 1989, 1).

This pattern for the financial support of research in the humanities at large is evident also within the field of religious studies: research is funded chiefly by the individual or by the university. Our examination of the financial resources for research will therefore focus principally on the immediate context of the universities and departments in which religious studies scholars do their research work and on which they rely for most of their support (other than their own pockets or purses).

The availability of internal sources for research grants and professional development expenses varied from one institution to another, but were uniformly important everywhere. The 1986 CFH survey of scholars in humanities cited earlier showed that 705 of 765 respondents who had sought research funding between 1983 and 1986 applied to their own university or faculty (including applications for the Social Sciences and Humanities Research Council's General Research Grants of up to $2500 administered by the university). About half of those surveyed (51.7%) had not applied to SSHRC for funding during the three-year period. Of these, 60.8% indicated, among other reasons why they had not applied, that they were able to carry on their research without funding (CFH, 1987a, 11-12). In several interviews conducted for the present study scholars similarly stated that their research was not of a kind requiring funding in order to be carried out.

At some institutions professors could apply to their dean or the university's research office for financial support for research, while at others the department head was provided with funds for distribution among the faculty in that department. Elsewhere, monies might be available to members of a religious studies department from an endowment, or from a connection with (for example) an affiliated college having its own funds apart from the university. Here individuals sometimes benefitted from joint appointments between religious studies departments and theological colleges, or other kinds of appointments that in effect made the resources of two affiliated institutions available to them.

Research needs have become more diverse in the past decade or two. Not so long ago the major (and perhaps sole) financial support for research from within one's own institution came in the form of a travel grant to a scholarly conference, often requiring that a paper be presented. But travel has become more expensive, while at the same time the number of conferences available offer greater opportunities for scholarly meetings. There are also other demands upon research funds. Field trips, travel to other libraries, equipment such as microcomputers and specialized software, long-distance telephone calls, typing and word-processing (or other forms of keyboarding and inputting where computers are used), photocopying, membership fees for learned societies, books, journal subscriptions, and research assistants – all these require funds.

Beyond the usual secretarial support for typing or word-processing and provision for telephone calls and photocopying, financial support additional to salaries still consists at a few institutions only of travel grants for attendance at scholarly conferences, often contingent upon the presentation of a paper, chairing a session, or being an executive member of a learned society. This requirement has sometimes resulted in individuals' seeking by almost any means to have their names appear on the programme for a meeting in order to have their travel expenses paid. As might be imagined, some have given papers more often than they should have, or importuned a programme organizer to be allowed to preside at a session. In one conference planning session it was announced, with regret that things were set up this way, that anyone needing to have their name on the programme to get a travel grant should be allowed the first chance to chair a session.

The policy of one institution where only $250 annually is allowed for conference travel contingent upon participation in the meeting in some substantial way was termed ''stupid'' by one professor who found such meagre support inadequate and the requirement for participation an extraneous demand. At the other end of the spectrum was a department where it is possible to receive up to $2000 annually for conference travel without any requirement to give a paper. This more generous provision was possible because of the availability of departmental funds in addition to those provided through the faculty.

While at least in one institution the amount available for travel to meetings and conferences had not increased substantially in fifteen years (e.g., the $400 which could provide up to three trips in 1975 might barely cover the expenses of one short trip in the 1990s), there appears to be a trend toward other funds for ''professional expenses.'' In addition to the usual travel allowances, individuals might be reimbursed $500 or more for such expenses as additional travel (e.g., for research), equipment, books, membership dues, subscriptions, research and secretarial assistance, and supplies.

The CFH survey on research needs asked Canadian scholars in humanities to what extent they subsidized their own research. Two-thirds (64%) of the respondents had spent more than $250 annually on scholarly books and journals for which they were not reimbursed, while more than half had spent at least that amount on conference attendance from their own pockets. And 60% had spent more than $250 on travel and living expenses related to research for which they were not reimbursed. About half the respondents had spent up to $250 of their own money in each of three additional areas — phone calls, professional memberships, and photocopying and microfilming.

While many faculty in religious studies may be able to conduct research without large grants, clearly a majority are subsidizing their own research, whether in small amounts related to individual book purchases or subscriptions or phone calls, or in large sums for the purchase of a microcomputer. People outside the academic world are frequently surprised to learn that academics often purchase their own equipment, such as microcomputers — though sometimes with special arrangements with their own institutions — for use in their university offices in the conduct of their daily work. Recently some faculty have had a part of their salary from the university paid to them in the form of a tax-free research grant from which they could deduct expenses such as those mentioned above.

Generally, greater diversity has appeared in the kinds of research funding available, especially as contrasted with the older standard travel grant. Institutions have provided professional expense allowances as well as internal research grants in small amounts for initiatory research, grants toward the publication of books and journals, stipends for student assistance, and funds for typing, proofreading, and editing.

7.3   Administrative Support of Research Time

In most institutions the typical major provision for time for research is the sabbatical leave. Usually available every seventh year, at a salary reduced to 75%-80% of the normal full salary, the sabbatical provides an opportunity for academics to devote themselves to research on a full-time basis, away from teaching and administrative duties. Church-related colleges have moved toward the university model for sabbaticals, though in such settings the leave is still sometimes seen as a time for refreshment, a change of venue and opportunity for reading or pursuing new directions, rather than for the completion of a specific project in research and writing with an eye to publication. A similar understanding of the purpose of the sabbatical leave was sometimes evident also within theological colleges.

In most places the sabbatical is granted upon application, dependent on approval of a proposed project, though such approval seems usually to be a routine matter. There were few instances reported in which sabbatical leave applications were turned down, though occasionally the leave had to be deferred because a number of individuals within a department were eligible to apply at about the same time. Most institutions reported that faculty members were taking their sabbatical leaves as soon as they were eligible and in rotation, so that there was not a backlog of applicants.

Several new developments came to light in interviews with professors and department heads about sabbatical leaves. One was the provision for a half-sabbatical (i.e., a leave of six months' duration), available after six years of teaching and at full salary, or after three years at reduced salary. This possibility has become popular with the increased number of "half" courses (i.e., a single term in length), as opposed to "full" courses extending from September to April (see chap. 8.2 below). Alternatively, it was sometimes possible to take a half-sabbatical at reduced salary, to be followed by an additional half-sabbatical after another year or so – in effect splitting the normal twelve months' leave in two. The half-sabbatical is useful when projects could be completed in the abbreviated time, or when family or other responsibilies did not allow for a year's leave at once.

Making personal arrangements for a sabbatical appears to be an increased difficulty for many. For couples where both partners are employed outside the home, but where just one is an academic, it is frequently difficult for both to relocate for a year (let alone the financial difficulties of getting by on reduced salary at a time when living expenses are bound to be higher and now that SSHRC leave fellowships have been eliminated). One would expect that among a middle-aged faculty with teenage children (or responsibilities for elderly parents) relocating is difficult. For these reasons, and especially in centres where library resources are good, sabbatical leaves spent "at home" (i.e., without relocating to another place) seem to have become more popular.

Flexible arrangements were evident at some universities where by various means scholars could extend the length of the leave, either to a period greater than a calendar year for a full sabbatical or to a full year for a half-sabbatical. Usually such arrangements involved doing extra teaching before or after the leave (for instance, teaching a spring- or summer-term course without additional stipend, or teaching more than the usual number of courses in a regular term). At other places, delaying the sabbatical leave beyond the initial point of eligibility meant increased financial support, so that if one waited as long as, say, ten years it might be possible to have a year's leave at full salary. At other institutions, however, delaying one's sabbatical meant simply that: eligibility years were lost, and fewer sabbaticals in the course of one's career was the net result.

Several institutions had provisions for the remission of one or more courses from a teaching load in order to devote more time to research.

Usually such arrangements were by application to the faculty dean and/or the research dean. Reportedly, competition was stiff for course remission for research, and while many had applied, very few were successful. Elsewhere it was reported that by informal arrangements courses could be scheduled in flexible ways over three terms to meet writing commitments, so that a professor might teach two courses (four half-courses) in the fall and winter and one (two half-courses) in the spring or summer to make up a three-course (six half-course) annual teaching load.

7.4   Publication and Scholarly Productivity

The Canadian Federation for the Humanities' national survey of research in humanities (CFH, 1987a) shows the number of "outputs" (i.e., publications and the presentation of papers) per researcher between May 1983 and May 1986. The most common form of output among humanists in Canada is the presentation of a paper, averaging slightly over one per year, with book reviews and refereed articles following close behind. The average humanist produces a book approximately every five years. The most frequent forms of publication over that three-year period, excerpted from the CFH explanatory table, are as follows for humanists in Canada:

Table 7-1
Average Research Output in the Humanities
in Canada, 1983-86*

Rank	Type of Production	Number in 3 Years
1st	Presentations of papers	3.81
2nd	Scholarly book reviews	3.04
3rd	Refereed journal articles	2.61
4th	Chapters in books	0.86
5th	Non-refereed journal articles	0.84
6th	Books	0.65

* Source: CFH, 1987a, 17

The assessment of scholarly productivity among professors of religious studies in Ontario done for our study is not strictly comparable to the CFH survey, having been conducted on a somewhat different basis. Whereas the CFH used a questionnaire sent to a random sample of humanists and covering a three-year period of research output, we extracted the information from c.v.s sent in by professors, evaluating and counting the outputs as reported in the c.v.s and covering their entire careers, which averaged fifteen years (see chap. 5.1.1 above). Where the c.v. did not contain the required information, a follow-up letter with a specific request for the missing data was sent (for instance, not everyone initially reported papers presented [see App. A below]).

The items included in our analysis of research and publications also differed from the CFH survey. We did not count book reviews; for our statistical purposes we reckoned a chapter in a book as the equivalent of a journal article; we attempted to differentiate between a paper presented in the context of a learned society meeting (i.e., for a peer audience) and a lecture that might be considered a form of teaching (and therefore was not counted for our study as a paper presentation); and rather than differentiating between refereed and non-refereed journal articles — because the evaluation process differs from one journal to another ("refereed" does not necessarily mean two or more readers' reports, for instance) — we attempted to assess an article's significance on the basis of its length and whether it was published in a recognized academic journal. By this measure, a 500-word meditation in an ecclesiastical publication would be excluded, though its author might include it as a "refereed journal article" in response to a questionnaire on the grounds that the publication's editor had not automatically published it, but made some evaluation of its worth.

While this process was laborious (students, whose work was checked by one of the three co-authors, were employed), the results are both stricter and more uniform than a questionnaire which asks individuals to conduct a kind of self-evaluation and report their outputs. While virtually every academic in Ontario has a curriculum vitae prepared and available when required, the form and content of these c.v.s vary widely, even within the same institution. Indeed, departments of religious studies might consider employing a standard form for the curriculum vitae throughout the province, perhaps following the model required by the Ontario Council on Graduate Studies for appraisal purposes.

The book is generally considered to be the most significant, though it is also the least frequent, form of academic output. Table 7-2 shows the total number of books published during their careers — once again, averaging fifteen years — by professors of religious studies and theology in Ontario.

An American survey of 5,000 faculty members found that 60% of them had never published or edited a book in their field (Hacker, 1986, 38). That would be true of nearly a fourth (23%) of the religious studies faculty (and over a third [36%] of the theological faculty) whose c.v.s we examined. About three out of four (70%) of the religious studies faculty had published between one and six books, while less than one in ten (7%) had published more than that. Two out of three (67%) of religious studies faculty had published a maximum of two books in their careers (once again, an average of fifteen years), while in theological colleges about nine out of ten faculty (87%) had no more than two to their credit.

We also examined c.v.s of Ontario religious studies faculty to see how many articles they had published during their scholarly careers. Again, theological college faculty are listed for comparative purposes. The results are summarized in Table 7-3.

Table 7-2
**Number of Books Published by Ontario Faculty in
Religious Studies and Theology: Career Totals**

Number of Books	Religious Studies		Theological College		All	Total Group
N	N	%	N	%	N	%
0	37	(23)	36	(36)	73	28
1	34	(21)	33	(33)	67	25
2	39	(24)	18	(18)	57	22
3	17	(10)	3	(3)	20	8
4	14	(9)	4	(4)	18	7
5	8	(5)	1	(1)	9	3
6	3	(2)	1	(1)	4	2
>6	12	(7)	4	(4)	16	6
Totals	164	(101)*	100	(100)	264	101*

* Rounding off to nearest whole number results in percentages
greater than 100.

Table 7-3
**Number of Articles Published by Ontario Faculty in
Religious Studies and Theology: Career Totals**

Number of Articles	Religious Studies		Theological Colleges		All	Total Group
N	N	%	N	%	N	%
0	9	(5)	13	(12)	22	8
1	14	(8)	10	(9)	24	8
2	15	(8)	13	(12)	28	10
3	13	(7)	13	(12)	26	9
4	12	(7)	8	(7)	20	7
5	13	(7)	7	(6)	20	7
6	10	(6)	3	(3)	13	4
7	9	(5)	3	(3)	12	4
8	6	(3)	7	(6)	13	4
9	9	(5)	3	(3)	12	4
10	10	(6)	1	(1)	11	4
>10	59	(33)	29	(26)	88	30
Totals	179	(100)	110	(100)	289	99*

* Rounding off to nearest whole number results in a percentage
less than 100.

At first glance, Ontario religious studies professors do not appear to be as
productive in publication of book chapters and journal articles as are the
humanities faculty surveyed by the Canadian Federation for the Humanities.
The average humanist in Canada was publishing the equivalent of about one
article per year in the three-year period surveyed (see Table 7-1). Our statis-

tics show that about one out of four (28%) of Ontario religious studies faculty had not produced more than three articles in their entire careers (for professors in theological colleges the ratio is almost one out of two [45%]). Only a third of Ontario religious studies faculty had produced more than ten scholarly articles in their careers.

An explanation of the apparent disparity between the productivity of religious studies faculty and humanities faculty in general may lie in the widespread increased productivity of the last few years, as compared with fifteen or twenty years ago. Among faculty in religious studies in Quebec, average annual scholarly production in all areas tripled in the ten years following 1972, from less than one output per year to almost two (Rousseau and Despland, 1988, 80). Our examination of the number of papers—the only form of scholarly production where our data allowed us to trace change in productivity over time—presented by Ontario religious studies faculty during roughly the same period (i.e., from the early 1970s to the early 1980s) showed a marked increase in individuals' scholarly output (see Table 7-4 below).

In the CFH's national survey of Canadian humanities scholars to which we have been referring it was found that the average number of paper presentations was 3.80 during the three-year period (an average of 1.27 per year). Again, it should be pointed out that these statistics were self-reported, whereas our count would exclude items that some individuals might consider to be valid paper presentations. Further, it might be reasonable to surmise that the CFH return rate of 42.7% includes a higher proportion of productive scholars, whereas our count included everyone who submitted a c.v., productive or not. (The perhaps unwarranted assumption is that those who voluntarily respond to a survey questionnaire are more likely to be those who have something to report.) We endeavoured to involve department chairs in encouraging their faculty's participation in our study, which probably contributed significantly to the very high response rate in our study (see App. A below).

Table 7-4 shows the number of papers presented by half-decade, from 1970 to 1984. This time, we counted only those individuals whose c.v. showed they had presented at least one paper; thus, there is no column for no papers presented. (Individuals not counted, then, may be either those who did not present a paper, those for whom we did not have a c.v., or those whose c.v. provided no information on papers presented.)

These statistics show, among other things, how productivity has increased from the early 1970s to the mid-1980s. One immediately notices how the percentage of individuals presenting only one paper during a five-year period steadily decreases, while the percentage of those presenting more than five papers increases. In the 1970-74 quinquennium 50 religious studies faculty presented 135 papers, an average of 2.7 per person. By the second half of the 1970s this figure had increased to 3.33 per person, with 87 individuals presenting 290 papers. In the 1980-85 quinquennium, the aver-

Table 7-4
Number of Papers Presented by Ontario Faculty in
Religious Studies and Theology,
by Half-Decades, 1970-84

Half-Decade	Number of Papers	Religious Studies	Theological Colleges	All	Total Group %
1970-74	1	16	5	21	36.8
	2	13	2	15	26.3
	3	12	0	12	21.1
	4	3	0	3	5.3
	5	2	0	2	3.5
	>5	4	0	4	7.0
1975-79	1	20	12	32	30.5
	2	14	2	16	15.2
	3	20	3	23	21.9
	4	10	1	11	10.5
	5	10	0	10	9.5
	>5	13	0	13	12.4
1980-84	1	19	16	35	25.5
	2	26	5	31	22.6
	3	20	2	22	16.1
	4	10	2	12	8.8
	5	7	2	9	6.6
	>5	25	3	28	20.4

age rose slightly, to 3.73 per person, with 107 religious studies faculty presenting 399 papers. In the first half of the 1980s, then, among faculty presenting papers the average per year was 0.75, still short of the CFH average of 1.27, though supporting our hypothesis of greater scholarly productivity in all areas (including books and journal articles) by the 1980s.

In the space of ten years, as well, clearly the overall participation rate of religious studies faculty is increasing, along with individual productivity. By "participation rate" we mean the proportion of scholars who presented a paper during a particular half-decade. It is worth noting that in this same period participation among theological college faculty increased at a greater rate than among religious studies faculty. In the first half of the 1970s only seven faculty from theological colleges presented papers, compared with 57 religious studies faculty. Ten years later, in the first half of the 1980s, 30 theological college faculty had presented papers, compared with 107 religious studies faculty. In other words, among those presenting scholarly papers, the participation of theological college faculty in this period increased from 10.9% of the total group to 21.9%, probably indicative of an increased emphasis on research and scholarship within theological colleges, as well as the hiring of new faculty trained in that mode.

Looking at the age profile of those presenting papers at scholarly conferences, one sees that in the first half of the 1980s a higher proportion of persons born between 1940 and 1944 presented papers: that is, faculty members in their early forties were about twice as likely to have read a paper as faculty in their early sixties (i.e., those born between 1920 and 1925). The next most active group in the first half of the 1980s, though small in numbers, was comprised of scholars in their early thirties, while those in their late thirties and those in their late forties were roughly comparable.

The presentation of papers by women might also be compared with that by men (in this case taking religious studies faculty and theological faculty together because of the small numbers of women involved). In the first half of the 1980s the participation rate of women scholars — again, the proportion of persons presenting papers, not the number of papers per person — was approximately the same as that of men. Sixteen women presented 47 papers (2.9 per person in the five-year period), compared with 500 papers presented by 115 men (4.4 per person). But if we set aside one man with the prodigious output of 80 papers (the next highest person presented 12 papers, while three men and one woman presented 11 each), the rate for the remaining group averages 3.7 papers per male scholar.

A look at the previous quinquennium reveals how markedly scholarly activity by women increased in the 1980s, especially when one compares the numbers of women participating in the presentation of scholarly papers. Between 1975 and 1979 only three women faculty in Ontario in religious studies and theology had presented papers: one presented four, the second presented six, and the third presented ten; the last woman exceeded the output of any man in the five-year period. In spite of the small sample involved, it is worth noting that each of these three women averaged 1.3 papers per year, at a time when the overall average for men and women taken together was 0.6 papers per year. (See, further, chap. 5.1.1.1 above on women in religious studies.)

Comparison of the number of articles, papers, and books prepared by one group of scholars with another is a difficult task, and it would be risky to generalize overmuch about the scholarly output of Ontario religious studies faculty as compared with humanists in Canada. As we have indicated above, the group being studied, and the method of selecting it, differ, as do the way "outputs" are counted and the period of time covered. These factors are bound to skew the results in varying degrees. Just as hazardous would be a close comparison with Quebec colleagues in religious studies, although we have noticed general trends. Here, especially, the avenues open for publication — and the areas of religious studies in which francophone publications are publishable — would make a difference in the number of books and articles produced, as would the research environment of the Quebec universities as compared with those in Ontario. Too many additional variables enter in here, complicating a picture already characterized by variables.

Some mention should be made too of opportunities for research and publication, and especially for the publication of research. Though it was not an area of questioning we systematically pursued, few, if any, Ontario faculty members interviewed complained of a lack of avenues for the publication of their research, though some did complain that the learned societies were not selective enough in screening papers to be presented at meetings (see chaps. 3.2.5 above and 7.7 below). It would appear that Ontario faculty find at least adequate opportunity to submit their articles for publication through existing journals in the field. Neither are they complaining about difficulties in placing book manuscripts with publishers. The existence of at least four major university presses in Ontario, as well as commercial publishing houses — to say nothing of the opportunities world-wide for scholarly publication — seems to afford ample means of publication.

7.5   Research Areas and Emphases; Methodologies

The information gathered from Ontario religious studies and theology faculty enables us to construct a comprehensive picture of the fields of research activity, which ones are popular and widely studied, and which ones are neglected. We sought categories for areas of research that researchers would find appropriate to describe their work. The categories were developed from those used in *Religious Studies Review* (see chap. 1 above), a review quarterly in religious studies published by the Council of Societies for the Study of Religion (on the Research and Teaching Inventory see, further, App. A below). They are a cross between the theoretical (i.e., how religious studies might or should be conceived) and the functional (i.e., how departments are commonly structured and how religious faculty commonly describe themselves and order their libraries). In addition, on the Inventory we supplied blank spaces, encouraging individuals to describe their major areas of research "in the terms that you customarily use." This method allowed a comparison of the terminology for categories of research as used by the researchers themselves with the terms supplied on the Inventory. In examining responses we soon became aware that the most frequently cited area of research for the "Other" category was "Women and Religion" (or something equivalent). Even considering that *Religious Studies Review* and some feminist scholars deliberately avoid such a category so as not to "ghettoize" feminist scholarship, its omission from our Inventory deprived us of an opportunity for useful statistical comparison with research in other fields of religious studies.

The responses of 189 individuals in Ontario religious studies departments who completed the Research and Teaching Inventory indicate that 20 (10.6% of the total group) reported that "Texts: Interpretation & Hermeneutics" was their primary area of research. Another 19 (10.1%) reported "Christian origins" as their primary area, while 9 (4.8%) reported "Ancient Near Eastern Religions." If, as seems likely, "Texts: Interpretation & Hermeneutics'' includes a fair, perhaps a preponderant number of biblical scholars, then these three groups taken together might be considered to comprise the researchers in biblical studies, totalling one quarter of the religious studies respondents. And if researchers in ''Psychology of Religion'' and ''Sociology of Religion'' are grouped together in the category ''Social-Scientific Study of Religion'' their numbers equal the religious studies faculty reporting ''Theology'' as their primary research area (that is, 15 individuals, or about 8% of the group). The next most popular area of primary research is ''History of Christianity'' (14 individuals, or 7%), while 12 individuals listed ''Ethics'' as their primary area of research, and 10 listed ''Philosophy of Religion.'' None of the other areas of research was reported as a primary area by as many as ten scholars. The responses for ''secondary area of research'' are similar, especially in those areas most often reported as primary research fields: Theology, Texts: Interpretation and Hermeneutics, and History of Christianity draw the largest number of researchers.

Table 7-5 gives a tabulation of the responses for the primary and secondary research areas, indicating whether the researcher is situated in a department of religious studies or a theological college. The order of the categories given here is identical with that on the Research and Teaching Inventory.

When faculty in religious studies and theological colleges are considered as a group, the strong concentration of research in Theology stands out. Theology was selected as the primary or secondary area of research by 85 individuals, or more than a quarter (26.3%) of the 318 respondents (since no one – it is hoped! – would have listed the same category for both primary and secondary research). As might be expected, those doing research in Theology who are based in theological schools (51 individuals) outnumber those in religious studies (33 individuals).

Looking at another category, Texts: Interpretation and Hermeneutics, 63 persons (almost 20% of the respondents) selected this as either a primary or secondary research area; this time, however, they were more equally balanced numerically between religious studies departments and theological colleges (32 to 31; cf. Table 7-6 below). A similar pattern is discernible in the next most frequently ''named'' areas (i.e., putting aside the ''Other'' category) – Ethics, Christian Origins, and History of Christianity – where researchers indicating one of these three as a primary or secondary area of research are fairly evenly divided between religious studies and theology.

Not surprisingly, given the distinctive natures of theological colleges and religious studies departments and programmes the research being done by professors in theological colleges is concentrated in a relatively small number of areas as compared with religious studies professors. Thus, in each of the five or six most frequently chosen research areas (see Tables 7-5 and 7-6) the numbers of theological college researchers are about the same as those in religious studies even though the theological professors are fewer

Table 7-5
Primary and Secondary Areas of Research
for Ontario Faculty in Religious Studies and Theology

	Primary		Secondary	
	R.S. Dept.	Theol. College	R.S. Dept.	Theol. College
Areas of Research	N	N	N	N
Methodology and Theory	7	5	6	5
Comparative Studies	6	0	11	0
Phenomenology of Religion	0	1	4	0
Ritual, Cult, Worship	1	8	3	3
Psychology of Religion	7	3	3	1
Sociology of Religion	8	0	3	2
Philosophy of Religion	10	2	9	4
Theology	15	29	18	22
Ethics	12	14	9	4
Religion, Literature, & the Arts	7	2	11	5
Texts: Interpretation & Hermeneutics	20	18	12	13
Ancient Near Eastern Religions	9	3	6	1
Greece, Rome, Graeco-Roman Period	5	0	9	0
Christian Origins	19	7	4	8
History of Christianity	14	10	10	14
History of Judaism	9	0	8	3
Islam	2	1	3	0
Africa	1	0	1	0
The Americas	1	0	5	2
Central Asia	1	0	0	0
South & Southeast Asia	6	0	4	1
East Asia	3	0	1	2
Buddhism	2	0	2	0
Practical/Pastoral	1	13	1	8
Other	18	9	12	7

(less than 40% of the two groups taken together). Their concentration in a relatively small number of areas as compared with religious studies professors is seen also when one notes that these 125 theological college professors selected only 15 (out of 25) areas of primary research whereas the 189 religious studies researchers were spread over 24 different areas. This pattern is less pronounced in areas of secondary research, where religious studies faculty are found working in all 25 possible areas, whereas theological researchers now increase their coverage to 19 areas.

Table 7-6 shows, in descending order in the left-hand column, the most common areas of research activity among faculty in religious studies in Ontario universities, combining reported areas of primary and secondary areas of research (e.g., the first line in the first column shows that 16% of the Ontario faculty in religious studies indicated that Theology was either their primary or secondary area of research activity). The responses from faculty in theological colleges and from the entire group studied are placed in the middle and right-hand columns respectively, an arrangement allowing comparison of the most frequently chosen research areas.

Table 7-6*
Ranking of Combined Primary and Secondary Research Areas for Ontario Faculty in Religious Studies and Theology

	Religious Studies %	Theological Studies %	Total Group %
Theology	16.0	40.8	26.8
Texts: Interp. & Hermeneutics	15.3	24.8	19.7
History of Christianity	12.9	19.2	15.4
Ethics	10.4	14.4	12.6
Religion, Literature, & the Arts	10.4	5.6	7.9
Comparative Studies	10.4	0	5.4
Christian Origins	9.8	12.0	11.9
Philosophy of Religion	9.8	4.8	7.9
History of Judaism	9.2	2.4	6.3
Ancient Near Eastern Religions	8.6	3.2	6.0
Methodology & Theory	6.8	8.0	7.2

* So as to give a clearer picture of the most frequently chosen areas of research specifically in religious studies, the 26 individuals holding a joint appointment in both a religious studies department and a theological college are not included in this table.

The ranking of these areas of research depends, of course, on the categories employed, and if and how they are grouped together. For instance, Psychology of Religion and Sociology of Religion are offered as separate options under the heading ''Social-Scientific Study of Religion'' in the ''Research and Teaching Inventory.'' But had we considered Social-Scientific Study of Religion a separate category including the psychology and sociology of religion, we could have reported that 12.3% of religious studies scholars in Ontario are doing research in this area, which would have moved it up to fourth place in Table 7-6, just behind History of Christianity.

Some comment, too, is in order about areas of research not appearing among the most frequently reported categories. Apart from Judaism, religions other than Christianity seem not to be attracting much research. To begin with, the number of persons teaching and doing research in those religious traditions is very small in comparison with those working in Western religious traditions, especially Christianity. It follows that the number of persons doing research in religions other than Christianity will also be small. For instance, only six scholars in the province report as a primary research area ''South and Southeast Asia'' (though it is listed as a secondary area of research by another six). We might also consider together the six categories comprising religious traditions other than Christianity and Judaism: Islam, Africa, The Americas, Central Asia, South and Southeast Asia, East Asia, and Buddhism. A total of 19 individuals report one of these categories as a primary research area. Twenty-two individuals (probably some of whom have a primary research area in another of those six categories) report one of these six categories as a secondary research area. Looked at another way, more than 10% of scholars in religious studies are conducting their primary research in other religious traditions than Christianity or Judaism, while more than 10% find their secondary area of research outside Christianity and Judaism. (An exception might be the category entitled ''The Americas,'' chosen by nine people, which might include Amerindian Religion or New Religious Movements in North America, but could also include American Protestantism or Religion in Canada with the major emphasis on Western Christianity.) Still, it is at least disappointing to discover that of 318 scholars in religious studies and theology in Ontario, only six report research in Islam as either a primary or secondary area, only four are doing research in Buddhism, only six in East Asia, only two in Africa, and two in Central Asia.

(See, further, 7.6 and chap. 2.4.6 and 2.4.7 above and chap. 8 below; the directories of departments and faculty published by the Council of Societies for the Study of Religion also provide an indication of areas of specialization beside the name of each faculty member.)

7.6 Directions of Research

In interviews at various campuses we asked faculty members how they perceived the new directions of research in their field. The intention was to discover what trends were being reported in various areas of religious studies and, further, what individual scholars thought of these trends and their significance.

Reflecting on research generally, one scholar maintained that a methodological consensus has been reached in religious studies, having to do with the understanding of religious myths and symbols, and how to decode them. But another scholar maintained that research in religious studies is scattered—''everything goes.'' While not disputing the practicality of the grouping together of various areas within religious studies, this person wanted to see better delineation and more careful focus in some of the new directions of research. For what it might be worth, the first scholar is a self-described ''generalist,'' who does comparative and phenomenological work in several areas; the other's research is confined to a fairly specific area traditional among the disciplines within theological studies. A third scholar, whose view might be seen as a mediating one, regarded fragmentation in religious studies as an enduring phenomenon, and a problem especially evident in the Canadian learned societies, where there is a lack of a common

perception of a shared task. While such fragmentation might make it difficult for some historians and philosophers (for example) to work together in
some respects, joint projects in teaching and research might compensate for
this overall problem. Yet another individual confirmed this view of fragmentation within religious studies, suggesting that to some extent it was a
negative effect of the multiplicity of small societies within the Canadian
learned societies. Though smaller societies have their advantages — for
example, by allowing small groups of scholars to find a common forum for
their work — the narrowing of focus with a proliferation of smaller societies
may distort one's sense of the field as a whole. In such an event, it was suggested, one society may become dominant over the rest, or some kind of
integrative measure may become necessary.

Accurate generalization about directions of research in one of the subfields of religious studies is hard to come by when only a few scholars from
each of the fields were interviewed. Some fields were not represented at all
among those interviewed, and others by only a single individual. In what
follows these factors should be kept in mind.

In the more frequently represented areas, some consensus was often evident. In theology, for example, the most widely shared area of research (see
above), several people referred to the importance of the experiential, or of
images and stories, in many aspects of theological research. One theologian
spoke of narrative theology as a "new" direction — these temporal designa-
tions are of course relative: some would regard narrative theology as "old"
by now — replacing an older doctrinal theology, with a greater fluidity as the
psychodynamics of narrative experience command more attention. Other
specialists in theology reported their interest in process thought, White-
headian studies, and theodicy — not new areas, by any measure. One individual spoke of collaborative research among theologians as of developing
importance.

Several philosophers of religion were interviewed. When asked about
new directions, one replied that such directions were difficult to characterize
because philosophers of religion tended to work as individuals rather than
as a group (suggesting perhaps their isolation in contrast to the more public
role among theologians). Another — a senior scholar — remarked that the
philosophy of religion had lost the position of dominance it had a generation
ago as theology had become ascendant in the meantime. A third, in a
church-related college federated with a university, had become involved in
church and campus concerns to the neglect of research. These comments
suggest an area formerly central that has lately become less important, raising questions about the fate of those whose graduate school research loses
its relevance or centrality, or about the fragmentation of work that is widely
scattered. Perhaps a certain "critical mass" of scholars working in a common area, with shared methods and objectives and content, is necessary for
the health and growth of a field. One might hypothesize that without such
collegiality many scholars drift into other areas or find that their own

research, lacking the interest and support of colleagues, comes to be subjected to less scrutiny on the part of peers, with a resulting isolation.

The question arose whether there is a distinctively Canadian emphasis in the academic study of religion, perhaps resulting from the influence of such prominent scholars and teachers as Wilfred Cantwell Smith, Bernard Lonergan, George P. Grant, and Northrop Frye. Clearly the careers of many Ontario faculty members in religious studies have been influenced by one or another of these individuals, whether through their teaching or their writing. One scholar ventured the view that certain narrow linguistic or analytic concerns are not so evident in religious studies in Canada as they are elsewhere. Further, that scholars such as Grant, Frye, and McLuhan may have a distinctively Canadian perspective in their concern for the aspect of cultural crisis in modern society. Other suggestions about the effect of learned societies in their distinctive Canadian aspects also came up (see 7.7 below).

The "Research and Teaching Inventory" included this question: "Do your research and teaching interests relate directly to religion in Canada? If so, please indicate how." The responses to this question assisted the authors in preparing for interviews with faculty members (see App. A below). In addition, the responses revealed that about one-third of religious study faculty and slightly less than a quarter of theological college faculty gave an affirmative answer to the question. However, the responses to the second part of the question — "If so, please indicate how" — showed a wide range in the understanding of what it might mean for teaching or research to "relate directly" to the study of religion in Canada. At one end might be the researcher with a major project dealing directly with a Canadian topic; at the other might be someone who reported that in their teaching they sometimes made reference to Canadian examples. Perhaps the most that might be said with respect to the responses to the question is that a sizeable portion of the respondents regarded their teaching or research as relating directly to the study of religion in Canada.

Among theologians interviewed a number of names arose of figures whose work they saw as significant in contemporary research: Tracy, Lonergan, Rahner, Whitehead, Hartshorne, Teilhard de Chardin, Schillebeeckx, Congar. In addition to the study of the thought of particular individual theological thinkers, several suggested that one of the new directions of theology lay in its being combined with or applied to a cognate field. Others spoke of inter-religious dialogue, such as that between Buddhists and Christians, as a developing new area. One theological college professor said that a growing Christian ecumenism in the study of theology facilitated dialogue between Christians and persons from other traditions. Particularly in theological college settings one found the application of theology to ethics or to social action. One scholar, speaking of historical theology in particular, claimed that it alternated between stodginess and faddishness: for example, displaying interest in Heidegger, Gadamer, Marxism, reception aesthetics, deconstruction and post-structuralism, and new historicism.

While a few were concerned about the possibility that biblical scholarship was merely following fads, most expressed a highly positive view of the way biblical studies had moved ahead and grown on many fronts: structuralism, hermeneutics, reader response and literary criticism, semiotics, and the search for fundamental cultural codes in texts made accessible through cultural anthropology and sociological methods. In working on Hebrew Bible narratives and other ancient Near Eastern texts, for example, one biblical studies scholar in an Ontario religious studies department draws on the work of Claude Lévi-Strauss, A. J. Greimas, and Vladimir Propp. Another individual summarized the situation in biblical studies this way: the current dominant interest is the notion of social description of people and movements which has come into the field from sociology, psychology, and anthropology. Other biblical scholars suggested that the influence of literary-critical techniques had attracted greater numbers of scholars, while agreeing that sociology may have sparked the keenest intellectual interest.

Though some were concerned about the possibility of going overboard in the pursuit of these new areas – one older scholar lamented that the great era of biblical scholarship was past – those who were conversant with and themselves involved in such developments by and large gave them a positive evaluation. One biblical scholar who found such new directions interesting and viewed them positively nonetheless found that he had returned to more traditional approaches to biblical texts (such as canon, form, and function). Another pointed to the continuing significance of archaeological work as a cognate area for biblical scholarship. We noticed repeatedly, by the way, that an older scholar might understand a ''new'' direction to be anything that was not around twenty or thirty years ago whereas a younger scholar might characterize as ''old'' a movement that had been evident for more than six months.

As the older form-critical and historical-critical approaches to the biblical texts give way to newer methods of literary analysis or to the use of sociological approaches, one person pointed out that literary-critical methods approach the biblical text as text (though another cautioned that such an approach has pushed things too far, in effect making the editors of biblical materials into ''authors'' – by no means a new claim but, at present, representing quite a different understanding of the issues than structuralists, say, would have). Yet another, using a badly mixed metaphor, maintained that the structural analysis of Bible provided scholars with a ''new Archimedean point to avoid plowing the same old ground.'' The point, perhaps, is that after decades of biblical scholarship based on form and redaction criticism and historical-critical approaches to the text, to the point where the employment of such methods becomes hackneyed, repetitious, or limited, the field of biblical scholarship experiences great vitality today as new approaches have emerged and new questions are being asked. Further, the result has not necessarily been to take the student of Bible into remote or irrelevant areas:

as another person explained, the use of a sociology of religion unites theoretical and empirical concerns.

The study of biblical texts is an area common to both religious studies and theological colleges. But it was suggested by more than one biblical scholar that in their experience many of the new directions stem from the influence of religious studies on the study of biblical materials (cf. chap. 3.3 above). (Such an influence was also evident in an interview with a moral theologian whose research on Christian views of marriage, homosexuality, divorce, and the family showed the impact of working in a religious studies environment.) One New Testament scholar pointed out that being situated in a department of religious studies, with responsibility for some graduate teaching, had resulted in a broadening of interests to include the second century (still claimed, though, to be cognate to the person's earlier work in New Testament). The Canadian context with involvement in the Canadian Society of Biblical Studies seminar on anti-Judaism had influenced and even determined the direction of these new interests. In fact, many scholars quickly pointed out that it was their involvement in societies for biblical studies (either the CSBS or the Society of Biblical Literature) that had directed their research.

The large number of scholars working in the area of Bible and their collaborative efforts highlight trends that appear in other areas as well. Scholars working on the religions of India mentioned in interviews the movement away from textual studies to field work on popular religions, festivals, comparative biographies of religious figures, and, in general, to cultural and social history. For one scholar the social and political aspects of Hindu religion — that is, its role in practice — and not simply "beliefs" are what matter. For instance, the beauty and persuasiveness of the text of the Bhagavad Gita frequently obscures its premises in caste and society, with attending political and social consequences. One researcher was studying Bengali art, another was engaged in "vernacular-based studies," while a third was doing research on the untouchables in India.

Specific mention was made of new interest in the Tantric tradition and of the fact that good translations of Sanskrit texts facilitated work. One scholar maintained that in Ontario interest in South India is "quite alive," referring to the initiatives university departments of religious studies are taking in community relations, and of the presence of multiracial groups on every campus. In May 1987 a small outreach conference on South Asia was held so that Ontario educators could learn what materials existed for high schools and public schools. There appeared to be in Ontario universities an identifiable core of South Asian specialists, all known to each other.

In those fields and subfields where the numbers of specialists is small (as in this case [see 7.5 above]) and sprinkled among various departments and universities, maintaining contact among them is regarded as especially important. In another field, sociology of religion, a scholar remarked that colleagues in Ontario universities with a specialization in the area were "ninety percent identifiable" among themselves, most of them belonging to the Association for the Sociology of Religion, the American learned society publishing the journal *Sociological Analysis*. With few colleagues close to hand, and with a greater specialization of work in the sociology of religion, such inter-university contacts are essential to the health and progress of the area and to counter isolation.

The kind of commonality of interests claimed for sociologists of religion did not seem to exist among scholars whose work is in the psychology of religion. There one found that some scholars are interested in the therapeutic, in depth psychology, and in dream analysis. Others are working on myth and symbol or might have a philosophical interest in the findings of psychology, while still others are doing various kinds of empirical research or clinical psychology. Still others are looking at the development of personality or maturational stages as related to religious faith. Unlike sociologists of religion, many of whom have strong links with departments of sociology, psychologists of religion seemed not to have close connections with a cognate department, not only because of the disparateness of their own field, but sometimes because their university's department of psychology was primarily behaviouralist in its methodological orientation.

Again, thinking of the possibility of a community of scholars in a particular area having shared interests, one notes that some francophone researchers in Ontario universities indicated that the directions of their research were determined by, or shared in common with, francophone colleagues in Quebec rather than anglophones in Ontario. But one has the impression that many of the earlier initiatives among colleagues in universities in Ontario and Quebec — in which, for example, an Ontario anglophone might collaborate with a Quebec francophone in joint research projects, a faculty exchange, and the like — have been discontinued. This change is in keeping with a growing tendency to a growing isolation of anglophones and francophones from each other in the Canadian Society for the Study of Religion with the move away from the working policy developed in the 1960s and 1970s of "passive bilingualism" at the annual meeting (i.e., a CSSR/SCER member could speak in either French or English and be comprehended by someone whose native tongue was the other language). In the 1980s francophones mostly went to sessions with papers in French while anglophones listened to papers presented in English. Meanwhile, with only some exceptions, French-speaking executive members no longer address an executive meeting (or annual business meeting) in French only with the expectation of being comprehended by all. The culmination of these tendencies is the recent founding by Quebec religious studies scholars of a learned society of their own, separate from, though related to, the Canadian Society for the Study of Religion. (See, further, chap. 2.7 above.)

In several fields, though not enough scholars were interviewed to be able to generalize about directions of research with any confidence, one heard confirmation of the tendency elsewhere to move from exclusively textual studies to an examination of the social context of texts. One scholar conducting research in late antiquity mentioned an emphasis in his research on social change during the period. Another, studying Mesopotamian literature, was looking at legal practices as revealed in the texts, and not just legal codes. Several scholars in the area of Japanese history and religion spoke of the current relevance of their work as well as of increased research on Japan. Whereas scholars used to cover the whole of Japanese history in their research, it was pointed out that now the tendency is toward specialization directed at particular aspects of that history, using the resources of anthropology and sociology.

One professor summed up trends in several "dialogical" areas involving religion and culture — religion and myth, religion and architecture, religion and art, religion and literature — with the comment that although there is much general interest in such areas, there is little in the way of substantive scholarship being carried on. In these as in other areas, for instance, women and religion or religion and ritual, the presence of one strong Ontario researcher whose work had attracted attention, especially in the United States as well as in Canada, could greatly enhance the visibility of that area in the context of religious studies in Ontario. Even where a scholar's research is isolated from that of other scholars, perhaps due to its specialization, one became aware of the positive exemplary effects of that individual's high reputation on colleagues in a department, in the university, or, indeed, in the province. Specific names of scholars whose reputations were strong in areas as diverse as Samaritan studies, ritual studies, women and religion, and Amerindian religion came up from time to time.

As indicated above, there are not many professors in Ontario whose principal or secondary area of research is Islam. We were told that the "politicization" of Islamic studies, especially for those whose research is on Shi'ite Muslims, has meant that scholars unacceptable to, say, Iran have been unable to go there for research and archaeology. That has had a deterrent effect on some graduate students, as well as on women scholars, but especially on those whose research might have taken them to Iran. The effect has been to restrict at least some aspects of Islamic studies to "insiders," who voice the charge of "Orientalism" against outsiders (see chap. 2.4.6 above). For example, a scholar could not both question the historicity of the Qur'an and be seen as "sympathetic." Many Muslim students, furthermore, would never enrol in a religious studies course in Islam not taught by an insider. Thus, someone who relativizes the texts or tradition is unacceptable to many Muslims. On the other side, though, a revisionist historian who made Islamic history conform to an ideology would not be acceptable in a department of religious studies. While many of these observations have general application to the academic study of religion (and to the much vexed insider-outsider debate), here the point is that research directions in at least one area of religious studies have reportedly been curtailed or discouraged. (See, further, chap. 2.4.6 above.)

7.7   Role of Learned Societies

In interviews religious studies faculty members were asked about the role of learned societies in their own professional lives. What societies were important to them? Did they go to meetings, and, if so, which ones and for what purposes? What role did they see for the Canadian learned societies? The data entered in our database from faculty c.v.s allowed us to compare the relative membership numbers as distributed across eight of the learned societies (listed in Table 7-7 according to numbers of members), as well as to count the number of faculty in Ontario having memberships in more than one learned society (see Table 7-8 below).

Table 7-7
Learned Society Memberships of
Ontario Faculty in Religious Studies and Theology*

Learned Society	R.S. Dept.	Joint R.S./Theol.	Theol. College	All	%
Canadian Society for the Study of Religion (CSSR)	66	13	11	90	33.2
American Academy of Religion (AAR)	40	5	21	66	24.4
Canadian Society of Biblical Studies (CSBS)	23	9	15	47	17.3
Society of Biblical Literature (SBL)	19	6	13	38	14.0
Canadian Theological Society (CTS)	18	4	14	36	13.3
Société canadienne de théologie (SCT)	4	0	16	20	7.4
Canadian Society of Church History (CSCH)	6	0	5	11	4.1
Canadian Society of Patristic Studies (CSPS)	7	2	2	11	4.1
Other	183	24	129	336	
Totals	366	63	226	655	

* N=271; maximum of 3 societies entered for each person

Among Ontario religious studies faculty with learned society memberships, approximately one-half belong to more than three learned societies, Canadian and otherwise (the proportion is similar for those having a joint religious studies/theological college appointment). By contrast, less than one-third of theological college faculty belong to more than three societies. On an overall basis, of the 271 persons counted, about 40% of Ontario faculty in religious studies and theology belong to more than three learned societies.

Fully half of the learned society memberships are in "other" societies than the eight societies whose names we listed and specifically counted numbers for. (A maximum of three learned society memberships for each person—and notice that 111 persons [see Table 7-8] had more than three learned society memberships—were entered into the database, beginning with memberships in the eight societies shown in Table 7-7 above.) On the other hand, fully 70% of the group have at least one membership in one of the eight societies coded for the database.

Table 7-8
Number of Learned Society Memberships
of Ontario Faculty in Religious
Studies and Theology

One or more	271
Two or more	231
Three or more	171
Four or more	111

Looking specifically at Canadian learned societies, do Ontario faculty tend to have memberships in more than one of the six constituent societies in the Canadian Corporation for Studies in Religion/Corporation Canadienne des Sciences Religieuses (i.e., CSSR, CSBS, CTS, SCT, CSCH, and CSPS)? Not many do:

- 16 persons belong to both CSSR and CTS; 14 belong to both CSSR and CSBS; one belongs to both CSBS and CTS;
- 18 individuals belonging to one of the three other societies in the Canadian Corporation for Studies in Religion—either the Société Canadienne de Théologie, the Canadian Society of Church History, or the Canadian Society of Patristic Studies—also hold membership in one of the other five societies in the CCSR (nine of these 18 belong to at least three of the constituent societies);
- none of these three societies—SCT, CSCH, CSPS—has more than 20 members from among the entire population surveyed for this study.

On the one hand, membership in more than one society within the CCSR does not provide another journal subscription: all society members automatically receive *Studies in Religion/Sciences Religieuses* (*SR*) as part of their membership. On the other hand, to belong to a second constituent society within the CCSR does not cost very much either, since the subscription fee to *SR* is paid only once. And, most of the societies have their annual meetings concurrently with the annual learned societies conference on a Canadian university campus in late May or early June, making attendance at the meetings of, say, both CSSR and CSBS, or CTS and CSSR, an easy matter. The six constituent societies in the CCSR might consider making joint or multiple memberships by Canadian scholars in religious studies more attractive or easier (in the way that some societies now do by combined billing through Wilfrid Laurier University Press).

When one compares membership of religious studies and theology faculty in the CSSR with that in the AAR, or in the CSBS with that in the SBL, membership in the Canadian learned society in each case outstrips that in the American counterpart by 25% or more. Forty religious studies and theological faculty belong to both the CSSR and AAR (i.e., 44.4% of the Ontario faculty who belong to the CSSR are also members of the AAR). And, 24 persons belong to both the CSBS and the SBL (i.e., half the Ontario members of the CSBS also belong to the SBL).

Theological college faculty not only belong to fewer societies, but their memberships tend to be found to a greater extent within the eight societies on our list. These results generally accord with the greater diversity of research to be found among faculty in religious studies: one would expect as well a greater diversity in their learned society memberships in comparison with their colleagues in theology. Whereas almost a third (31.8%) of the province's AAR members are to be found in theological colleges, only 16.7% of the province's CSSR members are in theological colleges, probably because there is no American counterpart for the Canadian Theological Society, which draws about half its Ontario membership from theological college faculty. (Although membership in the Catholic Theological Society of America is not restricted to Roman Catholics or to Americans, its concerns and its annual meeting programme focus on Roman Catholic theology and issues current in Roman Catholicism that affect Roman Catholic theologians.) That is, theological college faculty seeking an American equivalent for the CTS (or its francophone counterpart, Société Canadienne de Théologie [SCT]) are likely to join the American Academy of Religion. Perhaps even more remarkable is the relatively low degree of CTS membership among faculty in theological colleges in Ontario: only 14 members were counted from all of the colleges surveyed, a number surpassed by the 20 theological college faculty who belong to the francophone Roman Catholic equivalent of the CTS, the SCT.

What do Ontario faculty in religious studies report about the role of learned societies in their professional lives? And do the Canadian societies have a distinctive role to play? The reaction to learned society meetings was varied, ranging from that of one religious studies professor in a small department, a member of three societies with service on at least one executive, for whom they are "the highlight of the year" to that of a productive senior scholar at a large university who belongs to only one society and who long ago decided not to attend learned society meetings, finding them an inefficient means of communication and an unprofitable way to spend one's time and money. In keeping with this latter reaction was that of another person (again a member of only one society and, perhaps not coincidentally, located at the same institution) who described himself as a "lone wolf" and "not a conference-goer by temperament."

Those who spoke favourably of the role of learned society meetings often mentioned the importance of contacts and interchange with other scholars. In fact, one professor said that the value of such conferences is primarily as a forum to meet people and only secondarily as a means of scholarly exchange. Another spoke positively of the effects of meeting the authors of books one had read or used in courses. While one individual found learned societies important because her professional contacts are mostly outside her own department, another claimed that the large religious studies programme in his university provides all the intellectual support he needs. Demonstrably, then, the reaction to conferences and annual meetings depends to some extent on one's situation (the size and location of the academic institution) and the opportunity there for professional contacts with colleagues, as well as on one's disposition and temperament (the degree, perhaps, to which one is gregarious and enjoys public gatherings).

But there are other reasons for valuing learned societies (or not). One person stated that the value of learned societies meetings was to "gear people up to get a paper ready," though this person also mentioned that he found only occasional intellectual stimulation at conferences. Most journal articles, he thought, had first been presented as conference papers. Another confessed to going to meetings only when he himself was presenting a paper. Another claimed that learned societies provide good opportunities for graduate students to present their research, while someone else complained that such conferences are a source of frustration to him because of the "pointless papers," many by graduate students "wanting to get their names known." While we did not systematically explore the possibility, it is probably the case that doctoral candidates can advance their employment prospects by becoming "known" as they present papers at annual meetings of the learned societies. Graduate students who are visible in those settings are probably in an enhanced position when their c.v.s come before the members of a search committee (if some of that committee's members recall the candidate's name, face, and performance).

Several of those interviewed would have agreed with the complaint of a lack of coherence in conference programmes where the papers are, to quote one view, "all over hell's half-acre." Another individual was dismayed by the low calibre of the papers in the Canadian societies and urged more juried papers. While it was commented that many conferences are characterized by "oneupmanship," someone observed that the atmosphere in Canadian learned society meetings was different from that in the United States, being "less competitive and cutthroat." Many welcomed the alternative provided by the smaller scale of the Canadian meetings, where attendance is, at most, a few hundred people, to the "fourteen-ring circus" of the mammoth joint annual meetings of the Society of Biblical Literature and the American Academy of Religion (described by one scholar as "too big, too American, and too diffuse"), and where attendance in the late 1980s exceeded five thousand. The unique phenomenon presented by the annual

Canadian "Learneds," where most societies meet on a university campus in the spring, either concurrently or successively, and with subsidized travel for members, was regarded as an appropriate response to "the Canadian fact," a way of coping with extensive geography and a far-flung, but thinly spread, population. Another person, though, found the Canadian societies too small and limiting, preferring the spectrum of choice offered in the American versions. One religious studies professor found that the CSSR mixes history of religions with theology — he is against any kind of "reconvergence" of the two. For him, therefore, European meetings are preferable to North American ones. On the other hand, a theologian complained that many of the papers presented at CSSR meetings were too "esoteric."

One religious studies faculty member who said that learned societies meetings are "not important at all" for him preferred smaller working groups focussed on specific topics. Several spoke positively of on-going seminars in, for example, the SBL or CSBS on topics such as Anti-Judaism or Torah/Nomos. While some attend smaller meetings of more specialized societies for contact with scholars in narrowly defined areas of expertise (anthropologists, biblical scholars working on "Q," Assyriologists, mediaevalists, etc.), others go to meetings including all aspects of religious studies (such as the CSSR). Such widely based meetings, it was recognized, are useful for finding out about broad trends, but not for putting one in touch with work at the cutting edge of a particular field. At the CSSR, for instance, a specialized paper, if presented to the meeting at large, would be expected to be accessible to most of the membership rather than only to those having a technical expertise in the area. The AAR, though spreading across all areas of research in religious studies, consists of many caucuses, "consultations," and subgroups having more precise foci.

The comments in response to questions about the specific role for Canadian societies in religious studies were often appreciative and touched on several common themes. As well as providing general contact on scholarly matters, one person saw them as providing a self-understanding for religious studies in Canada, with commendable publishing enterprises. The last point was made frequently, with positive comments about the publications of the Canadian Corporation for Studies in Religion, such as SR Supplements, Editions SR, and various other series. This enterprise, widely known among scholars of religion in Canada, is also the envy of many learned societies outside of religious studies (see chap. 2.7 above). While, as already indicated, many people saw in the Canadian societies an alternative to their American counterparts, some expressed the view that Canadian scholars should be more involved in international conferences. For some this seemed to be a new direction for scholarly interchange. One faculty member who spoke of continuing a long-standing involvement in the Canadian societies was now beginning to alternate attendance at American meetings with European conferences. In this regard awareness on the part of Canadian scholars of such organizations as the International Association for the History of Religions (which met in Winnipeg in 1980) seems to be increasing. Canadian presence in the IAHR was highly visible at Sydney, Australia in 1985, as it was at Rome in 1990.

To sum up. It is evident that for some competent scholars in religious studies membership in learned societies or attendance at their meetings is not significant, while for others it is crucially important to their professional lives. Some older scholars regard such activity as appropriate at an early stage of their careers, but have become less involved over the years. Annual meetings of Canadian learned societies having to do with the academic study of religion were praised for their intimacy and informality, or criticized as being too limited. Some valued meetings for the opportunity to extend the boundaries of one's acquaintance with religious studies, or else stated that the directions of their own research were established by what they participated in at annual meetings, while others found the most worthwhile organizations to be those closely focussed in their own area of scholarly interest and expertise. (See, further, chap. 3.2.5 above.)

8

Undergraduate Curricula

Daniel Fraikin

8.1 Introduction

Undergraduate departments of religious studies have two functions. They offer courses which contribute to the liberal education of undergraduate students, and they provide a small number of students with a special competence in religious studies (majors, minors, honours or specialist degrees). General course offerings reflect the claim of the field to public status: they represent what the faculty thinks university-educated citizens should know about religion. Programmes, that is, planned courses of study for students aiming at a recognized competence in the field, reflect an additional concern for the integrity of the field. Hence the two main parts of this chapter, the first on course offerings in general, the second on programmes of study. Rather than providing an inventory or catalogue of course offerings, the chapter will focus on changes in undergraduate curricula in religious studies over the last 15 to 20 years and what these reveal about trends within the field from then until now.

8.2 Course Offerings

The number of courses listed in the calendars of Ontario's departments of religious studies has grown considerably since 1972, when the last survey was made (Anderson, 1972). The increase is not simply the result of the inevitable expansion of the departments. It results also from the fact that in the intervening years the standard length of a course in Ontario universities has changed from two terms to one. This move allowed for more flexibility. Within the same constraints of the B.A. programme twice as many courses

---

Notes to Chapter 8 can be found on page 231.

could be offered by the same faculty, and the students could take twice as many subjects. It provided an occasion to reduce the weight of some courses while keeping them on the books and to multiply courses on a given subject while not substantially expanding its share of the curriculum. As a result of this move, the number of entries in the calendar has practically doubled. For the purpose of comparing the present situation with that of the late 1960s and early 1970s we have chosen as one unit the one-term course and given two-term courses the value of two. Thus in Table 8-1 the figures given for 1972, as reported in Anderson's 1972 *Guide*, have been doubled and represent approximately twice the number of courses listed at that time, while those for 1986-88 represent the actual number of courses listed. One notices immediately that even with this adjustment the number of courses listed had doubled in this period. Since the number of instructors has not grown accordingly, this increase means that many courses listed are in fact offered only at irregular intervals. Table 8-1, therefore, shows the relative weight of different areas in the curriculum and allows a comparison between the two periods considered.

The great number of courses listed in the calendars of our religious studies departments can be distributed in a variety of categories. The classification used for Table 8-1 is intended in part to bring out the role of religions other than Christianity and Judaism, methodology, and languages and uses a common distinction between historical-descriptive and thematic courses.[1] The commentary that follows supplies details on subdivisions within the larger categories. Since curricula recall Heraclitus' dictum that "All things are in flux," it should be noted that some of the specifics for 1986-88 reported in the table and in our commentary will be somewhat dated, but the most recent calendars suggest that the overall trends persist.

Historical and descriptive courses introduce, describe, and explain religions or religious traditions as historical and cultural phenomena in time and space. Courses on the Christian tradition accounted for 15.4% of all courses listed. Counting in addition thematic courses presumably taught within the Christian framework of the West, Christianity occupied approximately the same 43% of the space in undergraduate courses in religious studies it did in 1972.

All religious studies departments or programmes in Ontario have at least one course on Eastern religions and non-Christian religions of the West. In light of controversies, past and present, over the distinction between religious studies and theological (i.e., Christian) studies (chap. 2.4.3 above), it may be said that the presence in a religious studies department of courses on "other religions" is a necessary condition of the department's credibility. With the inclusion of Judaism, such courses accounted for nearly a quarter (23%) of all courses listed in our departments. With the addition of courses on languages other than Hebrew and Greek (2%), the total reached 25%, one in every four of the courses offered.

Table 8-1[2]
Distribution of Undergraduate Courses in
Religious Studies in Ontario, 1972 and 1986-88

	Courses Listed		% of Total	
	1972	1986-88	1972	1986-88
Western roots	146	176	21.3	13.4
Christian tradition	62	202	9.0	15.4
Jewish tradition	15	86	2.1	6.5
Other traditions	131	216	19.0	16.4
Thematic (Western)	236	370	34.4	28.2
Thematic (comparative/ pluralistic)	17	48	2.4	3.6
Methodology	37	123	5.4	9.4
Biblical languages	22	63	3.2	4.8
Other languages	20	26	2.9	2.0
Totals	686	1310	100.0	100.0

The 2% increase in religions other than Christianity since 1972 (302 courses compared with 146) was unevenly distributed. Eastern traditions had in fact lost in percentage points. The major gains were on the side of Judaism and Islam. Judaism was poorly represented in 1972 and the situation has improved moderately nearly everywhere since then, but the large increase noticed in our data (86 courses, compared to 15!) occurred predominantly at Toronto and York. Courses on Islam also increased from 18 in 1972 (13 of which were at Toronto) to 35 in 1986-88 – still less than 3% of the total. Nearly every department of religious studies now has at least one course on Islam. (See, further, chap. 2.4.5 and 2.4.6 above.)

The place of courses in religions other than Christianity varies considerably from one department to another. Most departments have not only a general introduction to world religions but separate courses on a number of them. Choices have to be made on what religions will be taught among the many that compete for attention. Hinduism, Buddhism, Islam, and Judaism were the first candidates, as expected. Religions of China and Japan, indigenous religions of North America or Africa, and New Religions seemed to be less pressing concerns: fewer than ten courses on any one of these (which are not even offered every year) could be found in all of Ontario's departments of religious studies. More may have been added in the meantime.

Thematic courses are here defined as those dealing with aspects of religion such as myths and rituals; concepts such as providence, God, and immortality; social and psychological aspects of religion; and ethics. In religious studies departments one would expect many of those courses to be comparative, or pluralistic, that is, using data on such topics from different religions and cultures. Judging from the calendar descriptions, however, not many courses have a pluralistic bent. In most cases the course description makes no claim of moving beyond the frontiers of Western culture, and one should assume that the subject matter is discussed within the cultural and religious assumptions of the West, if not from those of Western Christianity (and its secular avatars) alone.

There are obvious reasons for this state of affairs. Except for the new generation of teachers whose graduate training was done in religious studies departments, most teachers are not sufficiently knowledgeable in other religious traditions to integrate them into their courses. It should be added in their defence that cross-cultural studies in most areas of the humanities and social sciences are a recent development and that religion scholars are no less, and possibly more, aware of their Western biasses than their colleagues in other departments (cf. chap. 2.4.4 above).

Courses in ethics are included in Table 8-1 among the thematic courses. All religious studies departments offer some. New subjects have appeared in recent years that have expanded the offerings beyond the basic introductions: courses on biomedical ethics, war and peace issues, business ethics, etc. The total number of courses has grown from 40 in 1972 to 60 in 1986, but their percentage of the total has dropped to 4.6% from the 5.8% they occupied in 1972. Many departments have still only one ethicist, if that, to teach the subject. Comparative ethics, a relatively new field, has made its appearance but is still rare.

Every religious studies department has a number of courses with labels such as "Religion and Literature," "Politics and Religion," "Art and Religion" (or "Religion and the Arts"), "Religion and Passages," "Women and Religion," "Health and Religion," "Religion and Symbols," "Religion and Human Nature," "Religion and Identity," "Religion and Law," etc.. Such "dialogical" titles reflect the current perception that religion is present in most areas of human life and also, perhaps, the hope of attracting students to the study of religion by associating it with better known human realities. With the exception of Religion and Literature and Religion and the Arts, which are already acknowledged specialties identified by graduate programmes in some universities of North America, "Religion and" titles signal emerging, or developing, interests in the study of religion. (See, further, chap. 2.4.9 above.)

Courses on the Bible and its historical contexts ("'roots'' of religion in the West) are offered on all campuses, as could be expected in a society shaped in so many respects by the Bible. They constitute 12.8% of all courses listed, 17.6% if biblical languages are included. Surprisingly, biblical courses have lost significantly since 1972 (when they occupied 27% of the curriculum). Even allowing for a good margin of error (although biblical courses are usually clearly identifiable in the calendar), this drop is an indisputable fact. A similar, but less dramatic, drop was observed in Quebec where, with the exception of Concordia (Loyola Campus, where the emphasis is on Theology), McGill, and the Université du Québec à Trois-Rivières, the drop averages four percentage points.[3] The facts in Ontario seem to call for further study and careful monitoring, considering that in the same province, in the last 15 years, one in four doctorates in both religious and theological studies was in the biblical area.

The titles, descriptions, and locations of biblical courses in departments of religious studies generally reflect a non-confessional and non-theological orientation. In titles such as ''Introduction to New Testament Literature,'' ''Introduction to the Study of the New Testament,'' the emphasis is respectively on literature (among other literatures) and on study rather than commitment, while in ''The Sacred Books of Judaism and Christianity'' the theologically loaded word ''Bible'' is replaced by an expression better suited to the study of religion in a pluralistic, secular university. Expressions such as ''literature'', ''social'', ''historical'', and ''scholarly reading'' usually signal the intention to study the Bible from some other perspective than a theological or devotional one.

Quite a few departments of religious studies offer courses in biblical languages, or accept for credit Greek courses offered in the classics department (Hebrew, Aramaic, and New Testament Greek are usually located in religious studies). Courses in Sanskrit and Arabic are offered only in large departments with graduate programmes, but it would be possible to get instruction on an individual basis wherever there is a specialist at hand. Such resources do not appear in the list of available courses but are known to exist.

Finally, there are courses named after the disciplines or methodologies employed, such as philosophy, sociology, anthropology, psychology, archaeology, literary criticism. The self-consciousness of religious studies (chaps. 1 and 2 above) seems to be reflected in the tripling of courses in this category (from 37 to 123), a near doubling of the percentages of the overall totals from 1972 to 1986-88 (5.4% to 9.4%). Courses in methodology of the social sciences are usually provided in the corresponding departments. Most religious studies departments have a course in which different methods in the study of religion are presented, but only some of the large ones, those with graduate programmes, offer separate courses on one particular methodology or another. Sociology and psychology of religion are singled out the most often, and in the same proportion.

Two more curricular items are of particular interest and deserve special consideration: courses dealing with women and religion and with religion in Canada. Specific courses on women and religion have appeared in the offerings of most departments in the last decade. At the time of our survey, 20 courses — 2.1% of the total — could be identified as having a particular emphasis on women in their content or perspective. Only two departments did not have at least one course on the subject. The presence or absence of women on faculty seems to be the determinant factor. Whether attention is paid to a feminist perspective in other courses is difficult to ascertain from course descriptions alone, but interviews revealed that a number of faculty, both men and women, are increasingly including primary sources by women and feminist scholarship in their courses.

Religion in Canada is also a new subject in Ontario departments of religious studies. In 1986-88 five of them had one course on the subject. In four others the number and variety of courses on various aspects of religion in Canada was significant enough to reveal a priority. Although only 25 courses, less than 2% of the total, were on religion in Canada, reference to the Canadian scene may occur in a variety of ways. A course on North American native peoples, for instance, will include consideration of Indians and Inuit in Canada, as will a course on native religions in general. In ethics, examples will often be drawn from the present Canadian context and in Religion and Literature courses some of the texts chosen for study are by Canadian authors.

Many departments distribute their courses according to "areas," "streams," or "profiles." Such groupings result from a blend of the following oppositions: East and West, past (origins) and present, historical and philosophical, Christian and non-Christian. The results are quite varied, as the following overview of department groupings shows:

- History of Religion (Jewish and Christian), History of Religion (other religions), Philosophical-Theological Studies of Religion;
- Judaeo-Christian Tradition, Religions of the World, Contemporary Religious Issues;
- Asian Religions, Biblical Studies, Western Religious Traditions, and a programme in Religion and Social Sciences;
- Religions of the World, Religion and Society, Religion and Psychology, Christianity;
- Religions of the West, Religions of the East, Scriptures, Religion, Ethics and Society, Philosophy of Religion;
- World Religions, History of the Christian Tradition, Biblical Studies, Theology-Philosophy-Ethics, and Religion, Society and Culture;
- Western Religions (Early to Modern), Ancient Near East and Mediterranean Religion (covers biblical area in a large sense), Asian and Folk Religions;
- Biblical and Near Eastern, Ethical, Historical, Theological, World Religions, Religion and Culture;
- Religion and Culture, Biblical Studies, Judaic Studies, Christian Studies.

There is clearly no agreement on these groupings in our Ontario departments. Some have abandoned areas altogether. In fact many courses in religious studies can be located in more than one area according to the religious tradition(s) they deal with, the method(s) they employ, and the historical and geographical location of the phenomenon examined. Usually the main focus determines the location. Since these various areas are not the basis for departments within departments or faculties, their main purpose is to provide guidelines for the distribution of courses in a programme.

What emerges from the survey of course offerings in religious studies departments is a consensus on a number of "musts" resulting from the demands of the public and the nature of the field. Departments of religious studies must be able to offer something on Christianity, world religions, the Bible, ethics, women, religion in Canada. But the requirements are uneven. At the time of our survey courses on world religions were no longer as much in demand as they were in the 1960s and 1970s and thus the need to offer them came more from a perception of the integrity of the field than from a strong demand on the part of students. Recently, demand again seems to be on the increase.

In comparison with the figures provided by Claude Welch for 1969-70 (1971, 191, Table 9-17), the present balance of courses in Ontario religious studies departments, seen across the board, is encouraging. At that time, in American and Canadian colleges and universities, courses on religions other than Christianity constituted less than 10% of the total. Courses on Judaism accounted for less than 3% of the total, those on sociology and psychology of religion also less than 3%, but those on the Bible 27%! Welch's survey included American colleges and universities, where there were significant differences between the curricula of religious studies departments in public and denominational institutions. It was in the former — the public institutions — that religions other than Christianity obtained the greatest visibility in the curriculum. Most departments and programmes of religious studies in Ontario fall in this category, but traces of denominational origins linger. In universities with a Catholic background, for instance, one will find courses in ecclesiology and sacraments. In the others, it seems that the curriculum is most distinctly one of religious studies precisely in those universities that also have a federated theological school (or schools), because, perhaps, the department does not have to assume the traditional role of providing students with religious or theological education, or is self-conscious about setting itself off from such education.

8.3   Programmes of Study

Every course is already an ordered process leading the students to a given competence on a subject. But there are degrees of competence, and it usually takes more than one unit of instruction to achieve it. Programmes of study appear when the university sets the norms for levels of recognized competence in a given area of knowledge, from a minor concentration to a Ph.D., and plans the instructional process leading to them. In most Ontario universities one can do a major, a minor, an honours and a combined honours concentration in religious studies (alternative nomenclature: major, minor, honours and medial concentration). Graduate programmes carry the process further. Although they are the subject of the next chapter, it is important to mention them here, for the norms of competence at the graduate level affect in part the level of competence expected at the highest level of undergraduate studies (cf., above, chaps. 3.1.3 and n. 8 there and 4.1.4).

Departments of religious studies in Ontario are under the control of the universities to which they belong and their general academic requirements are not different from those of other departments in the humanities. What interests us here is the understanding of competence in religious studies reflected in undergraduate programme requirements and processes.

A survey of first-year offerings in religious studies shows substantial differences in opinion on how best to introduce students to the subject. This is not surprising: the introductory course is a perennial topic on annual meeting programmes of religious studies learned societies. One Ontario department has no 100-level course in religion. Others all have one or more courses of a general nature such as Religion and Roots, the Drama of Human Life, Problems of Religion and Culture, Ideas of Love (or War), which are meant to open the eyes of students to the presence of religion in human affairs and to introduce "academic" thinking about religion. The stress is put on non-confessional and non-dogmatic perspectives. This latter intent is present in most other courses offered in first year, even when they start *in medias res*, that is, with courses on the Bible or some religious tradition. Only one department has a first-year course dryly entitled Religious Studies, which introduces students to methodology.

There is a propaedeutic intention in first-year courses. They are clearly devised with the assumption that the field is new to most students. They are meant to bridge the gap between secondary school and the university. If religious studies were part of high school curricula, those courses would possibly be superfluous. The university would pick up students where secondary schools left them, as is the case in other fields. The fact that religion is not an academic subject in most Ontario public schools puts the academic study of religion in universities at a clear disadvantage (see, further, chap. 9.5 below).

Ontario religious studies departments differ in their requirements for diversity and breadth of knowledge on the part of concentrators. The study of at least one religion different from one's own seems to be essential to the understanding of religion. Only four departments formally require of their concentrators a course on world religions. Other programmes require only that students take courses in areas of religious studies other than the one in which they intend to concentrate, which usually implies, but does not impose, deliberate attention paid to the variety of humanity's religious experience. Some departments require from students a variety of approaches to religion. In one of them, for instance, students must take courses dealing with religion either dialogically (religion and . . .) or thematically (myths and symbols, mysticism, etc.). In another, majors and honours students must take at least one course from each of the areas in which courses have been distributed.

One would expect reflection on the methods of religious studies to be an essential part of any programme in religious studies. There are different ways to make sure that this is done, and some departments insist on it more than others. We mentioned earlier that only a few had a general course on methodology. In one department, where it is not the object of a formal requirement, such a course does exist and everyone in fact takes it. In another, there is no course at all on the subject but it is expected that all courses will introduce their particular methodology. There is a substantial difference, however, between using particular methods and taking them as an object of formal reflection. The fact that a course in methodology is a requirement for honours students or graduate students seems to indicate a substantial consensus on the necessity of methodological awareness for anyone claiming competence in religious studies, but whether this should take place at the beginning or at the end of the process, at the undergraduate or at the graduate level, is probably the question at the root of the different practices presently observed.

At the time of our survey, nowhere in Ontario departments was the acquisition of languages, ancient or modern, required of undergraduates in religious studies, even at the honours level. The requirement of bilingualism at the University of Ottawa was the sole exception and is obviously related to the bilingual nature of that school. In the case of modern languages the practice of religious studies departments reflects that of the majority of Ontario universities to which they belong, which do not require from undergraduates the possession of another modern language, even French. As for the original languages of religious traditions, one could argue that concentrators in religious studies should not graduate without some knowledge of at least one of them. Not only is this not required but in some places courses in source languages do not count towards the specific requirements of the degree. There is clearly no encouragement along this line. In view of the heavy curricular demands on students resulting from the desire to provide them with some acquaintance with the whole field of religious studies and the spectrum of religious traditions it encompasses, it is not likely that language requirements will be introduced or stressed in Ontario religious studies departments and programmes. However, since a number of majors or honours students will want to pursue graduate studies and will be required to possess a sufficient knowledge of ancient and modern languages, the least one could expect in undergraduate programmes is encouragement to start early. Some graduate students we interviewed said as much, and one professor, asked to comment on the difference between graduate studies in Europe and in North America, mentioned poor preparation in languages as the most serious handicap of North American students entering graduate studies in the humanities. (See, further, chaps. 4.2.3 above and 11.4 below.)

8.4 Conclusions

The faculties of Ontario departments of religious studies have expanded modestly in the last fifteen years but the number of courses presented to students has grown nearly fourfold. The passage from a two-semester course system to one in which the one-semester course is the norm has allowed greater variety for both students and professors. When a three-year B.A. consisted of fifteen courses, not many students could afford to spend one of them on Hinduism, for instance. A one-semester excursion in the study of a religion represents a lower risk, and many discover the field because of this opportunity. Those who previously would have had to choose between a course on Hinduism and a course on Islam can now take both. Whether learning has gained in depth is a matter of discussion, but the advantages have been clear.

More subjects are also being taught. Judaism and Islam, among world religions, have scored some gains. Courses on women and religion have appeared and are multiplying, and interest in the Canadian scene is growing. Two areas deserve comment: it seems that biblical studies and the study of Eastern religions have lost some of their importance in the curriculum. It is true that Table 8-1 is based on courses listed and that the figures could have been different if we had been able to tell more precisely what was actually taught. It remains, however, that the addition of new courses (with or without a corresponding number of new professors) has the inevitable effect of altering the previous curriculum and reducing the relative weight of old, well-established areas. Biblical studies are in that category. They were well planted long ago. It is not in that area that curricula expanded. One may perhaps say the same of Eastern religions: they were the typical and most exotic "other" religions and well established in the 1970s. That Judaism and Islam have gained more attention is understandable. All things considered, then, the drop in those two areas is only the consequence of the expansion of course offerings in other, previously underdeveloped, areas.

Curricula have changed in response to a number of factors: new interests on the part of the professors themselves; response to obvious new challenges such as feminism and various ethical issues; social pressure for more Canadian content; response to events such as the new militancy of Islam, Christian fundamentalism, New Religions, etc. Religious studies departments in Ontario, unlike those of Quebec (Rousseau and Despland, 1988, 61-62), do not have to meet the needs of a profession such as school teaching. Curricula would be under new pressures if this situation were altered. The introduction of religious studies in the public school curriculum in Ontario would enhance substantially the presence of discourse on religion in the public sphere and, for the better or for the worse, create an interested public and a new instance of accountability. Just as curricula in religious education and theological training are sensitive to the demands of the denominations that support them, the growth of sensitivity to the study of religion in the public sphere and its eventual appearance in public schools will probably entail a greater dialogue between religious studies and the public and, possibly, pressures the consequences of which are still unknown.

Notes

1 The numbers represent courses listed, rather than actually offered in a given year in calendars dated 1971-72 and from 1986 to 1988 respectively, and exclude special honours seminars with undetermined content.

2 For the gathering of statistics used in this chapter courses were classified in the following way. (1) *Western Roots*: courses on the Hebrew and Christian Bible or the ancient world connected with the biblical period; (2) *Christian Tradition*: courses of a descriptive, historical nature on Christianity; (3) *Jewish Tradition*: courses on Judaism other than courses on the Hebrew Bible; (4) *Other Traditions*: courses on religions other than Christianity and Judaism; (5) *Thematic (Western)*: thematic or dialogical courses without explicit reference to non-Western religious data; (6) *Thematic (Comparative/Pluralistic)*: thematic or dialogical courses claiming to use data from non-Western religious traditions; (7) *Methodology*: courses on methodology or clearly defined as using a particular method; (8) *Biblical Languages*: Hebrew, Aramaic, and Greek; (9) *Other Languages*: courses on other source languages.

3 Rousseau and Despland (1988, 66) show a drop of 1.9% in the place of biblical studies in Quebec, but this figure does not reflect the average situation. Tables for each institution show that in the greatest number of them biblical studies have lost more than three percentage points. In Quebec biblical studies occupy 13% of the curriculum space, not counting biblical languages.

9

Graduate Education

Daniel Fraikin

9.1 Graduate Programmes in Ontario

The early seventies were a time of evaluation and planning in graduate religious studies. The Welch Report (1971) and Anderson's *Guide to Religious Studies in Canada/Guide des Sciences Religieuses au Canada* (1972) were followed in Ontario by a report of the Advisory Committee on Academic Planning of the Ontario Council on Graduate Studies (ACAP, 1974). This report had considerable impact, for its recommendations were generally followed by the Ontario government and established the status quo for the following decade.[1] The University of Waterloo abandoned its plans for a master's programme in religious studies, while Carleton went ahead in implementing one. A most interesting part of the ACAP report is the discussion of a graduate programme at the University of Toronto. The necessity of one in such a major university was not in doubt, but its nature and the conditions for its integrity were the subject of some debate (see chap. 2.5 above). The Centre for Religious Studies, in which graduate religious studies at the University are now located, was created after those discussions took place.

At present three universities, Carleton, Wilfrid Laurier, and Windsor, offer only an M.A. programme in religious studies, while McMaster, Ottawa, and Toronto offer the Ph.D. in addition. From 1985 to 1988 these six universities together granted an average of 40 M.A. and 9 Ph.D. degrees annually. Table 9-1 gives some figures on the number of students enrolled both full- and part-time in graduate religious studies programmes in Ontario, followed by the number of degrees conferred.[2]

It seems that the number of M.A.s and Ph.D.s awarded annually has dropped since 1972. Whether as a result of successful planning or thanks to

---

Notes to Chapter 9 can be found on pages 251-52.

Table 9-1
Enrolments and Degrees Granted in Graduate Religious Studies Programmes in Ontario Universities, 1972-88

	M.A.				Ph.D.		
	1972	1980	1984	1985-88	1972	1978-83	1983-88
							(averages)
Carleton	—	17/6	17/6	7/1.3	—	—	—
McMaster	32/10	29/15	15/7	22/6	72/12	44/7	42/4
Ottawa	33/32	8/7	12/2	5/6	38/5	19/3	23/2
Toronto	—	4/0	13/5	17/4.6	—	18/0	29/2
W. Laurier	15/1	31/5	42/13	33/11	—	—	—
Windsor	28/11	24/11	27/4	16/6	—	—	—
Totals	108/54	123/44	126/37	110/35	110/17	81/10	94/8

normal market forces, this is what the 1974 ACAP report recommended, except that the present number of Ph.D. graduates annually in religious studies is below the target of twelve a year envisaged at that time.

Theological schools also offer three graduate programmes, the M.A., the Th.D., and the Ph.D. (the distinction between the last two being of nomenclature only), which should be considered alongside graduate programmes in religious studies for a number of reasons. First, for these programs there is hardly any difference between the academic requirements of theological schools and those of religious studies departments: graduate studies in theology at their highest level are submitted to the same academic standards as apply to graduate studies in religion in colleges and universities. Second, in these graduate programmes in theology research is often no different in kind from much of that conducted in departments of religious studies, the prevailing approach being historical. Third, inasmuch as we are interested in the distinctiveness and specificity of religious studies, comparing graduate programmes in religious studies with those in theological schools (we shall keep them distinct) is appropriate.

That only the programmes mentioned above are considered in this chapter on graduate studies requires some explanation. There is a well-known ambiguity attached to the term "graduate" when referring to programmes in theology. The Master of Divinity degree (M.Div.) is a master's degree insofar as an undergraduate degree is required for admission to the programme and the students come to it with the corresponding education and maturity, but it is a first degree in theology. In addition, the M.Div. is a professional programme for ministry, about one third of which consists of the acquisition of pastoral skills of a sort not usually associated with the academic title of Master. The degrees of Master of Theological Studies (M.T.S.) and Master in Religious Education (M.R.E.) are also first degrees in theology.[3] The two programmes that follow on the M.Div., commonly called in theological circles graduate or advanced degree programmes, are the Master of Theology (Th.M. or M.Th.) and the Doctor of Ministry (D.Min.). The first is a one-year programme, with a thesis, in the M.Div. line. The second, also following on the M.Div. but at the doctoral level, is a programme done while in ministry and normally spreading over three years. All the above may be said to be confessional and ecclesial by their very nature, and thus outside of our field of inquiry.

The graduate programmes of theological studies of an academic type, that is the M.A., the Th.D., and the Ph.D., compare for that reason with graduate programmes in religious studies within secular universities in the province. The M.A. in theology is usually a first programme in theology like the M.Div., but in a more academic line (its declared purpose at the Toronto School of Theology is to prepare for admission to a doctoral programme). The Th.D. or Ph.D. in theology are academic doctoral programmes in theology. Thus the Th.M. or M.Th. and the D.Min. programmes are in the ministerial line, the M.A., Th.D. and Ph.D. in theology in the academic. Only the last three belong in a survey of graduate studies in religion.

In Ontario the two major institutions offering doctoral programmes in theology are the Toronto School of Theology (TST) and Saint Paul University. At TST, St. Michael's College, whose Faculty of Theology is one of TST's constituents, confers the M.A. and Ph.D. by virtue of its university status whereas the Th.D. degrees pursued in the various constituent schools are conferred jointly by those schools and the University of Toronto through an agreement reached in 1979 (see Table 2-1 and App. B). The Collège Dominicain de Philosophie et de Théologie in Ottawa also awards the Ph.D. by virtue of its university charter, but the numbers are relatively small (see Table 2-1 and App. B). The Institute for Christian Studies in Toronto, which awards the Ph.D. through the philosophy department of the Free University of Amsterdam, describes it as a degree in philosophy (Calendar, 1990-92, 10, 12; see Table 2-1 above).

At the time of our survey (1986-87) there were from 50 to 60 students in M.A. programmes at TST and Saint Paul together. There are between 150 and 175 students in doctoral programmes in those two centres (nearly twice as many as in the 1970s) and about a dozen graduates a year, 10 at TST and 2 at Saint Paul on average. According to the Director for Advanced Degree Studies at TST, it takes an average of six years to complete a doctorate.[4] Counting about 80 doctoral students between 1979 and 1981, there should have been about 13 graduates between 1985 and 1987, which is not far from the actual average of 12 for those years. The effects of recent large enrolments will first be felt in the 1990s.

Counting both religious studies departments and theological schools, about 20 Ph.D.s or Th.D.s and 100 M.A.s came out of Ontario graduate schools with degrees in religious studies or theology each year between 1976 and 1987.[5] One should note, however, that the number of degrees granted does not translate into an equivalent number of graduates then seeking employment, because a good number of M.A. graduates become doctoral students.

9.2   Doctoral Programmes

Although they are in the same general category of graduate studies, the
M.A. and the doctoral programmes in religious studies deserve separate
treatments. The latter has a much sharper institutional profile than the former. At present the doctoral programme prepares for both university teaching and scholarly work. In the field of religious studies, as in other areas of
the humanities, scholarship and teaching cannot usually be separated as they
often can in the sciences, where Ph.D.s may find employment in research
centres not related to universities. For most holders of doctoral degrees in
religious studies the university is the only place where research in religion
can be practiced for a living (scholars working independently of a university
have usually started there) and one enters it as a teacher. Conversely, one
can no longer be a university teacher without a Ph.D. Whether one seeks a
Ph.D. in religious studies for the sake of teaching or for research, it is as
teacher that one will first earn a living. The profession of academic is one of
the most well-defined in society. The Ph.D. is thus, as Claude Welch argued
in his landmark report, a professional degree (Welch, 1971, 47-51; cf. Pelikan, 1983 and many articles in Frankena, 1980).

In our interviews we heard no expression of doubt on the present institutional requirement of a Ph.D. for teaching religious studies in universities
and colleges (cf. chap. 3.1 above). The Ph.D. gives academic credibility to
both the individuals seeking employment and the institutions that hire them.
The match between this condition for employment and the realities of the
teaching profession, however, is the object of periodic questioning in North
America (see Frankena, 1980). If the thesis is the cornerstone of the Ph.D.
and it is understood as a work of advanced research, should it be required
for teaching undergraduates, which is what most university teachers spend
most of their time doing? In fact reality forces itself on the myth. Just as
against the stated ideal most university teachers are more teachers than
researchers, most theses, as we shall argue later, are more exercises of educational value to the graduates themselves than the feats of innovative
research they are supposed to be.

Although university calendars list the conditions for admission to the
doctoral programme and the requirements for the degree, the objectives are
not always clearly described. They are probably presumed to be known.
One department introduces both its master's and doctoral programmes by
citing the Council on Graduate Studies in Religion, according to which a
graduate must have demonstrated "excellence in the scholarly study of religion and the capacity for significant independent research, writing, and
teaching in recognized areas of specialization within religious studies."
Another sees specialization in a particular field (including related methodologies), experience in research, and competence in the chosen field as the
specific objective. The key words "excellence" and "competence" are left
undefined, of course. In practice, competence is defined empirically by the

present generation of scholars who pass judgment on their peers and admit others to the guild, and the Ph.D. programme is in many respects an apprenticeship during which the academic stock in trade is passed from one generation to another (see the discerning observations in Neusner, 1983, 144).

9.2.1   Admission Requirements

9.2.1.1   Prior Degree

In Ontario a master's degree is always required for admission to a doctoral programme. Given the diverse paths through which the degree can be earned (see below), one wonders what this requirement means. The M.A. guarantees neither sufficient background in the area of concentration, nor ability to do intensive research, nor possession of the languages, ancient or modern, necessary for scholarly work. Presumably the master's degree required is the one provided by the department itself, tailored as a preparation for the following degree. But what if a student comes with a master's degree earned elsewhere? What are the qualities that make an applicant ready for a doctoral programme? A student with an honours degree in religious studies, who has demonstrated his/her ability to write an undergraduate thesis in the course of obtaining that degree, could be better qualified than a student who has obtained an M.A. without a thesis. Why could that student not be accepted immediately in a doctoral programme, as is the case in some major American universities? In other words, why insist on a master's degree when there is no uniform definition of it and all the conditions for admission to the doctoral degree have to be spelled out and verified anyway?

9.2.1.2   Language Requirements

All programmes require a reading knowledge of foreign languages of scholarship. French and German are the ones usually specifically mentioned. One of them is a prerequisite, often part of the M.A. degree, the second has to be acquired in the course of the programme itself, but before the thesis is started. The ways to meet such requirements are usually spelled out in the university calendar or in department publications.

When it comes to the original languages of sources, such as Hebrew, Greek, Latin, and Arabic for the Western traditions, or Sanskrit, Japanese, Chinese, or other Asian languages for the Eastern traditions, the requirements are not as uniform. At the doctoral level it is always expected that a thesis on some ancient text will necessitate knowing the original language of the text. But in some institutions students are required to know one or more of the source languages pertinent to the religious tradition in which they will specialize, whether or not they work on the sources themselves. In one department, knowledge of Sanskrit is required of all those whose major area is Eastern religions. In doctoral programmes in theology at least one biblical language is usually required, sometimes two, with Latin added for good measure in at least two theological schools. How rigorous graduate programmes are in applying those requirements, it is difficult to say. Published data and interviews do not really disclose it. Students specializing in history of Christianity in the modern period or in ethics are not likely to make much use of whatever biblical language they brought to the programme. On the other hand, students in biblical studies will often have to know more than the one or two ancient languages they brought with them. Similar observations apply to those specializing in Eastern religions. In the doctoral programmes the standards of scholarship requiring knowledge of source languages are likely to be seriously applied, if only because the end result, namely, the thesis, is exposed to public scholarly scrutiny. One may argue, then, that departments and theological schools that require modern languages of scholarship and the source languages necessary for the student's specialization, rather than a pre-established set of languages, are the most realistic.

9.2.2   The Programme

9.2.2.1   Courses and Residency

All Ph.D. programmes require that students be in residence for a certain amount of time. It is not possible to start a Ph.D. on a part-time basis. Some institutions require two years of residence. One of them explicitly restricts the time spent in outside employment to ten hours. Others are not as clear on this matter, but the reason may be that it goes without saying. Considering the time it takes to complete a doctoral degree, it is unlikely that anyone would even apply or be admitted to a doctoral programme who is not prepared to spend a few years launching it. Usually doctoral students take at least two years of course work or readings to prepare for the comprehensive examination and another year at least to present a prospectus of their thesis. After this it may take any amount of time to reach the end. There is usually a limit placed on time for completion (six years is the norm) but it can be extended. Because most students work to support themselves while writing their dissertation and some accept a teaching position before they have finished,[6] the need for such an extension is not uncommon.

The first part of a doctoral programme always consists of course work leading to a comprehensive examination. The course requirements vary from two to three year-long courses or seminars in the area or areas of concentration. There are substantial variations between institutions on this section of the programme. Religious studies departments have the same concern for coverage of more than one religious tradition (typified in the common polarity of Eastern and Western religions) and diversity of methods as found in undergraduate programmes. In doctoral programmes in theology the degree is essentially understood as a specialization in a given area of theological scholarship and minimal attempt is made to balance it with breadth of knowledge in other areas. It is assumed that the theological degree on the basis of which the student was admitted, such as a Master of Divinity, has already provided sufficient coverage in the various branches of theology. Unfortunately, the basic theological degree does not often include serious coverage of other religions (cf. chap. 3.3 above).

9.2.2.2   The Thesis

In Ontario as in North America in general, the thesis process is so standard-ized that there are no substantial differences from one institution to another. The rigour of the process is of course better secured when it is in the hands of a graduate school dealing with the department at arm's length. One has to present a prospectus of the thesis, which has to be discussed and accepted by the department, not the supervisor only, and the thesis is always exam-ined by three readers at least, including one from outside the department, if not the university, and subject to an oral defence before a minimum of four (usually five) scholars. There are different traditions, however, among departments or schools regarding the nature of the defence. In those that fol-low the European custom, the defence is a public event including not only faculty and students but relatives and friends, an occasion for the candidate to show his or her mastery of the subject and for the institution to celebrate a high point of its academic life.

The distribution of theses among traditional clusters differs considerably from one centre of studies to the other, as Table 9-2 shows. The table offers only a general view for the sake of comparison, since the numbers are not comparable (a body of 61 theses for McMaster compared to 37 and 15 respectively for Ottawa and Toronto) and the assignment of theses to the second and third categories is somewhat subjective.

Table 9-2
Distribution of Doctoral Theses in Religious
Studies Graduate Programmes in Ontario Universities,
1970-86, by Area of Study

	McMaster	Ottawa	Toronto
Biblical Studies	25%	5%	25%
Western Religious Thought	32%	50%	20%
Religion and Society	11%	35%	30%
Eastern Religions or Philosophy	32%	—	25%

At the University of Ottawa the concentration is on Christianity and on the contemporary scene, with considerable emphasis on the social-scientific approach to religion. In the other two departments early Christianity and Eastern religions are strongly represented. Theological schools cannot be easily compared to religious studies departments in respect to the thesis because the categories are different. At the Toronto School of Theology, out of a hundred doctoral theses, 23% were in biblical studies, 15% in history, 57% in theology, and 5% in pastoral studies. At Saint Paul, out of 18 theses, 3 were in biblical studies, 7 in systematic theology, 2 in ethics, and 5 on various contemporary ecclesial and missionary developments. One cannot but notice the enduring presence of biblical studies even in departments of religious studies (on which see Rousseau and Despland, 1988, 147-48) and the absence of theses on religions other than Christianity in theological schools. The future of religiously pluralistic study would seem to be in the hands of religious studies departments.

Within the same areas, there seems to be little difference between doctoral theses originating from religious studies departments and those produced in theological schools. This is well known in the area of biblical studies, but it is also true of those dealing with the Western religious tradition in general. Compare "The Suffering God: A Study of Juergen Moltmann's Trinitarian Understanding of God" (McMaster) with "Martin Luther's Theology of Suffering in Modern Translation: A Comparative Study in the Roots of Dietrich Bonhoeffer's Theology of Suffering" (TST); or "Troeltsch's Historicism" (TST) with "Perspectivism in John Hick" (approved topic at McMaster). In most recognized theological institutions today (to some Christians' dismay, in fact) doctoral theses are objective, historical, descriptive, and explanatory rather than speculative and prescriptive, let alone confessional.

A large number of theses are in the form "The Thought [or an aspect of it] of X," or "Topic Y in X." The greatest number of doctoral theses are on texts, from scriptures or from a major author (the significance of some authors on whom dissertations are written is sometimes debatable). Theses on social and/or historical events, on socio-cultural problems, on contemporary religious movements, on rituals, on cross-cultural issues, in other words, on a problem for itself, without focusing on a particular author, are much rarer. Such theses would normally proceed from the application of sociological, psychological, and anthropological methods to some socio-cultural reality. That there are so few theses of this sort is probably due to the scarcity of persons with significant training or expertise in the social sciences in religious studies departments and schools of theology, but one may also suggest that it reflects the ongoing dominance of the traditional text-oriented approach of the humanities.

The very nature of doctoral dissertations has much to do with their relative conservatism. It is true that a thesis is supposed to be original and innovative, but that is rarely the case, for "true innovation in the humanities, as distinguished from the preservation of a tradition of scholarly understanding, is rare, unpredictable, and not an object that can be institutionally planned for or cultivated" (Quinton, 1980, 99). A truly creative thesis is rewarded by quick recognition and publication, but a thesis is usually acceptable to readers and examiners if it demonstrates knowledge of the field, control of data, and rigorous thinking, applied to some field not necessarily unknown but as yet relatively unplowed. Should it be creative and an original contribution to knowledge (and thus publishable), or is it enough that it be an exercise in scholarship esteemed for its educative value (Passmore, 1980, 56)? Doctoral programmes in the humanities in North American universities, including those in Ontario and those in religious studies and theology, seem to have accepted, willy nilly, the latter option.

9.2.2.3   Professional Training

According to the Council on Graduate Studies in Religion (as cited by the Graduate Student Handbook of McMaster's Department of Religious Studies), "capacity for significant independent research, writing, and teaching" is what students who earn graduate degrees should be able to demonstrate. No doctoral programme in Ontario, however, clearly declares that part of its task is to teach future teachers about teaching. Consequently, teaching abilities are not listed as a condition for graduation. The Welch report (1971, 48-51) had already noticed this nearly universal anomaly (one by no means restricted to doctoral programmes in religious studies). Teaching is probably considered a natural concomitant of those who possess knowledge. It is assumed that if you can do research and communicate to your colleagues what you have found, you can probably teach. It could also be argued that the doctoral programme is an apprenticeship and that one learns by being with a master. In any case, although a good number of doctoral students have occasion to gain some experience as teaching assistants, and some of those are fortunate enough to receive help in setting up a course entrusted to them, no course or seminar in pedagogy and didactics is part of our doctoral programmes. As one younger religious studies professor, a recent Ph.D., commented to one of us, "We spend more time [in graduate school] waiting for elevators than learning how to teach." University teaching is not often recognized by its practitioners as a special type of discourse deserving special reflection on their part. (See, further, chap. 6 above and chap. 12.7 below.)

9.3   M.A. Programmes

The M.A. programmes in religious studies in Ontario, sitting as they do between undergraduate and doctoral programmes, have an identity problem shared with most master's programmes in North America.[7] Even when it is distinguished from the many professional master's degrees, the academic M.A. stands for a number of different things. It may reward as little as the mere completion of a number of courses above the level of an undergraduate programme or as much as the competence which brings one to the threshold of the doctoral thesis. It is a terminal degree for some and a step towards the Ph.D. for others. Some do a thesis and others don't. When the programme is a step towards the Ph.D., students are usually advised or required to opt for the thesis. Their M.A. tends to look like a miniature

Ph.D., with the thesis the real centre of attention. Others look rather for broader or deeper knowledge. Finally, those for whom the M.A. in religious studies is a terminal degree cannot look forward, as Ph.D. candidates do, to a particular profession for which the programme would prepare them and whose demands would provide it with a focus.

Even when the M.A. is meant as a step towards the Ph.D., the necessity of a thesis is not self-evident. The problem is acknowledged in at least one programme description. At McMaster, where a student can either write a thesis or do a project, the project is described and justified in the following manner:

> Normally a project will cover broad areas of learning. It is designed to permit students to move into new areas, to read large and unfamiliar bodies of texts, and to deal comprehensively with large questions. The project route was devised because such studies, vitally important at the M.A. level, are often hindered by the requirements of a master's thesis.

What is acknowledged here is that the specialization and mobilization of energy required for a thesis is usually at the expense of the breadth of knowledge desired at the "M.A. level." Indeed, since the accepted length of time it takes to obtain an M.A. degree is one full year, two at the most, one cannot achieve both breadth and depth. The description cited above seems to say that the M.A. programme is the place to acquire the extended knowledge which will undergird a specialization at the doctoral level. But breadth of knowledge suits equally those who do not intend to become professional researchers or teachers and for whom a thesis is not the best use of their time. In fact most Ph.D. graduates at McMaster have also done a master's thesis there, and at TST, where the M.A. is explicitly described as a preparation for the doctoral programme, a thesis is required. On the other hand the Centre for Religious Studies, which has only one stream, requires instead a research paper. The least one can say is that the goals of the M.A. are many, that the relation between the M.A. and the Ph.D. is not clear, and that the role of a thesis needs clarification.

9.3.1 Admission Requirements

Admission to M.A. programmes is on the basis of a B.A. with a specialization in religious studies or theology, or some "cognate" discipline. One can compensate for lack of adequate preparation through a qualifying year. The reverse is true in master's programmes in theology. Because theology is not usually taught in undergraduate programmes, previous work is not expected for admission and, as a consequence, the programme is twice as long as in religious studies departments (advanced standing is given to those who do come with some preparation).

9.3.2 Language Requirements

Language requirements are not as rigorous for the master's degree as they are for the doctorate. The lowest requirement is that the students have a reading knowledge of whatever language is essential to the task. Most programmes do require one foreign language of scholarship, French or German. In addition, when research is done on original sources, on biblical texts, for instance, some competence in the language of the source is usually required as well. As in the doctoral programmes, the discrepancies in language requirements reflect two attitudes toward languages and their place in the master's programme. Languages can be understood and required as part of a scholar's general equipment giving her or him access to a larger pool of scientific knowledge, or they can be considered only as a tool for a special task. Requiring modern languages is to understand the M.A. on a competence model and, more precisely, on the model of competence expected of a Ph.D. Requiring languages only as the circumstances of research demand is to think of the M.A. in terms of a particular task. Not surprisingly, those departments with the stricter language requirements and verification procedures at the M.A. level are those which most clearly think of preparing students for a doctoral degree.

9.3.3 Residency and Course Requirements

M.A. programmes in religious studies departments, like other master's programmes in universities, are devised in such a way that it is possible for a student with all the prerequisites to complete the course work in one year (including the summer). Whichever option is chosen — thesis, project, major paper, or only courses — the total requirements amount to four or five full-year courses, the thesis having the value of two or three courses. In masters' programmes in theology, because most students now come to them without the appropriate specialization in theology or religious studies, the course requirements are heavier and the normal time required is two years. A number of graduate programmes in Ontario universities and theological colleges accept students at the master's level on a part-time basis. In fact, in Ontario as in Canada generally and the U.S.A., master's programmes attract a considerable number of people who seek university education beyond their undergraduate degree but do not intend to pursue a doctorate.

Religious studies M.A. programmes generally do not leave students entirely free to choose their courses. Some require that all take a course on methodology. Such a course has the advantage outlined above of bringing all students together. Some require that students know more than one religious tradition seriously and that they be exposed to more than one approach to religion. Those schools which see this as an imperative in undergraduate programmes tend to carry it over to the graduate level as well. Usually a given number of courses has to be taken in the student's chosen area of concentration. There is, in other words, no uniform pattern for course work in master's programmes. Some programmes are extremely structured, some are practically wide open, with guidance offered through an advisory system. There are advantages on both sides. Some students perceive the tight structure and control of a programme as regimentation and choose an open-ended one for the freedom it gives them to pursue their interests.

The thesis process is the usual one in universities. Whether or not to do a thesis in the first place, when there is a choice, is usually the decision of the student (which the faculty may veto in favour of course work) assisted by an advisor or an advisory committee. Departments differ in the control they exercise over its various steps. Some spell out clearly the areas within which topics can be chosen, the steps in submitting the thesis proposal and the form it must take, and assign the advisory role to a committee rather than a single advisor.

Procedures for the approval of the thesis vary from one university to another and are not always spelled out in the calendar. The thesis is always examined by one or more readers but a reader from outside the university is not always required, though one from outside the department is common. Sometimes the thesis is defended orally, sometimes not. Where a research paper (more modest than a thesis) or a project (not a thesis but a series of readings on which the student has to report) are part of the programme, some examination, written or oral, also takes place.

The topics covered by master's theses are generally in the same areas as those on which doctoral theses are written. It is noticeable, however, that at the Toronto School of Theology, where the M.A. is a preparation for the Ph.D. and the thesis is meant to offer a first occasion of writing a truly scholarly paper, the number of M.A. theses on the Bible is only half of what it is for the Th.M. students. A possible reason for this is that more Th.M. than M.A. students enter the programme with the knowledge of biblical languages required for a solid academic thesis on a biblical subject.

Judging from their titles, topics of master's theses seem to be more varied, and more imaginative, than those of doctoral theses. It may be because the stakes are not as high, or because there are fewer strictures on the exploratory urge of students, that they do not (as yet) have to submit as thoroughly to the canons of thesis writing. One wonders if some of the best ideas in religious studies may not be hidden in master's theses and, conversely, if the enormous importance given to methodological rigour in doctoral theses has not led to such extreme caution in the choice of dissertation topics that very few of them emerge as innovative or significant.

9.4   Graduate Students[8]

There are few demographic data on graduate students in religious studies, except in regard to immigration status and gender. Many Ontario graduate schools used to attract a significant number of foreign students, especially from the United States. In the last few years, due to the increased fees imposed on visa students, their number has diminished substantially. The situation may improve somewhat: the Ontario Ministry of Colleges and Universities has recently begun to grant a number of tuition scholarships to foreign students.

The proportion of women graduating in religious studies and theology in Ontario departments of religious studies and theological schools, on the other hand, has increased. Table 9-3 offers some figures on the proportion of women graduates at two different periods.

Table 9-3
Women Graduate-Degree Recipients
in Religious Studies and Theology in Ontario,
by Half-Decades, 1976-86*

| | 1976-1980 | | 1981-1986 | |
| | M.A. | Ph.D. | M.A. | Ph.D. |
	%	%	%	%
Religious Studies:				
Carleton	38	–	38	–
McMaster	33	16	22	41
Ottawa	42	28	11	28
Wilfrid Laurier (1970-80)	18	–	37	–
Windsor	52	–	54	–
Theology:				
Saint Paul	25	0	66	18
TST (1966-80)	18	5	40	23

* Comparative statistics are lacking for the Centre for Religious Studies at the University of Toronto since it did not come into being until 1976.

While the numbers involved are small and the time span is less, the increases shown in the table are roughly comparable to the increases in the proportion of Ontario masters' and doctoral degrees awarded to women in all fields in the two decades between 1968-69 and 1988-89 (chap. 5.1.1.1 and Table 5-3 above). The percentage of women receiving doctorates in Ontario religious studies graduate programmes is considerably greater than for Canadian women generally whether the latter obtained their degrees in Canada or elsewhere (see chap. 5.1.1.1 above, which also offers a number of comparisons between religious studies and other fields). The Ontario percentages in religious studies are comparable to those for religious studies doctoral programmes in the U.S.A. and Canada generally, judging from the annual list of completed doctoral dissertations in religious studies published in *Religious Studies Review* (though it must be used with some caution since not all institutions with doctoral programmes submit their lists of graduates or submit them every year). The percentage of women in these lists has grown from 21% (1985) to 24% (1988), 42% (1989), and 33% (1990).

For graduates in theological studies the figures compare well with those reported for 1985-86 by the Association of Theological Schools (ATS): 20% of doctoral and 18% of master's recipients are women. The ATS also recorded a considerable increase between 1970 and 1980, almost 10% (5.4% to 14.6%) for the doctorate and about 15% (7.7% to 23%) for the master's. For the period 1972-85 the ATS reported that the largest percentages of woman students were recorded in 1981-82 for both the master's and the doctoral degrees.

The single vocational goal of doctoral students in religious studies or theology (we are still dealing with Ph.D. and Th.D. degrees, not the Doctor of Ministry) is teaching in academic institutions. Students in master's programmes who are not working toward a doctorate have a variety of reasons for being there. Some, and not only Roman Catholics, think of school teaching. Many of the part-time M.A. students are teachers for whom an additional degree is an asset and who choose to do it in religious studies. Others are there simply out of interest, the master's programme being a way to remain a student of religious studies a bit longer or to become one, after a qualifying year. Others think that a master's degree is a better asset for employment than a mere B.A., even though they don't count the fact of having specialized in religious studies a particular advantage for employment. Still others see an M.A. in religious studies as an asset in professions where understanding people is in demand: social work, personnel management, international work, public service requiring abilities in intercultural relations, or journalism. Most students are aware that knowledge of religion does not offer the best guarantee of employment. Many of those who come into the programme do it for love of the subject and are, for this reason, enthusiastic students.

The attention and support graduate students receive varies greatly from one programme to another. At places where there is no doctoral programme, the group of M.A. students tends to be assimilated to the preceding group, namely, honours students. The problem is aggravated by the fact that at the master's level many are part-time students whose social life is elsewhere. Intellectually as well, graduate students are as much isolated as supported by their assignment to an area of the programme. It should insure the cohesion and mutual enrichment of graduate students in a given discipline or area of scholarship; but when there are not many graduate students, it isolates them instead.

The graduate school system always counts heavily on the relationship between students and their advisors, who will guide the students in their research, teach them skills, introduce them to other scholars, take them to meetings of learned societies, and push them to write and present papers for such occasions, in other words, relate to them as a master to apprentice. It is mostly thanks to the personal coaxing of their advisors that a good number of students attend the Canadian Learned Societies conferences or international meetings, present papers there, and eventually publish articles.

Most graduate students in religious studies and theology are poor. Institutions differ widely in their ability to support them through bursaries or scholarships (one student was offered $9,000 at one institution and nothing at another). Most students' choice of a graduate school is heavily influenced, if not determined, by considerations of money. It often affects their mobility. Unless they are offered financial aid, they will attend their regional university. Doctoral students often help support themselves through teaching or research assistantships. Graduate students in theology are sometimes able to find part-time employment in local churches or other religious institutions. Many graduate students are supported in part by their spouses. Some departments find resources to help students attend conferences. There is no easy way to know how many students are prevented from doing graduate studies or have to abandon them for financial reasons, but financial aid to graduate students is a growing concern of many religious studies graduate officers, department chairs, and heads of theological schools.

9.5   Employment of Graduates

Where do graduates in religious studies find employment? Unfortunately, very few departments or schools actively work at placing their students or keeping track of their graduates in a systematic fashion. One graduate programme affirms that three-quarters of its Ph.D. recipients have found employment in academic institutions and that the others are employed in church, university, or government service. Another department, on the basis of a 26% rate of response to a survey, finds that nearly half of their graduates are in teaching (from primary to university level!), while a third of them are in pastoral services (i.e., ministry).

The normal, expected employment of Ph.D.s is in academic institutions. That is where they find full use of their hard-earned degree. Judging from our data on the faculties of religious studies departments and programmes and of theological colleges in Ontario, employment of graduates holding doctoral degrees from Canadian universities (which means primarily Ontario universities, since they produce the majority of Canadian Ph.D.s in religious studies or theology) has grown substantially in the last twenty years. At the time of maximum expansion of those faculties, between 1965 and 1975, about 24% of the new faculty members had a Canadian degree. Openings for new professors have been fewer since, but the number of new appointees with Canadian degrees has grown to 46%, thanks in part to government pressure to give priority to Canadians, but also to the existence of a larger pool of qualified candidates. In the last few years the proportion of women obtaining academic positions has increased to more than a third (see chap. 5.1.1.1 above).

Those Ph.D.s in religious studies or theology who are denied employment in academic institutions join the M.A.s on the job market. A good number of them find employment with religious institutions. This is not a surprise in the case of graduates of theological schools. They benefit from the continuity between the churches and the educational institutions originally established to serve them. Most graduate students came to theological schools in order to serve their church in the first place. Many Ph.D.s and M.A.s from religious studies graduate programmes find employment in religious institutions as well. It seems that a good number of these religious institutions welcome the contribution of departments of religious studies and the specific expertise their graduates have to offer. One Roman Catholic school system is said to require from potential school teachers three courses in religious studies, and students are said to attend courses at the local university's religious studies department for that precise reason. The least that can be said is that religious studies is not in this case perceived as antagonistic to traditional religion. Does it mean, however, that the specific contribution of religious studies to established religious institutions is recognized or, rather, that the difference is not perceived at all?

The problem would seem to be that expertise in religion (as distinct from religious knowledge within a religious group) has yet to obtain in our society a recognized distinct place. The academic study of religion has now obtained institutional legitimacy in Ontario universities and many have acquired there a new kind of "religion knowledge," but outside the academic world such knowledge has been slow to find significant institutional recognition. At present, even when graduates of religious studies departments are hired by confessional schools or enter the service of a religious institution, it is not evident that the distinctiveness of their learning is recognized. The lag between an emerging area of knowledge and its institutional recognition is a problem for employment and calls for at least two tasks on the part of the present academic owners and dispensers of this knowledge.

First, since religious institutions are currently in fact major employers of religious studies graduates, religious studies departments would do well to survey this market and develop it. They should ask their employed graduates and their respective employers if, and how, the graduates' specific knowledge of religion and skills in analysing religious phenomena have made a difference. To raise these questions would promote awareness of the distinctive contribution of the study of religion to the life of religious institutions and thus work towards the recognition of its status in society.

The second task is to continue promoting religious studies (as distinct from the inculcation of religion) in the public school system. Because schools transmit mainly knowledge and skills recognized by society as "having to be transmitted," however, religious studies in public schools will impose themselves only when the knowledge of religion has gained recognition in the public mind as distinct from traditional religious knowledge and as both useful and enjoyable to society. The Ontario Supreme

Court ruling of September 1988 prohibiting prayer and religious exercises in public schools may lead to some form of religious studies there.[9]

What is needed, then, is the promotion of a more public status for discourse on religion and religion as an object of discourse. Religion is talked about in newspapers, magazines, and the media. One might want to call such discourse on religion "religion criticism." It exists already but, whereas the profession of literary or art critic is well-recognized, the profession of religion critic is not. Could one, at the present time, announce oneself as a religion critic? The recognition of such a profession would be greatly beneficial to the field. It would provide one possible focus to religious studies programmes, as we shall argue below, and some frame of reference for the accountability of religious studies to society. A joint session of the 1988 meeting of the American Academy of Religion and the Society of Biblical Literature in Chicago on "Reporting Religion," to which religion editors of major American newspapers were invited, and the presidential address of Martin Marty to the Academy entitled "Committing the Study of Religion in Public" (Marty, 1989), are recent evidence of a concerted effort to link public and academic discourse on religion (see also the piece by John Dart, Religion Editor of the *Los Angeles Times*, 1978).

The knowledge of religion acquired in religious studies departments also offers a specific contribution to other professions such as chaplaincies (institutional chaplains, e.g., have to serve people of all faiths), nursing, social work, and most other helping professions. That contribution is not well studied and is seldom recognized. Again, one would have to survey the market and work at influencing it.

9.6 Conclusions and Final Observations

Graduate studies in religion in Ontario are shaped by North American university standards through the university systems to which they belong. Some fall also under the academic standards of Roman Catholic universities' rules, which are no less stringent than public North American ones. The doctoral programme is the apex of graduate studies and concerns about its quality are high. Although there are plenty of other factors making for differences in style and quality between universities, there is little leeway and little variation in the conceptualization of doctoral programmes because it is focused on the dissertation and there is general agreement on what constitutes its academic validity.

The M.A. programmes are very different in that respect. Less encumbered by established norms, they are able to respond to a great variety of needs and, in North America, do in fact show extreme diversity. In Ontario the M.A. in religious studies (and in theology as well) has almost everywhere a dual purpose (a terminal degree or the first step towards a Ph.D.). This is a clear source of difficulty. If the M.A. is a preparation for the Ph.D., what it offers is probably not what is most useful to those for whom the

M.A. will be a terminal degree. Conversely, if the programme is adapted to the latter category of students, it will be of less use to the former. The more specific the objectives of the terminal M.A. and the Ph.D., the more difficult it is to plan a master's programme that meets the needs of both equitably. This may explain why descriptions of M.A. programmes are often specific on requirements and vague on educational objectives.

To design the M.A. programme specifically as a preparation for the Ph.D. is a solution that would deprive the large number of other students seeking simply to further their education beyond the B.A. or hoping to find employment other than college and university teaching. To run two parallel graduate programmes with two differently defined objectives does not seem feasible either.

If the M.A. has to remain a condition for the Ph.D., one way to avoid confusion would be to assign to each of the two a specific task, the second building on the first. The objective of the M.A. would be to provide knowledge of religions, understanding of methodology, a grasp of the issues, and the ability to interpret religious phenomena in contemporary cultures. That would prepare well for school teaching, journalism, social work, even undergraduate teaching, and be a solid foundation for specialization at the Ph.D. level. Writing a thesis is incompatible with this general objective within the usual time frame. A certain mastery of knowledge, rather than the ability to do advanced research per se, would characterize the M.A., while specialization in a given area and training for advanced research and university teaching would be the characteristic of the Ph.D.

The above suggestion is not foreign to the present situation, since at least one institution does not even mention a thesis for the M.A. and another suggests that breadth of learning and exploration of new domains of religious knowledge are what a master's programme often requires. But we suggest in addition that such a programme might be better focused if it were associated with some known public competence, such as the ability to interpret religious phenomena in different media, to speak intelligently about religion and its manifestations to a non-specialized audience, activities tentatively grouped here under the label "religion criticism." With such an objective in mind the criteria for admission to the M.A. programme, the nature of graduate courses, curriculum, and examination procedures could be more sharply defined.

The shape of the M.A. programme in religious studies, possibly its future, and certainly its health, will likely depend on the profile achieved by knowledge of religion in society, that is, on its eventual professional status. The word "professional" arouses suspicion in academic circles because it is not always recognized that being an academic is a profession. The M.A. in religious studies (unlike the M.A. in theology) need not be less academic simply because there are recognized uses for the knowledge acquired therein. The emergence of clearer roles for people knowledgeable in religion will help departments of religious studies sharpen their educational objectives.

We have suggested earlier that universities have not only a stake in the emergence of recognized professional uses for religion knowledge but a role to play in achieving that goal. One could imagine the creation of joint master's programmes in Religion and Journalism, Religion and Library Science, Religion and Social Work, etc., on the model of Wilfrid Laurier's joint Master of Divinity and Master of Social Work programme.

Notes

1 The only new graduate programme funded by the province since the ACAP report is the M.A. in Pastoral Care at Saint Paul University.

2 The figures for religious studies in Table 9-1 and in our text come from the annual statistical reports of the Ontario Council on Graduate Studies and the *Directory* published by the Council on the Study of Religion (now the Council of Societies for the Study of Religion)(especially for data on Master's programmes [Remus, 1981, 1985; Mills, 1987, 1988). For theological schools figures were harder to obtain and come from data provided by the schools themselves and the Association of Theological Schools' annual *Fact Book on Theological Education*. The latter, unfortunately, gives enrolment figures for each theological school by degree programme but not the number of degrees granted, does not distinguish between M.A.s and other master's degrees, and does not include figures for some schools pertinent to our survey. The figures for 1972 are from Anderson, 1972.

3 The M.T.S. programme is difficult to place. It can be as "academic" as the M.A. in its thesis stream. The reason for locating it among "ministerial" programmes is that courses taken are usually those of the M.Div. programme. (See, further, chap. 4.3.1 above.)

4 A comparison between the number of doctoral students in a given year and the number of graduates five or six years later, using data from the Association of Theological Schools for the years 1976 to 1985, gives roughly the same result. The average ratio of graduates to doctoral students five years earlier is 1 to 6.3 without counting the inevitable percentage of attrition along the way (the average will inevitably vary from year to year). Exact figures from McMaster showed an average of 6.3 years between admission to the doctoral programme (after the M.A.) and reception of the degree (the average will inevitably vary from year to year). In the U.S. the average time required between first enrolment in a Ph.D. programme and reception of the degree, in the field of Humanities, is now 6.2 years, the longest among all fields (National Research Council, 1987).

5 According to Statistics Canada's figures (Annual *Catalogue* 81-204 for 1978 to 1988), the average annual number of doctoral graduates in religious studies and theology was in fact 19 between 1977 and 1987. The figures for the masters graduates cannot be used to check ours because they include other masters' degrees than those considered in the present study.

6 According to our data on faculty members, in the period of rapid expansion of religious studies departments and theological schools in Ontario, between 1965 and 1975, the proportion of teachers hired before they had received their degree went as high as 39%. It fell to 24% between 1975 and 1980 and as low as 6% in the early 1980s, when there was little hiring and many seeking employment.

7 A good survey of the expansion and present complexity of this degree in the U.S.A. can be found in Glazer, 1986.

8 On this section cf., further, chap. 4.2 above.

9 In 1989 the departments of religious studies in Ontario joined in submitting a brief to this effect to Dr. Glenn Watson, who had been appointed by the Minister of Education to submit a report by January 1990 on religious education in public schools. Released by

the Minister in December 1990, it recommended for all public elementary schools a compulsory programme of "religion studies" (not "religious education") the purpose of which would be "learning about religion" rather than "indoctrination" (Watson, 1990, 59) and without which it would be "impossible to provide a comprehensive education" (ibid., 57). However, the Ministry, according to a background paper, rejected the recommendation because "there is no public consensus on the role of education about religion in the public elementary school curriculum, nor is there widespread experience in Ontario with this subject." Instead, the Ministry, continuing the interim policy instituted after the Ontario Supreme Court banning religious education that was indoctrinating in nature, ruled that school boards would be allowed to authorize non-indoctrinating instruction about religion for about an hour a week (Thompson, 1990). Responsiveness of religious studies departments to the needs of school teaching is not without some constraints, as the study by Rousseau and Despland on religious studies in Quebec has shown (1988, 61-63). See, further, chap. 12.10.3 below.

10

Libraries, Databases, Teaching and Research

Harold Remus

Things have changed since 1878 when the rules for the Victoria University library in Toronto specified the hours as "every Friday and Saturday from half-past two to half-past four, p.m." "during term time" and stipulated that books were to be checked out on Saturday afternoon and returned the following Friday but restricted the number per student to "one volume at a time, (unless the volume belongs to a set, and an additional volume is needed for the proper understanding of the other, of which necessity the Librarian shall be the judge)."

Library hours in small colleges with only part-time staffing may still resemble those of Victorian Victoria University, and some library staff today may still seem to construe library "holdings" to mean "hold closely" and a book on loan as a book waiting to be returned to its (proper) resting place on the shelves of the library. Those are exceptions, however: libraries and librarians today are committed to "user friendliness." But the most profound change since 1878 is the overwhelming volume of what libraries might be expected to collect or make accessible to faculties and student bodies that have also markedly changed since that time. There are also academic fields that did not exist in Ontario a century ago, religious studies among them. If technology is to a great degree responsible for many of the changes in universities and libraries, it is also technology that has changed the way library users learn about and, often, gain access to the present flood of information and then employ it in teaching and research.

Some things do not change, however. A century ago monies for education were scarce, priorities had to be set, and libraries were not at the top of the list. Priorities in collection policies, the areas in which collecting was to

Notes to Chapter 10 can be found on pages 266-67.

be done, and the scope of collecting also had to be determined. Today, these various concerns are, if anything, even more pressing than they were then.

It is these various issues, old and new, that we sought to address in examining library resources for religious studies in Ontario. We asked librarians to complete two questionnaires. The first (circulated in the late 1980s) asked for information on acquisition policies and budgets. The second (sent out in 1990) asked about electronic databases. (See Appendix A below.) In addition, in interviewing faculty and department or theological college administrators we asked about library resources and collection policies. Both in the interviews and on the first questionnaire we asked who is responsible for implementing policies and who makes the actual decisions on purchasing. We also asked faculty for their perceptions of the libraries at their institutions. As always in this study, we were interested in the picture for Ontario religious studies as a whole, rather than for individual institutions (see Preface).

Since policies and their implementation are geared to local needs and budgets, in what follows institutions are grouped according to whether they offer degree programmes in religious studies at the undergraduate level only, or have a master's programme as well, or offer both the master's and the doctorate. Libraries of theological colleges figured into the picture inasmuch as some offer academic graduate programmes (see chap. 9.1) and insofar as their resources may augment religious studies collections or, indeed, be factored into religious studies acquisitions policies. As with much in our study, limitations of time, energy, and money did not permit a thoroughgoing survey. What follows therefore is more in the nature of soundings and raising of issues, with some suggestions and recommendations, rather than full-scale reporting and analysis.

10.1 Collection Development and Acquisition Policies

Statements of collection development and acquisition policies were readily supplied to us, in writing in the case of librarians, at least orally by faculty. In addition, our questionnaire asked at which of five levels libraries developed their collections in 21 areas of religious studies: basic reference, undergraduate teaching, beginning research, comprehensive, and intensive.[1]

In institutions where instruction in religious studies is offered only at the undergraduate level, collecting is mostly to serve teaching requirements at that level, with some acquisition of beginning research materials. Acquisition of books and periodicals in languages other than English, or sources in original languages, is selective, often highly so. At one small institution, however, selectivity means including materials in Ojibway as well as some of the standard editions of early Christian sources ("the fathers") in Greek and Latin and in English translation that some libraries at institutions with graduate religious studies programmes do not possess. Although selectivity in universities with undergraduate religious studies degree programmes may focus on purchasing at the teaching level, acquisitions are generally said to take account of faculty research insofar as funds, regular or special, permit.

Collection policies at universities with M.A. programmes give more weight to the beginning research level, with comprehensive collecting reported for selected areas where departmental research and instruction are focussed. It is only in universities with both M.A. and Ph.D. programmes in religious studies that collection policies consistently embrace the comprehensive and intensive levels. However, collection policy at one theological college with both professional and graduate degree programmes is very close to these university M.A. and Ph.D. policies. Otherwise, collection levels at theological colleges tend to resemble those of university religious studies M.A. programmes but more concentrated in Christianity and related areas.

To what degree funds allocated for acquisitions support collection policies is another question. To our knowledge, no religious studies department in Ontario has tried to figure out what they might consider a budget adequate to support the study of religion at either the undergraduate or graduate levels. Twenty years ago Claude Welch (1971, 79) posited an annual acquisitions budget of U.S.$25,000 (about $116,000 in 1991 Canadian currency) as the basement figure necessary to support credible doctoral study. By that or almost any other measure, library budgets for religious studies in Ontario — graduate or undergraduate — are generally meagre. One notes, too, quite large differences among departments and programmes offering instruction at the same levels. Some of these have to do with the size of one institution in comparison with another or with relative degrees of penury from place to place. Others have to do with the proximity of other libraries and efforts on the part of acquisitions librarians and religious studies faculty to avoid duplications in holdings. Even taking such factors into account, and granting that collection policies represent desiderata and intentions more than actual practice, in some cases it is difficult to see any significant relation between policy and practice.

Faculty assessments of their libraries, offered in interviews, provide another perspective on collection policies and acquisition budgets. These correlated to some degree with the collection policies at their institutions, but probably even more with the budget realities there. At those offering only undergraduate religious studies degrees, with collecting restricted to the first two or three levels (basic reference, undergraduate teaching, beginning research), faculty found their libraries — large or small — inadequate for research. At one large institution offering only undergraduate religious studies degrees, one professor said that the library was all right for student use but that even in preparing lectures he found it necessary to resort to a nearby research library or to his personal library, while at a college associated with another university a professor said that even students found the college library inadequate.

At universities with M.A. programmes the picture painted was not all that different: the collections were adequate for undergraduate and most graduate instruction but deficient in resources for research. These assessments, however, varied by field, sometimes sharply. One specialist in Asian religions found the local library "the pits" for research. There were "the old classics" but not much more; serials and journals were especially lacking. This person had, with the co-operation of the library, been building up the collection since entering the department but had hesitated to order a great deal since no one else in the department was working in the same area. On the other hand, more than one professor working in a field with ties to another field (or fields) represented in the university by a strong undergraduate department or by a master's or doctoral programme — classics, history, psychology, anthropology, English were mentioned — commented on how that enhanced the resources for research in their own field. Some faculty specializing in Christianity or the fields traditionally related to it were quite content with their libraries: collecting in these areas had been going on a long time and continued strong inasmuch as many faculty were still specializing in them; in several instances a theological library was located nearby as well or was included as part of the university collection. Even within the Christian area, however, perceptions within an institution might vary, depending on individuals' specific subfields, their particular research interests, and the vigour with which they pursued them. One young and prolific scholar, for instance, found the local library quite inadequate in primary sources and foreign language serials and journals and so made frequent forays to a large research library.

At institutions with both master's and doctoral programmes in religious studies, again it was those faculty specializing in Christian studies who were much more likely to be content with their libraries than those working in other areas. Assessments by the former ranged from "excellent" and "superb" to "very good" and "adequate." And once again, the resources of theological libraries — one of which was labelled "fantastic" — figured into such assessments. Scholars of Asian religions were much more sombre in characterizing resources in their area: "pretty good if you don't push them"; "barely adequate"; "inadequate." The picture might be worse were it not for the Shastri Indo-Canada Institute Library Programme, which has helped Ontario religious studies departments to add to their collection many books and journals they would otherwise have been unable to acquire (see chap. 2.4.7 above and, e.g., Coward, 1986, 285).

These various assessments by faculty temper optimistic readings of collection policies and, not surprisingly, confirm what was suggested earlier, that budgetary restrictions hinder implementation of the policies. Sometimes, however, faculty nonchalance about submitting acquisition requests to libraries is also a factor (see 10.3 below). Not surprising, either, is that it was in the area of resources for research that most dissatisfaction was expressed but, also, that our interviewees had come to terms with the problem in various ways. They had come to accept, or resigned themselves to, the fact that library acquisition budgets are stretched thin and commonly well back in the queue for scarce funds; moreover, that comprehensive and intensive collecting are feasible only at large institutions, in effect confirming projections a quarter century ago of half a dozen or so major research centres across Canada (Graham, 1968, 24), but that even there funds are not necessarily adequate either. Accordingly, they had adopted various research strategies: they had extensive private research libraries, or they had worked hard over the years — sometimes against the opposition of librarians or administrators — to build up the research collection in their particular specialization(s), or they relied on neighbouring libraries or interlibrary loan or trips to research libraries to supply their needs, or they were turning increasingly to electronic databases for help (10.2 below), or various combinations of these options.

Recently the establishing of electronic databases has put at the disposal of scholars texts that hitherto were accessible only through interlibrary loan or through a visit to a major research library. Thus the texts of the "Corpus Christianorum Series Latina" as well as others not included in that series will soon be available in the CETEDOC Library of Christian Latin Texts (CLCLT) being developed by the Centre de Traitement Électronique des Documents of the Université Catholique de Louvain and Brepols Publishers. The Oxford Text Archive offers a voluminous (if that is not too anachronistic a term) collection both of Western and non-Western texts. The Archive has "Probably the most comprehensive catalogue of electronic data currently available" (Kraft, 1991b, 51). At least two Ontario institutions are assembling electronic databases. The Research Centre at St. Paul University is compiling a bibliography called "Repertoire bibliographique informatisé en histoire religieuse du Canada" that will be available in bilingual format on MULTILIS software. At Redeemer College the Pascal Centre is developing a bibliography on faith and science that it intends to make accessible also to users outside the College.

Electronically accessible resources are a great boon to scholars, especially those at smaller institutions. Electronic databases facilitate, for example, their research in what are standard, edited texts that because of cost can be acquired in hard copy only by large research libraries. It does not, however, obviate the continuing need for on-the-spot, first-hand examination of manuscripts and various documents and texts in hard copy and of materials not yet available in electronic form. Nor does it help if one's library does not possess desired texts on tape or disc or offer electronic access to them. Thus, while Ontario colleges and universities, large and small, are strong in bibliographic databases, either on line or on disc, so far they are weak in text databases, on line, on disc, or on tape. The King James Version of the Bible is commonly available electronically in Ontario college and university libraries, and the FABS Electronic Bible and Reference Bible as well as the Thesaurus Linguae Graecae and similar resources are available at a few places; however, the Oxford Text Archive tapes are accessible only as individuals write Oxford and ask for a specific text, which (for a fee) is then downloaded to a disc or tape and sent to the person making the request.

So while the need for travel funds for textual research may not be as pressing as it once was (Priestley, 1968, 13), they are still important. One scholar described what inadequate local resources for research mean for him: travelling, perhaps some distance, to a research library, during the week or on weekends or when classes are not in session; relying on interlibrary loan, which means a considerable delay in getting the books and sometimes putting aside what one is working on until the book arrives, and then having to work one's way into the issues again; or waiting for a sabbatical. In short, a scholar at a place that lacks a research library faces delays and frustrations and expenditures of time and energy that one at a major research centre does not. What may lighten the burdens now is the electronic library network that enables one to browse on-line catalogues at remote locations (for details and beginners' instructions see O'Donnell, 1990).

The best of worlds is when one has hard copy in abundance as well as access to at least some electronic databases. One interesting example in Ontario is a largish theological college with both professional and graduate degree programmes and a budget that by all indications is commensurate with them. Its annual acquisitions budget at the time of our first survey about four years ago was well above Claude Welch's minimum for doctoral study, seven times that of one of the Ontario universities with M.A. and Ph.D. programmes in religious studies, twice of that of another. Several variables can of course be adduced to account for these significant differences, but in the case of the theological college the commitment to scholarship on the part of faculty, administration, and governors, as demonstrated in acquisitions budget, is at the very least heartening. If accessibility is a condition of use, this library is a great boon to religious studies faculty and students in that particular area of Ontario who are doing work in Christianity. For many others, it is probably still an undiscovered country to whose bourne they might well wish to repair.

Texts in electronic form are much less expensive than in hard copy and make retrospective collecting much easier and less expensive as well as allow libraries to keep up to date with new editions of texts. (For example, the Thesaurus Linguae Graecae CD-ROM, containing the standard editions of 18,411 works by approximately 3,000 Greek writers from the eighth century BCE to 600 CE, is licensed to institutions for a registration fee of US$200 and an annual fee of US$100; for individuals these two fees are even less, US$60 each [Hughes, 1990, 38-39].) These alone are reasons for religious studies departments and programmes to make electronic databases an essential part of their collection policies. Perhaps even more important, however, is that texts in electronic form also offer new possibilities for research, facilitating translating and editing of texts as well as various kinds of concordance study and stylistic and content analysis that would otherwise be extremely laborious if not virtually impossible. Biblical scholars have for some time been carrying on such research (see, e.g., the electronic tools and texts cited in Zahavy, 1991 and Luc 1991). Some of the many computer applications to medieval studies are outlined in Gilmour-Bryson, 1984. For the modern period, the work on Kierkegaard by Abrahim Khan of Toronto (1985) and of his mentor, Alastair McKinnon of McGill (see the titles cited in ibid., 138, and McKinnon, 1982), offer early examples.

A boon to religious studies departments and programmes are the library resources of Ontario theological colleges in the Christian area and related areas. These resources amount to retrospective collections that would be prohibitively expensive or simply impossible for religious studies collections to acquire. On the other hand, religious studies acquisitions in areas where theological colleges do not generally make purchases, or cannot afford to do so given the necessity to keep their holdings current with publications in the Christian area, should be of benefit to the colleges. Our survey of collection levels by area of religious studies shows that religious studies' acquisitions are still heavily concentrated in the Christian area. As religious studies continues to acquire a profile distinct from the study of theology (see chap. 12 below), with more faculty working in religious traditions other than Christianity and in non-Western religions, library holdings in religious studies may also be expected to reflect these developments. However, it is also important that religious studies departments and programmes give attention to this question when, together with their libraries, they review their collection development policies.

This is a propitious time to review those policies. As is indicated elsewhere in this study (e.g., chap. 3.2.2), the 1980s were a time of transition in religious studies in Ontario. The changing of the guard in religious studies departments and programmes in the 1990s (chaps. 5.1.1.2, 5.3, and 12.2) will mark something like an end of the transition. The effects are already being seen as new faculty, with academic pedigrees and profiles different from those of the present incumbents (chaps. 4.2.1, 4.2.2, and 5.1.1), make their presence felt in faculty meetings, in classrooms, and in learned society gatherings. The 1990s, then, offer unique opportunities to realize some of the distinctives that religious studies scholars have perceived as setting the field apart (while not cutting it off) both from the theological colleges and from the cognate academic fields that contributed to its formation. If library collection policies mean anything, they should reflect these changes and indeed figure into bringing them about. In the area of Asian religions, for example, collections are well established at large universities where graduate programmes in those traditions have been in place for some time (though inadequate budget and other factors may hamper efforts to keep them current; see above). At other places, however, better representation of these traditions in curricula should be accompanied by appropriate changes in collection policies. Journal subscriptions might also come under scrutiny, both for reasons such as these and (in a time of tight budgets) with respect to the question which journals actually support present departmental aims and research. Electronic databases need to be included in collection policies either as CD-ROM or tape acquisitions or through licensing arrangements. These newer kinds of scholarly resources raise significant questions, both for libraries and for teaching and research.

10.2 Electronic Databases

As is indicated elsewhere in this study (chap. 3.2.5), use of electronic databases is an area where one is apt to observe a generational transition, with students and younger faculty more likely than older faculty to be availing themselves of electronic data. The first steps to computer literacy commonly begin when today's students are children. When they enter university, introduction to on-line library catalogues and electronic search facilities available in the library is a standard feature of orientation weeks. For religious studies concentrators it is important that further instruction follow, both in the use of databases in the humanities and social sciences generally and in religious studies specifically. At one university a senior faculty member versed in this kind of research and one of the reference librarians with an M.A. in religious studies co-operate in the instruction in the early sessions of the methodology seminar mandatory for all M.A. students. Included are assignments requiring them to develop, as for a thesis or paper, a full working bibliography based in part on searching of electronic databases. In the writing of papers and theses it is then assumed that the students will have conducted similar searches for previous scholarly literature on their topic. Still in the offing, as more texts become available electronically, says the professor, are exercises in the kind of textual study mentioned earlier (10.1 above).

While it is younger faculty who are likely to be the adepts, at home with electronic databases and the kinds of teaching and research they make possible, we observed a goodly number of older faculty, too, who were at various stages of acquaintance with the new ways of doing things. Not surprisingly, the traditional mentoring situation—older of younger—was often reversed, with younger faculty offering senior colleagues advice and assistance. Both for old hands and neophytes, the column "OFFLINE: Computer Assisted Research for Religious Studies," by Robert Kraft of the religious studies department, University of Pennsylvania, has proved invaluable. Appearing regularly in the *Council of Societies for the Study of Religion Bulletin* and in *Religious Studies News* as well electronically to members of the HUMANIST network prior to its publication in hard copy, it spreads the new gospel to the unconverted and keeps those already in the fold apprised of new resources and wrinkles. (A complete file of OFFLINE columns is available electronically through the HUMANIST network fileserver [humanist@brownvm.brown.edu].)

A recent OFFLINE column, for example, provides information on the American Bible Society's "ABS Reference Bible" CD-ROM, a database that includes Hebrew and Greek Bible texts and tools, English Bible versions and tools, Luther's translation, English translations of Josephus and the Apostolic Fathers, and Abingdon's *Dictionary of Bible and Religion* (Kraft, 1991b, 52). In another column Kraft (1990, 81) urges scholarly journals to review software and databases, alongside books. (The 1990 edition of *Critical Review of Books in Religion* includes two such reviews, comprehensive in scope and addressed to the uninitiated; see Hughes, 1990 and Scrimgeour, 1990.) Electronic journals are also coming into being. Thanks to the energetic efforts of persons like Kraft, displays of hardware and software are a regular feature of the joint annual meetings of the American Academy of Religion and the Society of Biblical Literature. Kraft is apt to show up, with appropriate displays, at the meetings of other learned societies as well.

Closer to home, John Hurd's work in computer-assisted instruction in New Testament Greek at the University of Toronto, and then beyond through his GreekTutor software, are well known (see the description in Hughes, 1990, 31-32 and cf. chap. 2.4.1 above). *Canadian Humanities Computing*, published by the Centre for Computing in the Humanities at the University of Toronto for the Consortium for Computing in the Humanities/le Consortium pour ordinateurs en sciences humaines, is an informative newsletter. A recent issue, for example, has an article on software (Zondervan's ScriptureFonts) that introduces pointed Hebrew and accented Greek into WordPerfect 5.1 (Johnson and Cioran, 1990). Another (Steele, 1990) reports on a new electronic network for students of Shakespeare. One of the liveliest networks has been the one called IOUDAIOS, begun in 1990 by Steve Mason of the religious studies programme at York University and with David Reimer, Department of Religion and Culture, Wilfrid Laurier University, recently added as "co-owner." Intended for scholars in Judaism in the first century CE but in practice extending several centuries each way, the network now includes over 200 members located in almost all parts of the world. An electronic journal devoted to reviewing of recent publications in the area is the most recent undertaking of the network.

Outside the academic world, electronic networks are now estimated at perhaps 50,000, on almost any subject (Kraft, 1991a, 26). The non-commercial network, BITNET, through its links with other networks connects colleges, universities, and research centres at 1,300 places in 38 countries with (in 1990) over 900 discussion groups (Scrimgeour, 1990, 51-52). *The User's Directory of Computer Networks* (Bedford, MA: Digital Press, 1990) provides information on how to locate resources, send mail, and gain access to academic and research networks. Discussion groups ("networks," in common parlance) are an interesting and lively way to stay in touch with much of what is going on in one's field, and a way to "meet" other scholars. Electronic acquaintanceships can then lead to face-to-face meetings which, without preliminaries, can continue scholarly discussion initiated electronically. In these respects networking is an inexpensive alternative to attending professional society meetings (see chap. 3.2.5 above), though not, we would suggest, a substitute for them (chap. 12.8 below).

Networking, we would also suggest, has its pitfalls. The flip side of staying electronically *au courant*, day to day and week to week, may be distraction from serious, steady research, or failing to set priorities amid the scholarly wonderland into which one can step electronically (Kraft, 1991a, 24). And the Faustian temptation beckons; as one adept observed recently,

> it is virtually impossible to keep up with the deluge of new and always faster hardware products and the ever growing software list. It seems unlikely that generalist types will be able to stay abreast of the field much longer. Active colleagues testified that the involvement in serious projects requires more than a full-time commitment (Zahavy, 1991, 25).

In the Ontario institutions we visited, this particular temptation seems remote, even taking into account the passage of several years since our visits to them which, in the world of electronic communication, approximates aeons.

As is noted elsewhere in this volume (chaps. 3.2.5, 7.7, 12.8), Ontario has its academic loners who produce important, often first-rate scholarship; networks will probably appeal to them as little as professional society meetings do. For most scholars, however, the choice increasingly is probably not whether to belong to a network, but which ones, and how — whether more as active contributor or as eavesdropper; whether to tune in to many channels or to focus on the one or the few (or on dialogue with the one or several scholars in a network) that will best contribute to pursuit of the long-term, carefully planned goals that, in the humanities, produce significant scholarship (Highet, 1950, 22-26, 85-88 might bear looking at again in this connection). Such dialogue is possible through electronic mail, apart from network symposia, of course. And of course much depends on the quality of the network(s) one tunes into, whether members commonly dash off opinions — the equivalent of hall and faculty-lounge chit-chat — or weigh what they say before they say it, and provide warrants. Worst is when they indulge in gamesmanship (sic), or even insult and invective. Networkers might ponder Francis Bacon's aphorism, "Reading maketh a full man [sic], conference a ready man, and writing an exact man" (*Of Studies*).

Another temptation is surface expertise. As the professor in one cartoon puts it as he sits before his terminal, "I'm accessing more and reading less." An Ontario religious studies professor cited to us the case of an American religious studies professor interested in a classic work by a Canadian scholar: she knew from daily vigils at the terminal who was doing research on the book and where each was located — but had not herself read the book.

Only in their form are these kinds of pitfalls new. In discussing electronic scholarship with Ontario religious studies faculty, during our interviews or subsequently, none cited them as reason to shut oneself off from the new world. Rather, they were excited about the possibilities and apt to be concerned about how to make the libraries at their institutions places that would facilitate the new kinds of research. Here, as with reviewing of collection policies, much depends on librarians and relations between academics and librarians.

10.3   Librarians and Academics

Academics scanning the pages of the *Canadian Association of University Teachers Bulletin Association canadienne des professeurs d'université* will probably have noticed articles and a column devoted to university librarians' activities and concerns. Members of faculty associations, especially those that have been certified as unions, will probably also be aware of the presence of librarians in meetings or on committees. And most academics and librarians will recognize that they have some obvious mutual concerns. Whether any of this leads to mutual respect and co-operation is another matter.

Many librarians do not have academic degrees beyond their undergraduate and professional library degrees. All are "schedule driven," not enjoying the flexible hours that academics take for granted. A goodly number are consumed by the heavy day-to-day demands on them, or preoccupied by necessity or choice with the technical aspects of their work. Some are determinedly managers and administrators, with little intrinsic interest in what they manage and administrate. It is just this, however, that interests academics: the books, periodicals, databases, the various resources for teaching and research that constitute "the library" for them. And librarians surely exist to assure that these various resources are there, adequately and available, every season and every day of the year and preferably nights as well.

These mutual incomprehensions are not helpful in a time when library budgets are lean, the annual volume of new publications is overwhelming, and modes of publication and use are changing rapidly. In the larger universities, and generally in theological colleges,[2] a number of faculty told us that the acquisitions librarians are competent and do their jobs well. At one smaller university we were shown a bibliography on Christianity and the visual arts compiled by one of the reference librarians; another reference librarian at the same school had done one on Christianity in Canada (both of these works known, unfortunately, only within the university and scarcely even there).

Many librarians need (and want) the academic training that would equip them to do this kind of work. And some at least would benefit from an enlarged understanding of academics' concerns, which have changed in recent decades as universities have changed. As for academics, it is probably safe to say they would benefit from knowing more about libraries and librarians' training, their working conditions, their concerns. University librarians are making efforts to increase better understanding of their profession (see, e.g., *Inside OLA* [i.e., Ontario Library Association] 15 [1991], 6). Another step in this direction was a conference entitled "The Academic Partnership/La solidarité universitaire" that brought librarians and academics together in Ottawa in November 1990 to consider issues such as workloads, promotion and tenure, faculty status for librarians, and professional development (CAUT *Bulletin* 37/8 [Oct. 1990], 18).

Academics have a stake in such concerns. Gender issues, a topic at one of the sessions, are not so different in libraries and in faculty settings. Study leaves, which academics regard as inalienable rights essential to professional growth and competence, are also important for librarians but are, instead, usually conceded to them only as privileges, hardly and infrequently won and commonly restricted to "release-time" provisions (Brett and Moore, 1991). "A Day in the Life of an Academic Librarian" — filled with committee meetings, administrative detail, demands of library users (Murchie, 1991) — rings distressingly familiar in academic ears. Only at the end of such a day (writes the Nova Scotia author of an article with that title) is there the time to do what

> brought me to libraries in the first place — reviewing and selecting books for possible acquisition, working on developing the collection which is after all what I still think a library is about. I will look through *Choice* and *British Book News*; I will sort through the box of flyers which I have collected over the past week; I will read reviews in a half dozen or more periodicals and scan the "books received" listings; I will review the bibliographies in two monographs; I will give some thought to the library's collections policies, the expressed concerns of faculty, the observed demands made by users, the growing information on what is available in other libraries (thanks, again, to co-operative automation), changes in the curriculum in the past few years and possibly in the future and, yes, the problem of money — all those aspects of selecting a few books out of the many available, the professional librarian's trusteeship to the future. The excitement of books and scholarship; reading and learning, the thought that a decision here might make a difference, the possibility of a reader's consciousness revolutionized by a book in the library . . . suddenly, I am no longer tired (Murchie, 1991).

These are the sorts of tasks that at least some faculty at the institutions we visited were also performing, systematically or otherwise, with sometimes one person or a committee assigned the responsibility on behalf of the rest of the faculty. These efforts got mixed reviews from faculty. In a couple of places — one offering only undergraduate religious studies degrees, the other with a graduate programme as well — they cited lack of coordination between faculty submitting requests to the library. At another university with a graduate programme the chair circulates publishers' catalogues in which faculty initial their requests for acquisition; the department's library committee consisting of two professors and one graduate student then allots the titles requested among the various areas, after which the graduate student records in the department's on-line acquisitions file (begun in 1980) what books have been ordered and in which areas. At still another university with a graduate programme books are selected through a combination of standing orders and faculty requests filtered through the departmental library representative, who noted that only three or four persons bothered to go through catalogues and reviews and pass on the requests (these few did a good job, however).

Faculty participation in acquisitions can make a difference. In one institution faculty took inventory of the books and periodicals in the collection and then compared these with a bibliography compiled by one of the faculty, with the result that the number of books ordered greatly increased, missing periodicals were acquired, and cataloguing was speeded up.

The responses to our questionnaire make clear that faculty can only advise and hope for consent: the control of acquisition budgets and purchasing decisions, both in universities and theological colleges, rests almost always with the library. Things do not always go smoothly. In one institution the faculty insisted on overseeing acquisitions because books were being purchased that the faculty did not want. At another, faculty members struggled with the library for years, trying to persuade it to acquire some primary sources essential both to faculty research and the graduate programme. One knowledgeable faculty member wondered about the standing order and approval plans that our questionnaires show are commonly in use. For example, if these exclude series purchases, as they sometimes do, then are important volumes in a series missed? Since faculty members usually do not participate directly in the decisions on these plans, that underlines the importance, he said, of librarians who are academically trained, and specifically with at least some acquaintance with religious studies. Failing that, consultation between librarians and faculty is especially important.

Cataloguing of acquisitions was another concern of some faculty we interviewed. Because religious studies is such a broad field, involving many cultures and languages, librarians with the requisite background and linguistic training are hard to find, which means that a book, wrongly catalogued, may become in effect inaccessible. Library of Congress cards are basic, but a cataloguer needs to know how to apply them consistently and so as to make sense in the local library. Moreover, a fair number of publications in religious studies come devoid of LC cards and require on-site classification by persons with the requisite linguistic competence and some knowledge of the fields involved. At another university, where faculty requested that volumes in a newly acquired series be shelved together for ease of reference and browsing, the library said that was technically impossible and, when told that other libraries had indeed done so, and after being instructed in how it could be done, refused. Foolish consistencies tend to perpetuate themselves, also after cataloguing decisions have been made, for example, pasting classification tags at uniform heights even if it means covering over the volume numbers of reference works.

These various examples point up the need, once again, for better understanding and co-operation between librarians and faculty and for faculty to be involved in collection and acquisition decisions. Perhaps even more important is that faculty lobby within their universities for better training for librarians and for measures to help them improve their training and to allow them to devote more of their time to tasks bearing on libraries' reasons for being. Inclusion of librarians in faculty associations and unions has contributed to these ends on some campuses. In urging their inclusion at Brock University, the editor of the faculty association newsletter observed that

> One of our most important resources, some say the very heart of the university, is the library. Anything we [faculty members] can do to contribute to the professional development of our librarians can only be of benefit to us as academics (Lye, 1991, 2).

10.4 Concluding Observations

To reiterate, the 1990s are a good time for religious studies departments and programmes and libraries to review collection policies in light of current and projected teaching and research aims and with a closer eye on budget realities. That might well mean more specific directives on the acquisition or leasing of electronic databases. In some places more attention to implementation of policies would seem to be in order, for example, through a departmental library representative or committee, with perhaps a student assistant assigned to help where funds for such are available. At least more coordination between faculty making book requests would seem wise. As electronic databases become part of a religious studies collection, instruction in their use should be part of professors' agendas, both for themselves and for students. Librarians might also be invited to classes and seminars to share in the instruction. That would be one way of recognizing and furthering a commonalty of interests and expertise between them and faculty that is increasingly important in a time of ''high-volume'' and ''high-tech'' publishing and research.

Notes

1 Descriptions of the collection levels:
  - *Intensive Level*: Supports doctoral and post-doctoral research with a high degree of adequacy and minimum reliance on interlibrary loan or other outside resources.
  - *Comprehensive Level*: Includes a wide range of published material, but probably little manuscript or special materials except in narrowly defined fields or for special needs. Expected to support with reasonable adequacy the doctoral work now offered or likely to be undertaken in the near future.
  - *Beginning Research Level*: Provides full support for undergraduate programmes and most of the materials required for work at the master's level.

- *Teaching Level*: Maintains a collection needed to support undergraduate instruction effectively and includes reference materials of all kinds, files of basic journals, and a wide range of subject indexes and bibliographies.
- *Basic Reference Level*: Designed to build collections selectively in subject areas in which no formal academic programme is offered, but which overlap with subject areas in which academic programmes are available.

  The 21 subject areas: Philosophy of Religion; Psychology of Religion; Sociology of Religion; Anthropology of Religion; Ethics; Ritual, Worship, Cultus; Religion and Literature; Religion and the Arts; South Asian Religions: Hinduism, Jainism, et al.; Southeast Asian Religions: Confucianism, Taoism, et al.; Buddhism; African Religions; Greek Religion; Roman Religion; Judaism; Islam; Christianity: History; Christianity: Theology; Christianity: Denominations; Bible; Religion in Canada.

2 Theological colleges, with a long library tradition and a professional society (the American Theological Libraries Association) constituted specifically for their libraries and librarians, are apt to have librarians with appropriate academic expertise; a university library, on the other hand, especially a smaller one, is less likely to have a librarian with the necessary expertise in religious studies.

11

Bible Colleges

Harold Remus

A peculiarly Protestant phenomenon, Bible colleges are something of a cross between a liberal arts college and a theological college.

As in a liberal arts college, Bible college curricula commonly include general education courses and extend over three or four years. Like university students concentrating in religious studies, Bible college students major in religion, specifically Christianity, usually Bible. However, in contrast to the way these are approached in a religious studies department, Christianity in some form is regarded as in some way normative, the Bible is posited as divinely inspired and uniquely authoritative, and one is expected to live a life that accords with its teachings.

Like a theological college, the Bible college is a professional school in that the curriculum includes practical courses to train students for various forms of Christian ministry. However, unlike students in most theological colleges, those in Bible colleges generally enter with only a high school diploma. In Canada, completion of the course of study generally culminates, not in a master's degree, as in a theological college, but in a diploma or a baccalaureate degree that, unlike the Bachelor of Arts or honours degree of religious studies, is likely to be professional in nature (Bachelor of Theology, Bachelor of Religious Education, Bachelor of Sacred Music).

While "college" often functions today as a generic name for these schools, often suggesting (to twentieth-century ears) post-secondary education, it is not a wholly suitable term. The first such schools were established originally as Bible institutes or Bible training schools, intended especially for persons without enough formal education to qualify them for entrance to a college or university, and today there are still many Bible institutes and training schools, some of which admit persons lacking a high school diploma. There is in fact a variety of institutions which common and current

---

Notes to Chapter 11 can be found on pages 284-85.

usage designates as "Bible colleges." Despite significant differences, they nonetheless share certain fundamental traits that distinguish them from other educational institutions. This chapter therefore uses "Bible colleges" as a generic term and tries, as much as the sources permit, to distinguish between "colleges" (some of which, it should be noted, bear the name "seminary") and "institutes" or "training schools.'

Their origins, their aims, their ethos, their curricula, their faculty and students, and the way religion is conceived and studied in Bible colleges set them apart from, and provide a useful contrast to, religious studies. Their origins and history, however, follow a course that often runs parallel to, even while distinct from, religious studies. There are other points of contact as well. Some of the similarities and dissimilarities, continuities and discontinuities will be examined in this chapter.[1]

11.1   Origins

Bible colleges have their roots in the late nineteenth and early twentieth centuries, amid the intellectual ferment and social transformations that contributed to the secularization and pluralism described in Chapter 2 and the attendant changes in the role, conception, and study of religion. Several factors figure prominently in their origin and development.

First, a fair number of Bible colleges represent one facet of the Christian revival movements associated with the names of such persons as Dwight L. Moody, the famous evangelist and founder of Moody Bible Institute in 1886. Moody and other American evangelists made impressive forays into Canada (Clark, 1948, 401-03), but there were indigenous revivalists as well who stood in a long tradition of revivalism in Canada (ibid., passim). The turn-of-the-century revivals were a response to what was perceived, by evangelists as well as others, as the irreligion and social malaise of the period. Students from the Bible colleges were to go into the slums of the large urban centres and minister to the physical and spiritual needs of the immigrants and workers there.

The settlement house movement of the same period had similar goals but was elitist in origin and conception (John Ruskin and Arnold Toynbee, uncle of the famous historian, were among its progenitors) and attracted university graduates (William Lyon MacKenzie King, among others) who were to go and live among workers and the poor, seeking to help with their physical needs as well as bring them education and culture (Fraser, 1979). By contrast, Bible colleges, as Moody conceived of them, would provide what he called "gap men" (1886; cited, Findlay, 1969, 328) — laypersons like himself and with little formal education but with enough education and training to serve in what historians commonly portray as indeed a yawning gap between the urban masses and the educated clergy and their congregations (Schlesinger, Sr., 1967 [1930-32]; in Canada, Clark, 1948, 391-424). The "gap men" (and women) would be sort of urban counterparts to the frontier circuit riders. Many of the schools were (and are) located in cities, and early graduates compiled impressive records of service there (e.g., Ringenberg, 165). One Bible college located in Toronto, Ontario Christian Seminary, offers an urban ministries programme designed expressly to train students for a similar kind of ministry today. Other Ontario Bible colleges have courses and programmes with similar goals.

Bible colleges also received much of their inspiration from the missionary movement in the late nineteenth century with its rallying cries of "All Should Go and Go to All" and "The Evangelization of the World in this Generation" (Brauer, 1953, 210-11). The original name of the school Moody founded (the second in North America) was The Bible Institute for Home and Foreign Missions of the Chicago Evangelism Society, and the name of the very first was the Missionary Training College for Home and Foreign Missionaries and Evangelists. Although the latter later moved to Nyack, NY, and was renamed Nyack Missionary College, it was started in New York City, by a graduate of Knox College in Toronto, A. B. Simpson. As a Presbyterian pastor in New York, he did not confine his activities to his congregation but went to the poor immigrants in the city as well. Eventually, he submitted his resignation to his congregation and in 1882 started the training school. It was modelled after the East London [England] Institute for Home and Foreign Missions begun in 1872 by H.G. Guiness, a British minister whom Simpson heard preach when Guiness was visiting Ontario while Simpson was still a teenager. Like Moody's institute, Guiness' and Simpson's schools admitted persons with insufficient education to pursue collegiate or seminary degrees and trained them for missionary work. Today, a hundred years later, the great majority of Protestant missionaries come from Bible colleges (Gangel, 1980, 35; Ringenberg, 1984, 164).

In their concern for urban or foreign missionary endeavour, the Moody and Nyack institutions shared common goals. But their emphases were different. Moody as an institute with three-year diploma programmes focused more on professional training, while Nyack as a degree-granting college included more general education and arts courses (Witmer, 1962, 37). These two general emphases have served to distinguish Bible colleges from one another and are related to where they are located on the theological and ecclesiastical spectrum.

The first Bible college in Canada, the Toronto Bible Training School, established in 1894, followed in the train of Guiness and Simpson and the schools they founded. These institutions represent what John G. Stackhouse, now teaching in the religious studies department at the University of Manitoba, has identified as the "churchly" strand in the Bible college movement (1990, 18). Like Guiness (an Anglican) and Simpson (a Presbyterian), the founders of the Toronto school were members of mainline Christian denominations, especially Baptist and Presbyterian but also Methodist, Anglican, and others (Rennie, 1984, 8; cited in Stackhouse, 1990, 9). Their efforts in founding the School were an extension of the missionary and social ministry endeavours of their denominations (ibid.). From the beginning the School, one of the forerunners of Ontario Bible College, was thus interdenominational and "churchly" rather than "sectarian." In the phrasing of its long-time president, John McNicol (1869- 1956), the School was "Fundamental, but Not Dispensational" (McNicol, 1946; cited in Stackhouse, 1990, 10); that is, it was theologically conservative, rather than sectarian fundamentalist. In Ontario, colleges in the "sectarian" tradition, such as Eastern Pentecostal Bible College and London Baptist Bible College, have stood quite apart from much in the social, cultural, and educational milieu; recently, however, they have added general education components to their curriculum (11.4 below).

The merger of Toronto Bible College (the later name of Toronto Bible Training School) with the London College of Bible and Missions in 1968 to form Ontario Bible College brought "churchly" and "sectarian" traditions together, presumably not without some attendant internal tensions. For a long time Ontario Bible College and other, similar "churchly" colleges that stand in a tradition of greater openness to the surrounding society and culture and to scholarship as practiced in universities than do sectarian schools have provided general education courses alongside those in professional training. Recently, however, Bible colleges generally have been moving to establish majors in liberal arts or in areas such as business administration and economics or (at Moody) even aviation (Eichhorst, 1984, 26). Indeed, about three-fourths of the recent graduates of accredited Bible colleges in the U.S.A. received B.A.s or B.Sc.s.

In Canada, where scale is smaller, Bible colleges are likely to carry out general education programmes in connection with a community college or a university, while retaining the traditional focus on Bible and training for Christian leadership (Eichhorst, 1984, 26-27). In Ontario, however, Bible colleges offering general education courses do so on their own but are not authorized by the Province to grant the B.A. or B.Sc. Recently, however, Ontario Bible College received provincial authorization to confer the B.R.S. (Bachelor of Religious Studies); enrolment in the programme is the second largest in the school. In addition, as in other provinces (see Neufeldt, 1983, 17), Ontario universities commonly give some transfer credit for Bible college courses or exempt students from Bible colleges from some courses.

Bible colleges — some more than others — also represent a protest against what many of their founders saw as an erosion of institutional Christianity, of traditional Christian beliefs, and of Christian values and morals in the society and culture around them. The announcement in a church paper of the founding of one such college in Ontario in the 1920s stated that it was "rendered necessary by the inroads of Modernism." One safeguard against such threats was the Bible, itself safeguarded against "the acids of modernity" (Lippmann, 1929, 8) by a doctrine of biblical inerrancy, some version of which is a traditional hallmark of Bible colleges. Various doctrinal standards also function in this way, with faculty and students being screened before entry and then expected afterward to teach and live in a way that accords with them.

Although the original impetus for the founding of Bible colleges came in the late nineteenth and early twentieth centuries, the great majority came into being after 1920 (see Witmer, 1962, 40, Table 1; "Bible Colleges in Canada," 1985). In Canada almost half the Bible colleges were established in the 1930s and 1940s, with a third more appearing in the 1970s and 1980s (ibid.). In Ontario, by contrast, the founding dates are sprinkled over nine decades, beginning with the oldest (both in Ontario and Canada), Toronto Bible Training School (later called Toronto Bible College and now Ontario Bible College) in 1894 (ibid.). The School had its beginnings in the home of the pastor of Walmer Road Baptist Church in Toronto (Witmer, 1962, 87). Origin in a local church or in the home of a minister was a common pattern in Ontario and elsewhere.

Today Bible colleges are found in almost every province and cover the denominational alphabet from Baptist to Wesleyan. However, interdenominational colleges and those connected with churches standing outside what was once the denominational "mainstream" predominate by far.[2] In Ontario, only Ontario Bible College is interdenominational. The rest are denominational or, if independent, tend to count on support from a particular denomination. However, none of the colleges restricts admittance to members of any one denomination.

11.2   Numbers[3]

Given the revival origins and missionary stance of many of the denominations that founded and today sponsor or participate in Bible colleges, the proliferation of the schools is not surprising. In North America today they number somewhere in the four hundreds (Editorial, 1982, 14). In Canada the figure is somewhere in the seventies,[4] divided about equally between "colleges," on the one hand, and "institutes," "training schools," and "training" or "leadership centres" on the other. In Ontario there are nine colleges and five or so training schools and institutes.

Enrolments in Canadian Bible colleges range from less than 50 full-time-equivalents to the three and four hundreds and as high as the six and seven hundreds in two colleges in Alberta and Saskatchewan, though none can match the numbers in the large American colleges where enrolments of more than a thousand are reported at a few institutions ("Enrollments During the Eighties," 1990, 11, Chart A).

Faculty in Canadian institutions range from few or no full-time-equivalents and a dozen or more part-timers in institutes and training schools, to a fairly typical 15 and 10, respectively, in the colleges, and as high as 42 and five in the largest college, Briercrest in Saskatchewan.

In the Ontario colleges, enrolments range from less then 50 to around 175 in two of the midsized schools, to the three and four hundreds in the two largest (Ontario Bible College and Eastern Pentecostal, respectively). In the Ontario training schools and institutes, enrolments in the forties are common. Faculty sizes vary accordingly.

11.3   Distinctives

The aims, curricula, and ethos of present-day Bible colleges reflect their origins. The original pattern, still fairly persistent, though with modifications (11.4 below), was that a religious experience of some kind produced a change in a person's life. Moved to serve Christ and to seek to win others to him, he or she enrolled in the Bible college and took courses that provided training in ways to do so. And since the Bible witnesses to Jesus, to whom the student had committed him- or herself, study of the Bible was central to the curriculum. It was central also in that it served as the guidebook for the changed life expected of the student. Since the Bible was written in three ancient languages, the student might study at least one, the Greek of the New Testament. But most courses used the Bible in English translation, and this sufficed since the Bible was seen as for all, not just an educated caste. Some schools might have subscribed to Moody's dictum, ''Never mind the Greek and Hebrew.'' Rather, ''Give them plain English and good Scripture. It is the sword of the Lord and cuts deep'' (cited, Findlay, 1969, 329). But for most, study of the ancient tongues — the languages of the divinely inspired autographs of the scriptures — was important. That required use of grammars, lexika, and commentaries. In addition, however, the Holy Spirit provided illumination. In the words of a historian of the Bible college movement, ''The teaching-learning process becomes three dimensional, for to pupil and teacher is added the interacting presence of the Holy Spirit'' (Witmer, 1962, 23).

Some Bible colleges are specifically denominational, founded to assure the continuance and growth of a certain (sometimes new) religious group. But, as in the Pietism of the last few centuries, students and faculty share an experiential bond more basic than denominational differentia: conversion or some other form of religious experience or commitment to Jesus Christ, from which flow a changed life, the desire to win others to him, and a desire and need to learn more about and from what is regarded as the divinely inspired and inerrant guidebook, the Bible, under the Spirit's leading. Inter-denominational colleges, which have some of the largest enrolments, are numerous therefore, and denominational colleges commonly enrol students from various denominations.

Amid these general similarities, there is much diversity, with variations in the specificity and stringency of doctrinal standards, the interpretation of the Bible, emphasis on evangelism and missionary spirit, curricula, qualifications of faculty and quality of education, attitudes to scholarship and to society and culture in general.

The variations often represent denominational or confessional distinctives. In Ontario, for example, one college describes itself in a recent calendar as an "Evangelistic, Fundamental, Baptistic, Premillenial" institution that fills "a void in Canada." A college in the Pentecostal tradition stresses in a 1980s calendar "the role of the Holy Spirit in all true instruction" and "as the Teacher, who reveals Christ, and as the One who endues with the power to witness for Christ." The college's most recent calendar states that one of the school's goals is "To help the student understand the biblical basis and historical development of our Pentecostal heritage and mission" and the role of "the Person and Ministry of the Holy Spirit."

11.4   Bible Colleges and Religious Studies

Some of the differences between Bible colleges and university departments and programmes of religious studies in Ontario are fairly obvious. Professional training is intrinsic to Bible colleges; in religious studies it is secondary at most. Unlike religious studies departments and programmes, which are located in or (in the case of church-related colleges) closely tied to provincial universities, Bible colleges are private institutions. Few have had even informal ties to universities, such as ad hoc arrangements for acceptance of Bible-college work for whole or partial credit (see, e.g., Gazard, 1980). Though more are moving in this direction (Eichhorst, 1984, 26; cf. 11.1 above), some stand in religious traditions strongly opposed to links between church and state.

As strictly private institutions, Bible colleges can serve, and choose to serve, religious, (specifically) Christian institutions. There is no need, and often a distinct disinclination, for curricula and the rest of the academic agenda to accommodate the secularism and pluralism of modern society and culture in general and of Canada and Ontario in particular, as universities, and religious studies in particular, have been obliged, and considered it essential, to do. Over against what many see as the "intellectual mélange" that is the modern university, bereft of the Christian faith that once gave it integrity and coherence (cf. chap. 3.1.1 above), Bible colleges see themselves as providing such a "faith dimension": *Education with Dimension* is the subtitle of Witmer's standard work on Bible colleges. In the words of one spokesperson, Bible colleges are characterized by an "integration of learning around a common core of interest" (Merrill C. Tenney, Preface to Witmer, 1962, 11). "Strange as it may seem," states an editorial in an influential evangelical magazine,

> a small Bible college committed to biblical Christian faith and dedicated to hard-headed, intellectually persistent integration of all truth is nearer the idea of a true university than the mammoth multi-versities that we have falsely come to call universities in our modern times (Editorial, 1982, 16).

"[E]ducation that promotes growth of the whole person" is the way Ontario Bible College characterizes its philosophy, with "broad exposure to studies in biblical, theological, professional and general education" alongside "the cultivation of Christian character, personal discipleship and skills for service" (Catalogue, 1990-91, 7). Calendars of other Ontario Bible colleges contain similar statements.

In accordance with these aims, Bible colleges commonly offer general arts courses alongside those in Christianity and the practical (professional) courses. Some tend to the Moody pattern, focusing more on specialized, professional training; others incline to the Nyack pattern, with more general education and liberal arts courses, though, as noted above (11.1), this distinction is being blurred. At Ontario Bible College, for example, the Bachelor of Religious Studies degree, a three-year programme with a Seminary Track and a University Track, seeks to provide "a strong foundation upon which to do more specialized undergraduate studies at university (courses are readily transferable for credit at many universities) or to go on to seminary" (ibid., 12). Specifically, the programme "is designed to provide the student with a solid foundation in Bible and theology as well as a broad base in the humanities and social sciences" (ibid.). The required core courses are biblical, Christian, and Western; in accord with Bible college principles, six credits of field education are also required (ibid.). Among the electives is a group of courses designated "Religious Studies" that includes one in comparative religions (ibid., 34).[5]

Some of the descriptions of arts and social sciences courses in Ontario Bible college calendars read much like those in a university calendar. For example, "Religions of Africa and Asia" is described in one calendar as

> An objective study of the history, major beliefs, practices and rituals of the major non-Christian religions: Animism, Hinduism, Buddhism, Islam and Shintoism. Communism as one of the major non-Christian ideologies will also be examined.

However, many such courses are apt to have also, or primarily, a professional purpose and an apologetic cast. At another institution the course entitled "Cults" examines "the established pseudo-christian cults, the new cults, the eastern-based cults, and to a limited extent the occult," after which "the key doctrinal points at which most cults differ from orthodox Christianity will be discussed." Courses in sociology, anthropology, linguistics, cross-cultural communication, world religions, or comparative religions may be directed to professional ends — to understanding contemporary urban society and culture, or immigrant populations or native peoples, or Third World cultures and peoples so that (as one calendar puts it) students "may be prepared [as missionaries] to adjust readily and labor efficiently among them." The course description of "Contemporary World Religions" at another college reads much like one in religious studies but goes on to say that the course will conclude with discussion of "strategies for effective Christian witness." The goal of the course in "Urban Anthropology" at the same school "is to establish a philosophy and strategy for multiplying churches in an urban setting." At still another institution, "World Religions and Modern Cults" is described as "A survey of major world religions and the dominant cults active in North America, dealing with their origins and error."

What religious studies course descriptions have come to call "new religions" are commonly designated as "cults" in Bible college calendars, and the course descriptions suggest an apologetic approach. Apologetics, once a mainstay of Ontario college and university curricula (chap. 2.1.2 and 2.4.3 above), appears frequently in Ontario Bible college calendars. In contrast to the study of the Hebrew Bible and the New Testament in religious studies contexts, such courses in Bible colleges, though cognizant of the historical-critical theories and approaches of biblical studies of the past century and a half (chap. 2.4.1 above), are predominantly opposed to them and directed to defending once regnant positions such as Mosaic authorship of the Pentateuch, literalistic readings of the Genesis accounts of creation, fall, and flood, and full historical reliability of the New Testament gospels.[6]

The leeway allowed teachers and students on these and related issues varies from place to place. One sees itself, according to a recent calendar, as distinct "from most Bible colleges" in that "each teacher states, after examining the various views, what the fundamental Biblical position is. The young person is not left to flounder, not sure what he [sic] should believe." Other Bible colleges would likely dispute this characterization of their practices: a concern for correct Christian teaching is common to all. Bible college calendars spell out doctrinal standards in some detail and make clear that faculty subscribe to them and that students may expect to do the same. Accordingly, in contrast to religious studies (chaps. 2, 3, and 5 above), religious beliefs and commitments are essential factors in the hiring of faculty. Once hired, they are generally continued on a contract basis. Although tenure policies do not seem to be high on the agenda of Bible college administrators and boards, there is a mutual understanding that faculty will not be terminated as long as they continue to comply with the confessional bases of the college.

There are similar expectations of students. Evidence of commitment to the college's doctrinal standards and to a Christian life figure into the admission process. One Bible college in the "sectarian" tradition (see 11.1 above) requires of applicants for both full-time study and extension courses a declaration of when they were "converted" or "saved." In addition, for those expecting to do full-time study their pastor and two Christians are to provide "testimonials . . . testifying to character and ability." "Churchly" Bible colleges are apt to be content with a more general stipulation such as "a personal belief and experience in Jesus Christ" coupled with "a genuine desire to learn the Word of God and to train for Christian service" (to quote one calendar). Upon entry, students in the more "sectarian" institutions may be required to sign or at least adhere to a code of conduct dealing with such things as movies, drinking, smoking, hair length, and dress. Similarly, attendance at chapel services is likely to be compulsory. One college stipulates that, in addition to completion of academic requirements, prospective graduates must be "in harmony with the Doctrinal Statement" of the school and be "deemed worthy in the matter of Christian character, attitude, testimony, practical service and achievement." The more "churchly" institutions are also concerned about educating "the whole person," but rules designed to achieve that goal are apt to be less noticeable. However, the calendar of one such college voices the expectation "that graduates will exhibit mature Christian character" and states that "On the basis of clear evidence that a student's behaviour is inconsistent with this expectation, the faculty reserves the right to postpone or deny graduation." Part of the ethos for both kinds of institutions is practice in some form of Christian ministry, for example, after classes, on weekends, or in internships of varying lengths. The degree to which students actually conform to such expectations will vary from school to school, indeed within a school, and may in fact be undergoing change (see below).

Professors holding earned doctorates in Ontario Bible colleges are relatively few. In the four largest colleges they constitute one-fourth of the total full-time instructional faculty, even less (20%) if one adds in part-time and associate faculty. If one includes doctorates in progress, the percentage rises to close to half (44%) and a little over a third if part-time and associate faculty are included. In these four schools, about half the faculty holding earned doctorates received them from educational institutions with theologically conservative or fundamentalist orientations such as Dallas Theological Seminary, Grace Theological Seminary, Southwestern Baptist Theological Seminary, and Trinity Evangelical Divinity School. However, the percentage of faculty with earned doctorates from mainstream universities and theological colleges increased in the 1980s,[7] and at the end of the decade two-thirds of faculty with doctorates in progress were studying at such schools, including a number of Ontario institutions.[8]

Those faculty without a doctorate commonly have graduated from a Bible college, then have acquired a professional degree at a seminary, sometimes in Ontario or elsewhere in Canada but also at conservative or fundamentalist educational institutions in the U.S.A. Those engaged in teaching arts, social sciences, or education courses are apt to have studied in a provincial university, at the undergraduate or graduate level, or in some cases both.

Although Bible colleges and religious studies thus largely follow divergent paths, sometimes they swim in some of the same waters. Bible college faculty occasionally study in the same universities as religious studies professors do, belong to the same learned societies, read and publish articles in some of the same journals, and stock their libraries with some of the same books. Some Bible college students find their way into religious studies departments and programmes, at both the undergraduate and graduate levels. At some Bible colleges students report experiences of change and growth similar to those of religious studies students (chap. 4.1 above). One graduate, now a pastor, told how he entered Bible college knowing "everything for sure," expecting his beliefs simply to be confirmed, and finding instead that "the quick, smart answers" he sought in order to "put Christ's detractors to flight" were not acceptable to his teachers. He saw them as his tormentors, but they "were themselves not tormented. . . . They wrestled with truth but were not exhausted. . . . They were spiritually fit. I was a spiritual misfit" (Cantelon, 1984).

Even though the English Bible is a staple of Bible college curricula, the biblical languages are also important and required for some degrees. Knowledge of at least one — Greek — is one advantage graduates of Bible colleges who enrol in religious studies sometimes have over religious studies students.

One graduate officer we interviewed felt that instruction in the biblical languages had passed from theological colleges and universities to Bible colleges. As respects numbers of students engaged in such study, this may be a correct observation. However, only one Bible college in Ontario, it seems, now offers all three biblical languages — Hebrew, Aramaic, and Greek — whereas they are available to religious studies students in a number of departments either within the department itself or through the department's ties with a local theological college. Several Ontario Bible colleges offer introductory Hebrew, and at least two of these a second year as well. All offer Greek at elementary and intermediate levels and exegetical courses that employ the Greek text of the New Testament. That accords with the character of Bible colleges as professional schools preparing students for Christian ministry. As such, they are more precisely compared with theological colleges than with religious studies departments. In Ontario, at least, religious studies departments have not found a way to induct undergraduate students into biblical languages while also requiring courses that make students aware of the multiplicity of religious traditions in the world (cf. chap. 8.3 above). Moreover, since many students decide to concentrate in religious studies relatively late in their university careers (chap. 4.1.1 above), those choosing to focus on the Hebrew Bible or Christian origins find it difficult to acquire proficiency in a biblical language alongside the required courses.

Though striving to be not of the world, Bible colleges are nonetheless in it: they too partake of the professionalization of higher education described in this volume as playing an important role in the changes in theological colleges in this century and in the development of religious studies in universities (chaps. 2 and 3 above). The original name of the American Association of Bible Colleges was the Accrediting Association of Bible Colleges (AABC).[9] It was formed in 1947 to raise standards, for example, through some standardization of Bible college curricula so they would more nearly approximate one another and, in their general education and arts courses, those of colleges and universities generally — but in a way that would accord with Bible college principles. The Association has assisted Bible colleges in their efforts to upgrade the quality of faculty and students, improve libraries, place financing and financial accountability on a sound footing, and introduce better management methods into administration.

In pursuing these aims, the AABC and the Bible colleges belonging to or seeking admission to it have not hesitated to draw on experts from outside the world of Bible colleges. The programme of the fortieth annual meeting of the AABC (1986), for example, included, alongside its speakers and resource persons from Bible colleges, seminaries, and churches, a vice-president for business and finance from a church-related college, a benefits-plan expert from a private company, a librarian from a state university, and a professor of higher-education administration from another state university. The plenary sessions and workshops were devoted to topics such as ''Legal Issues Facing Bible Colleges,'' ''Developing Faculty Through Team Mgmt. [sic],'' ''Keeping the Bible College Afloat — Raising Funds in a Competitive Environment,'' ''Evaluating Education Effectiveness Through Questioning Techniques,'' ''Writing Your Own Computerized Instructional Programs'' and ''Establishing an Instructional Computer Lab,'' building and evaluating libraries, and ''Integration of the Library and the Curriculum'' — all typical concerns of administrators, faculty, and librarians in academic institutions in North America. The display space given in the printed programme to the travel service, airline, and hotel for the meeting appears little different from what one sees in the programmes of the joint annual meetings of the American Academy of Religion and the Society of Biblical Literature.

In addition to its newsletter and an annual directory listing member schools and schools seeking membership, the AABC issues a long list of manuals and guidebooks on such matters as self-study and accreditation, academic administration, pedagogy and academic advising, libraries, publicity and recruitment, as well as various publications about Bible colleges and the AABC itself. As yet, the percentage of Bible colleges accredited by the AABC is small (less than one-fourth) in comparison with the total number of schools, with colleges far outnumbering institutes (AABC *Directory*, 1989-90, 1-32). Accreditation is seen as something desirable, however, as is evident from the lists of colleges in the annual AABC *Directory* that are either candidates for accreditation or have applicant status.

The AABC includes Canada in its purview and has a Commission on Canadian Bible College Education. Of the seventy-some Bible colleges in Canada (11.2 above), 10 (about 13%-14%) are accredited by the AABC. Three are in Ontario: Ontario Bible College, Emmanuel Bible College, and, recently, Eastern Pentecostal (AABC *Directory*, 1989-90). In the 1989-90 academic year eight more Canadian colleges were pursuing accreditation, including (in Ontario) London Baptist Bible College (applicant status) (ibid., 33-39). Some of the Ontario colleges that lack AABC accreditation are members of the Association of Canadian Bible Colleges, which is not an accrediting agency but seeks to help members improve standards.

The move to academic professionalization associated with the accreditation process and in general with keeping pace with social and cultural change seems to be reflected in changes in faculty and curricula in some colleges as well as in the way they present themselves to students, as seen in successive editions of their calendars. As was indicated earlier, the percentage of faculty with earned doctorates or doctorates in progress has risen and those earned or in progress at mainstream institutions is also on the increase. For example, prior to AABC accreditation, one college listed in its calendar one person with a Ph.D. and one as a Ph.D. candidate (out of a total full-time instructional faculty of 14). In the calendar issued after accreditation these numbers had increased to three, one (and 18) respectively. This same calendar also includes a General Studies component, re-named from "Historical and Contemporary Thought" and with more courses added, including one in world religions. A 1980s calendar of one college involved in the accreditation process listed one person with a Ph.D., another with the D.R.E. (Doctor of Religious Education), and a third as engaged in Th.D. studies (out of total of nine full-time instructional faculty). The most recent edition, however, lists two Th.D.s, one Ph.D., and three persons in studies leading to a professional doctorate (Ed.D., D.R.E., D.Min.), out of a total of ten regular and adjunct full-time instructional faculty. Here, too, a significant number of courses had been designated or added as "General Education" offerings. The College's distinctives, very prominent in the President's statement in the earlier calendar, have receded in the current President's message in the present edition. Another college, which sets itself apart from much in the ecclesiastical and educational mainstream, now includes in its curriculum general education courses in which students are to read John Milton, John Stuart Mill, Karl Marx, and Arthur Miller, among others. It also comments that "from long observation of the exaction of an educational ministry, we have become more charitable in our thought of heretical personalities, while still compelled to combat the erroneous principles to which their merely philosophical dreams give birth."

Healthy enrolments at Bible colleges such as these suggest that moving to the educational mainstream, and in general changing with the times, seem to appeal to today's students, success breeding success — or in the words of the Bible, "to those who have, more will be given" (Matt. 13.12). One wonders whether, by contrast, one school's lack of AABC accreditation and the various ways in which its calendar seemed to indicate a desire to stand apart from the mainstream contributed to the declining enrolments in the 1980s that led it to designate itself in its current calendar as a Leadership Training Centre and to scale down its three- and four-year degree programmes to a two-year leadership training programme.

As part of efforts to improve standards, some Bible colleges have established graduate divisions, that is, seminaries, alongside their undergraduate programmes. (Those in Ontario are listed in Appendix B below.) The President of Winnipeg Bible College and its graduate school, Winnipeg Theological Seminary, probably speaks for them when he says, "An undergraduate program *only* is now recognized, at best, as marginal for one's preparation for a lifetime of ministry" (Eichhorst, 1984, 26). Some Bible college students are now pre-seminary majors, even as some university students major in religious studies as preparation for theological college (chap. 4.1.3 above). According to a survey conducted about ten years ago by a professor at Winnipeg Theological Seminary, 70% of AABC member schools offer such a major (Gangel, 1980, 35).

Bible colleges and religious studies in Ontario both reflect their origins, but with some significant differences. Bible colleges have espoused a "perennialist" philosophy of education with roots in the Christian tradition epitomized in the Christian Bible (Moncher, 1988). In the terms of this study, they have sought to identify with the values and ethos of the "Then" of religion study — ante-bella Ontario, when a Christian ethos and inculcation of religion, that is, Christianity, and "religious knowledge" courses were the rule in colleges and universities — more than with those of the "Now" and the movement to religious studies and the pluralistic study of religion following World War II (chap. 2.4.10 above). They stand — with notable exceptions in the churchly tradition — in the separatist, sectarian tradition of Christianity, of "Christ Against Culture" (Niebuhr, 1952, chap. 2). But even as early Christianity moved from margin to mainstream, both in numbers and ethos, so also many of the denominations that gave birth to, sustain, and are sustained by Bible colleges have moved increasingly into the mainstream of Canadian society. As in early Christianity, too, the large influx of new members resulting from vigorous evangelistic efforts and the attendant pressures of institutionalization threaten sectarian identities. Bible colleges are not immune to these developments, as Bible college sources make clear (cf. Witmer, 1962, chap. 12; Editorial, 1982). As academic institutions, they are also experiencing the tension between religious loyalty and academic professionalization.

Some of these tensions seem to be tugging at one another in a magazine interview by an administrator in an Ontario Bible college. Asked about maintaining a balance between "legalism and dogmatism" and "true spirituality and freedom of thought," he drew a distinction between education and indoctrination.

> In education there is an openness to study alternatives and a liberty to reach different conclusions realizing that great people of God have differed in some areas. . . . Real education exposes students to the options and the alternatives. It gives them the resources and teaches them how to think and interpret the scriptures.

Indoctrination, on the other hand,

> is simply communicating a narrowly defined form of truth. There is no
> exploration, no inductive study of the Scriptures, no freedom in reaching
> conclusions. Students are presented with conclusions, required to accept
> them and leave committed to them. . . . Some schools are too committed
> to their distinctives and simply indoctrinate. Some students graduate with
> a very neat package of truth, convictions and distinctives but have never
> really learned to study the Bible.

Nonetheless, indoctrination in at least some "fundamentals" is intrinsic to
Bible colleges:

> every evangelical Bible college indoctrinates. There is indoctrination on
> the deity of Christ, on the inerrancy of the Scriptures, the Virgin birth
> and other great fundamentals.

However, when one gets "beyond these, there needs to be freedom." The
ideal is to "keep them [education and indoctrination] in perfect balance."

In the analysis of present-day Bible colleges by a sometime president and
now professor at an American Bible college one also sees Then and Now
straining at each other. What he calls the "traditional" Bible college "is
marked by an exclusive commitment to vocational Christian ministry; a
single and simple curriculum; an emphasis on terminal training; and complete separation from secular education" (Gangel, 1980, 36). The "progressive" Bible college, on the other hand, is marked by a broader definition of
Christian ministry that encompasses "a wider range of majors" and greater
openness to the outside world. In the progressive colleges the

> leaders push their institutions to join consortia; seek licensing where
> applicable; move on to the highest possible levels of accreditation; join
> state and national professional organizations at professorial and adminis-
> trative levels; and through it all affirm that the fear of the Lord is indeed
> the beginning of wisdom (ibid.).

In tune with this description of the "progressive" colleges is *Christianity
Today*'s call to Bible colleges to aim for the highest possible academic
standards, whether their students are preparing for a specifically Christian
vocation or one of the professions such as medicine or elementary or secondary school teaching, or are seeking a general, liberal arts education (Editorial, 1982).

> For better or for worse, the Bible college has taken over post-high school
> Christian education for a vast segment of evangelical young people. It
> has become an evangelical substitute for a four-year liberal arts college
> education (ibid., 14).

These kinds of judgments reflect changes in North American society and
culture. Bible college students are changing, too. According to an AABC

survey of its colleges in the 1970s, entering students were less apt to conform to the original and customary pattern indicated at various places in this chapter. They

> are not so settled on distinctives traditional in Bible colleges. They are less likely to be committed in the early stages of their education to full-time Christian ministry, less excited over the specialized ministry programs, less certain that when they graduate they will find opportunities for appropriate ministry available, and less certain about God's specific call and the gifts he has given them (ibid.).

Then and Now, confessionalism and pluralism, religious loyalty and academic respectability will likely continue to pose questions of identity and integrity for Bible colleges even as they have for church-related colleges and for religious studies departments.

Notes

1 Since budgetary and time constraints did not permit sending of questionnaires to faculty in Bible colleges, or interviews with administrators or faculty, this chapter is based chiefly on published materials. A number of Ontario Bible colleges graciously supplied copies of their calendars; various publications were also obtained from the American Association of Bible Colleges, Fayetteville, Arkansas. Professor John Franklin, who chairs the Department of General Arts at Ontario Bible College, and Mr. Garry Peters, Librarian at Emmanuel Bible College, offered valuable bibliographical assistance.

  For the history and general nature of Bible colleges, presented in summary form in our text, the most accessible treatments are Witmer's volume (1962), which, though dated, is still useful, providing a brief history along with a description of the nature of Bible colleges generally and of a number of schools in particular, plus statistics and discussion of various other matters; and, more recently, Ringenberg, 1984, 157-73, which treats the origins and nature of Bible colleges within the larger context of American culture and Protestant higher education in the U.S.A. More detailed are the dissertations by Boon, 1950 (which treats Canadian as well as American Bible colleges) and Moncher, 1988 (U.S.A. only). Stackhouse, 1990 is an illuminating historical and typological study of Canadian Bible colleges; see also his Ph.D. dissertation (1987) and Sawatsky, 1985. McKenzie, 1982 provides a history of Ontario Bible College (1894-1968). For comparison with Bible colleges in another province (Alberta) see Neufeldt, 1983, chap. 1.2.4 and 121-39. Other publications are cited, where pertinent, in our text.

2 Interdenominational Bible colleges account for about 18% of the total in Canada ("Bible Colleges in Canada," 1985). Of the denominational institutions, those with Baptist, Mennonite, or Pentecostal connections are best represented, each with about 13% of the total (ibid.).

3 Unless otherwise noted, figures cited in the text are for 1985 and are based on the table "Bible Colleges in Canada," 1985. It is designated as an "annual" guide, but no successors have appeared in *Faith Alive* (now *Faith Today*). It supersedes the useful but earlier and much less comprehensive tables in Harder, 1980, 38-43.

4 The figure is approximate. "Bible Colleges in Canada," 1985 includes institutions that are not Bible colleges in origin or intent and in Ontario fails to include at least one institution (Northland).

5 The C.R.S. (Certificate of Religious Studies) at Toronto Baptist Seminary is a graduate degree programme of two semesters, with required courses in Issues in Old Testament

Introduction, Old Testament Theology, Introduction to Theology, Church History, Introduction to Public Speaking, and 14 hours of electives (Prospectus [Calendar], 1989-91,
24).

6 Cf., further, the descriptions of biblical courses in Alberta Bible colleges in Neufeldt,
1983, 121-39; note, however, that they are from the early 1980s.

7 Represented (one Ph.D. each): St. Andrews in Scotland, University of Iowa and New
York University in the U.S., and McMaster, St. Michael's College, and University of
Waterloo in Ontario. Of the two part-time faculty, both have the Ed.D, one from Har-
vard, the other from Seattle University.

8 Represented in the two-thirds: Laval, Guelph, York, Ontario Institute for Studies in Education, Toronto School of Theology; plus (outside Canada) New York University.

9 A brief account of the origins of the AABC and of accreditation is given in Witmer,
1962, 41-47; more detailed is the personal account by Mostert (1986), the long-time
Executive Director of the AABC.

12

Conclusions and Recommendations: 2001 and All That

Harold Remus, William Closson James, and Daniel Fraikin

12.1 Religious Studies in Ontario in the 1990s

As is pointed out in the Preface, no full-scale review of religious studies in Ontario had been undertaken prior to the present study. A good bit of the study has been devoted, therefore, to looking back — how did we get where we are? — and, as is appropriate in a state-of-the-art review, to recording and analyzing of statistical data, reporting of perceptions and attitudes of persons both in and outside the field, and placing what we found and reported in larger academic and cultural contexts. Along the way we have ventured some conclusions and recommendations. Now we do so in a more systematic way, both drawing things together and looking ahead.

It is clear that religious studies is now firmly established in Ontario universities. Even in the few places where there is no religious studies department or programme, religious studies courses are sometimes available in affiliated colleges or in what amount to religious studies courses in departments such as history or philosophy; or religious dimensions of various subjects are included in some way in courses offered in various university departments (chap. 2.6). All this attests, as founders of religious studies departments argued and as their successors have maintained, that, for better or for worse, religion as a large and perduring area of human experience is a fit subject of study in a university. Quite apart from its intrinsic interest and importance, religion deserves to be studied also on utilitarian grounds: it is a

---

Notes to Chapter 12 can be found on pages 324-25.

fundamental feature of Ontario society and culture as well as of the "global village" in which we live. Moreover, knowledge and understanding of the various religious traditions of humankind can contribute to the overcoming of prejudices and to more equitable and harmonious human relations, while for Canadians working or traveling in other countries, some acquaintance with the religions of the peoples of those countries is often essential.

Religious studies in Ontario reflects these changes, not only around the globe but specifically in this province, where multiculturalism supplanted a society more homogeneous than the present one while a religious pluralism replaced the sometime predominant Christian ethos (chap. 2.1-3). The field reflects, too, changes in the way religion is studied and in the broadening of the focus of study to include religions other than Christianity and traditions considered contextual to it (chap. 2.4). Religious studies, in Ontario as well as in North America generally, is still in the process of discerning the implications of these changes and drawing conclusions from them. In Ontario, there is still some distance to go, as we have pointed out in various places in this study. The religious traditions of Africa, Asia, and Oceania are still underrepresented in faculty numbers, in curricula, and in research; so, too, are those of the indigenous peoples of Canada, or of Jews and Muslims (chaps. 2.4.4-8, 7.5, 8.2).

Religious studies departments need to keep in mind, of course, that the religious consciousness and allegiances of the majority of Ontarians are still predominantly Christian in some sense (chap. 2.3). As departments plan for the future they will need to include courses in Christianity, with professors to teach them. At present, however, such courses and the distribution of courses and faculty among the various religious traditions are still more a matter of certain givens and of institutional inertia than of forethought and planning. When religious studies departments were established they were commonly a transmutation of religion or ("religious knowledge") departments offering mainly Christian courses taught by Christian professors. Even when departments were wholly new creations, the faculty available to teach them had commonly received their graduate degree from religious studies programmes that were Christian in conception and structure. The critiques of the *Encyclopedia of Religion* cited in Chapter 2.4.10 give some indication of how much allegiance religious studies still owes to that past and to other inherited patterns and how far it needs to go to appropriate new approaches to the study of religious traditions – including Christianity – and recent research on them. This became apparent, too, in our interviews with faculty regarding new directions of research: with a number of them, it seemed the conversation could have been taking place a decade or more earlier. Also apparent in our study has been movement to hiring of women and inclusion of feminist research and concerns in curricula and departmental agenda; however, despite encouraging trends, here too there is still considerable distance to travel (chaps. 3.2.4, 4.1.4, 4.2.6, 5.1.1.1, 5.2.2, 9.4).

12.2   Faculty and Curricula

These various manifestations of legacies from the past are not surprising in a period of transition (chap. 3.2.2). But that time is coming to an end, providing Ontario religious studies departments and programmes with a signal opportunity to look ahead. The key is the retiring of faculty in considerable numbers in the nineties (chap. 5.1.1.2). Departments and programmes can critically examine curricula and faculty resources and plan for the future freer than usual of vested interests of incumbent faculty and of concerns about faculty "re-tooling" to meet new needs. The usual attention would presumably have to be paid to such factors as service courses specific to a particular institution (e.g., ethics courses for business or nursing students) or courses with large enrolments that contribute to a department's viability in the university as well as some of the other factors listed in Chapter 6.1. The great diversity in undergraduate religious studies curricula noted in Chapter 8 reflects such factors, along with others mentioned there: self-consciousness about religious studies as an academic field reflected in thematic courses or courses in methodology; the perception of religion as present in many non-"religious" areas of life, leading to "dialogic" courses; recognition of the great variety of religious traditions and the need to provide coverage of a broad spectrum of them.

The changes in curricula since 1972 outlined in Chapter 8 are not insignificant. The number of courses in Christianity, for example, decreased significantly. Nonetheless, they still constituted almost four out of ten of the total offerings (chap. 8.2). In part this proportion may be seen as reflecting social and cultural realities mentioned earlier as well as the importance of Christianity as a religion. In part, however, as is pointed out in Chapter 8, it resulted from the fact that faculty had been trained primarily in Christian studies and were not equipped to offer courses in other traditions or, in thematic and dialogic courses, to venture much beyond Christian and related phenomena or to follow some of the suggestions made by a religious studies professor (chap. 3.2.2) such as broadening courses in "Bible" or "scripture" beyond Jewish and Christian canons. Morton Smith has presented an impressive brief against what he calls "the maleficent effects of our inherited terminology" on study of ancient Near Eastern texts and religions (1983, 306). Perhaps as simple a move as changing the title of a course from "Old Testament" to "Hebrew Bible" or "Jewish Bible," or from "New Testament" to "Christian Origins," might lead to a different perception of the texts and movements studied on the part of both teacher and student.

Generally, and sometimes from their inception, Ontario departments and programmes, or pockets within them, have done more than change course titles. However, at this point in the unfolding story of religious studies, and with new faculty coming onto the scene, they might ask themselves whether still more is needed and would be possible. They might turn into questions addressed to themselves some comments made by Van Harvey two decades ago characterizing "the very definition of the field and the resulting structure of the curriculum and the department" as "uncriticized" and still basically Protestant in nature, with "the study of religion [isolated] from the methods and content of such disciplines as anthropology, sociology, linguistics, archaeology, philology, and the like," and "these fields . . . [not being] permitted to inform materially the very conception of the field of religious studies" (1970, 25).

This is not to make a whipping post of Protestantism. As Jacob Neusner pointed out a few years ago, after indeed lamenting what he sees as the infection of religious studies by an individualistic notion of disembodied religion deriving from (especially) Lutheranism, religious studies owes a great debt to certain Protestant scholars of religion and their "openness to diversity," their "capacity to pursue an other-than-narrow-theological program" (1988, 28). It is they

> who took seriously and responded to the program of the Enlightenment, with its interest in the critical examination of religion. They are the ones who saw the study of religion as a generalizing science. . . . who asked not only about religions but also about religion. They are the ones who invited to give testimony not only those they understood but also those they did not understand (ibid.).

Even they, however, were inclined to study religions insofar as they touched ecclesiastical concerns (ibid., 29), which, while appropriate for them, is not for religious studies scholars in universities.

Having said this, nonetheless it is the "state of the art" in religious studies both in Ontario and elsewhere that many would argue for a continuing place for tradition-specific courses rather than or alongside generic courses. Religious traditions and literatures have their own integrities and bodies of scholarship attached to them which scholarship and teaching need to respect. Moreover, there are numerous practitioners of religion, as well as cultured enquirers about religion, who do respect them and want to learn more precisely about the Bhagavad Gita or Gandhi, or the Tanak—the Torah, prophets, and "writings"—or about Muhammed and the Qur'an, or about Jesus and Paul and the New Testament. Religious studies planners ignore these potential students and their ties to religious communities at their peril (12.4 below). Pedagogically, one academic term hardly suffices to study any one religious corpus or figure, let alone others alongside them. Methodologically, there are traditions of scholarship that warrant tradition-specific courses, such as the various historical- and other -critical approaches in the study of the Hebrew Bible and the New Testament, or the study of Indian literature applying techniques of textual analysis derived from the Indian philosophical tradition. Moreover,

> To study any one religion in depth the student should expect to study
> more than one, but to study more than one religion she or he should
> expect, over several semesters, to achieve a detailed, cumulative knowl-
> edge of at least one religion, generally through a series of courses
> devoted to different periods of its history and to different aspects of its
> ongoing life (Crites, 1990, 9).

However, since such study "in depth" is "not only of a culture but of a
society," it requires "the application of sociological and anthropological
methods" (ibid.) — and those from other fields as well.

As they weigh the relative merits of tradition-specific and generic
courses, religious studies departments and programmes might consider Van
Harvey's comment cited above and ask: Is a course being taught in isolation
from scholarship in other academic fields in the university, especially tradition-specific courses in view of their great indebtedness to scholarship
within religious communities? As has been noted in various places in this
study, the study of religion is being pursued in university departments
besides religious studies. Striking confirmation of this is the bibliography
of work on Religion and Canada entitled "Religious Studies" by Laperrière
and Westfall (1990), which cites almost exclusively works by persons outside religious studies departments and programmes.

With the impending retirements in the nineties, religious studies departments and programmes are now in a better position to ask serious questions
about curricula and department or programme structures and to hire persons
to fit courses and areas, rather than the reverse. The fact that graduates of
religious studies doctoral programmes in Ontario and Quebec are now
required to study a religious tradition other than the one in which they specialize, and to acquire some expertise in methodology (chap. 9.2.2.1),
means that if departments and programmes define faculty positions and
design curricula to reflect changes in the study of religion, there is a good
chance faculty will be available to teach them, even from doctoral programmes strictly within Canada itself. And if not, then "second-tier"
searches — that is, looking outside Canada — are legally permissible.

In some cases, that may be important, if another concern is to be
addressed: quality of faculty. One might say that, other things being equal,
it is the single most important factor in the future of religious studies in
Ontario. Hence the importance of the hiring, tenure, and promotion policies
mentioned earlier in this study (chaps. 3.1.1, 3.2, 5.2). Though hardly as
stringent in formulation or application as those of a place like Harvard
(Rosovsky, 1990, chap. 11), they go a long way toward excluding non-academic factors and to providing mechanisms for assessing the academic
ones. At the university level, these are taken seriously. At the departmental
and programme level, they need to be taken with utmost seriousness. The
point of hiring is the moment when "the temptation to be nice at the wrong
time" (Barzun, 1954, 178) needs to be resisted. Prospective faculty need to
be told, in plain language — orally and in writing — what the requirements

are for tenure and, later, promotion. Recommendations for tenure and promotion must then take the requirements seriously, again avoiding the nice-at-the-wrong-time temptation and basing decisions on merit: competence in teaching, solid evidence of scholarship as demonstrated in presentation of papers and (especially) publications, and responsible shouldering of departmental chores and participation in university life. And if there was ever time to discard any vestiges of the "zoo theory" (chap. 5.2.3.1; Welch, 1971, 16), it is now: confessional background or membership may be important in hiring in a church-related college (chap. 3.1.1) or a theological college (chap. 5.2.4.2), but in religious studies in an Ontario university it is competence in one's area of specialization that should count. (Integrity is presupposed but, unfortunately, can't be assumed, and, equally unfortunate, turpitude is not readily detectable at the hiring stage.) Given expertise and empathy, a scholar standing in the Jewish tradition can teach, and teach well, courses in Christianity, a person in the Christian tradition can teach courses in Judaism, and an atheist courses in Islam (chap. 3.2.3). This is not to overlook the fact that a scholar who has grown up in a particular religious tradition or in a culture or society imbued with it may have an academic headstart on one who comes to it later in life. Nor is it to deny that having persons from a variety of cultures in a department — religious studies or otherwise — can enrich discourse within the department. Such factors need to be taken into account in hiring and tenure decisions, but in each case they presuppose competence in one's area of specialization.

Affirmative-action or equity-employment policies now being put into place in Ontario universities should in no way diminish the preceding recommendations: women, it is safe to say, want to be hired on the basis of merit, not because they are women. Their records as productive scholars (chap. 7.4) indicate that that has been the case in religious studies in Ontario, and our interviews, anecdotal evidence, and our own experience confirm that finding. The same can be said of their performance as teachers and department chairs. It is hard to imagine that if and when another state-of-the-art review is undertaken in Ontario women scholars will not be included among the investigators. Religious studies departments and programmes have been seeking, with some success, to hire more women (chap. 5.1.1.1 and 5.2.2). Their increasing numbers in Ontario graduate programmes (chap. 5.1.1.1) and specifically in religious studies graduate programmes (chaps. 5.1.1.1 and 9.4) offer some hope that there will be a pool of candidates on which to draw in the 1990s. The presence of women in greater numbers on religious studies faculty should serve to increase awareness of women's concerns, and use of feminist scholarship and should help to encourage women students to pursue advanced degrees (chap. 5.2.2). Now is the time for departments and programmes to include such matters in their planning. (On the effect of such developments on male doctoral students and their job opportunities see 12.11 below.)

In Chapter 3.2.4 we reported that at the time of our interviews relations between men and women faculty were, with some exceptions, reasonably good. At the end of our study, a few years later, that is still our perception, but there also seem to be more exceptions, for some of the same reasons cited earlier. The issues are valid ones, and complex, to be resolved (it would seem) through negotiations, *Auseinandersetzungen*, and various "learning experiences." There will be tensions, there may be pains. It is another kind of transition.

Among other employment equity issues is the hiring of persons who belong to minority groups or are physically disabled (the "physically challenged," in one terminology). It is an issue that concerns universities increasingly in the 1990s. Such groups are but faintly represented among Ontario religious studies faculty. Among other things, this means that some students have had few role models from such groups for a career as a religious studies academic. This is one reason the pool of applicants from such groups for teaching jobs in religious studies departments will likely not be proportionate to their numbers in Ontario society. Policies of preferential hiring are directed to overcoming the effects of this and other legacies such as discrimination in graduate education and hiring. It is important to point out that any persons thus hired would be entering department and university not as representatives of their group—a new version of the "zoo theory"—but because they are qualified for the job.

12.3   Religious Studies and Litigation

Some general characteristics of the academic scene in the nineties, and concerns associated with them, call for attention at this point. One is the climate of litigation attendant on such things as the introduction of the Charter of Rights with the new Constitution of 1982, government regulations on hiring of Canadian candidates, and a greater militancy of faculty associations and movement to their certification as unions in some places. Especially where there is a faculty union, but not only there, departments and especially department chairs or other department officers, need to be looking over one shoulder at the administration and over the other at the faculty collective and their respective lawyers while peering ahead to descry the possible consequences of any decisions taken, all the while keeping a meticulous "paper trail."

What a department or programme puts on paper for public consumption also requires close scrutiny: promises—or what might be construed as promises—of courses available, faculty to teach them, and vocational opportunities following graduation are all possible subjects of litigation if they are false or misleading or can interpreted as such. Course listings and academic regulations in calendars must be kept current and accurate. Rules on such matters as academic dishonesty and statements of course requirements must be spelled out in detail. At one university recently court action

was threatened if transfer credit, which the student took to have been prom-
ised, was not granted for a course taken at another institution. This happened to be in the area of religious studies, but none of the preceding is
peculiar to religious studies — it is part of the general climate in Ontario
universities.

12.4   Religious Studies and Religion(s)

Also not peculiar to religious studies, though religious studies is involved
more than many fields, is the movement away from ethnocentrism, especially Eurocentrism (chap. 2.4). The issue has provoked a new "battle of
the books" in American universities and is beginning to do the same in
Ontario (see, 12.8.1 below). Earlier in this chapter (12.2) we recommend
revising curricula, courses of study, and hiring priorities in ways that recognize the plurality of religious traditions and reflect the religious pluralism of
Ontario society. In doing so, however, it would be important to provide a
continuing place for the Western heritage of Ontario culture. And while
methodological, thematic, dialogic courses are important, our interviews
with students indicate there is a strong desire to study religions themselves,
religion in the particular rather than in general or in the abstract. Ernst
Käsemann observed years ago that most of the theology students in Germany came from a pietistic background, that is, one in which religion was
practised (Käsemann, 1957, 4 [1964, 14]). So, too, our classes are populated
with students many of whom practise a particular religion, sometimes Eastern, more likely Western. Some are mature students with an interest in religion, often Christianity (chap. 4.1, 4.1.1). If some observers are right,
among intellectuals, old and young, there is a renewed interest in religion
(Schumer, 1984), with a new periodical, *New Oxford Review*, avowedly
addressed to such persons. Not having grown up under the thumb of an
inherited religious tradition, "we didn't have traditional religion to rebel
against," observes one Harvard professor who has returned to Judaism
(cited in Schumer, 1984, 93). "Those of us who are going back to some
degree of traditionalism never really experienced in our own lives the negative side of tradition" (ibid.). Some of the mature students in universities
are aging baby boomers who, according to some accounts, are turning to
organized religion, especially Christianity, though often more of a mix-
your-own concoction than one of the straight denominational potions
(Woodward et al., 1990). Some of these students, both the older and the
younger, will certainly want to learn about Eastern religions, or if they are
majors or in honours a department can insist that they do as part of distribution requirements, but many elective students will want courses in Western
religions instead or as well. In either case, a religious studies department or
programme would do well to ponder Martin Marty's postulate (1989, 7) that
"without the enduring activities of religious communities that stimulate

curiosities and concerns'' and ''provide constituencies for the academic study of religion'' religious studies enrolments would shrink considerably.

Our interviews also indicated that both among practitioners and non-practitioners of particular religious traditions some of the same kinds of ''searchings,'' ''quests,'' or ''hungers'' that brought students to religious studies in the early days of the field in the 1950s and 1960s persist today (chap. 4.1.1). Whether religious studies professors will want to come out of the ''objectivity'' closets in which most have hidden and acknowledge their own (present or sometime) religious proclivities and loyalties (or disloyalties) will continue to be a matter of individual choice (chaps. 3.2.3 and 4.1.2). Should they do so, in a way that does not edge into proselytizing or compromise their scholarly credentials (which would be a serious breach of religious studies etiquette), it would not go against academic protocol in various other fields where professors often make no secret of personal premises and leanings (chap. 3.2.3). It might also be good pedagogy:

> Arguing that a teacher can have opinions and convictions but denying them a place in the classroom robs both students and teacher of a valuable means of fostering learning. Few subjects are value-free, and honesty about where one stands, illumination about how one has arrived there, and respect for the beliefs of others form a better basis for teaching than does a resolute, ultimately dogmatic posture of impersonal objectivity (Eble, 1977, 13).

Such self-disclosure, reported to colleagues in other departments, would probably not arouse their suspicions to the degree it would have before religious studies gained acceptance as an academic field. Those suspicions are still there, however, if for no other reason than guilt by association with the ''televangelism'' of electronic religion and its eccentricities or with other unsavoury aspects of the practice of the religion. Moreover, self-disclosures that allow students to compress professors into preconceived, stereotyping boxes can be pedagogically self-defeating (chap. 3.2.3). There will probably never be a time when religious studies is ''just like any other field'' in this respect.

That distinctiveness, for better or for worse, brought hordes of students to religious studies in the 1960s, and with it the temptation to offer (in Ivan Strenski's words) courses in ''mock mysticism and pseudo-soul-saving'' (1986, 334). Response to students' existential concerns is integral to responsible professoring. At the same time, however, religious studies professors, it seems to us, would do well to contemplate Strenski's warnings about religious studies departments becoming ''the walk-in therapy center for the university,'' to the possible neglect of ''knowledge and education, hard thinking and good writing—which themselves put the existential concerns of adolescents—whether narcissistic or not—into perspective . . .'' (ibid.).

12.5   Religious Studies — and Theology, and Other Fields

One of the paths religious studies took to establish its academic credentials was away from theological colleges and "theology." Much attention has been paid to both in this study (chaps. 2.4.3 and 3.3), especially as compared with the less extensive treatment in the Alberta counterpart to the present volume (Neufeldt, 1983). That is not surprising, given the different histories of the two provinces. As in Quebec (see Rousseau and Despland, 1988, especially 142-50), so also in Ontario the study and teaching of theology has a long and continuing history. It is also true that the "state of the art" in Ontario — though not only there (chap. 2.4.3) — is that the place of "theology" in religious studies is disputed (chap. 2.4.3).

"Theology" is a multivalent and protean term, and our discussion of the relation between theology and religious studies in Chapter 2.4.3 suggests there are varieties of theology, or even ways of "doing theology," that on academic grounds could pass muster in a religiously pluralistic university setting and would constitute study *of* rather than instruction *in* religion, but also others that would not. For example, in addition to caveats noted in Chapter 2.4.3, a professor planning to "do theology" in a religious studies course — that is, to "theologize" rather than offer an exposition of, say, Augustine's or Calvin's theology — would have to announce that intention explicitly — along with the premises from which the "doing" would proceed — both at the beginning of the course and at other points along the way as well as in the course description. Assent to them could not be a requirement of the course. Nor could the course itself be required of a student, any more than one in, say, Zen meditation, except as one of a number of options in a course-distribution scheme. Successful completion of the course would require the student's being able to think in a particular theological vein, or to solve theological problems drawing on the premises of a particular theological tradition, whether one with long historical roots or only nascent, for example, a "meta-theology" or a "secular theology" (see Harvey, 1970, as cited in chap. 2.4.3 above). It does not seem to us that, in a religious studies setting, doing theology in a particular historical tradition would have to be by an insider to that tradition — to insist on it would be still another variation on the "zoo" theory. Moreover, in such a setting "explaining" that leaves open the possibility of "explaining away" is also legitimate (Wiebe, 1988, 13; chap. 2.4.3 above). Whether such a theology should be called "hermeneutics" (Strenski, 1986, as cited in chap. 2.4.3 above) or perhaps more properly be construed as "philosophy of religion" (cf. Wiebe, 1988) is one of a number of interlocking questions that it is safe to say will remain *sub iudice* for some time to come.

Institutionally, there continue to be ties in Ontario between religious studies and theological colleges and, nationally, between learned societies in religious studies and theology. These need to be scrutinized periodically, to assure that neither is trying to do the job of the other, that in areas of cooperation neither is co-opted by the other, and to explore possibilities of further cooperation. For example, theological college faculty may be able to offer courses in the history of Christianity for which a particular religious studies department lacks expertise. Conversely, religious studies professors could offer courses in areas in which theological college faculty may not be competent, for example, Asian or indigenous religions, should theological colleges take a greater interest in those areas than at present (cf. chap. 3.3). Religious studies departments and theological colleges will doubtless continue to divide up responsibility for the teaching of biblical languages.

In the area of scholarship the edges of the religious studies-theology antinomy are not keen: professors in theological colleges publish in religious studies journals, and religious studies professors in theological journals, and many journals are neither one nor the other and accept articles from both sources as well as from others. The publication of journals and books by the Canadian Corporation for Studies in Religion/Corporation Canadienne des Sciences Religieuses is an area in which religious studies and theological societies have successfully cooperated. The Corporation's publication programmes are one of the significant and distinctive achievements of our learned societies, often envied by other fields, and Ontario religious studies professors and departments surely do well to continue their support of them (chap. 2.7).

While cooperation between religious studies and theology is of long standing, religious studies departments and programmes also have a variety of working arrangements with other university departments or with faculty in those departments. Such arrangements are sine qua non for a programme or a centre in religious studies (chap. 2.6.5). However, some departments, too, draw on professors from other departments to teach, or to teach in, religious studies courses, or to serve as adjunct professors in a graduate programme, teaching courses and serving as thesis supervisors or readers. As in relations with theological colleges, careful forethought has to be given to such cooperation and, once initiated, it needs to be carefully monitored to assure that the instruction offered by persons not trained in religious studies accords with the department's aims (chap. 4.2.4). Such initiatives are to be encourged, in view of budgetary restraints in Ontario universities, the nature of religious studies as in many ways "multi-disciplinary" — like history, "a field encompassing field" (Harvey, 1966 [cf. chap. 2.4.9 above]) — and the increasing awareness that in many respects religious studies is more closely related to other university fields than it is to theology. Appropriate attention must of course be paid to the integrity of religious studies when drawing upon or hiring persons from outside the field (chap. 4.2.4). From the other direction there is the recent case of a religious studies student admitted to a specialization in religion in an anthropology doctoral programme with the understanding that a religious studies professor in the university would serve as a dissertation reader.

Also to be encouraged is the work that some Ontario religious studies professors are doing with representatives of some of the various religious traditions in the province. Especially important, it seems to us, is work with indigenous peoples and research on their traditions. Some such research is being done, and there are courses devoted to native traditions or that include study of them in some way (chap. 2.4.8), but it is small in comparison with the importance of these traditions in Canada and North America generally and in Ontario in particular. This is certainly an area where interdepartmental cooperation, for example, with anthropology or history, suggests itself. That would make more feasible what we see as a prime desideratum, namely, a doctorate in indigenous religions in one of the Ontario religious studies graduate programmes.

With respect to teaching, our observations of practices in religious studies departments and programmes prompt some comments on working with representatives of religious traditions. On the one hand, research proposals routinely have to meet ethical standards laid down by universities and granting agencies. In teaching, however, that is not necessarily the case, and we would urge departments and programmes to adopt comparable guidelines for bringing representatives of religious traditions into the classroom and for field trips to sanctuaries or to interview individuals. Moreover, any such contacts require pedagogical preparation: What methodological perspectives are useful to first-hand study of a religion, and specifically this particular religion, and how are they to be applied (cf. chap. 2.4.4 above and 12.8.2 below)? Without such guidelines and preparation serious misunderstandings, and abuse, can result. At the least, it is bad pedagogy. Nor does it take seriously religious studies' claim that the academic study of religion is something more than the collection and recording of data.

12.6   Indigenization of Textbooks

In religious studies courses generally, Canadian phenomena are now often included as aspects of a larger subject (chaps. 7.6 and 8.2). That is one way professors supplement (especially) textbooks written by American professors and issued by American publishers. Some textbooks, of course, include chapters or sections on Canadian religious traditions (e.g., Handy, 1985) or discuss a particular field or methodology in relation to religion in Canada (O'Toole, 1984, 226-32 [with bibliographical footnotes]; Dawson, 1991). And there are textbooks devoted wholly or in part to specific Canadian religious traditions (e.g., Walsh, 1966; Moir, 1972; J.W. Grant, 1972/1988), or monographs that might serve as supplementary reading on a particular religious tradition in Canada (Waugh and Prithipaul, 1979) or Ontario (J.W. Grant, 1988; Westfall, 1989) or a particular aspect of religion in Canada (e.g., Allen, 1970; Fraser, 1988) or on the sociology of religion in Canada (Clark, 1948, 1962; Crysdale and Wheatcroft, 1976; Mol, 1985; Bibby, 1987). However, a perusal of a recent bibliographical survey of scholarly publications on religion in Canada bears out the authors' statement that "the subject of religion in Canada still remains for them [i.e., religious studies departments and programmes] only a minor focus of scholarly interest" (Laperrière and Westfall, 1990, 43): although the survey is headed "Religious Studies," only a small number of the items are by persons in religious studies departments and programmes.

It is welcome news that so much attention is being devoted to the study of religion in Canada by those outside religious studies. However, we would urge religious studies professors in Ontario who are doing research on the subject, or who may be teaching courses on various aspects of religion in Canada, to think of producing textbooks which would be focussed on specifically Canadian religious traditions and take fuller account of Canadian scholarship and Canadian concerns than do those produced outside Canada. Copying services and publishing firms that now print textbooks or other teaching aids designed by professors for specific courses have made the task much simpler by looking after copyright permissions, printing quantities to order, and providing for revisions from one year to the next. We would encourage professors who have produced aids of this kind to inform others through electronic networks. Professor-produced textbooks using materials in the public domain can be transmitted electronically, whole or in selected portions, to enable others to use them in their courses or in making textbooks of their own. And we would urge our learned societies to find avenues for the authors of textbooks and other teaching aids to announce them, for example, in society newsletters, and to provide sessions at their annual meetings in which they might be discussed. The Canadian Corporation for Studies in Religion might consider issuing the best of these in a series, even as Scholars Press has recently launched a series of "teaching books" in religious studies and theology (*Religious Studies News* 6/1 [Jan.-Feb. 1991], 32).

12.7   Teaching

Having annual meeting sessions on teaching was one of the suggestions made by faculty in interviews (chap. 3.2.5). We commend this suggestion to our learned societies. A few years ago, for example, the Eastern International Region of the American Academy of Religion held a successful three-day workshop at one of the Ontario universities on teaching the introductory course in religious studies. That many religious studies professors are working hard at teaching became evident in our interviews (chap. 6.5). We would encourage society newsletters and *Studies in Religion/Sciences Religieuses* to consider devoting a section to teaching in which professors would report, briefly or at length, on new approaches they are trying or on publications or other aids they have found useful, or would discuss problems in teaching generally or connected with particular courses or kinds of courses. Such a section would take some planning and might require an editor assigned specifically to the gathering, sifting, and assessing of materials for inclusion. The section on teaching in *Horizons*, the journal of the College Theology Society, has been quite successful and might provide a model. So, too, the lively and extremely helpful monthly (except July and August), *The Teaching Professor,* which we would commend to departments, programmes, and individuals (Magna Publications, 2718 Dryden Drive, Madison, WI 53704-3086). Contributors include Canadian as well as American professors. (Among the articles in the December 1990 issue: ''On Being Vague,'' ''How Old Dogs Learn New Tricks,'' ''Instructional Evaluation,'' and an ''Open Letter to Teaching Professors'' that recommends, among other ''extreme suggestions,'' useful books on university-level teaching [e.g., Eble, 1977 and McKeachie, 1990].) Indeed, the time may be right to consider an *SR Newsletter*, published by the Canadian Corporation for Studies in Religion/Corporation Canadienne des Sciences Religieuses, in co-operation with the religious studies learned societies, departments, and programmes, that would contain a section on teaching, news from departments and programmes, and announcements of common interest.

Within departments and programmes, planning for the future should take teaching into consideration more than has often been the case in the past. Curricula and graduate preparation sometimes, of necessity, do not match well (chap. 6.1), but is it necessarily the case that senior faculty should have freedom to select courses to their liking while faculty fresh from graduate school must shoulder courses quite unrelated to their preparation and background (chap. 6.1)? Or is it necessarily the case that senior faculty are the ones best qualified to teach graduate seminars? The sometime dean of the Faculty of Arts and Sciences at Harvard suggests (without wanting to make a rule of it) that the reverse may be desirable: new Ph.D.s are on the cutting edge of research in comparison with older faculty whereas the latter have a store of wisdom more important in teaching undergraduates than ''the latest specialist wrinkles. . . . Life experience is a valuable part of the liberal arts no matter what the subject'' (Rosovsky, 1990, 217). A recent study suggests something similar. There are different kinds of scholarship, commensurate with different stages in a professorial career. A professor may move from specialist scholarship to ''scholarship of integration'' — synthesizing earlier, specialized research and correlating it with work in other fields — to ''scholarship of teaching,'' for example, writing of textbooks or preparation of audio-visual teaching aids, as well as working hard at classroom teaching (Boyer, 1990).

Basic to this perception of professorial life, and to a professor's career in general, is specialist scholarship. To that end, for the development of young colleagues as scholars — and teachers — and for the long-term health of a department or programme, it would seem wise to assign them, right from the beginning, as many courses as possible that build on their specialization and, as much as university policy permits, to reduce their course load in their first year or two when course preparations will be particularly burdensome (chap. 6.4). Some faculty mentioned in interviews how older colleagues, sometimes in team-taught courses, had given them help and guidance in developing courses or in pedagogy (chap. 6.1). The reverse is certainly true too, however, as more than one aging professor will attest. Mentoring programmes might be mutually advantageous, therefore, especially in larger institutions, where there are more waters to chart and the sharks may lurk deeper.

Part-time instructional faculty are a fact of life in Ontario universities, one of the less cheering aspects of academic life in the 1980s and probably into the next millennium (chap. 3.2.4 and 3.2.6). Some are better scholars and teachers than the full-time faculty who hire them. Most are unknown quantities until they have taught a course for the department. Careful hiring, in which they are interviewed not only by the department chair but by other faculty members as well, has proved helpful in some cases, and we recommend it. Beyond that, part-time instructors should be provided, as much as possible, with the supports to teaching that regular faculty enjoy: secretarial help, office space, computer time, etc. Mentoring by faculty who teach or who have taught the same course may also be helpful. Inclusion in faculty gatherings and recognition of work well done are important to their morale and hence to their teaching. They can offer much to a department (cf. Rabinowitz, 1991).

As to aims and methods in teaching, it is likely that the present diversity will continue along with the self-awareness of religious studies as a field noted in Chapter 6.2 and 6.3. Uniformity is hardly a desideratum. Here, too, discussions of aims and methods at annual meetings, in the pages of society newsletters, and in *Studies in Religion/Sciences Religieuses* could prove stimulating, especially with respect to the Canadian scene.

Course loads is another subject that needs more airing. We confess dismay at learning of the heavy loads at certain places (chap. 6.4). While normal load requirements are set by university policy, some faculty opt for "overload" courses in the evening, in distance education programmes, or in spring and summer terms. Whatever their reasons, financial or otherwise, they thereby expend time and energy that might otherwise go to research or just to plain keeping abreast of one's field. But university policies also sometimes allow for reduced teaching loads, fewer "contact" hours, and other variations from the norm (chap. 6.4). More communication among Ontario religious studies departments and programmes, in learned society meetings, in print, or electronically might lead to changes from one university to the next. It is in the interests of overburdened departments and professors to pursue the possibilities — if they can find the time. Tenured faculty might decide to forego extra teaching duties, thus providing more opportunities for young part-time lecturers in places where stipends are available to hire them.

Much is at stake. More time for research, or for course preparation, should mean better teaching. More research should mean more and better scholarship and publications and thus a better department or programme and a higher profile on campus, and, for the individual, advancement.

As is pointed out in Chapter 6, religious studies professors have enjoyed a good reputation as teachers. For the future of religious studies in Ontario, it is important to continue good pedagogy and to work toward improving it further. The 1990s, when many new faculty will be entering departments and programmes, is a propitious time to consider new initiatives for doing so.

12.8   Research and Publication

Faculty research and publication is another area where religious studies, like other fields, is in transition (chaps. 3.1.3, 7.4). One notices it in the research modes of the older and younger professors. The latter are more likely to be the ones sitting at a computer terminal, not only entering lecture notes, syllabi, and copy for a book or an article, but also monitoring and contributing to electronic networks of scholars in their field in all parts of the world (chaps. 3.2.5 and 10.2). Their c.v.s are also apt to be thicker than were those of their older colleagues at a comparable stage of their careers.

These are generalizations to which there are numerous exceptions. But both in Ontario (chap. 7.4) and Quebec (Rousseau and Despland, 1988, 136) they are borne out by statistical data and in interviews. For various reasons suggested earlier (chap. 3.1.3; cf. chap. 7.4), a goodly number of older faculty have not been productive scholars, whereas for many younger faculty, trained in a different time and mode and prodded by more stringent tenure and promotion policies, research and publication are just part of the academic way of life. As the authors of the Quebec study observe, ''Ceux qui publiaient publient de plus en plus,'' while the rest have not been prolific scholars in the past and are not likely to be so in the future; however, thanks to their experience and their years they can nonetheless make important contributions to the field (Rousseau and Despland, 1988, 136; cf. 12.7 above).

The data reported in Chapter 7.4 indicated that while Ontario religious studies professors have not been as productive as Canadian humanities professors generally, in the one area where we were able to measure change over time, namely, presentation of papers, productivity has increased over a decade, both for individuals and with respect to the number of individuals involved (''participation rate''). Given the changing nature of religious studies faculty noted above, it is to be expected that their scholarly productivity will increase still further.

If nothing else, tenure and promotion policies now in place will provide incentives for research and publication. But if our reading of younger faculty is not way off the mark, they will be publishing books and articles and presenting papers because they are energetic scholars and want to communicate the results of their research to others and seek their reactions. Love of learning, we perceive (and fondly hope), is at least as important as the external pressures. If so, that will likely function as a safeguard against publication for the sake of publication at a time when "publish or perish" has become a prime paradigm of academic life. Fifty years ago Jacques Barzun was already lamenting

> that commentaries have swamped originals and that scholarship is now a task of slogging through a jungle of books. We have felled the Canadian forests for paper to print on, and we cannot see the truth for the wood-pulp (1954 [1945], 272).

Refereeing manuscripts submitted for publication is a weighty responsibility laid on faculty. If they take religious studies and their subfields seriously as academic endeavours in a university, they will exercise it rigorously. That would render less attractive a wry scheme of promotion proposed by "an unknown genius" to encourage publication of only truly significant research: all faculty begin as full professors and drop one rank for every book published, a by-product of which would be the blunting of criticism that undergraduates are taught by junior faculty and never see the authors of all those books, since now the "junior" faculty would be those very authors (Rosovsky, 1990, 89, n.14). Prodigality in publication such that would call for such a scheme among Ontario religious studies scholars is not foreseeable until the millennium. But the point is well taken: referees should use a fine-toothed comb.

In our survey of research areas, the breadth of areas covered by religious studies is one indication of how religious studies has moved away from theology and its focus on Christianity and related areas (chap. 7.5). Even so, the percentage of religious studies scholars working primarily in areas other than Christianity is small (ibid.). That, and the significant proportion of persons whose primary and secondary areas of research are Christian theology, underline the importance of the kind of planning recommended earlier in this chapter that would make religious studies in Ontario a field much more inclusive and representative of the religions of humankind than at present.

In our interviews with faculty regarding directions of research there were few surprises (chap. 7.6), little one would not have learned from attending professional society meetings or from perusal of journals of recent (and sometimes not-so-recent) vintage. More important is what the responses to our question about directions of research revealed about Ontario religious studies faculty and how they perceive scholarship and themselves as scholars.

One predictable observation is that some stay well abreast of what is happening in their field or in religious studies generally. A few are at the cutting edge of research internationally. There are more such persons, whom we didn't interview, as is evident from their c.v.s. One of the disappointments, however, was that others are living their scholarly lives a decade or more ago, as though nothing had happened since then, or have given up the game while maintaining — or not — the appearances. That there are more such is also evident from c.v.s. Perhaps it should not have occasioned disap-

pointment: it happens in other university departments and in other professions, where, however, a tenure system does not shield congealed competence.

One antidote we prescribe for that malady is active membership in one or
more learned societies, which will bring journals to one's desk, provide the
stimulus (and the pain) of giving and hearing papers, and, for many at least,
serve as an annual tonic (chaps. 3.2.5, 7.7). Antidote is not panacea, however. Others will find electronic networks more stimulating, more au
courant — and cheaper (chap. 10.2). Some faculty in thinly populated subfields or in departments where they were the only ones working in their
areas of research mentioned isolation and how important to them are gatherings with colleagues, regionally, nationally, or internationally. For them
electronic networks should prove especially valuable. Then there are the
loners, self-professed and otherwise, whose scholarly productivity shames
many of the learned society types and who stay at home sipping aged port
while poring over ancient texts. They are the exceptions, however, and even
they occasionally emerge from their lairs to enter the scholarly lists. In general, the strong impression our interviews left with us is that there is a positive (unfortunate) correlation between scholarly somnolence and scholarly
isolation.

It is encouraging that a healthy number of Ontario religious studies faculty belong to learned societies, about half to three or more, in fact, both
Canadian and otherwise (chap. 7.7). That many belong to no more than one
of the Canadian religious studies societies (ibid.) is not a bad sign, in our
opinion: provincialism always lurks (see 12.10.1 below), and belonging to
societies other than those in religious studies or in Canada, as some religious studies faculty do, diminishes the possibility. On the other hand,
membership in more than one of the Canadian religious studies societies
gives a fuller perspective on the field of religious studies in Canada and is
not that burdensome for persons on a regular salary since much of the cost
of the first membership goes to pay for a subscription to *Studies in Reli-
gion/Sciences Religieuses* (chap. 7.7). We would encourage the societies to
consider ways to make joint or multiple memberships easier and more
attractive.

Also very useful to society officers and a way of raising members' consciousness of the various Canadian learned societies in the field would be an
annual directory of the societies belonging to the Canadian Corporation for
Studies in Religion/Corporation Canadienne des Sciences Religieuses that
would include for each a brief self-description and a listing of officers with
addresses and phone numbers (see the directories published in the February
and April issues of the *Council of Societies for the Study of Religion Bulletin*). It could be published in *Studies in Religion/Sciences Religieuses* or in a
newsletter (see 12.7 above).

12.8.1 · "Fragmentation" and a "Battle of the Books"

One view of research in religious studies, expressed by several faculty, is that it is unfocused and fragmented (chap. 7.6). The breadth of the field and its rapid expansion — explosion? — in recent decades lends some support to this view, as does riffling through the pages of the hefty programme the American Academy of Religion and Society of Biblical Literature turn out each year for their joint annual meeting, or even the much more modest production of the Canadian Society for the Study of Religion for its annual gathering plus the syllabi for the annual meetings of other, smaller societies in the field. Whether religious studies is any more diffuse and fragmented than, say, modern-day anthropology or geography is doubtful. On the other side is the view (expressed in interviews) that there is consensus in religious studies at least to the effect that the field is non-confessional in nature. Beyond that, it is doubtful that there is much methodological consensus if one considers the "-isms" and "-ologies" that come and go and come and which faculty seek to impart to students as important to understanding religious traditions and to "doing" religious studies. There is nothing peculiarly Ontarian or Canadian here. At issue is something that religious studies departments and professors in North America generally wrestle with and that affects more than research. What in religious studies is "the knowledge most worth having," and how does one impart or attain it? What does or should a B.A. or an M.A. or a Ph.D. in religious studies "have" upon receipt of the degree? Is there a common fund of knowledge, a core of learning, a critical mass of method?

These are particularly vexing questions in the 1990s if, when, and insofar as the "battle of the books" mentioned earlier migrates or has already migrated northward. Religious studies may be a step ahead, with its efforts, noted in various places in this volume, to make study of religion more than the study of just one (Western) religion (Christianity) or two (Christianity and Judaism), less ethnocentric, less androcentric. Perhaps other fields and departments might find our experience thus far instructive. The "multi-cultural scope" of religious studies, observes an American report on the field, "is not unique to the study of religion, but it is rare, and it is one of the paramount values the study of religion in depth offers the liberal arts student in an increasingly cosmopolitan world" (Crites, 1990, 12). By intention (though not necessarily, in practice), "The academic study of religion is not ethnocentric": "It is directed to the cultural specificities of each religious tradition under study" (ibid., 10).

However, when it comes down to questions of "core," of what the holder of a religious studies degree should know and share with other holders of such a degree, consensus among religious studies faculty is still around the corner. Partly it is a question of quantity. A department that undertakes to set down a list of "essential" books for its concentrators and graduate students by asking each faculty member for nominations will likely end up with a shopping list of classics of East and West as well as of the "greats" of modern study that none of the nominators has or ever will read in full. It can be whittled down, of course. However, it is then that battle lines are apt to be drawn, and if American experience is any indication, by competing orthodoxies firing opposing canons. But Canadians are not Americans (so far), and when the department forms the inevitable committee to study the problem the members would presumably apply to the positions of opposing factions the skills acquired in studying religious traditions, teasing out and examining premises and warrants, examined and otherwise. From our interviews, from attendance at learned society meetings, and from our general knowledge of religious studies in Ontario acquired over the years, we do not as yet see a self-proclaimed "cultural left" like that in American universities which contends one cannot simply add to the Western canon since that would be to retain the oppressive, colonialist, androcentric biasses of those writings: if, indeed, "social transformation is the primary goal of education," then that must be achieved with the help of a new canon, compiled from writings outside the old, oppressive one (Searle, 1990, 35, citing Gerald Graff in Gless and Smith, 1990).

The extended review by John Searle, professor of philosophy at the University of California — Berkeley, offers a critical look at the American debate and the debaters' premises. One conclusion he draws (1990, 37), applicable, it seems to us, also to religious studies and its once and still largely Western curriculum, is that

> there never was, in fact a fixed "canon"; there was rather a certain set of tentative judgments about what had importance and quality. Such judgments are always subject to revision, and in fact they were constantly being revised.

In recent years various readers of the Jewish and Christian scriptures have contended, sometimes insisted, that interpretation should adhere to those texts in their present, canonical form (e.g., J. Sanders, 1972, 1984, 1987; Childs, 1985, 1986; Alter and Kermode, 1987). For quite different reasons, subscribers to doctrines of verbal, plenary inspiration of the same scriptures have also resisted efforts to look behind the text as it stands. But the Christian canon at least has always had loose edges, was "not finally closed" (Barth, 1956, 481 [cf. 476-81]), even for some strict constructionists of inspiration doctrines (Pieper, 1950, 292, 331-37). It is true, as Frank Kermode points out (in Alter and Kermode, 1987, 604), that there have been no actual deletions or additions. On the other hand, disuse of certain books, by design or neglect, and canons within canons have had the effect of altering the canon. Interestingly, closure of Jewish and Christian canons, rather than dampening further literary efforts, soon evoked them (Cohen, 1987, 292, 331-32; Cullmann, 1959), and these have long been the object of scholarly study by students of the canons themselves.

There have also been borers from within, efforts to get behind the canons. "J," "E," "D," and "P" were discerned behind "Moses," while Jesus was looked for in pre-canonical traditions embedded in those recorded in the four canonical gospels and then, beyond any of these, in non-canonical traditions and writings (some of which were, for some Christians and Christian groups at some time, canonical). Jesus' "forerunner," John the Baptizer, turns out in such "excavating" study to be a prophet and founder of a movement in his own right, as Mount Allison (Scobie, 1964) and York University (Mason, 1991) scholars have nicely demonstrated (as have others before them, e.g., Dibelius, 1932). The stories and roles of women have been recovered from the canons and beyond them (chap. 2.4.9). In short, these have hardly been "fixed" canons. Usage that assumes they are — for example, "biblical studies" or "extra-biblical" — while comfortable and convenient,

> conceals the fact that there is no such thing as "*the* Bible." There are many different "Bibles," accepted by many different religious organizations, but it hardly needs arguing that the question of what was or is accepted by the Samaritans or the Ethiopians or the Mormons or the Council of Trent or the sanhedrin of Yabneh has no importance for questions about the original significance of books written before their times. On such matters the Holy Ghost was not a reliable source of information (M. Smith, 1983, 296).

While some factions in the battle of the books may insist on replacing entirely the present "oppressive" canon, others dissent from that view. The *Norton Anthology of Afro-American Literature* by the Afro-American scholar Louis Gates, Jr., of Duke University exemplifies his preference for "an alternative, minority canon of works that can be taught alongside the classics of European culture" (D'Souza, 1991, 71). Similarly, Searle argues that "the student should have enough knowledge of his or her cultural tradition to know how it got to be that way" (1990, 42). "However," he goes on to say, "you do not understand your own tradition if you do not see it in relation to others. Works from other cultural traditions need to be studied as well." And rather than excluding the works by white males that have so dominated reading lists, the reasons why males were the authors of those works "should be explained and understood" (ibid.).

These conclusions have a familiar ring. From "Moses" (though maybe not the Yahwist [thus Bloom and Rosenberg, 1990]) to "Matthew" to Paul to Augustine, Aquinas, Luther, Feuerbach, Freud, Otto, Eliade, Bultmann, and beyond, the "canon" of religious studies curricula consisted almost exclusively of writings by white males. It was then expanded to include, first, works from other religious traditions, usually by males (and usually of colour), and then later by women, white and of colour. The reasons for the whiteness and maleness were given some attention since critical study was essential to the shifts in focus. Critical examination of the non-Western writings would presumably reveal that males of colour and beyond the pale of the West were also androcentric and oppressive.

In Ontario, the "state of the art" in religious studies, as we have observed it, is that departments and programmes have decided on a mixture of the various options outlined in the preceding paragraphs. The traditional Western canon of religious traditions has been retained, but viewed critically, often expanded to include overlooked writings, figures, and movements, and commonly examined from a variety of perspectives. Other canons, from other cultures and religious traditions, have also been introduced, these too viewed critically and approached using a variety of methodologies. So far, Ontario departments and programmes have not chosen complete displacement of the "old" canon by a new canon or canons.

These are "truth" questions. If, for reasons enunciated elsewhere in this study (chaps. 2.5, 3.2.3), religious studies professors are skittish about taking stands on the "truth" of the traditions represented in the writings they study and teach, they are not reluctant—in their publications, in their classes, and through their choice of readings for students—to assess the worth of these writings as representative of a particular tradition. Moreover, whereas the debate outlined has concentrated on texts, specifically certain texts in the humanities (Searle, 1990, 36), more is involved in the study of religion. Unlike literary critics for whom (it has been argued) "Writing constitutes the canon for the West" (Readings, 1989, 169), religious studies scholars have come to perceive that the "texts" of religion are more than texts: they include food, clothing, body markings and body language, social customs, institutions, play, rituals, dance, music, art, architecture, artifacts—none of these confined to the West and all of them, and more, crucial to understanding religion (cf. chap. 2.4.9). For religion is not simply individuals thinking, believing, professing, but also, and especially, it is behaviours—"something that people do, and they do it together" (Neusner, 1988b, 27). Some behaviours are recorded in texts, others are not and require direct observation—field study, diachronic and synchronic. Such perceptions of religion and the study of it carry with them the corollaries that fields outside the humanities have much to contribute to the study of religion—the academic study of religion is not confined to religious studies—and that the study of such "doing" cannot be confined to a few, familiar religions—"the West"—or even to behaviours not commonly perceived as "religious" (chap. 2.4.9).

Such perceptions and how they came to be, a story told at greater length earlier in this volume (chap. 2; cf. chap. 3.2.3) and elsewhere, constitute, it seems to us, something of an aetiology for present religious studies faculty in Ontario and elsewhere, one they recount to themselves, to one another, and to students to explain their presence in the university and what they do there. If (one might argue) they know something about the origins of religious studies in the scholarly study of Christianity and Judaism, they can look with some understanding on it, some of them can continue to study those traditions and offer courses in them, and students from those traditions can see them as possible and viable forms of the religious life even as they also acquire some acquaintance with the critiques of those religions and of religion generally and learn to ponder the question *"Why* religion?" (Preus, 1987). But faculty and students can also, with some equanimity, move beyond those origins to the study of other religious traditions, as indeed they have. The aetiology may also help to understand the "fragmentation" in research mentioned earlier as, in the first place, a consequence of some moves attendant on the coming-to-be of religious studies.

How one proceeds from there is moot. Most simply, one might hail the multifariousness of research in religious studies as healthy diversity and a sign of vitality. Or, having decided "that the study of religion itself is still living in a 'pre-paradigmatic' state, given the ongoing competition between incommensurable approaches," one may then "take care to protect the pluralism afforded by tolerance of competing paradigms" (Preus, 1987, xi-xii), while nonetheless pursuing the question of a suitable paradigm, as Preus's study does. Or one might choose to tolerate (or perhaps ignore) the diversity and concentrate on one's particular specialty, as many do. Or one might interpret it as intrinsic to a phenomenon as many-faceted as "religion" which, to be grasped in its complexity, requires multiple, interdisciplinary methodologies (Fenton, 1970). Or one might perhaps prescribe methodological therapy en route to "a science of religion" on the way to "a science of man [sic]" (Penner, 1989a, 178). As this (itself fragmentary) listing of divergent interpretations suggests, "fragmentation" in research (and teaching) in religious studies will persist into the (next) millennium, also in religious studies in Ontario. It is a persistence deriving partly from institutional inertia (there is much intellectual and institutional capital invested in it), partly because deeply embedded scholarly and personal convictions and premises are involved, partly because "religion" is indeed a complex subject, partly because religious studies faculty and students are still expanding the horizons of the field and questioning its points of reference. At a recent American Academy of Religion meeting, for example, an Ontario religious studies professor asked what have been the geographical and ethnic coordinates from which the history of religion in the southwestern United States has been written (Grimes, 1990b). Similar questionings in other areas, and along methodological lines, are to be encouraged as continuations of the story of religious studies in Ontario. Only further research and discussion, however, will tell what directions it will take.

12.8.2 *Methodology and Diversity*

However, some words about methodology may be in order at this point. Those who undertake something new may have to explain what it is they are doing, and why, especially in a venue that has certain basic ground rules and a suspicion of anyone perceived as having a longstanding habit of ignoring or violating them. Not surprisingly, then, religious studies has devoted much attention to methodology or methodologies (chap. 2.4), to the weariness of some: as far back as 1970 Van Harvey spoke of religious studies' "inordinate preoccupation with methodology" and related it to "the search for identity and self-understanding by members of departments of religion" (1970, 29). Whether or not religious studies' identity is still in "crisis" (Welch, 1971, chap. 2), as some contend (Preus, 1987, xvii), methodology continues as a perennial topic, both in the subfields of religious studies and for religious studies as an academic field in the modern, secular university. It has come up for discussion at various places in this study.

One way of looking at these "wearying" discussions of "methodology" and to explain their staying power is to see lurking in them "truth" questions that have driven critical debate over religion in the West, especially over the last four centuries but not only then (Cicero's *De natura deorum* or some of Lucian of Samosata's satires come to mind). Are religious phenomena to be "regarded as manifestations of a universal sense of transcendence and/or of its archetypal expressions" (Preus, 1987, 211)? Is there an "x" (or are there "x's") "out there" corresponding to such a sense; that is, what is the ontological status of any such sense or belief (cf. chap. 2.4.3 above)? Since in the academy such questions cannot be placed off limits to critical study, and since the academy has no magisterium to hand down decisions on them, methodological debates over them continue. They are, one might say, part of religious studies' continuing effort to find its place and its way within the university, wearying though it may be.

Weariness with methodological discussions may also be related to the fact that methodological approaches are so many and diverse — not surprisingly since "religion" is complex, to say nothing of the "truth" questions just mentioned. These questions have been complicated recently by some deconstructive readings apparently subversive both of religious scriptures and of the ways they have been received in religious communities or by scholars. One suspects, too, that people "want to get on with it" — actually work on the data of religion rather than focus on working up to them. That is in fact what at least some of those known for their concern with methodology profess as their motivation (e.g., Penner, 1989b, 2-3). To that end we would encourage publication of studies that test or exemplify particular methodological approaches. For instance, the volumes in the Guides to Biblical Scholarship series published by Fortress Press include examples showing how the methods discussed by the authors are used in practice.[1] The disservice done to readers and scholarship when an author, persuaded by a publisher, omits the methodological theory underlying her examples is pointed out by David Jobling (1991, 7, 8) in the case of Mieke Bal's *Lethal Love* (1987).

If previous Canadian debates over methodology are any indication, it is a safe bet that methodology will continue to be a concern in religious studies in Ontario. The new journal *Method & Theory in the Study of Religion* (chap. 2.7 above), based in the Centre for Religious Studies in Toronto, and a recently inaugurated series "Toronto Studies in Religion" edited by Donald Wiebe of Trinity College, University of Toronto, and published by Peter Lang in association with the Centre provide focussed fora for continued discussion; so, too, another new series entitled "Religion and Reason: Method and Theory in the Study and Interpretation of Religion" edited by Jacques Waardenburg (Université de Lausanne) and published by Mouton de Gruyter. It can also be safely predicted that the present diversity in the way religion is approached and studied at the tertiary level in Ontario will persist given the variety of institutions devoted to such study, the diverse historical circumstances in which these came into being, their various institutional allegiances, and their commitment to the serving of often distinct constituencies (chap. 2.6). In this context some observations by Van Harvey (1970, 29) seem apropos:

> Religions surely can be significantly studied from many different standpoints and perspectives and one's contribution to the field will depend not so much on the application of some method so much as on the knowledge, insight, and imagination he [sic] brings to his [sic] work.

Also apropos is the interest many of the faculty we interviewed expressed in what is happening in other fields, for example, sociology and literature, and the readiness to apply what they learned to their own work (chap. 7.6). This kind of cross-disciplinary fertilization has been one of the marks of religious studies in the past two decades, and the faculty we interviewed were, with a few exceptions, in favour of it. It is of a piece with the general movement of religious studies in the direction of university and away from theological college. There is the danger of faddishness, as one professor pointed out, but that did not seem to be the case with those we interviewed: new modes of thought and new methods provided fresh vantage points on their work and heuristically useful ways of approaching it.

12.9   Anglophone, Francophone

Another kind of movement in religious studies in Canada, reported earlier (chaps. 2.7 and 7.6), is that of francophone scholars away from their anglophone counterparts. The establishing of a separate Quebec society for the study of religion is widely viewed by both francophones and anglophones as the logical consequence of what was, en effet, two solitudes. So far, discussions have been amicable, and we would hope that politicization of the kind reported above in the "battle of the books" or in Islamic studies (chap. 7.6) would not develop. The mutual seeking of ties between the new Société québécoise pour l'étude de la religion and the Canadian Society for the Study of Religion and the Société's participation in the Canadian Corporation for Studies in Religion/Corporation Canadienne des Sciences Religieuses are welcome signs. In a time of debate and acrimony over national unity, cultivation of these ties and of ties between individual francophone and anglophone scholars, within the CSSR and between the two societies, is certainly to be encouraged. Failure to do so will impoverish anglophone scholars and, we are inclined to believe, francophone ones as well.

12.10   Graduate Study

In the graduate study of religion in Ontario one notes that both M.A. and Ph.D. programmes exist today where three decades earlier there were none (chap. 9). This has meant that persons wishing to pursue studies one level beyond the baccalaureate have been able to do so in a provincial university, often close by or even in their own municipality. It has also meant that students inclined to the academic life who formerly would have trekked outside the country for their graduate education (chaps. 2.1.3, 5.1.1.4) could now complete their study within the province itself. This raises several important issues.

12.10.1   *Provincial Education and Provincialism*

Thanks to the new doctoral programmes as well as to Canadian immigration regulations and the desire of religious studies departments for more Canadian staff, religious studies faculty in Ontario are increasingly hiring graduates of the Ontario programmes, some of whom have also done their undergraduate work in the province. It is a copsummation long wished by many, an antidote to what they saw as a plague of outsiders brought in to staff new and burgeoning departments of religious studies in the 1960s. But is there anyone besides us who is worrying just a little about the future when what might become a preponderance of faculty educated within the province may foster provincialism? Will indigenization (chap. 2.7) have been bought at the cost of forfeiting diversity and vitality such as were brought to religious studies in Ontario, and in Canada generally, by Canadians and outsiders who had studied in some of the best doctoral programmes in North America and Europe?

One hopes not, and a possible shortage of provincial or Canadian doctoral graduates as the decades wears on (chap. 5.1.1.2, 5.3) may mean hiring of persons from outside Canada and thus more possibility of diversity, especially if Ontario departments with religious studies graduate programmes are serious about quality (12.1 above). However, they would also do well, it seems to us, to position Post-it notes in strategic and prominent places to remind themselves of ways to preserve and foster vitality and diversity in their programmes. One note might read: Encourage participation of faculty in learned societies in Canada and elsewhere. Another might urge students to do the same. (Involvement of Ontario religious studies faculty in the Eastern International Region of the American Academy of Religion, for example, fosters contact with counterparts in adjacent American states.) Other reminders might seek to maintain or initiate programmes for students to do some of their study or research at another Ontario university or outside the province or outside Canada; another to bring guest lecturers and guest professors to campus. Still another note might read: Talk to colleagues in other subfields in the department or university about collaboration in research or about serving as thesis readers. Such moves would do much to expand horizons of professors and students and in some instances make it possible for students to approximate at home what they would otherwise achieve only by studying outside Ontario or outside Canada.

For Ontario religious studies departments and programmes, but also, and especially, for graduate students, it is lamentable that the opportunities to study in the U.S. or Europe of which many present Ontario religious studies faculty availed themselves are now largely denied to the present generation because of the enormous increases in tuition in the U.S. and the weakness of the Canadian dollar against American and European currencies. Short of our learned societies winning big in the lottery and allocating the interest from the winnings to scholarships, we see no solution to this problem. Related to it is the paucity of scholarship and assistantship monies for study even within the province, and the unfortunate circumstance that students sometimes settle for study at a graduate school that is not their first choice because only there can they survive financially (chap. 4.2.5). Again, we have no solution to offer. However, it is issues such as these that we would commend to the attention of the Canadian council on graduate religious studies that seems to be in process of formation (chap. 2.7).

12.10.2   Agenda Items for a Canadian Council on Graduate Religious Studies

The council-to-be would also seem to be the agency most suited to consider various recommendations made in Chapter 9.5 and 9.6 as well as others that are no doubt occupying graduate officers. Near the top of the agenda, it seems to us, would be a survey of all departments and programmes of religious studies as well as theological colleges in Canada to determine how many faculty openings each foresees in the next half-decade and decade, and in which areas. Institutions with doctoral programmes should be asked how many graduates are expected in those same areas and time periods. The results would yield data to supplement those available from sources like those cited in Chapter 5 and would shed further light on whether the 1990s will see a shortage or surplus of faculty. The data would be crucial both for faculty as they plan curricula and future appointments and for students contemplating graduate study.

Another kind of survey (suggested in chap. 9.5) would be of recipients of religious studies graduate degrees who are employed by religious institutions such as churches and church agencies, as well as the employers themselves, to learn their perceptions of how the knowledge and skills gained in a religious studies graduate programme have contributed — or not — to the work the person is doing for the institution. The same might well be done with graduates employed in the helping professions. Such surveys would increase awareness of the value—if any—of graduate work in religious studies and could help to achieve further recognition of the academic study of religion in society. The answers would also provide religious studies graduate programmes with valuable "feedback" on the kind of education they are seeking to offer and its efficacy.

For appraisal submissions to the Ontario Council on Graduate Studies Ontario as well as for other purposes, religious studies departments with graduate programmes keep tabs on which of their graduates go on to further study and sometimes where they find jobs: another agenda item for any council-to-be might be the gathering and analyzing of such data from across the country. Also very useful (and long overdue) would be the publication in *Studies in Religion/Sciences Religieuses* of annual lists of titles of M.A., Ph.D., and Th.D. theses completed or in progress country-wide, following the pattern in *Religious Studies Review* or some other model.

Several concerns were mentioned to us by graduate officers. One has to do with inadequate information on just what sort of preparation institutions with doctoral programmes expect of students contemplating study beyond the master's level. This makes it difficult for students to decide between one programme and another, or to know how to prepare themselves better or, lacking sufficient preparation, what additional hurdles they would face as doctoral students; graduate officers, too, may be at a loss to advise them on specifics. One person envisaged written guidelines circulated among graduate officers that would give more specifics than are provided in calendars or in the annual directories of the Council of Societies for the Study of Religion (Mills, 1987ff.). Visits by graduate officers to each other's institutions were also suggested. Trading syllabi at least on core courses such as methodology was another suggestion. The transition from undergraduate to master's study, or from master's to Ph.D study, can also prove difficult, and more attention to orientation to the new situation was suggested, beginning when students begin to think seriously about applying to a programme and continuing well into the first term or first year of study. Treating students as "people," rather than as items to be run through bureaucratic and academic mazes (see 12.11 below), was another concern. As to the nature of graduate programmes, one graduate officer reported that some students contemplating graduate study found graduate curricula disappointing—staid, unimaginative, too tied to traditional theological, philosophical, and "seminary" fields of study, and unlike the innovative, more university-oriented curricula they had come to know and appreciate.

As is pointed out in the Preface, it was not our purpose or mandate to assess individual institutions or their programmes. Our discussion of graduate study in religious studies in Ontario (chap. 9.2) treats the province as a whole, therefore, rather than specific programmes. However, it seems to us that some areas of the academic graduate programmes in Ontario—M.A.,

Ph.D., and Th.D. — are more equal than others. Since we are not in a position to make specific assessments and recommendations of the kind Claude Welch's study did (1971, chap. 5), we would encourage those responsible for these programmes to scrutinize the nooks and crannies of their programmes, asking whether they have the faculty and other resources to offer a graduate degree in this area or that and, if they do, whether they are actually allotting them for this purpose. We would recommend that such soul-searching take place *after* provincial assessment rather than on the eve of it, when "putting-best-foot-forward" is uppermost in mind. Some discussion of whether such internal self-scrutiny is needed in Canadian graduate religious studies programmes generally, and procedures for conducting it, might be another item on the agenda of any council-to-be.

Twenty years ago Claude Welch remarked on "the (sometimes unfortunate) hunger" of some clergy and laity of that day for doctoral titles for ministers (1971, 37). In Ontario, and perhaps in other provinces as well, at present there seems to be a hankering in some institutions for doctoral (or masters') programmes that may begin to spread to religious studies departments (and perhaps theological or church-related colleges) that lack them at present. Talk of new graduate programmes in universities is in some measure part of the competition for scarce provincial dollars: a university proposes launching new programmes or elevating existing ones in order to strengthen their bid in the inter-university bidding. It is a sort of "creative" fiscal dreaming or wild-card poker play and not a good reason for inaugurating a graduate programme. (Maybe a certain element of "empire-building" is involved as well.) Faculty desire to "teach graduate/doctoral students" is not, in itself, a good enough reason either. Neither is the desire to enhance the prestige of an institution. A new programme may do that — but it could also diminish it with a programme that is a non-starter, in which students would be ill-advised to enrol and which they themselves would soon see as not doing much for them in the job market.

To be credible a new programme has to be premised on fundamental *academic* considerations of the kind required by the Ontario Council on Graduate Studies. For example, will the proposed programme be distinct from other, existing programmes and fill a gap in the field? (A doctoral programme in indigenous religions [12.5 above] would be a case in point.) Are there faculty qualified to serve in the programme (what do their c.v.s show?), are there enough of them, and can enough of them be relieved of other duties so they can devote the time needed to provide instruction at that level and do the research commensurate with it? Are there faculty in cognate fields who can be involved in the programme and sufficiently so for their participation to be responsible and credible? What will be the admission standards for students, and what would be a critical mass so they can learn from one another? Will the programme provide for specifically doctoral or masters' courses, rather than throwing students in with those at a lower level of instruction? What are the steps students will have to follow on the way to the degree? And so forth. Institutions contemplating a graduate programme could do worse than to study closely Claude Welch's "critical appraisal" of doctoral programmes in religion (1971), which contributed to the discontinuation of certain existing programmes, put a damper on proliferation of new ones, and certainly raised consciousness in the field of what mounting and sustaining a credible doctoral programme entailed.

These kinds of issues and others mentioned in Chapter 9 would seem to be of concern both to anglophone and francophone graduate professors and students, and participation from both language groups in any council to be formed would be important.[2]

12.10.3   Religion as a "Teachable" Subject

Particular to Ontario at this time and therefore not necessarily of concern to such a council is the granting to the study of religion status as a "teachable" subject in public secondary schools. Ontario religious studies departments and programmes have been active in lobbying efforts on this matter (chap. 9, n. 9). Further efforts are in the offing as of this writing. Religious studies at the secondary level seems a logical extension of its establishment in universities. The Ministry of Education has left to school boards the decision whether or not to offer courses relating to religion, and if so, what kind (ibid.). Should at least some of them decide to do so, it seems there are secondary school teachers who are interested in teaching them or in fact have been teaching world religion courses. Sessions on the study of religion in public schools offered on a professional development day in 1989 by two Ontario religious studies professors, for example, drew a sizeable number of such teachers.

Some religious studies professors, perhaps with experience of discrimination in the public schools and memories of the old, indoctrinating kind of instruction, have misgivings about offering any kind of instruction having to do with religion. We share those concerns. So, while we would encourage lobbying efforts like those mentioned above, we note some essential qualifiers. It goes without saying, but doubtless needs to be said to school boards and others, that religious studies is distinct from and something other than the previous religious education classes taught by outsiders, usually local Christian clergy often with little study of Christianity beyond their own (sometimes narrow) tradition and sometimes intent on indoctrination and "conversion." Lobbying efforts should also distance themselves from lobbying efforts of other groups, for example, ecclesiastical groups, even those that advocate study of religion similar to what religious studies departments would recommend. Drawing on their particular expertise, religious studies departments need to make clear what kinds of courses can be offered in a pluralistic environment, that teachers who staff them require training in religious studies to do so, that such training is available in university religious studies departments and programmes, and that these same departments and programmes are ready to work together with boards of education and Ontario teachers' colleges toward making religion a subject teachable in this way in Ontario public schools.

12.10.4   M.A. Programmes

Maybe the purpose and nature of the M.A. in religious studies, examined and questioned in some detail in Chapter 9.3 and 9.6, should not be subjected to further scrutiny — "if it ain't broke, don't fix it." Perhaps M.A. programmes as presently constituted in Ontario religious studies are what are appropriate to specific local conditions. Still, if the 1990s (as was suggested earlier) are a good time for departmental self-scrutiny, and if the M.A. is an important degree in its own right, apart from preparation for the Ph.D., and if many persons have profited from terminal M.A. study, then M.A. programmes too might bear examination, by departments and by any Canadian council-to-be on graduate religious studies, in light of the questions and recommendations in Chapter 9.

We call attention especially to one of them: the opportunity and obligation to interpret religion and religions to persons outside the field and to offer insight into how religion affects politics, economics, ethics, social movements, wars and rumours of war, and many other aspects of our culture. Looking at the United States, Ivan Strenski observed that it "disgraced" religious studies that "Americans look to almost any other discipline than ours when it comes to matters where religion itself is central" (1986, 334). Perhaps Canada, being smaller, is different — religious studies professors do get called by the media, but often they are passed over on issues where they are in fact the persons most qualified to speak. Maybe they themselves are partly to blame insofar as they write strictly for an academic audience and not also for a literate public, or both at once.[3]

This concern about the public role of religious studies is not new, as the following, written by a religious studies professor two decades ago, indicates:

> What should the politician know about religion? What do the advertising copy writer, the journalist, the diplomat, the city planner, the business executive, or the doctor need to know about religions to carry out their professions more adequately? In the secular situation there is a new public clientele to whom educational service is due . . . (Fenton, 1970, 74-75).

A new journal, *The Fourth R* (Polebridge Press, Sonoma, CA), is devoted to this kind of literate informing. So, too, might a terminal M.A. programme in which students, building on their religious studies baccalaureate, seek to acquire a comprehensive grasp of religion(s) in the context of contemporary culture on the way to becoming "religion critics" (chap. 9.5).

12.11   Students — and Professors

Considerable attention has been devoted to students in this study (chaps. 4 and 9.4). We reported on satisfactions and dissatisfactions, on the contented and somewhat malcontented, and made various suggestions and recommendations to both students and their professors. Many more, along with sage advice, are offered by the former Dean of the Faculty of the Arts and Sciences at Harvard in Chapters 4-8 of his "owner's manual" for the university (Rosovsky, 1990), and we recommend those pages to readers.

The kind of students Rosovsky sees as most suited to graduate study in present-day academia are those who, *inter alia*, "find it difficult to distinguish between work and pleasure when it comes to academic tasks" (ibid., 151). The joy of study — or lack thereof — is a theme that haunts numerous novels, biographies, and autobiographies; and seeking to make it a joy for students suffuses works on pedagogy by humanists such as Gilbert Highet (*The Art of Teaching* [1952]) and Kenneth Eble (*The Craft of Teaching* [1977]). Often that consists primarily of teachers' removing hindrances to study, for it is in study itself — rather than in the seeking of joy — that joy is found. In our interviews with students, none suggested there should be no hurdles in their studies. They might even have assented to the adage *per aspera ad astra* in (rough) translation ("Through toils to [academic] titles"). But along with the joy many expressed in their studies, they regretted hurdles turned into hindrances. Insofar as faculty may be responsible for doing so, or are perceived thus by students, some professorial self-examination may be in order.

Granted that students do the learning, and that professors don't "learn" them but, rather, strive to teach them, in what ways did students perceive their teachers to be hindering learning? We cited some examples earlier (chap. 4.1.4 and 4.2.6), for example, poorly organized courses and outdated lectures. However, professors also teach through their behaviour and through the rules they set down, in writing or otherwise, and it is these as much as anything that seem to generate anxiety and discouragement. For example (summarizing characterizations by students and some faculty):

- Professors are pompous and hide behind a starched front or behind academic titles.
- Their "much learning" (or something) makes them arrogant and impatient of dissenting, albeit perhaps less-learned views.
- They are inflexible: this is the way things are done; these are the topics one may study or not study; "I never give anything higher than a B+" (on which see Barzun's mordant comments [1954, 191]).

Underlying these sorts of perceptions would seem to be another: professors seem to forget they are human, and that students are too. The distance essential to the teacher-student relationship should presuppose mutual respect, for teacher qua teacher and student qua student, but, at the very least, for each other as humans. Sexual harassment is a blatant form of disrespect, and a hindrance to learning, if there ever was one. But there are other forms, like those mentioned above, or (what some students reported as extremely distracting) faculty infighting. Sexist language, or other kinds of discriminatory speech, is another, one mentioned by students. If a university or college does not yet have guidelines on inclusive language, a department or programme should develop its own or adopt or adapt one from another school (Remus, 1990 is thus available; Milne, 1989 [see chap. 2.4.9 above] is a persuasive statement of rationale). Support and encouragement of women students, especially, is also a concern to which faculty need to give more thought and attention (chap. 5.1.1.1).

Mentoring of graduate students by faculty — urging them to attend professional society meetings, present papers, and publish articles (chaps. 4.2.4 and 9.4) — is an implicit recognition of a student's worth. So, too, is consulting of students on hiring and tenure decisions, and their inclusion in colloquia sponsored by the department, both as participants in discussion and as presenters; or faculty encouragement of mentoring of new students by those already in the programme, or faculty efforts to offset feelings of isolation (chap. 9.4) by arranging (or at least fighting for) a gathering place for students, or study space, or computer facilities.

If the study of religion has impressed on us faculty the value of symbols, we should have no difficulty seeing that such expressions of concern and respect should help to raise and maintain students' morale, important at any time but especially now when employment prospects seems dim or distant — the mid-1990s? the end of the decade? Male graduate students, especially, are prone to discouragement in view of affirmative-action or employment-equity hiring policies (see 12.2 above). Those we talked to support the policies as a just widening of the pool of qualified candidates but also perceive them as diminishing their own prospects if gender is the deciding factor in hiring of equally qualified candidates. It may be, however, that by mid-decade the number of applicants will be smaller than the number of positions available. We have dispensed whatever wisdom present data and projections seem to warrant on job prospects in academia (chap. 5.1.1.2, 5.3; but cf. 12.10.2 above), and have suggested ways religious studies faculty might work to broaden employment opportunities for religious studies graduates (12.10.3 and chap. 9.5, 9.6), to which we might add that the present high rate of participation in university education[4] entails a continuing need for faculty. Nonetheless, advising students, present or prospective, about the future is a risky business, heavy with responsibility, in which the "bottom line" may be whether a student deems a concentration or a graduate degree in religious studies worth pursuing even if it may perhaps not result in a job, at least not one directly related to religious studies.

If we have devoted more space to professors' failings than to those of students, it is because they are the ones in positions of power. As for students, one can expect that in those cases where a professor does not earn a student's respect he or she will avoid courses by that instructor or drop out after enrolling and seeing the light — unless it is a required course, in which case they will put other coping devices into play, including grousing among themselves, approaching the instructor, or even registering a complaint with the department chair or dean. In our experience, written complaints or formal lodging of grievances (as opposed to mere complaining) occur infrequently. Undergraduates are fearful of consequences, often too preoccupied with studies and life to make the effort, and probably unaware of the importance of doing so, while graduate students shrink from emerging from the but small anonymity afforded by small classes to offer themselves as potential targets of professorial thunderbolts. All of them may be sceptical that a university grievance procedure or a sexual harassment policy with safeguards for complainants will actually provide them adequate protection. Without formal protests, however, departments, department chairs, and deans find it hard to right wrongs or impossible even to approach the object of the complaint, who may in fact be surprised to learn that a problem exists or that it is serious (the surprise may be part of the problem).

One kind of disrespect mentioned by a woman professor should be noted: reluctance or refusal (usually by male students) to accord a hearing to feminist scholarship. Though not mentioned in our interviews, but related to this professor's experience, is the evidence that is being brought forward of a "chilly climate" for women faculty which the President of the Canadian Association of University Teachers recently called "secretive petty terrorism" — "graffiti, unsigned nasty letters, sick pranks, and even vandalism" — the anonymity of which renders them extremely difficult to deal with (Kerr, 1991). A chilly climate for professors who belong to visible minorities is also not hard to envisage.

It does not seem, judging from our interviews, that religious studies majors and honours students or graduate students are likely to be among the secret terrorists — or, one hopes, the not-so-secret sort either who in at least one institution constituted themselves as vigilantes publicly accusing of sexual harassment a faculty member who was later exonerated of any such behaviour. Religious studies students have generally been listening to diverging viewpoints, and learning. Religious studies faculty can take some satisfaction in these students' perceptions of religious studies as a field: some of the concerns dear to faculty hearts, including feminist issues and respect for diverse cultures in a university setting, would seem to be getting through to them (chap. 4.1.2).

Noting that religious studies continues to attract students in goodly numbers and from a broad spectrum of backgrounds and age groups, religious studies departments and programmes will want to pay close attention to the reasons students give for taking religious studies courses or for deciding to concentrate in religious studies (chap. 4.1.1) and consider these in relation to curricular matters discussed earlier in this chapter and in Chapter 8.

At the graduate level, it is evident that in Ontario a religious studies "type" has developed and now predominates (chap. 4.2.1.2 and 4.2.2) that contrasts both with students in professional, theological degree programmes (chap. 4.3.1) and with students in research and teaching graduate degree programmes in Ontario theological colleges (chap. 4.3.2). The latter are strong in the traditional Christian subfields and build on a degree from a theological college, as did religious studies graduate programmes at one time (chap. 4.2.1.1 and 4.3.2). Students in the former—the professional degree programmes—usually do not come to theological college with a religious studies degree, and many do not seem much interested in graduate religious studies courses where they are available, or cannot fit them into a full schedule. The considerable number of students in M.T.S. programmes—what one might call a "general interest" theology degree—evidently find study in a theological college more attractive than a religious studies M.A. programme (chap. 4.3.1) or see it as an alternative in places where there is no M.A. programme in religious studies.

Each of these kinds of programmes has distinctive strengths and roles. The strengths have been enhanced in recent years by accrediting agencies and by more professional academic policies. While each kind can learn from the other and will find co-operation mutually beneficial at times, each will do better if the distinctions are not blurred. M.T.S. students, for example, are usually active in churches and seem to feel comfortable in a Christian academic setting and find there more courses more to their liking (chap. 4.3.1). Religious studies M.A. programmes will continue to offer courses in Christianity, taught (one hopes) according to religious studies models; but for religious studies to "Christianize" in order to attract these students would sap the integrity of such programmes as religious—not simply *Christian*—studies. At some point, M.T.S. graduates and clergy who while in seminary had no time for religious studies may want the kind of instruction offered in religious studies and turn there for help in understanding and living in our pluralistic, secular society.

Another kind of student has also been showing up in religious studies classes: Bible college graduates. We noted earlier (chap. 11.4) that the pluralism and academic professionalization noted at various places in this study have also affected Bible colleges, both those in churchly and in sectarian traditions. Our perception is that this will continue, with Bible colleges becoming more like junior universities, on the one hand, and, on the other, moving to establish affiliated graduate institutions—that is, seminaries—if they have not already done so (ibid. and App. B). Moreover, we will likely see more Bible college graduates or erstwhile students continuing their education in universities, with some of them enrolling in religious studies courses, commonly those in Christianity but, increasingly, also in courses in the other religions they encounter in Ontario life. A few (in some cases from the ranks of the disaffected) will end up concentrating in religious studies or going on to graduate study in the field, their initial interest in religion continuing, as for many other students, in this way.

12.12   Religious Studies and Community Colleges

Lack of time and budgetary restraints did not permit any investigation of the study of religion in Ontario's community colleges. Louis Rousseau and Michel Despland's state-of-the-art review of religious studies in Quebec (1988) likewise did not include them as such in its purview. Bruce Porter's survey two decades ago of 73 anglophone community colleges in Canada turned up a picture rather the opposite of what is reported in this volume regarding the study of religion in Ontario universities: of the 65 responding to his "modest questionnaire" over half had no religious studies courses, about one in five offered the study of religion in other courses, about one in six offered from one to four religious studies courses, and eight of the 65 had full religious studies programmes (1972, 41-43). Of the 29 Ontario community colleges listed in Porter's Appendix B (49-51), three offered one course, three offered two to four, and one was planning to begin offering courses in 1972-73 (45, Table II).

The picture in Alberta is somewhat similar, according to Ronald Neufeldt's survey (1983, 8-10). Since "there is little or no support for humanities courses or programs in the junior colleges, certainly there will be little or no support for religious studies" (1983, 8). Usually, "whether anything in religious studies is taught depends very much on the initiative of individual instructors and/or pressure for specific courses from the community" (ibid.).

By contrast, Freeman Sleeper and Robert Spivey's survey of the study of religion in two-year colleges in the U.S. found that it was "recognized in a majority of colleges as an integral part of the liberal arts curriculum" and was taught "as a legitimate, academically respectable subject," usually on "the 'seminary' model (focusing on biblical studies and theology)" or stressing world religions (1975, 85). Instruction was apt to be by persons holding the equivalent of a theological master's degree (43%), rather than a doctorate (14%; ibid., 22, Table VI), and often by persons teaching, either part-time or full-time, in a field such as literature of philosophy who had done some graduate study in religion as well (ibid., 22, Table VII; 85). Perhaps this has changed in the interval, but what has likely not changed is the stress on teaching and ability to teach in a cognate field as well as in religious studies (ibid., 88), for which the usual specialist, research-oriented Ph.D. programme is not necessarily the best preparation (ibid., 88).

One conclusion Neufeldt drew is that, with a couple of exceptions,

> As long as there is on the part of the administration of community and regional colleges little or no vision of the importance of the humanities one should not expect anything of consequence to happen with reference to the development of religious studies courses and programs (1983, 31).

Porter concluded his survey by, in effect, suggesting that one not wait for something to happen. On the one hand, he encouraged religious studies graduates to seek jobs in community colleges and not "as 'last resort' employers, or as steps to a *real* job in a university"; on the other hand, he suggested that religious studies departments work "to establish good and productive relations with the community college sector of higher education" (1972, 44). While there are some recent indications of movement to more co-operation between universities and community colleges in Ontario, with a deputy minister recently suggesting that each should accept the other's courses for credit (Gutschi, 1991), one suspects that what Neufeldt observed in Alberta is likely true in Ontario as well. These are issues we must leave to future investigators.

12.13   In Conclusion

The various suggestions and recommendations in this chapter and the ones preceding often entail choices and decisions, many extremely difficult to make and often frustrating because religious studies departments and programmes don't hold all the cards. When it comes to curricula, for example, tight budgets offer little hope of expansion through increase in faculty size. That renders dubious one way Ontario religious studies departments in the 1960s and 1970s responded to academic, social, and cultural changes and to the need to extend their coverage from West to East, namely, by adding courses to their curricula. Moreover, the previously successful strategy of doubling course offerings without doubling teaching time by replacing full-year courses with semester offerings (chap. 8.2) has now exhausted the possibilities. For faculty to assume heavier teaching loads in order to offer more courses, or to teach slightly fewer courses each with much larger enrolments, is also no answer. Faculty are already over-extended as a result of freezes on hiring or actual cuts in faculty in the 1980s in Ontario. What courses or sequence of courses should (and reasonably can) be required of major or honours students is also a perplexing question given that quite a few students decide on a religious studies concentration when well into their university career (chap. 4.1.1). Whether and how language courses, so essential to serious study of so many religions and important, often crucial, in graduate study, can be maintained or shoe-horned into curricula or into students' already crammed schedules is another crux (chaps. 4.2.3, 8.3, 9.3.2, 11.4).

Hard choices will have to be made. Suggestions and recommendations made earlier in this chapter and in Chapter 8 may offer some help. But priorities among them (and others) will need to be established. One that we believe deserves a place near the top of the list is the vision of religious studies as offering a liberal, liberating education, as some of the students we interviewed found it to be and as pioneers in the field have envisaged it should be (chap. 4.1.1) — one that dispels religious illiteracy and fosters a life-long habit of study and inquiry. That would be a welcome contrast to the ignorance, obscurantism, and repression of thought that have often characterized religion and are no strangers in university life. Insofar as departments can learn from one another, sessions at the Learned Society meetings could facilitate the re-plotting of curricula in the 1990s. An annual gathering of Ontario department chairs and programme co-ordinators at the Learneds, similar to those convened at one time by the Council on the Study of Religion during the annual meetings of the American Academy of Religion and the Society of Biblical Literature, could also be helpful, for this as well as other concerns.

In Chapter 2.2 we sketched a profile of a "typical" religious studies department today as contrasted with the way religion was studied in Ontario colleges and universities at the end of the last century. What might an Ontario religious studies department or programme in the year 2001 look like? There are certain things one might safely predict, such as a younger and more productive faculty and a leaner but more carefully drawn curriculum. Beyond that it would be foolhardy to venture — Will the ratio of women to men faculty be more evenly balanced? Will the curriculum more adequately reflect the plurality of religious traditions, studied in their own right, and the importance of other fields for the study of religion? Will teaching be methodologically self-conscious and respecting of students? Will faculty and students do more research using electronic databases, and will library resources change accordingly? — since the shape of departments and programmes, what is expected of students, how faculty relate to students, what funds are available in universities, and various other elements that determine the institutional lineaments of religious studies in Ontario universities will depend on what decisions are made in the 1990s not only by faculty but by all those who "own" religious studies and universities in Ontario: faculty and students, administrators, governments and governing boards, alumnae/i, the general public. If our study assists these "owners," however imperfectly, in making better informed decisions, we believe it will have served its purpose.

Notes

1 More sustained examples, representative of particular approaches: literary (Via, 1967; Meagher, 1979); historiographic (McDannell, 1986); ethnographic (Peacock and Tyson, 1989); psychological (Chernus, 1991); structuralist (Polzin, 1977; Penner, 1989b); sociological (Robbins, 1988; Remus, 1983 [sociology of knowledge]).

2 Although much has happened in graduate religious studies since Claude Welch's state-of-the-art study (1971), it is still worth a look, both to gain some perspective on what has changed and, especially, what remains much the same after two decades.

3 Recent samples of the last sort, mostly by religious studies scholars: Outside Canada: Rahman, 1979, 1982; Eck, 1982; Gager, 1983; Wilken, 1984; Gill, 1987; Gadon, 1989; Segal, 1990. In Canada: Despland, 1979, 1984; Hurtado, 1988. Specifically in Ontario: Goldenberg, 1979, 1982, 1990; Moir, 1982; Hospital, 1985; R. Cook, 1985; Kinsley, 1986, 1989; J.W. Grant, 1984, 1988; P.D. Young, 1990.

4 According to Statistics Canada, in the 1990-91 academic year full-time university enrolment rose 4.1% across Canada (to a record 536,000 students) and 4.7% in Ontario; in the

18-24 age group about 14.5% were enrolled in university compared with 10% in 1982; students over 30 constituted 10.5% of full-time enrolments compared with 8% in 1982 (Cox, 1991). The picture in the U.S. colleges and universities is similar:

> despite the end of the baby boom, the expected crisis [in enrolments] never materialized. As Harrington and Sum have shown [1988, 17], "This is because demographics alone do not determine enrolment trends." Between 1970 and 1983, the college-age population increased by 22 percent, and college enrolment rose by 45 percent. From 1980 to 1987, enrolments still rose by 3.8 percent, although college-age population has been projected to decline 17 percent between 1983 and 1993 (Rosovsky, 1990, 146).

Appendix A
Gathering and Processing of Data

William Closson James

For the three co-authors of this study the task has been in progress, intermittently, and with periods of varying intensity, and through changes in database, personnel, and scope (see Preface above) since the Learned Societies meetings in the spring of 1984. It was then that Harold Coward, the indefatigable general editor for the series of which this volume is a part, set the Ontario portion of the project in motion when he began to assemble the team to do this review. By that time the State-of-the-Art Review of Religious Studies in Alberta had already been published, and the companion studies of Quebec and Atlantic Canada were underway.

By the summer of 1984 we found ourselves preparing budgets and charting our course in a preliminary way; by fall, we were involved in conference calls with authors from other parts of Canada and planning to meet with them while in Chicago for the joint annual meeting of the American Academy of Religion and the Society of Biblical Literature.

Beginning in the spring of 1985 letters were sent to universities, church-related colleges, and theological colleges in Ontario, inviting them to participate in this review. We wrote to heads and chairs of religious studies departments, to co-ordinators of programmes, to principals of theological colleges, and to "contact persons" at campuses with neither a programme nor department nor seminary but known to be involved or interested in the teaching of courses related to the academic study of religion. In that letter of invitation the background to the "State-of-the-Art" review was described and its aims and sponsorship by the Canadian Corporation for Studies in Religion/Corporation Canadienne des Sciences Religieuses laid out. We included a copy of Professor Coward's Foreword to the first volume, *Religious Studies in Alberta*, by Ronald Neufeldt (1983). The three co-authors introduced themselves and the basic procedures were described: "We will be collecting information on course offerings, curriculum vitae of faculty, and relevant data on the history and development of each institution.'' We expressed our hope of visiting each institution.

Each administrative officer (chair, head, co-ordinator, principal) was asked to provide the following documentation for their institution: a copy of the current calendar; a list of courses offered in the previous three years; the annual report submitted by their academic unit, or other relevant self-study, whether for external or internal use; founding documents or general history; publicity for curriculum or programmes, including handbooks or guides; any statements or reports on institutional standards, especially as pertaining to appointments, promotion, and tenure; and a recent copy of the librarian's annual report or an assessment of library holdings. We also asked each administrative officer to estimate the number of faculty members in the department or programme, explaining that we would be sending the appropriate number of individual envelopes containing survey material to be distributed to each faculty member. By enlisting the assistance of administrative officers in the distribution and collection of questionnaires we hoped to get a higher rate of return than if we had approached faculty members on our own. We provided a sealable envelope for each individual to return to their head, chair, co-ordinator, or principal, for forwarding to us. We assured administrative officers and individual faculty members that material submitted would be kept confidential and used solely as contributing to a province-wide picture of religious studies in Ontario (see Preface).

In the envelopes provided for distribution to faculty members we provided a covering letter explaining that we were seeking four things from each person: a curriculum vitae from each full- and part-time member; a completed copy of the ''Research and Teaching Inventory'' (see chap. 7.5); a copy of the annual report submitted to the faculty dean (or departmental chairperson or other official); and course descriptions or syllabi from courses taught within the previous two years. Once this invitation to participate had been issued, we were able to proceed to the preliminary collection of documentation from the participants.

From the c.v.s we extracted information for entry into the database programme, including such things as name; gender; institution (which we divided between theological institutions and university departments or programmes in religious studies); the person's highest degree, its source, field, and year awarded; year of birth; rank; learned society memberships; and the year appointed to one's current position. Using student assistants under the supervision of one or more of the co-authors, we counted the number of books and articles published, including only significant publications (e.g., articles of a certain size in academic journals). We also counted the number of papers presented before peers in the context of learned society meetings (in this last case, we broke down the presentation of papers by quinquennia — 1970-74, 1975-79, etc.). We also indicated whether or not an individual held an ''M.Div.'' degree, interpreted as meaning post-baccalaureate theological study associated with professional training for the ministry, priesthood, or rabbinate. From the "Research and Teaching Inventory" we entered two areas of research for each individual and up to eight areas of teaching. We also indicated whether or not the individual's research or teaching included a focus on "Religion in Canada" (one of the questions asked in the "Research and Teaching Inventory").

We soon found out as we attempted to enter data that some c.v.s lacked essential information. For instance, not every professor included in the c.v. their membership in learned societies, the titles and dates of papers presented, their date of birth, or their current rank. In fact, the disparity among c.v.s submitted posed some unforeseen problems, necessitating follow-up letters to individuals in which we requested the missing items of information. Sometimes when information was entirely lacking for a particular person — some people seem not to respond to such requests, especially at periods when multiple requests for similar information have come from other agencies, as, for instance, when a graduate programme is under review — the department was able to supply at least a c.v. Overall, though, the rate of response was high and our colleagues across the province were helpful, courteous, and responsive to our requests. Almost 300 individuals submitted a c.v. and/or completed a Research and Teaching Inventory. We also found useful the *Directory of Departments and Programs of Religious Studies in North America* edited by one of our co-authors (Remus, 1985). Much of the information on faculty members needed for our database — name, rank, year appointed, highest degree and its source, etc. — could be gleaned from this *Directory*. In all, we obtained from various sources data for approximately 370 academics in religious studies and theology in Ontario, though we did not (see above) have for each person as much information as was requested in our mailing to individuals. Depending on how one calculates it, the response rate to our requests for information was somewhere around 75%, quite high especially considering the amount of material we requested from each individual.

Entering the information from individuals' c.v.s into the database programme began in 1985, continued throughout 1986, and extended into 1987. It will be appreciated that counting books, articles, and papers presented from scores of c.v.s, and then entering that data into computer files, along with other information, was a formidable task. And when the database we initially were using was unable to perform (or performed poorly) some of the jobs we asked it to do, it was necessary to start over with our cross-tabulations in the fall of 1988, when the entire database was transferred from one software programme to another (with, of course, all the attendant difficulties of learning a new, albeit much better functioning, piece of software).

In the seven years this study has been in progress the three of us have made great strides toward some kind of functional computer literacy. In 1984 two of us had just acquired our first microcomputers (by today's standards, woefully under-memoried and horrendously over-priced) and were learning some such word-processing programme as the cumbersome old Wordstar (we were told, and believed it at first, that it was like learning a new language). As we finished up this study, we moved on to hard disks and modems and desktop inkjet printers or were doing word processing, from office or home, on the university mainframe. In the latter stages we zipped electronic messages back and forth between Queen's and Wilfrid Laurier University and effortlessly (almost) shipped to one another, via electronic mail, completed chapters for perusal and editing.

For those aspects of our research focusing on undergraduate curricula and graduate education (see chaps. 8 and 9), the course syllabi, calendars, and other published materials proved essential. Invaluable for those aspects of our study, but for almost all others as well, were the visits we made to campuses around the province. These began in late 1985 with most conducted in 1986. In preparation for these visits and the interviews they provided, we reviewed the publications provided by the department, programme, or college in the form of calendars, handbooks, brochures, self-study documents, and appraisal materials — in short, whatever we received in response to our request in the letters of invitation. In most cases there was no shortage of material on hand in advance of the visit; where a few things were missing or more up-to-date material was required, we sent a request to the administrative officer. Since we mostly knew in advance which persons we would be interviewing, we reviewed their c.v.s, course descriptions, and other material provided ahead of time. (For further information on the selection of faculty to be interviewed see chap. 3.2 above.) Frequently we found it difficult to snatch enough time from other duties (each of us had full teaching loads and/or administrative duties on our own campuses) not only to get away for a two- or three-day visit to another institution, but to prepare for the visit in advance (see once again the laments in our Preface about lack of time).

In our meetings at Queen's before embarking on our visits we developed the questions to be used in interviews with various categories of individuals. Since we most usually split up and conducted interviews separately even when we went to an institution as a team, it was important that our interview questions be identical (although we allowed ourselves the freedom to explore different areas in depth as the occasion demanded). As a result of this advance collaboration we produced six different colour-coded sets of questions, ranging in length from a single sheet of three questions (for undergraduate students) to eleven pages with almost 50 questions and follow-up questions for religious studies chairs or theological college principals or deans. (The remaining sets of questions were tailored for our interviews with graduate students, individual faculty members, undergraduate deans of arts and graduate deans, and departmental graduate officers.) We used the interview questions somewhat flexibly. We might pass over questions deemed to be irrelevant at a particular institution. The time given to a particular question also varied. A question on morale, for example, might elicit the simple response "good" or a fifteen-minute discourse. We learned through experience how to use most efficiently an hour-long session with a faculty member, sailing through questions of little relevance or evoking a clearcut or straightforward response, but pausing to delve a little deeper or follow up a bit more if the answer seemed a bit too perfunctory or the question not well understood (or if we failed to understand the answer and needed clarification). In interviewing undergraduates we found ourselves adding questions to the three with which we began.

After a visit we wrote up our notes from interviews, not just for each other's use, but as the first step each of us took individually in the process of distillation of our findings toward the writing of the chapters in this study. What emerged typically was a write-up of ten or a dozen pages on each department or institution visited, and divided into sections corresponding to the relevant chapters — perceptions, students, research, teaching, and so on. Though we were not reporting on departments or programmes or colleges individually (this is not an institution-by-institution study), each summary from a single visit became a part of the larger, global picture that was being built up gradually. We made these summaries available for each other so that they could be canvassed in the process of writing the chapters for which each of us had responsibility.

On each visit we also left a copy of our "Questionnaire on Library Resources" to be filled out and returned (usually by mail) by the person responsible for collection development and acquisitions for the religious studies department or theological college. The questionnaire asked for a copy of whatever published statement existed on collection development and acquisition policies, as well as details on how and by whom the policy was implemented. It also asked about standing-order agreements, co-operation with nearby academic libraries, and specific aspects of acquisition policies with respect to such areas as original sources, periodicals, faculty research, materials in languages other than English, and retrospective collection. The questionnaire concluded with a checklist on collection development policy to cover matters that might not be dealt with in the published statement. This checklist was in a form familiar to most library personnel, in which typical subject areas in the academic study of religion (philosophy of religion, South Asian religions, sociology of religion, Islam, etc.) were listed; beside each subject listing a letter code for the collection level (ranging from the basic reference level to the intensive level appropriate to doctoral research) was to be placed. (For further details see chap. 10.1 above.)

In the late 1980s, after we had distributed the library questionnaire, electronic databases began to come into their own. We therefore distributed a second questionnaire, on electronic resources, which was distributed to librarians in 1990 and was also used in the preparation of Chapter 10. This second questionnaire is reproduced below.

SURVEY OF COMPUTERIZED LIBRARY RESOURCES

Does your library have access to any of the following <u>**ON-LINE DATABASES**</u>?

A.   Bibliographic:

        Art Index
        Arts and Humanities Search   _____
        ATLA Religion Database/Religion Index   _____
        Current Contents Search   _____
        Dissertation Abstracts Online   _____
        Essay and General Literature Index   _____
        Historical Abstracts   _____
        Humanities Index   _____
        Philosopher's Index   _____
        PsycINFO   _____
        Social Sciences Index   _____
        Social Scisearch   _____

B.   Full Text:

        Bible (King James Version)   _____
        Catholic News Service   _____
        Catholic Trends   _____
        ChurchNews International   _____
        Lutheran News Service   _____
        National Catholic Register   _____
        Origins: Catholic Documentary Service   _____
        RNS Daily News Reports   _____
        United Methodist Information   _____

Does your library own or have access to any of the following <u>**CD-ROM DATABASES**</u>?

A.   Bibliographic:

        Art Index
        Dissertation Abstracts Ondisc   _____
        Essay and General Literature Index   _____
        Humanities Index   _____
        PsycLIT   _____
        Religion Indexes   _____
        REX on CD-ROM   _____
        Social Sciences Citation Index Compact
            Disc Edition   _____
        Social Sciences Index   _____
        Sociofile   _____

B.   Full Text:

                    Die Bibel   _____
                    The Bible Library   _____
                    FABS Electronic Bible   _____
                    FABS Reference Bible   _____
                    Master Search Bible   _____
                    Thesaurus Linguae Graecae CD-ROM   _____

Does your library own or have access to any of the following **DISKETTE DATABASES**?

A.   Full Text:

                    Die Bibel   _____
                    CompuBIBLE   _____
                    Novum Testamentum Graece   _____

Does your library own or have access to any of the following **MAGNETIC TAPE
DATABASES**?

A.   Bibliographic:

                    Arts and Humanities Search   _____
                    Dissertation Abstracts   _____
                    Psychological Abstracts on Tape   _____
                    Social SciSearch   _____

B.   Full Text:

                    CETEDOC   _____
                    Oxford Text Archive   _____

Does your library own the **IBYCUS** System?   _____

Is your library or department involved in the assembly of any bibliographic or
full-text computerized database relevant to Religious Studies? If so, please
describe.
_____
_____
_____
_____
_____

Thank you for your assistance. Please return this form at your earliest
convenience to: Dr. Harold Remus, Department of Religion & Culture, Wilfrid
Laurier University, Waterloo, Ontario N2L 3C5.

Appendix B

Ontario Theological Colleges and Theological Faculties

Locations, Denominations, Founding Dates, Affiliations/Federations, Degree and Non-Degree Programmes,[1] Accreditation[2]

Harold Remus

Hamilton:

McMaster Divinity College. Baptist Convention of Ontario and Quebec. Established and affiliated with McMaster University, 1957, at the time of provincialization of the University, where theology had been taught since its founding in 1887. Affiliated with Toronto School of Theology, 1969. Degrees conferred by the University. M.Div., M.R.E., M.T.S., Certif.Th. ATS. (See, further, Toronto School of Theology and chap. 2.6.10 and 2.6.11 above.)

Theological College of the Canadian Reformed Churches. Established 1968. M.Div.

Kingston:

Queen's Theological College. United Church of Canada. Established and affiliated with Queen's University, 1912, at the time of provincialization of the University, where theology had been taught since its founding in 1841. Degrees conferred by the University. M.Div., B.Th., M.T.S., Th.M. ATS.

Notes to Appendix B can be found on page 339.

London:

Huron College, Faculty of Theology. Anglican Church of Canada. Established
    1863. The college and its theological faculty affiliated with University of West-
    ern Ontario (formerly Western University), 1878. Affiliated with Western as
    Huron College Faculty of Theology, 1975, with the Faculty's M.Div. degree
    being conferred by the University. ATS. (See, further, chap. 2.6.2 above.)

London Baptist Seminary. Independent. Established 1976. Affiliated with London
    Baptist Bible College, 1976. M.Div. (See, further, chap. 11 above.)

St. Peter's Seminary. Roman Catholic Church (Diocese of London). Established
    1912. Affiliated with University of Western Ontario through Ursuline College
    of Arts, ca. 1920; affiliated with Western on its own as St. Peter's Seminary
    College of Arts, 1939; in 1966 affiliated with Western through King's College
    but granted theology degrees on its own by virtue of its provincial charter; since
    1975, by an agreement between the Seminary and Western, the University con-
    fers the Seminary's M.Div. degree. ATS. (See, further, chap. 2.6.2. above.)

Ottawa:

Collège dominicain de philosophie et de théologie. Roman Catholic Church.
    Established 1900 as Studium Generale of the Dominican order in Canada. Rec-
    ognized by the international Dominican order as a seminary in 1909. Consti-
    tuted by Rome as a Pontifical Faculty empowered to grant ecclesiastical degrees
    (B.Th., L.Th., D.Th.) to members of the Dominican order, 1965; granted a uni-
    versity charter by Province of Ontario with power to confer civil degrees in the-
    ology (B.Th., M.Th., M.A.[Th.], Ph.D.), 1967.

*St. Paul University/Université Saint-Paul, Faculty of Theology/Faculté de Théolo-
    gie.* Roman Catholic Church. Established 1965 at the time of the creation of a
    new provincial University of Ottawa/Université d'Ottawa as the successor to
    the original Université d'Ottawa, where a Faculty of Theology had existed
    since 1889. Federated with the present University of Ottawa/Université
    d'Ottawa, 1965. Confers ecclesiastical degrees on its own and civil degrees
    (indicated by * in the following list) through the University of Ottawa/Univer-
    sité d'Ottawa. B.Th., *B.Th., *M.A.(Th.), L.Th., *Ph.D.(Th.), Th.D., B.C.L.
    (Canon Law), *B.C.L., *M.C.L., L.C.L., *Ph.D.(C.L.), D.C.L., *M.A. (Pastoral
    Studies), *Dipl.(Past.St.), *M.A.(Mission Studies), *Certif. (Missiology), *Cer-
    tif. I, II (Social Communications). (See, further, chap. 2.6.10 and 2.6.11 above.)

St. Catharines:

Concordia Lutheran Theological Seminary. Lutheran Church–Canada. Established
    1976 as an extension of Concordia Theological Seminary, Fort Wayne, IN.
    Affiliated with Brock University, 1982. Degrees conferred by the University.
    M.Div., M.T.S. ATS Associate Status.

Toronto:

Central Baptist Seminary. Fellowship of Evangelical Baptist Churches in Canada.
    Established 1949. Affiliated with college division of Central Baptist Seminary.
    M.Div., M.T.S., Certif.T.S., B.Th., B.R.S. (See, further, chap. 11.)

Centre for Christian Studies. Anglican Church of Canada and United Church of Canada. Established 1969 as a co-operative venture of the Anglican Women's Training College (established 1892 as the Church of England Deaconess and Missionary Training House) and the United Church's Covenant College (formerly United Church Training School, formed in 1926 through a merger of the Methodist National Training School [established 1894] and the Presbyterian Missionary and Deaconess Training Home [established 1897 as the Ewart Training Home]). Diploma, leading to Christian (especially lay) ministry in Anglican Church or to diaconal or lay ministry in United Church.

Emmanuel College. United Church of Canada. Established 1928. Created through a merger of Victoria University Faculty of Theology and Union College, which had been constituted (1927) by the faculty and eighty percent of the student body of Knox College after the Ontario Legislature awarded Knox College to those Presbyterians who had not joined in the formation of the United Church of Canada (1925). A constituent college of Victoria University; federated with the University of Toronto, 1928; federated with Toronto School of Theology, 1969. Since 1979 the M.Div., M.R.E., M.Div./M.R.E., M.Div./M.A., M.Div./M.S.W., Th.M., and Th.D. are awarded jointly by Victoria University and the University of Toronto, through the Toronto School of Theology. The M.A. and Ph.D. are conferred through St. Michael's College, the L.Th. and D.Min by Emmanuel. ATS. (See, further, St. Michael's College, Toronto School of Theology, and chap. 2.6.11 above.)

Knox College. Presbyterian Church in Canada. Established 1844. Affiliated with University of Toronto, 1885; federated with University of Toronto, 1890; with Toronto School of Theology, 1969. Since 1979 it confers the M.Div., Th.M., and Th.D. jointly with the University of Toronto, through the Toronto School of Theology. The M.A. and Ph.D. are conferred through St. Michael's College, the D.Min. by Knox. ATS. (See, further, St. Michael's College, Toronto School of Theology, and chap. 2.6.11 above.)

Ontario Theological Seminary. Interdenominational. Established 1976. Affiliated with Ontario Bible College, 1976. M.Div., M.T.S.., Certif. Biblical Studies. ATS. (See, further, chap. 11 above.)

Regis College. Roman Catholic Church. Established 1930 as College of Christ the King which in 1943 inaugurated a curriculum in theology and since 1961 has offered only theology courses. Since 1956 Regis has been the Toronto section of the Pontifical Facultés de la Compagnie de Jésus au Canada, thus authorizing it to offer ecclesiastical degrees in theology. From 1957 to 1978, it was the School of Sacred Theology of St. Mary's University (Halifax), the University conferring the students' civic degrees in theology. Federated with Toronto School of Theology, 1969, with University of Toronto, 1979. It offers the S.T.B., S.T.M., and S.T.L. on its own. Since 1979 it offers the M.Div., Th.M., and Th.D. jointly with the University, through the Toronto School of Theology. The M.A. and Ph.D. are conferred through St. Michael's College. ATS. (See, further, St. Michael's College, Toronto School of Theology, and chap. 2.6.11 above.)

St. Augustine's Seminary. Roman Catholic Church (Archdiocese of Toronto).
Established 1913. Affiliated with St. Paul University/Université Saint-Paul (see
above), 1965, through which it confers the ecclesiastical degree of S.T.B.
Federated with Toronto School of Theology, 1969, with University of Toronto,
1979. Since 1979 it confers the M.Div. jointly with the University of Toronto,
through the Toronto School of Theology. It confers the ecclesiastical degrees of
M.T.S. and Dipl.T.S. on its own. ATS. (See, further, Toronto School of Theology and chap. 2.6.11 above.)

University of St. Michael's College, Faculty of Theology. Roman Catholic Church.
Established 1852. The University affiliated with University of Toronto, 1881;
federated with University of Toronto, 1887, 1901; the Faculty of Theology
federated with Toronto School of Theology, 1969. Since 1979 it confers the
M.Div., M.R.E., Th.M., and Th.D. jointly with the University of Toronto,
through the Toronto School of Theology, and the M.A., Ph.D., and D.Min. on
its own. ATS. (See, further, Toronto School of Theology and chap. 2.6.4 and
2.6.11 above.)

Toronto Baptist Seminary. Association of Regular Baptist Churches (Canada).
Established 1926. Affiliated with the college division of Toronto Baptist Seminary. M.Div., M.T.S., C.R.S. (Certif. of Religious Studies), Cert.Div.

Toronto School of Theology. Christian interdenominational. Established 1969 as a
Federation of Emmanuel College, Knox College, Regis College, St. Augustine's Seminary, St. Michael's College Faculty of Theology, Trinity College
Faculty of Theology, and Wycliffe College, and as the successor to the Toronto
Graduate School of Theological Studies (est. 1944). Affiliated with University
of Toronto, 1978. Affiliated with McMaster Divinity College (see above) at the
basic degree level (1969) and with Waterloo Lutheran Seminary (see below) at
the advanced degree level (1972). ATS. (See, further, under each of the member
schools and chap. 2.6.11 above.)

Trinity College, Faculty of Theology. Anglican Church of Canada. Established
1852. Trinity College federated with the University of Toronto in 1903; the Faculty of Theology federated with Toronto School of Theology, 1969. Since 1979
it confers the M.Div., Th.M., and Th.D. jointly with the University of Toronto,
through the Toronto School of Theology. The M.A. and Ph.D. are conferred
through St. Michael's College, the L.Th. and D.Min. by Trinity. ATS. (See, further, St. Michael's College, Toronto School of Theology, and chap. 2.6.11
above.)

Victoria University, Faculty of Theology. United Church. Established 1871 (Methodist Church). Victoria College was federated with the University of Toronto in
1892 when Victoria moved from Cobourg to Toronto. (See, further, Emmanuel
College.)

Wycliffe College. Anglican Church of Canada. Established 1877 (as the Protestant
Episcopal Divinity School). Affiliated with the University of Toronto, 1885;
federated with University of Toronto, 1890, with Toronto School of Theology,
1969. Since 1979 it confers the M.Div., M.Rel., M.Th., and Th.D. jointly with
the University of Toronto, through the Toronto School of Theology. The M.A.

and Ph.D. are conferred through St. Michael's College, the L.Th., Dipl. Christian Studies, and D.Min. by Wycliffe. ATS. (See, further, Toronto School of Theology and chap. 2.6.11 above.)

Waterloo:

Conrad Grebel College. Mennonite Conference of Eastern Canada. Established 1957. Affiliated with University of Waterloo, 1957. M.T.S. (inaugurated 1988).

Waterloo Lutheran Seminary. Evangelical Lutheran Church in Canada. Established 1911. Federated with Wilfrid Laurier University, 1973; affiliated with Toronto School of Theology at the advanced degree level, 1972. Degrees conferred by the University. M.Div., M.T.S., M.Th., M.Div./M.T.S.-M.S.W (with Faculty of Social Work, Wilfrid Laurier), Dipl.Th. ATS. (See, further, Toronto School of Theology and chap. 2.6.9 above.)

Notes

1 Excluded are degrees in philosophy at Collège dominicain and St. Paul University/Université Saint-Paul and the arts programme of St. Peter's Seminary.
2 ATS = accredited by the Association of Theological Schools in the United States and Canada.

References

AABC *Directory*
    1989-90   *American Association of Bible Colleges Directory*. Fayetteville, AK: American Association of Bible Colleges.

Abdul-Rauf, Muhammad
    1985   "Outsiders' Interpretations of Islam: A Muslim's Point of View." In Martin, 1985, 179-88.

ACAP
    1974   *Perspectives and Plans for Graduate Studies*. Vol. 12, *Religious Studies 1974*. Prepared by the Advisory Committee on Academic Planning, Ontario Council on Graduate Studies. Toronto: Council of Ontario Universities/Conseil des Universités de l'Ontario.

Adams, Charles J.
    1967   "The History of Religions and the Study of Islam." In Kitagawa et al., 1967, 177-93.
    1974   "The History of Religions and the Study of Islam." *American Council of Learned Societies Newsletter* 25/3-4, 1-10.
    1983   "The Development of Islamic Studies in Canada." In Earle H. Waugh, Baha Abu-Laban, and Regula B. Qureshi, eds., *The Muslim Community in North America*, 185-201. Edmonton: University of Alberta Press.
    1985   "Foreword." In Martin, 1985, vii-x.

Adams, Charles J., ed.
    1977   *A Reader's Guide to the Great Religions*. 2nd ed. New York: Free Press and London: Collier Macmillan.

Adams, Doug
    1985   "Recent Religion and Visual Arts Scholarship." *Religious Studies Review* 11/2, 159-65.

Adams, Doug, and Diane Apostolos-Cappadona, eds.
    1987   *Art as Religious Studies*. New York: Crossroad.

Ahmad, 'Aziz
    1967   *Islamic Modernism in India and Pakistan, 1857-1964*. London et al.: Oxford University Press.

Alexander, W.J., ed.
1906   *The University of Toronto and its Colleges, 1827-1906.* Toronto: University Library.

Algar, Hamid
1980   "The Study of Islam: The Work of Henry Corbin." *Religious Studies Review* 6/2, 85-91.

Allen, Richard
1970   *The Social Passion: Religion and Social Reform in Canada, 1914-1928.* Toronto: University of Toronto Press.
1985   "Providence to Progress: The Migration of an Idea in English Canadian Thought." In Westfall et al., 1985, 33-46.

Alter, Robert, and Frank Kermode, editors.
1987   *The Literary Guide to the Bible.* Cambridge, MA: Harvard University Press.

Alton, Bruce
1986   "Method and Reduction in the Study of Religion." *Studies in Religion/Sciences Religieuses* 15/2, 153-64.
1988   "On the Idea of a Quebec Society for the Study of Religion." *The Canadian Society for the Study of Religion Bulletin La société canadienne pour l'étude de la religion* 11/3 (May), 5-8.

Anderson, Charles P., and T.A. Nosanchuk, eds.
1967   *The 1967 Guide to Religious Studies in Canada.* N.p.: Canadian Society for the Study of Religion.

Anderson, Charles P., ed.
1972   *Guide to Religious Studies in Canada/Guide des Sciences Religieuses au Canada.* N.p.: Corporation for the Publication of Academic Studies in Religion in Canada.

Armour, Leslie, and Elizabeth Trott
1981   *The Races of Reason: An Essay on Philosophy and Culture in English Canada 1850-1950.* Waterloo, Ont.: Wilfrid Laurier University Press.

Arnal, Oscar L.
1979   "A New Society within the Shell of the Old: The Millenarianism of the Wobblies." *Studies in Religion/ Sciences Religieuses* 8, 67-81.
1985   *Ambivalent Alliance: The Catholic Church and the Action Française 1899-1939.* Pittsburgh: University of Pittsburgh Press.
1986   *Priests in Working-Class Blue: The History of the Worker-Priests (1943-1954).* New York and Mahwah, NJ: Paulist Press.

Arnal, Oscar L. (with the assistance of Erich Schultz et al.)
1988   *Toward an Indigenous Lutheran Ministry in Canada: The Seventy-Five Year Pilgrimage of Waterloo Lutheran Seminary (1911-1986).* Waterloo, Ont.: Waterloo Lutheran Seminary.

Ashby, Philip H.
1965   "The History of Religions." In Ramsey, 1965, 1-49.

Assemblée générale de la section des sciences religieuses de l'ACFAS
1989   "A l'item: Projet de fondation d'une Société québécoise pour l'étude de la religion." Agenda item, May 18.

ATS
Annual   *Association of Theological Schools in the United States and Canada
            Fact Book on Theological Education.* Vandalia, OH: Association of
            Theological Schools.
1986   *Policy Statements.* Bulletin 37, Part 5. Vandalia, OH: Association of
            Theological Schools.

Bal, Mieke
1987   *Lethal Love: Feminist Literary Readings of Biblical Love Songs.*
            Bloomington and Indianapolis: Indiana University Press.
1988a   *Murder and Difference: Gender, Genre, and Scholarship.* Trans. by
            M. Gumpert. Bloomington and Indianapolis: Indiana University
            Press.
1988b   *Death and Dissymetry: The Politics of Coherence in the Book of
            Judges.* Chicago and London: University of Chicago Press.

Baltzell, E. Digby
1957   "Bell Telephone's Experiment in Education." In Goldwin and Nel-
            son, 1957, 11-21.

Band, Arnold J.
1966   "Jewish Studies in American Liberal-Arts Colleges and Universi-
            ties." *American Jewish Yearbook* 67, 1-30.

Barth, Karl
1956   *Church Dogmatics.* Vol. 1/2, *The Doctrine of the Word of God.* Trans.
            by G. T. Thomson and Harold Knight. New York: Scribner's.

Barzun, Jacques
1954   *Teacher in America.* Garden City, NY: Doubleday Anchor Books.
            Originally published 1945 (Boston: Little, Brown).

Baum, Gregory
1974-75   [Response to Charles Davis, 1974-75]. *Studies in Religion/Sciences
            Religieuses* 4/3, 222-24.

Baumgarten, Albert I.
1985   "The Torah as a Public Document in Judaism." *Studies in Religion/-
            Sciences Religieuses* 14/1, 17-24.

Beare, Frank W.
1962   *The Earliest Records of Jesus: A Companion to the Synopsis of the
            First Three Gospels by Albert Huck.* New York and Nashville: Abing-
            don Press.

Benson, Thomas L.
1987   "Religious Studies as an Academic Discipline." In Eliade, 1987, vol.
            14, 88-92.

Bestor, Dorothy K.
1977   *Aside from Teaching English, What in the World Can You Do?* Seat-
            tle: University of Washington Press.

"Bible Colleges in Canada" (Table)
1985   *Faith Alive: Canada's Evangelical Newsmagazine* (November), 42-54.

Bibby, Reginald W.
1987 *Fragmented Gods: The Poverty and Potential of Religion in Canada.* Toronto: Irwin.

Bloom, Alfred
1976-77 "Reflections on the Center for the Study of World Religions, Harvard Divinity School." *Studies in Religion/Sciences Religieuses* 6/5, 497-98.

Bloom, Harold, and David Rosenberg
1990 *The Book of J.* (Translation of "J" [the Yahwist document] by Rosenberg; interpretation by Bloom.) New York: Grove Weidenfeld.

Boon, Harold W.
1950 "The Development of the Bible College or Institute in the United States and Canada since 1880 and its Relationship to the Field of Theological Education in America." Ph.D. dissertation, New York University.

Bowen, William, and Julie Sosa
1989 *Prospects for Faculty in the Arts and Sciences.* Princeton: Princeton University Press.

Bowers, Kenneth S.
1990 "Psychology's been trying to hire women profs." *University of Waterloo Gazette* 31/10 (Nov. 7), 2.

Boyer, Ernest L.
1990 *Scholarship Reconsidered: Priorities of the Professoriate. A Special Report for the Carnegie Foundation for the Advancement of Teaching.* Princeton: Princeton University Press.

Boyle, John P.
1985 "The Academy and the Church Teaching Authority: Current Issues." In George Kilcourse, ed., *The Catholic Theological Society of America: Proceedings of the Fortieth Annual Convention San Francisco, June 5-8, 1985,* vol. 40, 172-80. Bellarmine College, Louisville, KY: Catholic Theological Society of America.

Brauer, Jerald C.
1953 *Protestantism in America: A Narrative History.* Philadelphia: Westminster Press.

Bregman, Lucy
1979 "Religion and Psychology: Recent Scholarship." *Religious Studies Review* 5/2, 111-15.

Brett, Jim, and Bob Moore
1991 "Release Time Provisions for Librarians." *Canadian Association of University Teachers Bulletin Association canadienne des professeurs d'université* 38/1 (March), 2.

Bridston, Keith R., and Dwight W. Culver
1965 *Pre-seminary Education: Report of the Lilly Endowment Study.* Augsburg Publishing House.

Brief to the Royal Commission on Education of the Province of Quebec
1961   Submitted under the authority of the Board of Governors, and with the approval of the Senate, November 19, 1961. Montreal: McGill University.

Brooks, Douglas R.
1989   "Hinduism in *The Encyclopedia of Religion.*" *Critical Review of Books in Religion 1989*, 77-104.

Brown, Joseph Epes
1964   *The Spiritual Legacy of the American Indian.* Pendle Hill Pamphlet 135. Wallingford, PA. Reprinted, 1982 (New York: Crossroad).
1976   "The Roots of Renewal." In W. Capps, 1976, 25-34.

Brown, Karen McCarthy
1978   "Heretics and Pagans: Women in the Academic World." In David G. Jones, ed., *Private and Public Ethics: Tensions Between Conscience and Institutional Responsibility*, 266-88. New York: Edwin Mellen Press.

Brown, Peter
1967   *Augustine of Hippo: A Biography.* Berkeley and Los Angeles: University of California Press.
1971   "The Rise and Function of the Holy Man in Late Antiquity." *Journal of Roman Studies* 61, 80-101.
1981   *The Cult of the Saints: Its Rise and Function in Latin Christianity.* Chicago: University of Chicago Press.
1982   *Society and the Holy in Late Antiquity.* Berkeley and Los Angeles: University of California Press.

Burwash, Nathaniel
1906a   "The Development of the University, 1853-1887." Chapter 2 in Alexander, 1906, 39-56.
1906b   "The Development of the University, 1887-1904." Chapter 3 in Alexander, 1906, 57-70.
1927   *The History of Victoria College.* Toronto: Victoria College Press.

Butler, Samuel
1948   [1903] *The Way of All Flesh.* New York and Toronto: Rinehart.

Buttrick, George A., et al., eds.
1962   *The Interpreter's Dictionary of the Bible.* 4 vols. New York and Nashville: Abingdon.

Cain, Seymour
1987   "Study of Religion: History of Study." In Eliade, 1987, vol. 14, 64-83.

Campbell, Bruce F.
1980   2nd, rev. ed., 1981 *Career Guide for Graduate Students in Religion.* Waterloo, Ont.: Council on the Study of Religion.

Canadian Journal of Theology
1955   "The Purpose of the Journal: An Editorial." *Canadian Journal of Theology* 1/1, 1.

Cantelon, Jim
1984   "Recollections of a Spiritual Misfit." *Faith Alive: Canada's Evangelical Newsmagazine* (March), 27.

Capps, Donald
1988   "The Psychology of Religious Experience." In Lippy and Williams, 1988, vol. 1, 51-70.
Capps, Walter H.
1987   "Society and Religion." In Eliade, 1987, vol. 13, 375-84.
Capps, Walter H., ed.
1976   *Seeing with a Native Eye: Essays on Native American Religion.* New York: Harper & Row.
CAUT
1990a   "CAUT and Canadianization." *Canadian Association of University Teachers Bulletin Association canadienne des professeurs d'université* 37/9 (October), 7, 14-16.
1990b   "A Statistical Glance at the Changing Status of Women in Ontario Universities." Prepared by the Council of Ontario Universities Committee on the Status of Women. In ibid. 37/10 (December), 6.
1990c   "Blind Reviewing of Journal Articles." In ibid., 7.
1991a   "A Statistical Glance at the Changing Status of Women in the Ontario Universities." In ibid. 38/1 (Jan.), 4.
1991b   "Status of Women Supplement/Supplément du statut de la femme." Supplement to ibid. 38/4 (April).
Census of Canada
1981   *Population: Religion.* Ottawa: Statistics Canada.
1981   *Population: Ontario: Religion.* Ottawa: Statistics Canada.
CFH
1984   "Scholars . . . And Teachers? The Academic Career Prospects of Ph.D. Graduates in the Humanities." *Canadian Federation for the Humanities Bulletin* 7/2, 4-12.
1987a   "National Survey on Research Needs and Research Funding in the Humanities: Statistical Summary of Responses Received from April to June 1986." *Canadian Federation for the Humanities Bulletin* 10/1, 10-22.
1987b   "Profile of Canadian Humanists." *Canadian Federation for the Humanities Bulletin* 10/1, 23.
1987c   *History of the Affiliated Learned Societies of the Canadian Federation for the Humanities/Historique des sociétés savantes affiliées à la Fédération canadienne des études des humaines.* Ottawa: Canadian Federation for the Humanities/Fédération canadienne des études humaines.
Chernus, Ira
1991   *Nuclear Madness: Religion in the Psychology of the Nuclear Age.* Albany: State University of New York Press.
Chernus, Ira, and Edward T. Linenthal
1984   "Teaching Religious Studies in the Nuclear Age." *Council on the Study of Religion Bulletin* 15/5, 141, 143.

Childs, Brevard S.
1985   *The New Testament as Canon: An Introduction.* Philadelphia: Fortress Press.
1986   *Old Testament Theology in a Canonical Context.* Philadelphia: Fortress Press.

Christ, Carol P.
1977   "The New Feminist Theology: A Review of the Literature." *Religious Studies Review* 3/4, 203-12.

Clark, S.D.
1948   *Church and Sect in Canada.* Toronto: University of Toronto Press.
1962   *The Developing Canadian Community.* Toronto: University of Toronto Press.
1976   *Canadian Society in Historical Perspective.* Toronto: McGraw-Hill Ryerson.

Clarkson, Shannon
1989   "Language about God." *Studies in Religion/Sciences Religieuses* 15/1, 37-49

Classen, Hans George
1978   "Religious Studies in Canada." *Queen's Quarterly* 85, 389-402.

Clebsch, William A.
1981   "Apples, Oranges, and Manna: Comparative Religion Revisited." *Journal of the American Academy of Religion* 49/1, 3-22.

Clifford, Michael D.
1987   "Psychotherapy and Religion." In Eliade, 1987, vol. 12, 75-81.

Clifford, N. Keith
1969   "Religion and the Development of Canadian Society: An Historiographical Analysis." *Church History* 38, 506-23.
1973   "His Dominion: A Vision in Crisis." *Studies in Religion/Sciences Religieuses* 2, 315-26. Reprinted in P. Slater, 1977, 23-41.
1990   "Universities, Churches and Theological Colleges in English-speaking Canada: Some Current Sources of Tension." *Studies in Religion/-Sciences Religieuses* 19/1, 3-16.

Clothey, Fred W.
1983   *Rhythm and Intent: Ritual Studies from South India.* Madras et al.: Blackie and Son.

Cohen, Shaye J.D.
1987   *From the Maccabees to the Mishnah.* Philadelphia: Westminster Press.

Collins, Mary
1987   "Ritual Symbols and the Ritual Process: The Work of Victor W. Turner." In Collins, *Worship: Renewal to Practice,* 59-71. Washington, DC: Pastoral Press.

Combs, Eugene
1976-77 "Learned and Learning: CSSR/SCER, 1965-1975." *Studies in Religion/Sciences Religieuses* 6/4, 357-63.

Commission of Inquiry
1970   *A Commitment to Higher Education in Canada: The Report of a Com-
          mission of Inquiry on Forty Catholic Church-Related Colleges and
          Universities.* Ottawa: National Education Office, Canadian Catholic
          Conference.
Commonwealth Universities Yearbook 1988
1988   Vol. 2, *C-H.* London: Association of Commonwealth Universities.
Conway, John S.
1959   "The Universities and Religious Studies." *Canadian Journal of The-
          ology* 5/4, 269-72.
Cook, Ramsay
1985   *The Regenerators: Social Criticism in Late Victorian English Can-
          ada.* Toronto: University of Toronto Press.
Cook, Terry
1972   "John Beverly Robinson and the Conservative Blueprint for the
          Upper Canadian Community." *Ontario History* 64, 79-94.
Corbett, John
1986   "The Pharisaic Revolution and Jesus as Embodied Torah." *Studies in
          Religion/Sciences Religieuses* 15/3, 375-91.
Coward, Harold
1986   "The Canadian Contribution to Study of South Asian Religions."
          *Revue Canadienne d'études du Développement/Canadian Journal of
          Development Studies* 7/2, 281-91.
Coward, Harold, and Roland Chagnon
1988   "Religion." In Marsh, 1988, 1850-51.
Cox, Bob
1991   "University enrolments continue surprising rise." Canadian Press
          dispatch in *Kitchener-Waterloo Record* (Jan. 8), D14.
Cragg, Gerald R.
1955   "The Present Position and the Future Prospects of Canadian Theol-
          ogy." *Canadian Journal of Theology* 1/1, 5-10.
Craig, Gerald M.
1959   "The Canadian Setting." In Rose, 1959, 3-13.
Crim, Keith, General Editor
1976   *The Interpreter's Dictionary of the Bible.* Supplementary vol. Nash-
          ville: Abingdon.
1981   *Abingdon Dictionary of Living Religions.* Nashville: Abingdon.
Crites, Stephen D.
1990   *Liberal Learning and the Religion Major: A Report to the Profession.*
          The American Academy of Religion Task Force for the American
          Association of Colleges. Atlanta, GA: American Academy of Reli-
          gion.
Crysdale, Stewart, and Les Wheatcroft, eds.
1976   *Religion in Canadian Society.* Toronto: Macmillan.

CTSA (Catholic Theological Society of America)
1980   "CTSA Committee Report on Cooperation between Theologians and the Church's Teaching Authority." In Luke Salm, ed., *The Catholic Theological Society of America: Proceedings of the Thirty-fifth Annual Convention San Francisco, California, June 11-14, 1980,* vol. 35, 325-36. Manhattan College, Bronx, N.Y.: Catholic Theological Society of America.

Cullmann, Oscar
1959   "Infancy Gospels." In Edgar Hennecke and Wilhelm Schneemelcher, eds., *New Testament Apocrypha,* English trans. (1963) ed. by R. McL. Wilson, vol. 1, 363-69. Philadelphia: Westminster Press.

Daly, Mary
1968   *The Church and the Second Sex.* New York: Harper & Row.
1973   "Introduction." In Plaskow Goldenberg, 1973, 1-3.

d'Angelo, Mary Rose
1986   "Remembering Her: Feminist Readings of the Christian Tradition." *Toronto Journal of Theology* 2/1, 118-26.

Dart, John
1978   "Religious Journalism as a Vocation." *Council on the Study of Religion Bulletin* 9/3 (June), 71.

Davis, Charles
1974-75   "The Reconvergence of Theology and Religious Studies. "*Studies in Religion/Sciences Religieuses* 4/3, 2-21
1980   "Editorial: The Fourteenth International Congress of the IAHR." *Studies in Religion/Sciences Religieuses* 9/2, 123-24.
1984   " 'Wherein There Is No Ecstasy.' " *Studies in Religion/Sciences Religieuses* 13/4, 393-400.

Davis, Winston
1987   "Sociology of Religion." In Eliade, 1987, vol. 13, 393-401.

Dawsey, James
1988   *A Scholar's Guide to Academic Journals in Religion.* American Theological Library Association Bibliography Series, 23. Metuchen, NJ: Scarecrow Press.

Dawson, Lorne L.
1985   " 'Free-Will Talk' and Sociology." *Sociological Inquiry* 55, 348-62.
1986   "Neither Nerve nor Ecstasy: Comment on the Wiebe-Davis Exchange." *Studies in Religion/Sciences Religieuses* 15/2, 145-51.
1987   "On References to the Transcendent in the Scientific Study of Religion: A Qualified Idealist Proposal." *Religion* 17, 227-50.
1988   *Reason, Freedom, and Religion: Closing the Gap Between the Humanistic and Scientific Study of Religion.* Toronto Studies in Religion, 6. New York: Peter Lang.
1991   "Religion and Legitimacy." In Singh Bolaria and Peter Li, eds., *Sociology.* Mississauga, Ont.: Copp, Clark, Pitman.

De Jong, Arthur
  1990   *Reclaiming a Mission: New Directions for the Church-Related College.* Grand Rapids, MI: Eerdmans.
Desjardins, Michel
  1985   "Law in 2 Baruch and 4 Ezra." *Studies in Religion/Sciences Religieuses* 14/1, 25-37.
Despland, Michel
  1977   "Religion and the Quest for National Identity: Problems and Perspectives." In P. Slater, 1977, 525-51.
  1978a   "Church History, History of Christianity, and History of Religions." *Studies in Religion/Sciences Religieuses* 7, 259-61.
  1978b   "New Approaches to Religious Historiography in France." *Studies in Religion/Sciences Religieuses* 7, 323-27.
  1979   *La religion en occident: Évolution des idées et du vecu.* Montreal and Paris: Fides et Cerf.
  1984   *The Education of Desire: Plato and the Philosophy of Religion.* Toronto: University of Toronto Press.
Detweiler, Robert
  1978   "Recent Religion and Literature Scholarship." *Religious Studies Review* 4/2, 107-17.
Dibelius, Martin
  1932   "Jungfrauensohn und Krippenkind: Untersuchungen zur Geburtsgeschichte Jesu im Lukas-Evangelium." In *Sitzungsberichte der Heidelberger Akademie der Wissenschaften, philologische-historische Klasse*, Abhandlung 4. Reprinted in his *Botschaft und Geschichte: Gesammelte Aufsätze*, vol. 1, edited by Günther Bornkamm with Heinz Kraft (Tübingen: Mohr [Siebeck], 1953), 1-78.
Dillenberger, John, and Claude Welch
  1988   *Protestant Christianity Interpreted Through Its Development.* 2nd ed. New York: Macmillan and London: Collier Macmillan.
Dinur, Benzion (Dinaburg)
  1971   "Wissenschaft des Judentums." *Encyclopaedia Judaica.* Vol. 16, 570-84. Jerusalem: Encyclopaedia Judaica, Macmillan, Keter Publishing.
Dittes, James
  1969   "Psychology of Religion." In Gardner Lindzey and Elliot Aronson, eds., *The Handbook of Social Psychology,* 2nd ed., 602-59. Reading, MA: Addison-Wesley.
Dix, Gregory
  1945   *The Shape of the Liturgy.* Westminster: Dacre Press.
Doherty, Robert E.
  1950   *Development of Professional Education: The Principles Which Have Guided the Reconstruction of Education at Carnegie Institute of Technology 1936-1950.* Pittsburgh: Carnegie Press.
Doty, William G.
  1986   "Ritual: The Symbolic Intercom." In Doty, *Mythography: The Study*

of Myths and Rituals, chap. 3. University, AL: University of Alabama Press.

Driver, Anne Barstow
1976   "Review Essay: Religion." *Signs: Journal of Women in Culture and Society* 2/2, 434-42.

Driver, Tom
1970   "The Study of Religion and Literature: Siblings in the Academic House." In Ramsey and Wilson, 1970, 304-21.

D'Souza, Dinesh
1991   "Illiberal Education." *The Atlantic* 267/3 (March), 51-79.

Duke, James O.
1989   "That Than Which Nothing (Much) Greater Can Be Conceived: A Review of the Treatment of Christianity in *The Encyclopedia of Religion*." *Critical Review of Books in Religion 1989*, 41-55.

Eble, Kenneth E.
1977   *The Craft of Teaching: A Guide to Mastering the Professor's Art.* San Francisco et al.: Jossey-Bass.

Eck, Diana
1982   *Banaras, City of Light.* New York: Knopf.

Eckel, Malcolm David
1989   "*The Encyclopedia of Religion* and the Study of Buddhism." *Critical Review of Books in Religion 1989*, 105-16.

Edinburgh, Arnold, ed.
1978   *The Enduring Word: A Centennial History of Wycliffe College.* Toronto: University of Toronto Press.

Editorial
1982   "To Build a Better Bible College." *Christianity Today* (February 5), 14-16.

Eichhorst, Bill
1984   "Bible Colleges . . . for what purpose?" *Faith Alive: Canada's Evangelical Newsmagazine* (March), 26-27.

Eliade, Mircea
1963   "The History of Religions in Retrospect: 1912-1962." *Journal of Bible and Religion* 31, 98-109.

Eliade, Mircea, Editor in Chief
1987   *The Encyclopedia of Religion.* 16 vols. New York: Macmillan and London: Collier Macmillan.

Eliade, Mircea, and Joseph Kitagawa, eds.
1959   *The History of Religions: Essays in Methodology.* Chicago: University of Chicago Press.

Elliott, John H.
1986   "Social-Scientific Criticism of the New Testament: More on Methods and Models." In Elliott, ed., *Semeia 35, Social-Scientific Criticism of the New Testament and Its Social World*, 1-33. Decatur, GA: Scholars Press.

"Enrollments During the Eighties"

1990 *American Association of Bible Colleges Newsletter* 34/1, 8-9, 11.

Fackenheim, Emil F.

1967 *The Religious Dimension in Hegel's Thought*. Bloomington: Indiana University Press.

1968 *Quest for Past and Future: Essays in Jewish Theology*. Bloomington and London: Indiana University Press.

1970 *God's Presence in History: Jewish Affirmations and Philosophical Reflections*. New York: New York University Press.

1978 *The Jewish Return into History: Reflections in the Age of Ausschwitz and a New Jerusalem*. New York: Schocken Books.

1982 *To Mend the World*. New York: Schocken Books.

1987 "The Development of My Thought." *Religious Studies Review* 13/3, 204-06.

Fairbairn, A.M.

1905 "Introduction" to Jordan, 1905, vii-ix.

Fairweather, Eugene R.

1970 "Canadian Journal of Theology: 1955-1970." *Canadian Journal of Theology* 16/3-4, 127-28

Falk, Nancy

1978 Review of Marina Warner, *Alone of All Her Sex: The Myth and Cult of the Virgin Mary* (New York: Knopf, 1976); Fatima Mernissi, *Beyond the Veil: Male-Female Dynamics in a Modern Muslim Society* (New York et al.: Schenkman and John Wiley, 1975); Manisha Roy, *Bengali Women* (Chicago and London: University of Chicago Press, 1975). *Religious Studies Review* 4/2, 81-85.

Farquhar, John Nicol

1913 *The Crown of Hinduism*. London: Humphrey Milford.

Feilding, Charles.

1966a *Education for Ministry* = title of *Theological Education* 3/1.

1966b "Twenty-three Theological Schools: Aspects of Canadian Theological Education." *Canadian Journal of Theology* 12/4, 229-37.

Fennell, William O.

1985 "The Canadian Theological Society: An Anniversary Retrospective." *Studies in Religion/Sciences Religieuses* 14/4, 409-13.

Fenton, John Y.

1970 "Reductionism in the Study of Religion." *Soundings* 53, 61-76.

Ferguson, Everett, et al., eds.

1989 *Encyclopedia of Early Christianity*. New York and London: Garland.

Findlay, James F., Jr.

1969 *Dwight L. Moody: American Evangelist 1837-1899*. Chicago and London: University of Chicago Press.

Fiorino, Albert F.

1978 "The Moral Education [lege: Foundation] of Egerton Ryerson's Idea of Education." In McDonald and Chaiton, 1978, 59-80.

Fisher, Ben C.
1989   *The Idea of a Christian University in Today's World.* Macon, GA:
          Mercer University Press.
Fisher, Robin, and Kenneth Coates
1988   *Out of the Background: Readings on Canadian Native History.*
          Toronto: Copp Clark Pitman.
Fraikin, Daniel
1986   "The Rhetorical Function of the Jews in Romans." In Richardson
          and Granskou, 1986, 91-105.
Frankena, William F., ed.
1980   *The Philosophy and Future of Graduate Education: Papers and Com-
          mentaries Delivered at the International Conference on the Philoso-
          phy of Graduate Education at The University of Michigan, April
          13-15, 1978.* Ann Arbor: University of Michigan Press.
Fraser, Brian J.
1979   "Theology and the Social Gospel among Canadians: A Case Study."
          Studies in Religion/Sciences Religieuses 8/1, 35-46.
1988   *The Social Uplifters: Presbyterian Progressives and the Social Gos-
          pel in Canada, 1875-1915.* Waterloo, Ont.: Wilfrid Laurier University
          Press for the Canadian Corporation for Studies in Religion/Corpora-
          tion Canadienne des Sciences Religieuses au Canada.
Freedman, David Noel, and Gary A. Herion, eds.
Forth-   *Anchor Bible Dictionary.* Garden City, NY: Doubleday Anchor
coming   Books.
French, Goldwin S.
1978   "Egerton Ryerson and the Methodist Model for Upper Canada." In
          McDonald and Chaiton, 1978, 45-58.
Friesen, John
1988   "A Social History Interpretation of Bishop Irenaeus of Lyons." Paper
          presented at Annual Meeting of the Canadian Society of Patristic
          Studies/Association canadienne des études patristiques, University of
          Windsor, June 3.
Funk, Robert W.
1977-78   "Issues in Scholarly Publishing." *Scholarly Publishing* 9, 3-17,
          115-29.
Gadon, Eleanor W.
1989   *The Once and Future Goddess: A Symbol for Our Time.* San Fran-
          cisco et al.: Harper & Row.
Gager, John G.
1983   *The Origins of Anti-semitism: Attitudes toward Judaism in Pagan and
          Christian Antiquity.* New York and Oxford: Oxford University Press.
Galling, Kurt, ed., with Hans von Campenhausen et al.
1957-65   *Die Religion in Geschichte und Gegenwart.* 7 vols. Tübingen: Mohr
          (Siebeck).

Gamelin, Francis C.
1975   *Church-Related Identity of Lutheran Colleges.* Washington, DC: Lutheran Educational Conference of North America.

Gangel, Kenneth
1980   "The Bible College: Past, Present, and Future." *Christianity Today* (Nov. 7), 34-36.

Gazard, Peter R.
1980   "A Needs Assessment of Transfer Credit Procedures in Canadian Bible Colleges." Ph.D. dissertation, Universityof Calgary.

Geertz, Clifford
1973   "Thick Description: Toward an Interpretive Theory of Culture." In Geertz, *The Interpretation of Cultures: Selected Essays,* 3-30. New York: Basic Books.

Gilbert, Arthur
1969   "Jewish Theological Education in a Secular Academic Setting." *Journal of Ecumenical Studies* 6, 549-72.

Gilkey, Langdon
1981   "A Theological Voyage with Wilfred Cantwell Smith." *Religious Studies Review* 7/4, 298-310.

Gill, Sam D.
1978   "Native American Religions." *The Council on the Study of Religion Bulletin* 9/5, 125, 127-28.
1979   "Native American Religions: A Review Essay." *Religious Studies Review* 5/4, 251-58.
1987   *Mother Earth: An American Story.* Chicago and London: University of Chicago Press.

Gilmour-Bryson, Anne, ed.
1984   *Computer Applications to Medieval Studies.* Studies in Medieval Culture, 17. Kalamazoo, MI: Medieval Institute Publications.

Glatzer, N. N.
1964   "Beginnings of Modern Jewish Studies." In A. Altmann, ed., *Studies in Nineteenth-Century Jewish Intellectual History,* 27-45. Cambridge, MA: Harvard University Press.

Glazer, Judith S.
1986   *The Master's Degree: Tradition, Diversity, Innovation.* ASHEERIC Higher Education Report, 6. Washington, DC: Association for the Study of Higher Education.

Gless, Darryl J., and Barbara Herrstein Smith, eds.
1990   *The Politics of Liberal Education.* Durham, NC: Duke University Press.

Goethals, Gregor T.
1981   *The TV Ritual: Worship at the Video Altar.* Boston: Beacon Press.

Goldenberg, Naomi R.
1979   *Changing of the Gods: Feminism and the End of Traditional Religions.* Boston: Beacon Press.

1982   *The End of God: Important Directions for a Feminist Critique of Religion in the Works of Sigmund Freud and Carl Jung.* Ottawa: University of Ottawa Press.

1990   *Returning Words to Flesh: Feminism, Psychoanalysis, and the Resurrection of the Body.* Boston: Beacon Press.

Goldwin, Robert A., ed., and Charles A. Nelson, consultant

1957   *Toward the Liberally Educated Executive.* White Plains, NY: Fund for Adult Education.

Graham, John F.

1968   "The Social Sciences: Specific Needs." In Hubbard, 1968, 17-25.

Granskou, David

1986   "Anti-Judaism in the Passion Accounts of the Fourth Gospel." In Richardson and Granskou, 1986, 201-16.

Grant, George M.

N. d. [1894?] *The Religions of the World in Relation to Christianity.* Guild Text Books. New York: Fleming H. Revell.

Grant, George P.

1951   "Philosophy." In *Royal Commission Studies*, 1951, 119-34.

1968   "The Academic Study of Religion in Canada." In Hubbard, 1968, 59-68.

1986   "Faith and the Multiversity." In G. P. Grant, *Technology and Justice*, 35-77. Toronto: Anansi.

Grant, John Webster

1972   *The Church in the Canadian Era: The First Century of Confederation.* A History of the Church in Canada, 3. Toronto: McGraw-Hill Ryerson. 2nd, rev. ed., 1988 (Burlington, Ont.: Welch).

1972-73   " 'At least you knew where you stood with them': Reflections on Religious Pluralism in Canada and the United States." *Studies in Religion/Sciences Religieuses* 2, 340-51.

1977   "Religion and the Quest for a National Identity: The Background in Canadian History." In Slater, 1977, 7-21.

1984   *Moon of Wintertime: Missionaries and the Indians of Canada in Encounter Since 1534.* Toronto et al.: University of Toronto Press.

1988   *A Profusion of Spires: Religion in Nineteenth-Century Ontario.* Toronto et al.: University of Toronto Press.

Gray, Patrick T.R.

1988   "Legislation and Religion in the Reign of Justinian." Paper presented at the Annual Meeting of the Canadian Society of Patristic Studies/ Association Canadienne des études patristiques, University of Windsor, June 2.

Greeley, Andrew M.

1969   *From Backwater to Mainstream: A Profile of Catholic Higher Education.* New York: McGraw-Hill.

1972   *Unsecular Man: The Persistence of Religion.* New York: Schocken Books.

Greeley, Andrew M., with William van Cleve and Grace Ann Carroll
1967   *The Changing Catholic College*. Chicago: Aldine.
Green, William Scott
1989   "Old Habits Dic Hard: Judaism in *The Encyclopedia of Religion*."
         Critical Review of Books in Religion 1989, 23-40.
Griffith Thomas, W.H.
         N.d. "Old Testament Criticism and New Testament Christianity."
         The Fundamentals: A Testimony to the Truth. Vol. 8, 5-26. Chicago:
         Testimony Publishing Co.
Grimes, Ronald L.
1975   "Masking: Toward a Phenomonology of Exteriorization." *Journal of
         the American Academy of Religion* 53, 508-16.
1976a   "Ritual Studies: A Comparative Review of Theodore Gaster and Vic-
         tor Turner." *Religious Studies Review* 2/4, 13-25.
1976b   *Symbol and Conquest: Public Ritual and Drama in Santa Fe, New
         Mexico*. Ithaca: Cornell University Press.
1979a   "The Actor's Lab: The Ritual Roots of Human Action." *Canadian
         Theatre Review* 22, 9-19.
1979b   "Modes of Ritual Necessity." *Worship* 53/2, 126-41.
1982a   "Defining Nascent Ritual." *Journal of the American Academy of
         Religion* 50/4, 539-55.
1982b   *Beginnings in Ritual Studies*. Washington DC: University Press of
         America.
1982c   "The Lifeblood of Public Ritual." In Victor Turner, ed., *Celebration:
         Studies in Festivity and Ritual*, 272-83. Washington, DC: Smithsonian
         Institution Press.
1983   "Tempest on Snake Island." In Tony Coult and Baz Kershaw, eds.,
         Engineers of the Imagination, 164-81. London: Methuen.
1984a   "The Need for Ritual Practice: Weddings that Wed." *Liturgy* 4/2,
         9-13.
1984b   "Bibligraphy: Sources for the Study of Ritual." *Religious Studies
         Review* 10/2, 134-45.
1985   *Research in Ritual Studies: A Programmatic Essay and Bibliography*.
         ATLA Bibliographical Series, 14. Metuchen, NJ and London: Ameri-
         can Theological Library Association and Scarecrow Press.
1986a   "Of Words the Speaker, of Deeds the Doer." *Journal of Religion*
         66/1, 1-1
1986b   "Desecration of the Dead: An Inter-Religious Controversy." *Ameri-
         can Indian Quarterly* 10/4, 305-18.
1987   "Ritual Studies." In Eliade, 1987, vol. 12, 422-25.
1988a   "Infelicitous Performances and Ritual Criticism." *Semeia* 43, 103-22.
1988b   "Ritual in the Toronto Towneley Cycle of Mystery Plays." *Studies in
         Religion/Sciences Religieuses* 16/4, 473-80.
1988c   "Victor Turner's Social Drama and T.S. Eliot's Ritual Drama."
         Anthropologica n.s. 27/1-2, 79-99.

1988d   "Ritual Criticism and Reflexivity in Fieldwork." *Journal of Ritual Studies* 2/2, 217-39.

1989   "Liturgical Renewal and Ritual Criticism." In Proceedings of the Georgetown Conference on Liturgy.

1990a   *Ritual Criticism.* Columbia, SC: University of South Carolina Press.

1990b   "Mapping Religions: Geopiety and Holy Historiography — A View from the Southwestern United States." Paper delivered at Annual Meeting of the American Academy of Religion, New Orleans, November.

Gutschi, Monica

1991   "Broaden the appeal of courses, college told." *Kitchener-Waterloo Record* (April 4), B3.

Gwynne-Timothy, John R.

1978   *Western's First Century.* London, Ont.: Universityof Western Ontario.

Hacker, Andrew

1986   "The Decline of Higher Learning." *New York Review of Books* (Feb. 13), 35-42.

Hague, Dyson

N.d.   "The History of the Higher Criticism." *The Fundamentals: A Testi-*
[1909]   *mony to the Truth.* Vol 1, 87-122. Chicago: Testimony Publishing Co.

Hahn, Herbert F.

1956   *The Old Testament in Modern Research.* London: SCM Press and Philadelphia: Muhlenberg Press. 2nd ed., supplemented with a survey of recent literature by Horace D. Hummel, 1968 (Philadelphia: Fortress Press).

Hall, Anne A.

1980   "Teaching Amy Counterpoint." *The Radical Teacher* 17 (Nov.), 39-41.

Hall, Douglas John

1985a   "On Contextuality in Christian Theology." *Toronto Journal of Theology* 1/1, 3-16.

1985b   "Barmen: Lesson in Theology." *Toronto Journal of Theology* 1/2, 180-99.

1989   *Thinking the Faith: Christian Theology in a North American Context.* Minneapolis: Augsburg.

Handy, Robert

1977   *A History of the Churches in the United States and Canada.* New York: Oxford University Press.

1985   "Dominant Patterns of Christian Life in Canada and the United States: Similarities and Differences." In Westfall et al., 1985, 344-55.

Harder, Ben

1980   "The Bible Institute-College Movement in Canada." *Canadian Church Historical Society Journal* 22 (April), 29-45.

Harrington, Paul E., and Andrew M. Sum

1988   "Whatever Happened to the College Enrollment Crisis?" *Academe:*

Bulletin of the American Association of University Professors (Sept.-Oct.).

Harvey, Van A.

1966   *The Historian and the Believer: The Morality of Historical Knowledge and Christian Belief.* New York: Macmillan.

1970   "Reflections on the Teaching of Religion in America." *Journal of the American Academy of Religion* 38/1, 17-29.

Hastings, James, ed., with John A. Selbie, A. B. Davidson, S. R. Driver, and H. B. Swete

1898-   *A Dictionary of the Bible.* 5 vols. New York: Scribner's.
1904

Hastings, James, ed., with John A. Selbie

1906-08 *A Dictionary of Christ and the Gospels.* 2 vols. New York: Scribner's.

Hastings, James, ed., with John A. Selbie et al.

1908-26 *Encyclopaedia of Religion and Ethics.* 13 vols. New York: Scribner's and Edinburgh: T. & T. Clark.

Hastings, James, ed., with John A. Selbie and John C. Lambert

1915-18 *Dictionary of the Apostolic Church.* 2 vols. Edinburgh: T. & T. Clark.

Heisig, James W.

1987   "Psychology of Religion." In Eliade, 1987, vol. 12, 57-66.

Henderson, J. L. H., ed.

1969   *John Strachan: Documents and Opinions.* Carleton Library, 44. Toronto and Montreal: McClelland and Stewart.

Highet, Gilbert

1947   *The Classical Tradition.* New York: Columbia University Press.

1952   *The Art of Teaching.* New York: Knopf.

Hill, Samuel S., ed.

1984   *Encyclopedia of Religion in the South.* Macon, GA: Mercer University Press.

Hiller, Harry D.

1976-77 "The Contribution of S.D. Clark to the Sociology of Canadian Religion." *Studies in Religion/Sciences Religieuses* 6/4, 415-27.

Hocking, William Ernest

1940   *Living Religions and a World Faith.* London: Allen & Unwin.

Holbrook, Clyde

1963   *Religion, a Humanistic Field.* Humanistic Scholarship in America: The Princeton Studies. Princeton: Princeton University Press.

Hollis, Martin

1977   *Models of Man: Philosophical Thoughts on Social Action.* Cambridge and New York: Cambridge University Press.

Holsten, W.

1961a   "Religionsgeschichte." In Galling, 1957-65, vol. 5, 986-91.

1961b   "Religionswissenschaft." In ibid., 1038-42.

Homans, Peter

1968   "Toward a Psychology of Religion: By Way of Freud and Tillich." In

Homans, ed., *The Dialogue Between Theology and Psychology*, 53-81. Essays in Divinity, 3. Chicago and London: University of Chicago Press.

1987   "Psychology and Religion Movement." In Eliade, 1987, vol. 12, 66-75.

Hopper, Stanley Romaine, ed.

1957   *Spiritual Problems in Contemporary Literature.* New York: Harper Torchbooks.

Hospital, Clifford G.

1985   *Breakthrough: Insights of the Great Religious Discoverers.* Maryknoll, NY: Orbis Books.

Howard, Oswald

1963   *The Montreal Diocesan Theological College: A History from 1873 to 1963.* Montreal: McGill University Press.

Hubbard, R.H., ed.

1968   *Scholarship in Canada, 1967: Achievement and Outlook: Symposium Presented to Section II of the Royal Society of Canada.* Toronto: University of Toronto Press for the Royal Society of Canada.

Hughes, John J.

1990   "Beyond Word Processing." *Critical Review of Books in Religion 1990*, 1-43.

Hultkrantz, Åke

1976   "The Contribution of the Study of North American Religions to the History of Religions." In W. Capps, 1976, 86-106.

1983   *The Study of American Indian Religions.* Ed. by Christopher Vecsey. American Academy of Religion Studies in Religion, 29. New York: Crossroad and Chico, CA: Scholars Press.

Hurd, John C.

1986   "Paul Ahead of His Time: 1 Thess. 2:13-16." In Richardson and Granskou, 1986, 21-36.

Hurtado, Larry

1988   *One God, One Lord: Early Christian Devotion and Ancient Jewish Monotheism.* Philadelphia: Fortress Press.

James, William

1958   [1902] *The Varieties of Religious Experience: A Study in Human Nature, Being the Gifford Lectures on Natural Religion Delivered at Edinburgh 1901-1902.* New York: New American Library.

James, William Closson

Forth-   "What Do I Know? The Generalist in Religious Studies." In Klaus
coming   Klostermaier, ed., *Religious Studies: Directions for the Next Two Decades.* University of Manitoba Studies in Religion. Atlanta, GA: Scholars Press.

Jasper, R.C.D.

1989   *The Development of the Anglican Liturgy 1662-1980.* London: SPCK.

Jencks, Christopher, and David Riesman
1969   *The Academic Revolution.* Garden City, NY: Doubleday.

Jobling, David
1991   "Mieke Bal on Biblical Narrative." *Religious Studies Review* 17/1, 1-10.

Johnson, Benton
1980   "A Fresh Look at Theories of Secularization." In Hubert M. Blalock, Jr., ed., *Sociological Theory and Research: A Critical Appraisal*, 314-31. New York: Free Press and London: Collier-Macmillan.

Johnson, Joanne M., and Samuel D. Cioran
1990   "Scripture Fonts: Word Processing Greek and Hebrew." *Canadian Humanities Computing* 4/4 (Nov.), 6-8.

Johnson, Luke T., ed.
1973   *Teaching Religion to Undergraduates: Some Approaches and Ideas from Teachers to Teachers.* N.p.: Society for Religion in Higher Education.

Jones, Cheslyn, Geoffrey Wainwright, and Edward Yarnold, eds.
1978   *The Study of Liturgy.* New York: Oxford University Press.

Jordan, Louis Henry
1905   *Comparative Religion: Its Genesis and Growth.* Edinburgh: T. & T. Clark.

Jungmann, Josef A.
1941   *Liturgical Worship.* Trans. by a monk of St. John's Abbey. Collegeville, MN et al.: Frederick Pustet Co.

1949   *Missarum sollemnia: Eine genetische Erklärung der römischen Messe.* 2 vols. Vienna: Herder Verlag.

1960   *The Early Liturgy to the Time of Gregory the Great.* London: Darton Longman and Todd.

1962   *Pastoral Liturgy.* New York: Herder and Herder.

Käsemann, Ernst
1957   "Neutestamentliche Fragen von heute." *Zeitschrift für Theologie und Kirche* 54/1, 1-21. Reprinted in his *Exegetische Versuche und Besinnungen*, vol. 2 (Göttingen: Vandenhoeck & Ruprecht, 1964), 11-31.

Kayfetz, Ben
1959   "The Evolution of the Jewish Community in Toronto." In Rose, 1959, 14-29.

Kerr, Robert W.
1991   "President's Message: Warming the Chilly Climate." *Canadian Association of University Teachers Bulletin Association canadienne des professeurs d'université* 38/3 (Mar.), 3.

Khan, Abrahim H.
1985   *Salighed as Happiness? Kierkegaard on the Concept Salighed.* Waterloo, Ont.: Wilfrid Laurier University Press.

Kiesekamp, Burkhard
1973   "Presbyterian and Methodist Divines: Their Case for a National

Church in Canada, 1875-1900.'' *Studies in Religion/Sciences Religieuses* 2/4, 289-302.

King, John
1914   *McCaul: Croft: Forneri: Personalities of Early University Days.* Toronto: Macmillan.

King, Ursula
1990   "Women Scholars and *The Encyclopedia of Religion.*'' *Method & Theory in the Study of Religion* 2/1, 91-97.

King, Winston L.
1965   *Introduction to Religion: A Phenomonological Approach.* New York: Harper & Row.

Kinsley, David
1986   *Hindu Goddesses: Visions of the Divine Feminine in the Hindu Religious Tradition.* Berkeley: University of California Press.
1989   *The Goddesses' Mirror: Visions of the Divine from East and West.* Albany: State University of New York Press.

Kitagawa, Joseph M.
1959   "The History of Religions in America.'' In Eliade and Kitagawa, 1959, 1-30.
1967   "Primitive, Classical, and Modern Religions: A Perspective on Understanding the History of Religions.'' In Kitagawa et al., 1967, 1-19.

Kitagawa, Joseph M., et al., eds.
1967   *The History of Religions: Essays on the Problem of Understanding.* Essays in Divinity, 1. Chicago and London: University of Chicago Press.

Klauser, Theodor
1974   *Gesammelte Arbeiten zur Liturgiegeschichte, Kirchengeschichte, und christlichen Archäologie.* Ed. by Ernst Dassmann. *Jahrbuch für Antike und Christentum,* Supplementary Vol. 3. Münster: Aschendorffsche Verlagsbuchhandlung.

Klein, Charlotte
1978   *Anti-Judaism in Christian Theology.* Trans. by Edward Quinn. Philadelphia: Fortress Press.

Klostermaier, Klaus
1976-77 "From Phenomenology to Metascience: Reflections on the Study of Religion.'' *Studies in Religion/Sciences Religieuses* 6/5, 551-64.

Knutson, Mary, and June O'Connor
1986   "Recent Works in Feminist Theology.'' *Religious Studies Review* 12/3-4, 197-205.

Koenker, Ernest B.
1954   *The Liturgical Renaissance in the Roman Catholic Church.* Chicago: University of Chicago Press.

Kraeling, Emil G,
1955   *The Old Testament Since the Reformation.* London: Lutterworth Press.

Kraemer, Ross S.
1983   "Bibliography: Women in the Religions of the Greco-Roman World." *Religious Studies Review* 9/2, 127-39.
1985   Review of Schüssler Fiorenza, 1983. *Religious Studies Review* 11/1, 6-9.

Kraft, Robert A.
1990   "OFFLINE: Computer Assisted Research for Religious Studies— 28." *Council of Societies for the Study of Religion Bulletin* 19/3 (Sept.), 79-82. (Also in *Religious Studies News* and electronically.)
1991a   "OFFLINE: Computer Assisted Research for Religious Studies— 31." *Council of Societies for the Study of Religion Bulletin* 20/1 (Feb.), 24-27. (Also in *Religious Studies News* and electronically.)
1991b   "OFFLINE: Computer Assisted Research for Religious Studies— 32." *Council of Societies for the Study of Religion Bulletin* 20/2 (April), 50-52. (Also in *Religious Studies News* and electronically.)

Landy, Francis
1991   "On the Gender of God and the Feminist Enterprise: A Response to Shannon Clarkson." *Studies in Religion/Sciences Religieuses* 19/4, 485-87.

Langevin, Gilles
1968   "L'Evolution récente et l'état actuel de l'enseignment de la théologie au Canada français: Dossier." *Canadian Journal of Theology* 14/3, 169-79.

Laperrière, Guy, and William Westfall
1990   "Religious Studies." In Alan Artibise, ed., *Interdisciplinary Approaches to Canadian Society: A Guide to the Literature*, 9-76. Montreal and Kingston: McGill-Queen's University Press for the Association of Canadian Studies.

Laporte, Jean-Marc
1985   "Editorial." *Toronto Journal of Theology* 1/1, 1-2.

Lawrence, Bruce B.
1978   Review of Annemarie Schimmel, *Mystical Dimensions of Islam* (Chapel Hill: University of North Carolina Press, 1985); J. Spencer Trimmingham, *The Sufi Orders in Islam* (New York: Oxford University Press, 1971); Martin Lings, *What is Sufism?* (Berkeley: University of California Press, 1977).
1990   "Current Problematics in the Study of Islam." *Religious Studies Review* 16/4, 293-300.

Lincoln, Bruce
1981   *Emerging From the Chrysalis: Studies of Women's Initiation.* Cambridge and London: Harvard University Press.

Lindbeck, George, with Karl Deutsch and Nathan Glazer
1976   *University Divinity Schools: A Report on Ecclesiastically Independent Theological Education.* N.p. [U.S.A.]: The Rockefeller Foundation, Working Papers.

Lippmann, Walter
1929   *A Preface to Morals.* New York: Macmillan.
Lippy, Charles H., ed.
1986   *Religious Periodicals of the United States: Academic and Scholarly Journals.* New York: Greenwood Press.
Lippy, Charles H., and Peter W. Williams, eds.
1988   *Encyclopedia of the American Religious Experience.* 3 vols. New York: Scribner's.
Long, Charles H.
1977   "The History of the History of Religions." In Adams, 1977, 467-75.
Luc, Alex
1991   "LBase and Bible Word Program." *Council of Societies for the Study of Religion Bulletin* 20/1 (Feb.), 25-26. (Also in *Religious Studies News* and electronically in OFFLINE [see above *s.v.* Kraft].)
Luckmann, Thomas
1967   *The Invisible Religion: The Problem of Religion in Modern Society.* New York: Macmillan and London: Collier-Macmillan.
Lye, John
1991   "Editorial." *BUFA Memo* (Brock University Faculty Association) 9/5 (April), 2-3.
Macklem, T.C. Street
1906   "The Art Colleges (continued): Trinity College." Chapter 8 in Alexander, 1906, 137-48.
MacLennan, Hugh, ed.
1960   *McGill: The Story of a University.* London: Allen & Unwin.
Macmillan, Cyrus
1921   *McGill and Its Story 1821-1921.* London and New York: John Lane and Toronto: Oxford University Press.
Macpherson, John
1967   "A History of the Canadian Society of Biblical Studies." Presidential Address to the Canadian Society of Biblical Studies, 1962. First published in the CSBS *Bulletin.* Updated to 1967 and published in Norman E. Wagner, ed., *Canadian Biblical Studies*, 1-16. Waterloo, Ont.: Canadian Society of Biblical Studies.
MacRae, George W., ed.
1972   *Scholarly Communication and Publication.* Waterloo, Ont.: Council on the Study of Religion.
Maier, Harry O.
1989   "The Charismatic Authority of Ignatius of Antioch: A Sociological Analysis." *Studies in Religion/Sciences Religieuses* 18/2, 185-99.
1991   *The Social Setting of the Ministry as Reflected in the Writings of Hermas, Clement, and Ignatius.* Dissertations *SR*, 1. Waterloo, Ont.: Wilfrid Laurier University Press for the Canadian Corporation for Studies in Religion/Corporation Canadienne des Sciences Religieuses.

Marsh, James H., Editor-in-Chief
1988   *The Canadian Encyclopedia.* 2nd ed. Edmonton: Hurtig Publishers.
Martin, Richard D., ed.
1985   *Approaches to Islam in Religious Studies.* Tucson: University of
          Arizona Press.
Marty, Martin E.
1986   "Academic Religion Today." *Theology Today* 43/2, 244-48.
1989   "Committing the Study of Religion in Public." *Journal of the Ameri-
          can Academy of Religion* 57/1, 1-22.
Mason, Steve
1991   "Fire, Water, and Spirit: John the Baptist and the Tyranny of Canon."
          Public Lecture, York University, Jan. 31.
Massey, Marilyn Chapin
1977   "David Friedrich Strauss and His Hegelian Critics." *Journal of Reli-
          gion* 57, 341-62.
Masters, Donald C.
1966   *Protestant Church Colleges in Canada: A History.* Toronto: Univer-
          sity of Toronto Press.
Maurice, F. D.
1847   *The Religions of the World and Their Relations to Christianity.* Lon-
          don: J. W. Parker.
May, William F.
1984   "Why Theology and Religious Studies Need Each Other." *Journal of
          the American Academy of Religion* 52/4, 748-57.
McAuliffe, Jane Dammen
1989   "Moments of Delight and Disappointment: Islamic Studies in *The Ency-
          clopedia of Religion.*" *Critical Review of Books in Religion 1989*, 57-76.
McCluskey, Neil G., ed.
1970   *The Catholic University: A Modern Appraisal.* Notre Dame: Univer-
          sity of Notre Dame Press.
McCool, Gerald A.
1977   *Catholic Theology in the Nineteenth Century: The Quest for a Unitary
          Method.* New York: Seabury Press.
McDannell, Colleen
1986   *The Christian Home in Victorian America, 1840-1900.* Bloomington:
          Indiana University Press.
McDonald, Neil, and Alf Chaiton, eds.
1978   *Egerton Ryerson and His Times: Essays on the History of Education.*
          Toronto: Macmillan.
McGill, Arthur C.
1970   "The Ambiguous Position of Christian Theology." In Ramsey and
          Wilson, 1970, 105-38.
McKeachie, Wilbert J.
1990   *Teaching Tips: A Guidebook for the Beginning College Teacher.* 8th
          ed. Lexington, MA: D.C. Heath.

McKenzie, Brian A.
1982   "A History of the Toronto Bible College (1894-1968)." Theme paper
        for the Ph.D. degree, University of Toronto.
McKillop, A. B.
1979   *A Disciplined Intelligence: Critical Inquiry and Canadian Thought in
        the Victorian Era*. Montreal and Kingston: McGill-Queen's Univer-
        sity Press.
1987   *Contours of Canadian Thought*. Toronto: University of Toronto Press.
McKinnon, Alastair
1982   "The Shape of Kierkegaard's Authorship." In McKinnon, ed.,
        Kierkegaard: Resources and Results, 122-57. Waterloo, Ont.: Wilfrid
        Laurier University Press.
McLelland, Joseph C.
1976-77   "Editorial." *Studies in Religion/Sciences Religieuses* 6/5, 483-84.
McMullin, Neal
1989   "*The Encyclopedia of Religion* : A Critique from the Perspective of
        the History of the Japanese Religious Traditions." *Method & Theory
        in the Study of Religion* 1/1, 80-96.
McNicol, John
1946   "Fundamental, but Not Dispensational: An Answer to Criticism."
        Evangelical Recorder 52 (March).
Meagher, John C.
1979   *Clumsy Construction in Mark's Gospel: A Critique of Form- and
        Redaktionsgeschichte*. New York and Toronto: Edwin Mellen Press.
Meek, Theophile J.
1927   "The Interpenetration of Cultures as Illustrated by the Character of
        the Old Testament Literature." *Journal of Religion* 7, 244-62.
        Reprinted as "The Fusion of Traits through Contact" in Wilson D.
        Wallis and Malcolm M. Willey, eds., *Readings in Sociology* (New
        York: Knopf, 1930), 81-86.
1936   *Hebrew Origins*. New York: Harper. 2nd, rev. ed., 1950 (New York:
        Harper and Toronto: University of Toronto Press).
Merton, Robert
1967   *On Theoretical Sociology: Five Essays, Old and New*. New York:
        Free Press and London: Collier-Macmillan.
Meyer, Ben F.
1988   "Monographs from the McMaster Project on Judaism and Christian-
        ity." Paper delivered to Annual Meeting of the Canadian Society of
        Biblical Studies, University of Windsor.
Meyer, Ben F., and E.P. Sanders, eds.
1982   *Jewish and Christian Self-Definition*. Vol. 2, *Self-Definition in the
        Greco-Roman World*. Philadelphia: Fortress Press.
Michaelsen, Robert
1972   "The Engaged Observer: Portrait of a Professor of Religion." *Jour-
        nal of the American Academy of Religion* 40, 419-24.

Miller, Casey, and Kate Swift
  1988   *The Handbook of Nonsexist Writing*. 2nd rev. ed. New York: Harper
            & Row.
Mills, Watson E.
  1987,   *The Council of Societies for the Study of Religion Directory of*
  1988,   *Departments and Programs of Religious Studies in North America*.
  1989,   Macon, GA: Council of Societies for the Study of Religion.
  1990
Milne, Pamela
  1989   "Women and Words: The Use of Non-sexist, Inclusive Language in
            the Academy." *Studies in Religion/Sciences Religieuses* 18/1, 25-35.
Milne, Pamela, with Edward Crowley
  1984   *Teaching Monograph Series. 1: The Learning Cell*. Windsor: Office
            of Teaching and Learning, University of Windsor.
Moir, John S.
  1968   "The Upper Canadian Roots of Church Disestablishment." *Ontario
            History* 60, 247-58.
  1972   *The Church in the British Era: From the British Conquest to Confed-
            eration*. A History of the Christian Church, 2. Toronto: McGraw-Hill
            Ryerson.
  1982   *A History of Biblical Studies in Canada: A Sense of Proportion*. Soci-
            ety of Biblical Literature: Biblical Scholarship in North America, 7.
            Chico, CA: Scholars Press.
Mol, Hans
  1985   *Faith and Fragility: Religion and Identity in Canada*. Burlington,
            Ont.: Trinity Press.
Moncher, Gary R.
  1988   "The Bible College and American Moral Culture." Ph.D. disserta-
            tion, University of California, Berkeley.
Morgan, Robert
  1977   "F. C. Baur's Lectures on New Testament Theology." *Expository
            Times* 88/7, 202-06.
Mostert, John
  1986   *The AABC Story: Forty Years with the American Association of Bible
            Colleges*. Fayetteville, AK: American Association of Bible Colleges.
Murchie, John
  1991   "A Day in the Life of an Academic Librarian." *Canadian Associa-
            tion of University Teachers Bulletin Association canadienne des pro-
            fesseurs d'université* 38/4 (April), 22-23
Myerhoff, Barbara
  1978   *Number Our Days*. New York: Simon & Schuster.
National Research Council
  1987   *Summary Report. Doctorate Recipients from United States Universi-
            ties*. Washington, D.C.: National Academy Press.

Neufeldt, Ronald W.
1983 *Religious Studies in Alberta: A State-of-the-Art Review.* The Study of Religion in Canada/Sciences Religieuses au Canada, 1. Waterloo, Ont.: Wilfrid Laurier University Press for the Canadian Corporation for Studies in Religion/Corporation canadienne des Sciences Religieuses.

Neusner, Jacob
1970 "Modes of Jewish Studies in the University." In Ramsey and Wilson, 1970, 159-89.
1983 "Judaism within the Discipline of Religious Studies." *Council for the Study of Religion Bulletin* 14/3 (Dec.), 141, 143-45.
1985 *The Public Side of Learning: The Political Consequences of Scholarship in the Context of Judaism.* American Academy of Religion Studies in Religion, 40. Chico, CA: Scholars Press.
1988a "Judaism in Contemporary America." In Lippy and Williams, 1988, vol. 1, 311-23.
1988b "The Theological Enemies of Religious Studies: Theology and Secularism in the Trivialization and Personalization of Religion in the West." *Religion* 18, 21-35.

New Catholic Encyclopedia
1967-79 Edited by an Editorial Staff at Catholic University of America. 17 vols. New York: McGraw-Hill.

Nicholls, William
1971 "A New Journal and its Predecessor." *Studies in Religion/Sciences Religieuses* 1/1, 1-3.

Nickelsburg, George
1978 Review of Klein, 1978. *Religious Studies Review* 4/3, 161-68.

Niebuhr, H. Richard
1952 *Christ and Culture.* London: Faber & Faber.

Nisbet, Robert
1987 "Sociology and Religion." In Eliade, 1987, vol. 13, 385-93.

OCUFA
1990a "The Future of the Professoriate." *Ontario Confederation of University Faculty Associations Forum* 6/22 (May-June), 3.
1990b "Status of Women Committee Report." In ibid. 6/24 (October), 4. Data reported and calculated from Statistics Canada, *Universities: Enrolment and Degrees, 1988. Catalogue 81-204.* Ottawa.

O'Donnell, James
1990 "OFFLINE: Computer Assisted Research for Religious Studies— 29." *Council of Societies for the Study of Religion Bulletin* 19/4, 102-05. (Also in *Religious Studies News* and electronically [see above, *s.v.* Kraft].)

Ogden, Schubert M.
1972 "What Is Theology?" *Journal of Religion* 52, 22-40.
1988 *Theology in the University: The Question of Integrity.* A Lecture in

the SMU-Dallas Series, The University and Contemporary Issues, 22 September. Dallas, TX.

Ong, Walter J.
1981   *Fighting for Life: Contest, Sexuality, and Consciousness*. Ithaca, NY: Cornell University Press.

Ontario Council on Graduate Studies/Conseil des Universités de l'Ontario
Annual   *Macroindicator Data*

Ontario Education Act
1987   (June) Regulation 262. Toronto: Ministry of the Attorney General.

Oppenheim, Michael
1987   "Theology and Community: The Work of Emil Fackenheim." *Religious Studies Review* 13/3, 206-10.

Orlinsky, Harry M.
1965   "Old Testament Studies." In Ramsey, 1965, 51-109.

O'Toole, Roger
1984   *Classical Sociological Approaches*. Toronto: McGraw-Hill-Ryerson.
1985   "Society, the Sacred and the Secular: Sociological Observations on the Changing Role of Religion in Canadian Culture." In Westfall et al., 1985, 72-85.

Pacala, Leon
1981   "Reflection on the State of Theological Education in the 1980s." *Theological Education* 18/1, 9-43.

Pamp, Frederic E., Jr.
1957   "Liberal Arts as Training for Executives." In Goldwin and Nelson, 1957, 36-48.

Paper, Jordan
1983   "Amerindian." In Margaret Lindsay Holton, ed., *Spirit of Toronto: 1834-1984*, 1-9. Toronto: Image Publishing Co.

Passmore, John
1980   "The Philosophy of Graduate Education." In Frankena, 1980, 40-63.

Peacock, James L., and Ruel W. Tyson, Jr.
1989   *Pilgrims of Paradox: Calvinism and Experience among the Primitive Baptists of the Blue Ridge*. Washington, DC: Smithsonian Institution Press.

Peckham, Morse
1960   *Humanistic Education for Business Executives: An Essay in General Education*. Philadelphia: University of Pennsylvania Press.

Pelikan, Jaroslav
1983   *Scholarship and its Survival: Questions on the Idea of Graduate Education*. A Carnegie Foundation Essay. Princeton: Carnegie Foundation for the Advancement of Teaching.

Penner, Hans H.
1989a   "Accounting for Origins." *Journal of the American Academy of Religion* 57/1, 173-80.
1989b   *Impasse and Resolution: A Critique of the Study of Religion*. Toronto Studies in Religion, 8. New York: Peter Lang.

1989c   *"The Encyclopedia of Religion." Critical Review of Books in Religion 1989*, 1-21.

Pieper, Francis
1950   *Christian Dogmatics*. Vol. 1. Translated by a committee. St. Louis: Concordia Publishing House.

Plaskow Goldenberg, Judith, ed.
1973   *Women and Religion: 1972. Proceedings*. Waterloo, Ont.: American Academy of Religion.

Polzin, Robert M.
1977   *Biblical Structuralism: Method and Subjectivity in the Study of Ancient Texts*. Philadelphia: Fortress Press and Missoula, MT: Scholars Press.

1980   *Moses and the Deuteronomist: A Literary Study of the Deuteronomic History*. Part 1, *Deuteronomy, Joshua, Judges*. New York: Seabury Press.

1989   *Samuel and the Deuteronomist: A Literary Study of the Deuteronomic History*. Part 2, *1 Samuel*. San Francisco: Harper & Row.

Porter, Bruce
1972   "Religious Studies in Canadian Community Colleges." In Anderson, 1972, 41-51.

Porter, John
1965   *The Vertical Mosaic: An Analysis of Social Class and Power in Canada*. Toronto: University of Toronto Press.

Preus, J. Samuel
1987   *Explaining Religion: Criticism and Theory from Bodin to Freud*. New Haven: Yale University Press.

Priestley, F.E.L.
1968   "The Humanities: Specific Needs." In Hubbard, 1968, 11-16.

Prospectus
1975   "University of Toronto School of Graduate Studies Centre for Religious Studies *Prospectus*." Unpublished typescript.

Pummer, Reinhard
1987   *The Samaritans*. Iconography of Religions, sec. 23, Judaism, fascicle 5. Leiden: Brill.

Quinton, Anthony
1980   "Reflections on the Graduate School." In Frankena, 1980, 86-109.

Rabb, J. Douglas
1983   "Introduction." In Rabb, ed., *Religion & Reason: A Symposium*, ix-xvii. Winnipeg: Frye Publishing.

Rabinowitz, Celia E.
1991   "The Introductory Course and the Adjunct." *Council of Societies for the Study of Religion Bulletin* 20/2, 29, 31.

Rahman, Fazlur
1979   *Islam*. 2nd ed. Chicago et al.: University of Chicago Press.

1982 *Islam and Modernity: Transformation of an Intellectual Tradition.* Chicago: University of Chicago Press.

1985 "Approaches to Islam in Religious Studies: A Review." In Martin, 1985, 189-202.

Ramsey, Paul, ed.

1965 *Religion.* Englewood Cliffs, NJ: Prentice-Hall.

Ramsey, Paul, and John F. Wilson, eds.

1970 *The Study of Religion in Colleges and Universities.* Princeton: Princeton University Press.

Rawlyk, George A.

1984 *Ravished by the Spirit: Religious Revivals, Baptists, and Henry Alline.* Kingston: McGill-Queen's University Press.

Rawlyk, George, and Kevin Quinn

1980 *The Redeemed of the Lord Say So: A History of Queen's Theological College 1912-1972.* Kingston: Queen's Theological College.

Readings, Bill

1989 "Canon and On: From Concept to Figure." *Journal of the American Academy of Religion* 57/1, 149-72.

Reed, Thomas Arthur, ed.

1952 *A History of the University of Trinity College, Toronto, 1852-1952.* Toronto: University of Toronto Press.

Reimarus, H.S.

1777 "Unmöglichkeit einer Offenbarung die alle Menschen auf eine gegründete Art glauben könnten." Reprinted in K. Lachmann, ed., *Gotthold Ephraim Lessings Sämtliche Schriften.* 3rd ed., revised by F. Muncker. Vol. 12, 316-58. Leipzig: Göschen'sche Verlagsbuchhandlung, 1897.

Reinhartz, Adele

1986 "The Meaning of Nomos in Philo's *Exposition of the Law.*" *Studies in Religion/Sciences Religieuses* 15/3, 337-45.

Remus, Harold

1971 "Origins" (of graduate study in religion in North America). In Welch, 1971, 113-33.

1983 *Pagan-Christian Conflict Over Miracle in the Second Century.* Patristic Monograph Series, 10. Cambridge, MA: Philadelphia Patristic Foundation.

1984 "Authority, Consent, Law: *Nomos, Physis,* and the Striving for a 'Given.' " *Studies in Religion/Sciences Religieuses* 13/1, 5-18.

1986 "Justin Martyr's Argument with Judaism." In S. Wilson, 1986b, 59-80.

1987 "Inside/Outside: Celsus on Jewish and Christian Nomoi." In Jacob Neusner et al., eds., *New Perspectives on Ancient Judaism.* Vol. 2, *Religion, Literature, and Society in Ancient Israel, Formative Christianity, and Judaism,* 133-50. Lanham, MD: University Press of America.

1988   "Religion as an Academic Discipline: Origins, Nature, and Changing
         Understandings." In Lippy and Williams, 1988, vol. 3, 1653-64,
         1668.
1990   *Equity in Communication: Guidelines.* Waterloo, Ont: Wilfrid Laurier
         University.

Remus, Harold, ed.
1978,   *The Council on the Study of Religion Directory of Departments and*
1981,   *Programs of Religious Studies* [1978: *Religion*] *in North America.*
1985   Waterloo, Ont.: Council on the Study of Religion.

Rennie, Ian
1984   "Gratitude for the Past." *Evangelical Recorder* 90 (Spring), 6-11.

Richardson, Peter
1986   "On the Absence of 'Anti-Judaism' in 1 Corinthians." In Richardson
         and Granskou, 1986, 59-74.

Richardson, Peter, ed., with David Granskou
1986   *Anti-Judaism in Early Christianity.* Vol. 1, *Paul and the Gospels.*
         Studies in Christianity and Judaism/ Études sur le christianisme et le
         judaïsme, 1. Waterloo, Ont.: Wilfrid Laurier University Press for the
         Canadian Corporation for Studies in Religion/Corporation Cana-
         dienne des Sciences Religieuses.

Ricoeur, Paul
1969   *The Symbolism of Evil.* Boston: Beacon Press.

Rietschl, Georg, and Paul Graff
1951-52 *Lehrbuch der Liturgik.* 2nd rev. ed. 2 vols. Göttingen: Vandenhoeck
         & Ruprecht.

Riley, Philip Boo
1984   "Theology and/or Religious Studies: A Case Study of *Studies in Reli-*
         gion/Sciences Religieuses, 1971-1981." *Studies in Religion/Sciences*
         Religieuses 13/4, 423-44.

Ringenberg, William C.
1984   *The Christian College: A History of Protestant Higher Education in*
         North America. Grand Rapids, MI: Eerdmans and Christian Univer-
         sity Press.

Robbins, Thomas
1988   *Cults, Converts, and Charisma.* London: Sage.

Robinson, John Beverly
1840   *Canada and the Canada Bill.* London: J. Hatchard and Son; reprinted,
         1967 (East Ardley, Wakefield, Yorkshire: S.R. Publishers and New
         York: Johnson Reprint Corporation).

Rose, Albert, ed.
1959   *A People and Its Faith: Essays on Jews and Reform Judaism in a*
         Changing Canada. Toronto: University of Toronto Press.

Rosovsky, Henry
1990   *The University: An Owner's Manual.* New York and London: Norton.

Rousseau, Louis
    1989   "Memoire concernant la fondation d'une Société québécoise pour
              l'étude de la religion." Unpublished memorandum. January 28.
    1990   "Rome: Admission de la S.Q.É.R. au sein de l'A.I.H.R." Reprinted
              from the 1st issue of the *Bulletin* of the Société québécoise pour
              l'étude de la religion in *Canadian Society for the Study of Religion
              Bulletin/La Société Canadienne pour l'Étude de la Religion* 14/2
              (April), 31.
Rousseau, Louis, and Michel Despland
    1988   *Les sciences religieuses au Québec depuis 1972.* Sciences religieuses
              au Canada/The Study of Religion in Canada, 2. Published by Wilfrid
              Laurier University Press for the Corporation Canadienne des Sciences
              Religieuses/Canadian Corporation for Studies in Religion.
Ruether, Rosemary Radford
    1985   *Womanguides: Readings Toward a Feminist Theology.* Boston: Beacon.
*Royal Commission Studies: A Selection of Essays Prepared for the Royal
Commission on National Development in the Arts, Letters and Sciences.*
    1951   Ottawa: Edmond Cloutier.
Said, Edward
    1978   *Orientalism.* New York: Pantheon Books.
Sanders, E. P.
    1986   "Paul on the Law, His Opponents, and the Jewish People in Philippi-
              ans 3 and 2 Corinthians 11." In Richardson and Granskou, 1986,
              75-90.
Sanders, E. P., ed.
    1980   *Jewish and Christian Self-Definition.* Vol. 1, *The Shaping of Chris-
              tianity in the Second and Third Centuries.* Philadelphia: Fortress
              Press.
Sanders, E. P., ed., with A. I. Baumgarten and Alan Mendelson
    1981   *Jewish and Christian Self-Definition.* Vol. 2, *Aspects of Judaism in
              the Graeco-Roman Period.* Philadelphia: Fortress Press.
Sanders, James A.
    1972   *Torah and Canon.* Philadelphia: Fortress Press.
    1984   *Canon and Community: A Guide to Canonical Criticism.* Philadel-
              phia: Fortress Press.
    1987   *From Sacred Story to Sacred Text: Canon as Paradigm.* Philadelphia:
              Fortress Press.
Savory, Roger
    1980   *Iran under the Safavids.* Cambridge: Cambridge University Press.
Sawatsky, Ronald G.
    1985   " 'Looking for that Blessed Hope': The Roots of Fundamentalism in
              Canada." Ph.D. dissertation, University of Toronto.
Schlatter, Richard
    1967   "The Nature and Formulation of Academic Disciplines." In Karl D.
              Hartzell and Harrison Sasscer, eds., *The Study of Religion on the*

Campus of Today: Selected Papers from the Stony Brook Conference on Religion as an Academic Discipline, 16-21. Washington, DC: Association of American Colleges.

Schlesinger, Arthur M., Sr.
1967   *A Critical Period in American Religion 1875-1900.* Philadelphia: Fortress Press. Reprinted from *Massachusetts Historical Society Proceedings* 64 (1930-32), 523-46.

Schoenfeld, Stuart
1978   "The Jewish Religion in North America: Canadian and American Comparisons." *Canadian Journal of Sociology* 3, 209-31.

Schoof, T.M.
1970   *A Survey of Catholic Theology 1800-1970.* Trans. by N. D. Smith. Paramus, NJ: Paulist Newman Press.

Schuller, Eileen M.
1989   "The 40th Anniversary of the Dead Sea Scrolls." *Studies in Religion/Sciences Religieuses* 18/1, 61-65.

Schumer, Fran
1984   "A Return to Religion." *New York Times Magazine* (April 15), 90-98.

Schüssler Fiorenza, Elisabeth
1983   *In Memory of Her: A Feminist Theological Reconstruction of Christian Origins.* New York: Crossroad.

Schwartz, Leo
1978   *Wolfson of Harvard.* Philadelphia: Jewish Publication Society.

Schweyer, J. Douglas
1973   "The History and Development of Religious Education in Ontario Schools." STM Thesis. Concordia Theological Seminary, St. Louis, MO.

Scobie, Charles H. H.
1964   *John the Baptist.* Philadelphia: Fortress Press and London: SCM Press.

Scott, Nathan A., Jr.
1968a   "Introduction: Theology and the Literary Imagination." In Scott, 1968b, 1-25.
1987   "Religious Dimensions of Modern Literature." In Eliade, 1987, vol. 8, 569-75.

Scott, Nathan A., Jr., ed.
1968b   *Adversity and Grace: Studies in Recent American Literature.* Essays in Divinity, 4. Chicago and London: University of Chicago Press.

Scrimgeour, Andrew D.
1990   "The Computer as a Tool for Research and Communication in Religious Studies." *Critical Review of Books in Religion 1990*, 45-59.

Searle, John
1990   "The Storm Over the University." *The New York Review of Books* 37/19 (Dec. 6), 34-42.

Seasoltz, R. Kevin
    1987   "Editorial Notice." *Worship* 61/1, 80-83.
Segal, Alan F.
    1990   *Paul the Convert: The Apostolate and Apostasy of Saul the Pharisee.*
               New Haven: Yale University Press.
Sekaquaptewa, Emory
    1976   "Hopi Indian Ceremonies." In W. Capps, 1976, 35-43.
Shapiro, Susan
    1987   " 'For Thy Breach is Like the Sea: Who Can Heal Thee?' " *Religious*
               Studies Review 13/3, 210-13.
Sharpe, Eric J.
    1975   *Comparative Religion: A History.* London: Duckworth.
    1977   *Faith Meets Faith: Some Christian Attitudes to Hinduism in the Nine-*
               teenth and Twentieth Centuries. London: SCM Press.
Sheraton, J. D., assisted by W. Caven, F. H. Wallace, T. C. Street
    1906   "The Theological Colleges." Chapter 12 in Alexander, 1906,
               184-200.
Shook, Laurence K.
    1971   *Catholic Post-Secondary Education in English-speaking Canada.*
               Toronto: University of Toronto Press.
Shriver, George
    1988   *"Religious Studies Review."* In Lippy, 1988, 459-61.
Shukster, Martin B., and Peter Richardson
    1986   "Temple and *Bet Ha-midrash* in the Epistle of Barnabas." In S. Wil-
               son, 1986b, 17-31.
Simeone, Angela
    1987   *Academic Women: Working Towards Equality.* South Hadley, MA:
               Bergin & Garvey.
Sinclair-Faulkner, Tom
    1977   "A Puckish Look at Hockey in Canada." In P. Slater, 1977, 383-405.
    1981   "Theory Divided from Practice: The Introduction of the Higher Criti-
               cism into Canadian Protestant Seminaries." *Studies in Religion/-*
               Sciences Religieuses 10/3, 321-43.
    1989   "Editorial: Inclusive Language." *Studies in Religion/Sciences Reli-*
               gieuses 18/1, 3-4.
Sissons, C. B.
    1952   *A History of Victoria University.* Toronto: University of Toronto
               Press.
Slater, Peter
    1972   "Religion as an Academic Discipline." In Welch, 1972b, 26-36.
Slater, Peter, ed.
    1977   *Religion and Culture in Canada/Religion et Culture au Canada.*
               Waterloo, Ont.: Canadian Corporation for Studies in Religion/Corpo-
               ration Canadienne des Sciences Religieuses.

Slater, Robert L.

1961   "The Meeting of World Religions." *Harvard Divinity School Bulletin* 25 (January), 1-8. French translation by Albert Jordan, "La rencontre des religions," in *Studies in Religion/Sciences Religieuses* 6/5 (1976-77), 499-506.

Sleeper, C. Freeman, and Robert A. Spivey

1975   *The Study of Religion in Two-Year Colleges*. Missoula, MT: Scholars Press for the American Academy of Religion.

Smart, Ninian

1973   *The Science of Religion and the Sociology of Knowledge: Some Methodological Questions*. Princeton: Princeton University Press.

1974   "Religion, Study of." *Encyclopaedia Britannica*. 15th ed. *Macropaedia*. Vol. 15, 613-28. Chicago et al.: Helen Hemingway Benton, Publisher.

1988   Review of Eliade, 1987. *Religious Studies Review* 14/3, 193-99.

Smith, Huston

1981   "Faith and Its Study: What Wilfred Smith's Against, and For." *Religious Studies Review* 7/4, 306-10.

Smith, Jonathan Z.

1975   "The Social Description of Early Christianity." *Religious Studies Review* 1/1, 19-25.

1987   *To Take Place: Toward Theory in Ritual*. Chicago and London: University of Chicago Press.

Smith, Morton

1983   "Terminological Boobytraps and Real Problems in Second-Temple Judaeo-Christian Studies." In Peter Slater and Donald Wiebe, eds., with Maurice Boutin and Harold Coward, *Traditions in Contact and Change: Selected Proceedings of the XIVth Congress of the International Association for the History of Religions*, 295-306. Waterloo, Ont.: Wilfrid Laurier University Press for the Canadian Corporation for the Study of Religion/Corporation Canadienne des Sciences Religieuses.

Smith, Wilfred Cantwell

1957   *Islam in Modern History*. Princeton: Princeton University Press.

1959   "Comparative Religion — Whither and Why?" In Eliade and Kitagawa, 1959, 31-58.

1972   *The Faith of Other Men*. New York: Harper Torchbooks.

1976   *Religious Diversity: Essays by Wilfred Cantwell Smith*. Ed. by Willard G. Oxtoby. New York: Harper & Row.

1978   *The Meaning and End of Religion: A Revolutionary Approach to the Great Religious Traditions*. London: SPCK. First published, Macmillan, 1962.

1981   *Towards a World Theology: Faith and the Comparative History of Religion*. Philadephia: Westminster Press.

Solberg, Richard W., and Merton P. Strommen

1980   *How Church-Related are Church-Related Colleges? Answers Based on a Comprehensive Survey of Supporting Constituencies of Eighteen LCA Colleges.* Philadelphia: Board of Publication, Lutheran Church in America and New York: Division for Mission in North America.

Spivey, Robert A.

1968   "Modest Messiahs: The Study of Religion in State Universities." *Religious Education* 63, 5-12.

Stackhouse, John G., Jr.

1987   "Proclaiming the Word: Canadian Evangelicalism since World War I." Ph.D. dissertation, University of Chicago.

1990   "Canadian Evangelicalism in the Twentieth Century: One Heart, Two Minds." Paper presented to the Canadian Evangelical Theological Association, Ontario Theological Seminary, Willowdale (Toronto), Ontario, May 14.

Stamp, Robert M.

1986   *Religious Exercises in Elementary and Secondary Schools.* Toronto: Ontario Ministry of Education.

Stark, Rodney, and William Sims Bainbridge

1985   *The Future of Religion: Secularization, Revival, and Cult Formation.* Berkeley: University of California Press.

Statistics Canada

Annual   *Universities: Enrolment and Degrees. Catalogue 81-204.* Ottawa.

1988   *Universities: Enrolment and Degrees. Catalogue 81-204.* Ottawa.

Steele, Ken

1990   "New Electronic Discussion Group: Shaksper." *Canadian Humanities Computing* 4/4 (Nov.), 2-3.

Stoesz, Donald B.

1988   "Don Wiebe: A Shift in His Method?" *Toronto Journal of Theology* 4/1, 71-85.

Stokes, G. Allison

1978   "Bibliographies of Psychology/Religious Studies." *Religious Studies Review* 4/4, 273-79.

Stover, Dale

1981   "The Amerindian Liberation of European Religious Consciousness." *Council on the Study of Religion Bulletin* 12/3, 65, 67.

1988   "Orientalism and the Otherness of Islam." *Studies in Religion/Sciences Religieuses* 17/1, 27-40.

Strenski, Ivan

1986   "Our Very Own 'Contras': A Response to the 'St. Louis Project' Report." *Journal of the American Academy of Religion* 54/2, 323-35.

Suchocki, Marjorie

1985   "Theological Education as a Theological Problem II: The One and the Many Revisited." In George Kilcourse, ed., *The Catholic Theological Society of America: Proceedings of the Fortieth Annual Con-*

vention San Francisco, June 5-8, 1985, vol. 40, 67-73. Bellarmine
College, Louisville, KY: Catholic Theological Society of America.

Sullivan, William J.
1972   "The Catholic University and the Study of Religion." In Welch,
        1972b, 37-45.

Sweet, Leonard I.
1990   "Straddling Modernism and Postmodernism." *Theology Today* 47/2,
        159-64.

Symonds, T. H. R.
1975   *To Know Ourselves: The Report of the Commission on Canadian
        Studies*. Vols. 1 and 2. Ottawa: Association of Universities and Col-
        leges in Canada.

Talman, James J., and Ruth Davis Talman
1953   *"Western" — 1878-1953: Being the History of the Origins and Devel-
        opment of the University of Western Ontario during its First Seventy-
        Five Years*. London, Ont.: University of Western Ontario.

Taylor, Marvin J.
1982   "A Theological Faculties Profile: 1981 Data Compared with the 1971
        Study." *Theological Education* 19/1, 119-43.

Thompson, Catherine
1990   "School boards allowed to teach religion." *Kitchener-Waterloo
        Record* (Dec. 7), A3.

Thorp, John
1989   "The Humanities Lobby." *Canadian Federation for the Humanities
        Bulletin* 12/2, 1-3.

Thwaites, Reuben Gold, ed.
1896-   *The Jesuit Relations and Allied Documents: Travels and Explorations
1901   of the Jesuit Missionaries in New France, 1610-1791*. 73 vols. Cleve-
        land: Burrows Brothers. Reprinted, 1959 (New York: Pageant Book
        Co.).

Tiele, C.P.
1888   "Religions." *Encyclopaedia Britannica*. 9th ed. Popular Reprint.
        Vol. 20, 358-71. New York: Henry G. Allen.
1893   "Study of Comparative Theology." In J. W. Hanson, ed., *The
        World's Congress of Religions: The Addresses and Papers Delivered
        before the Parliament and an Abstract of the Congresses Held in the
        Art Institute, Chicago, Illinois, U.S.A., August 25 to October 15, 1893
        Under the Auspices of The World's Columbian Exposition*, 280-86.
        Chicago: Mammoth Publishing Co.

Tillich, Paul
1957   *The Protestant Era*. Abridged ed. Trans. by James Luther Adams.
        Chicago: University of Chicago Press.

Toelken, Barre
1976   "Seeing with a Native Eye: How Many Sheep Will It Hold?" In W.
        Capps, 1976, 9-24.

Tolbert, Mary Ann
1983 "Defining the Problem: The Bible and Feminist Hermeneutics." *Semeia* 28, *The Bible and Feminist Hermeneutics*, 13-26.

Toombs, Lawrence, E.
1985 *Tell el-Hesi: Modern Military Trenching and Muslim Cemetery in Field I (Strata I-II)*. Waterloo: Wilfrid Laurier University Press.

Tracy, David
1991 *Dialogue with the Other: The Inter-Religious Dialogue*. Grand Rapids, MI: Eerdmans.

Tracy, David, and John B. Cobb, Jr.
1983 *Talking about God: Doing Theology in the Context of Modern Pluralism*. New York: Seabury Press.

Trible, Phyllis
1978 *God and the Rhetoric of Sexuality*. Philadelphia: Fortress Press.
1984 *Texts of Terror: Literary-Feminist Readings of Biblical Narratives*. Philadelphia: Fortress Press.

Trigger, Bruce G.
1988 "The Historians' Indian: Native Americans in Canadian Historical Writing from Charlevoix to the Present." In Fisher and Coates, 1988, 19-44. Reprinted from *Canadian Historical Review* 67/3 (1986), 315-42.

Trinity 1852-1952
1952 Special Centennial Issue of the *Trinity Review*. Toronto: Trinity College.

Turner, A. Richard
1970 "The Religious As it Appears in Art." In Ramsey and Wilson, 1970, 281-303.

Tyson, Ruel, Jr., James L. Peacock, and Daniel W. Patterson, eds.
1988 *Diversities of Gifts: Field Studies in Southern Religion*. Urbana and Chicago: University of Illinois Press.

University of Toronto President's Committee
1965 *Graduate Studies in the University of Toronto: Report of the President's Committee on the School of Graduate Studies 1964-1965*. Toronto: University of Toronto.

University of Waterloo
1990 "Historian traces Lutheran origins of UW." *University of Waterloo Gazette* 31/15 (Dec. 12), 1, 4.

Vallée, Gérard
1980 "Theological and Non-theological Motives in Irenaeus's Refutation of the Gnostics." In Sanders, 1980, 174-85.

Vaudry, Richard W.
1987 "Theology and Education in Early Victorian Canada: Knox College, Toronto, 1844-1861." *Studies in Religion/Sciences Religieuses* 16, 431-47.

Via, Dan O., Jr.
1967 *The Parables: Their Literary and Existential Dimension*. Philadelphia: Fortress Press.

Von Zur-Muehlen, Max

1986   *Myths and Realities: The Misconception of Faculty Shortages in the Next Decade.* Ottawa: Canadian Higher Education Research Network. Working Paper 86-3.

1987   "Myths and Realities: The Fallacy of Faculty Shortages in the Next Decade." *Canadian Journal of Higher Education* 17/1, 13-25.

Waardenburg, Jacques

1973,   *Classical Approaches to the Study of Religion: Aims, Methods and*
1974   *Theories of Research.* Vol. 1, *Introduction and Anthology.* Vol. 2, *Bibliography.* The Hague and Paris: Mouton.

Wach, Joachim

1967   "Introduction: The Meaning and Task of the History of Religions (*Religionswissenschaft*)." In Kitagawa et al., 1967, 1-19.

Wade, Francis C.

1978   *The Catholic University and the Faith.* Milwaukee: Marquette University Press.

Wagner, Norman E.

1972   "Early Bronze Age Houses at 'Ai (et-Tell)." *Palestine Exploration Quarterly* 104, 5-25.

1976   "Scholars as Publishers: A New Paradigm." *Scholarly Publishing* 7, 101-12.

Wagner, Norman E., and Aarne J. Siirala

1968   "Theological Education as Ministry." *Canadian Journal of Theology* 14/3, 149-59.

Wagner, Norman E., Lawrence E. Toombs, and Eduard R. Riegert

1973   *The Moyer Site: A Prehistoric Village in Waterloo County.* Waterloo, Ont.: Wilfrid Laurier University Press.

Waldman, Marilyn Robinson

1976   Review of Marshall G. S. Hodgson, *The Venture of Islam: Conscience and History in a World Civilization*, 3 vols. (Chicago and London: University of Chicago Press, 1975); W. Montgomery Watt, *The Formative Period of Islamic Thought* (Edinburgh: Edinburgh University Press, 1973), and *The Majesty That Was Islam: The Islamic World 661-1100* (New York: Praeger, 1974); F. E. Peters, *Allah's Commonwealth: A History of Islam in the Near East 600-1100 A.D.* (New York: Simon and Schuster, 1973). *Religious Studies Review* 2/3, 22-35.

Wallace, Dewey D., Jr.

1988   Review of Eliade, 1987. *Religious Studies Review* 14/3, 199-206.

Wallace, Malcolm W.

1951   "The Humanities." In *Royal Commission Studies*, 1951, 99-118.

Wallace, W. Stewart

1927   *A History of the University of Toronto 1827-1927.* Toronto: University of Toronto Press.

1937   *The Encyclopedia of Canada.* Vol. 5. Toronto: University Associates of Canada.

Walsh, H.H.
  1966   *The Church in the French Era: From Colonization to the British Con-*
            quest. A History of the Christian Church in Canada, 1. Toronto:
            McGraw-Hill Ryerson.
Washbourn, Penelope
  1973   "Differentiation and Difference: Reflections on the Ethical Implica-
            tions of Women's Liberation." In Plaskow Goldenberg, 1973, 95-105.
Watson, Glenn A.
  1990   *The Report of the Ministerial Inquiry on Religious Education in*
            Ontario Public Elementary Schools. Toronto: Ministry of Education,
            Province of Ontario.
Waugh, Earle H., and K. Dad Prithipaul, eds.
  1979   *Native Religious Traditions.* Waterloo, Ont.: Wilfrid Laurier Univer-
            sity Press for the Canadian Corporation for Studies in Religion/Cor-
            poration Canadienne des Sciences Religieuses.
Wegman, Herman A. J.
  1985   *Christian Worship in East and West: A Study Guide to Liturgical His-*
            tory. Trans. by Gordon W. Lathrop. New York: Pueblo Publishing.
Welch, Claude
  1971   *Graduate Education in Religion: A Critical Appraisal. Report of a*
            Study Sponsored by the American Council of Learned Societies with a
            Grant from the Henry Luce Foundation, Inc. Missoula, MT: Univer-
            sity of Montana Press.
  1972a,   *Protestant Thought in the Nineteenth Century.* Vol. 1, *1799-1870.*
  1985a   Vol. 2, *1870-1914.* New Haven and London: Yale University Press.
  1972b   *Religion in the Undergraduate Curriculum.* Washington, DC: Associ-
            ation of American Colleges.
  1985b   "Theological Education as a Theological Problem I."In George Kil-
            course, ed., *The Catholic Theological Society of America: Proceed-*
            ings of the Fortieth Annual Convention San Francisco, June 5-8,
            1985, vol. 40, 64-67. Bellarmine College, Louisville, KY: Catholic
            Theological Society of America.
Wellhausen, Julius
  1878   *Die Geschichte Israels.* Berlin: G. Reimer. Later editions are entitled
            Prolegomena zur Geschichte Israels. English translation, *Proleg-*
            omena to the History of Ancient Israel (Edinburgh: A. & C. Black,
            1885).
West, Cornel
  1985   Review of Schüssler-Fiorenza, 1983. *Religious Studies Review* 11/1,
            1-5.
Westerholm, Stephen
  1986   "*Torah, Nomos,* and Law: A Question of 'Meaning.' " *Studies in*
            Religion/Sciences Religieuses 15/3, 327-36.
Westfall, William
  1976   "The Dominion of the Lord: An Introduction to the Cultural History

of Protestant Ontario in the Victorian Period.'' *Queen's Quarterly* 53, 47-70.

1989   *Two Worlds: The Protestant Culture of Nineteenth-Century Ontario.* Kingston: McGill-Queens University Press.

Westfall, William et al., eds.

1985   *Religion/Culture. Canadian Issues/Thèmes Canadiens 7. Proceedings of a conference sponsored by the Association for Canadian Studies and the Graduate Centre for Religious Studies, University of Toronto, held at the Ontario Institute for Studies in Education, Toronto, on May 23-26, 1984/Communications presentées lors d'un colloque tenu a l'Institut Ontarien des Études en Éducation, Toronto, du 23 au 26 Mai 1984, sous les auspices de l'Association des Études Canadiennes et du Graduate Centre for Religious Studies, University of Toronto.*

Wevers, John W.

1956   ''Canadian Universities and the Teaching of Religion.'' *Canadian Journal of Theology* 2, 151-62.

Whittaker, John H.

1981   ''Neutrality in the Study of Religion.'' *Council on the Study of Religion Bulletin* 12/5, 129-31.

Wickens, G. A., trans.

1964   *The Nasirean Ethics.* London: Allen & Unwin.

Wiebe, Donald

1978   ''Is a Science of Religion Possible?'' *Studies in Religion/Sciences Religieuses* 7/1, 5-17.

1984   ''The Failure of Nerve in the Academic Study of Religion.'' *Studies in Religion/Sciences Religieuses* 13/4, 401-22.

1986   ''The 'Academic Naturalization' of Religious Studies: Intent or Pretence?'' *Studies in Religion/Sciences Religieuses* 15/2, 197-203.

1988   ''Postulations for Safeguarding Preconceptions: The Case of the Scientific Religionist.'' *Religion* 18, 11-19.

Wilder, Amos Niven

1958   *Theology and Modern Literature.* Cambridge: Harvard University Press.

Wilken, Robert L.

1971   *Judaism and the Early Christian Mind: A Study of Cyril of Alexandria's Exegesis and Theology.* New Haven and London: Yale University Press.

1980   ''The Jews and Christian Apologetics after Theodosius I *Cunctos Populos.''* *Harvard Theological Review* 73, 451-71.

1983   *John Chrysostom and the Jews: Rhetoric and Reality in the Late 4th Century.* Berkeley: University of California Press.

1984   *The Christians as the Romans Saw Them.* New Haven: Yale University Press.

1989   ''Who Will Speak *For* the Religious Traditions? AAR 1989 Presidential Address.'' *Journal of the American Academy of Religion* 57/4, 699-717.

Wilson, John F.

1970   "Introduction: The Background and Present Context of the Study of
          Religion in Colleges and Universities." In Ramsey and Wilson, 1970,
          3-21.

Wilson, Stephen G.

1986a   "Marcion and the Jews." In S. Wilson, 1986b, 45-58.

Wilson, Stephen G., ed.

1986b   *Anti-Judaism in Early Christianity.* Vol. 2, *Separation and Polemic.*
          Studies in Christianity and Judaism/Études sur le christianisme et le
          judaïsme, 2. Waterloo, Ont.: Wilfrid Laurier University Press for the
          Canadian Corporation for Studies in Religion/Corporation Cana-
          dienne des Sciences Religieuses.

Winnett, Fred V., and W. Stewart McCullough

1977   "A Brief History of the Department of Near Eastern Studies (for-
          merly Oriental Languages) in the University of Toronto to
          1976-1977." Addendum: "Additions and Corrections for the History
          of the Department of Near Eastern Studies in the University of
          Toronto." Unpublished typescripts. Toronto: Department of Near
          Eastern Studies, University of Toronto.

Witmer, S. A.

1962   *The Bible College Story: Education with Dimension.* Wheaton, IL:
          Accrediting Association of Bible Colleges.

Woodward, Kenneth L., et al.

1990   "A Time to Seek." *Newsweek* (Dec. 17), 50-56.

Wright, R. Ramsay, and W. J. Alexander

1906   "The Arts Faculty." Chapter 5 in Alexander, 1906, 78-99.

Wrong, Dennis H.

1959   "Ontario's Jews in the Larger Community." In Rose, 1959, 45-57.

Yinger, J. Milton

1974   "Religion, Social Aspects of." *Encyclopaedia Britannica.* 15th ed.
          Macropaedia. Vol. 15, 604-13. Chicago et al.: Helen Hemingway
          Benton, Publisher.

Young, Pamela Dickey

1990   *Feminist Theology/Christian Theology: In Search of Method.* Min-
          neapolis: Fortress Press.

Younger, Paul

1974-75   [Response to Davis, 1974-75.] *Studies in Religion/Sciences Reli-
          gieuses* 4/3, 231-33.

Yu, Anthony C.

1987   "Literature and Religion." In Eliade, 1987, vol. 8, 558-69.

Zahavy, Tzvee

1991   "Report on New Orleans." *Council of Societies for the Study of Reli-
          gion Bulletin* 20/1 (Feb.), 25. (Also in *Religious Studies News* and
          electronically in OFFLINE [see above *s.v.* Kraft].)

Zimmerman, Joyce A.

1988   *Liturgy as Language of Faith: A Liturgical Methodology in the Mode of Paul Ricouer's Textual Hermeneutics.* Lanham, MD: University Press of America.

Zuesse, Evan M.

1979   *Ritual Cosmos: The Sanctification of Life in African Religions.* Athens, OH and London: Ohio University Press.

Index

Abdul-Rauf, Muhammad, 41
"academic revolution," 84
ACAP, *see* Advisory Committee on
Academic Planning
Adams, Charles J., xvi, 33, 41, 42, 89
n. 16
administrators, interviews with, 330;
in government agencies, xv; in
universities, *see* chap. 3.1; xv, 20,
101, 159; in church-related colleges,
see chap. 3.1.1; in theological col-
leges, 110, 111, 117 n. 12, 119
Advisory Committee on Academic
Planning (ACAP), 61, 233
Aitken, Brian, xvi
African religions, *see* religions, *s.v.*
Algar, Hamid, 40, 41
Alton, Bruce, xvi, 30, 31, 85
American Academy of Religion, 2, 31,
49, 51, 102, 109, 113, 117 n. 14,
122, 141, 166, 181, 186, 217, 218,
219, 249, 261, 280, 305, 309, 324;
Eastern International Region, 299,
312
American Association of Bible Col-
leges, *see* Bible colleges, *s.v.*
American Association of Theological
Schools, *see* Association of Theo-
logical Schools (ATS)
American Society of Church History, 2
American Theological Libraries Asso-
ciation, 267 n. 2
Americanization of Canada, 7
Amore, Roy, xvi
Ancient Near Eastern studies, 21, 59,

76; *see also* religions, *s.v.* Ancient
Near Eastern
Anderson, Charles, 5, 58; *Guide to
Religious Studies in Canada/Guide
des Sciences Religieuses au Canada*, 233
Anglicanism/Anglicans, 7, 8, 9, 11, 14,
17, 18, 74, 77, 87 n. 7, 97, 115 n. 3,
166, 271
anthropology/anthropology of religion,
1, 2, 32, 34, 45, 46, 48, 49, 51, 52,
61, 62, 69, 72, 158, 182, 183, 187,
211, 214, 219, 240, 256, 267 n. 1,
276, 290, 298, 305
Aquinas, Thomas, 307
Arabic, 13, 225, 237
Aramaic, 225
Arapura, J. G., 44
archaeology, 1, 2, 21, 34, 47, 115, 187,
211, 214, 225, 290
Arnold, Thomas, 15
arts, literature, and religion, *see* religious studies, subfields, *s.v.*
Asia, 120; Asian religions, *see* religions, *s.v.*
Association canadienne-française pour
l'avancement des sciences, 85
Association for the Sociology of Religion, 213
Association of Canadian Bible Colleges, *see* Bible colleges, Canada,
s.v.
Association of Theological Schools
(ATS), 12, 87, 111, 156, 157, 164,
165, 168, 170 n. 3, 188, 246, 251 n. 2

385

Ontario, *s.v.* curricula, undergraduate

Religionsgeschichte, 90 n. 20

"religious knowledge" courses and departments, Ontario: 5, 12, 59, 74, 76, 97, 98, 104, 160, 169, 288; inculcation of religion as aim, 11, 15, 58, 282; typical courses, 12; required/elective, 11, 12; apologetics, 24; *see also* University College

religious studies, general
• nature of, *see* chaps. 1, 2.4.3;
• origins/history, *see* chap. 1; 3 n. 2, 88 n. 15; Protestantism, "Protestant seminary" curriculum/dominance 21, 24, 38, 101, 290; teaching of/about religion, 56, 183; comparative study, 88 n. 15 (terminology for, 89 n. 19, 90 n. 20); identity search/crisis, 141, 310; growth of, 305; reference works in, *see* chap. 2.4.10; journals in, 3 (*see also entries for specific journals*); related/relation to other academic fields, 1, 2, 3, 20, 23, 34, 49, 57, 61, 62, 68-70, 290, 297, 305, 308, 311; and social sciences, 29, 31, 48, 90 n. 27, 91 n. 32, 176, 177, 181, 191, 213, 291; (*see also* psychology/psychology of religion, sociology/sociology of religion, anthropology/anthropology of religion);
• departments/programmes of, 1, 3, *et passim*; departments, rationale for, 58, 92 n. 39;
• as haven for academic "refugees," 122-23;
• faculty, qualifications, 2 (*see also* religious studies, Ontario, *s.v.* faculty, preparation and background); as "engaged observer"/"participant observer," 31;
• dilettantism, 49;
• Western orientation, 38, 182, 187, 207-08, 294, 305; ethno/Eurocentrism, *see* chap. 12.8.1; 54; *see also*: religious studies, methodology/theory, *s.v.* "battle of the

books"; religious studies, Ontario, *s.v.v.* curricula, undergraduate (*s.v.* courses: Western/non-Western) *and* State-of-the-Art Review (*s.v.* curricula);
• learned/professional societies, *see* chaps. 3.2.5, 7.7, 12.8; xiii, 2, 82, 83, 84, 303; *see also*: religious studies, Canada; religious studies, Ontario, *s.v.v.* learned/professional societies *and* State-of-the-Art Review (*s.v.* recommendations); *and entries for specific societies*;
• learned/professional societies, publishing programmes, 3, 82, 297, 299; *see also* Canadian Corporation for Studies in Religion/Corporation Canadienne des Sciences Religieuses, *s.v.*

religious studies, graduate study, *see* chaps. 4.2, 4.3.2, 9; 90 n. 21; *also*: Welch Report; religious studies, Ontario, *s.v.v.* graduate study *and* students, graduate

religious studies, graduate students
• with professional degrees, *see* chap. 4.2.2.1; age, 130; male/female ratio, 130; backgrounds/religious commitments, 130; fields of study, 131;
• without professional degrees, *see* chap. 4.2.1.2; age, 131; male/female ratio, 131; backgrounds/religious commitments, 131; preparation for graduate study, 130-31; full/part-time status, 131; fields of study, 131;
• *see also* religious studies, Ontario, *s.v.v.* graduate study *and* students, graduate

religious studies, subfields, *see* chap. 2.4.9; 2;
• arts, literature, and religion, *see* Tabs. 7-5, 7-6; 2, 47, 48, 49, 51, 52, 70, 187, 212, 214, 224, 225, 226, 263, 267 n. 1, 308, 311;
• biblical studies/scholars, *see* chap. 2.4.1; 21, 49, 72, 73, 113, 118 n. 14, 128, 142, 171, 188, 205,